JERI LABER is the author of more than 100 articles that have appeared in the *New York Review of Books*, *New York Times* and many other newspapers and magazines. She is the co-author of *"A Nation is Dying": Afghanistan Under the Soviets* (Northwestern University Press). In November 2000, in recognition of her human rights work, she was awarded the Order of Merit by President Václav Havel on behalf of the Czech Republic. Jeri Laber lives in New York City and in Walton, New York.

Praise for *The Courage of Strangers*

"This is the memoir of a brave woman, who left her traditional middle class life to confront the varieties of human depravity as a leading operative in the human rights movement. What this occupation can do to one's soul is not dwelled upon. Her story, with its inevitable moments of high drama, is instructive as history and quietly moving as the statement of a person called to the ministry of humanism. It reminded me that the American Dream is something more than corporate thievery, celebrity worship, and political cant." —E. L. DOCTOROW

"Jeri Laber has written an important book, indispensable for understanding the emergence of the human rights movement in the United States. Part personal memoir, part history of the movement, part gripping narrative of dangerous missions behind the Iron Curtain, *The Courage of Strangers* is brutally honest and gracefully written."   —*Human Rights Watch Council Book Review*

"An affecting tale of personal growth and global activism . . . Laber is a strong, natural writer"   —*Publishers Weekly*

"*The Courage of Strangers* is neither conventional autobiography nor history but a case study of the way 'ordinary people' can make a difference and in doing so become extraordinary. . . . Read this book. Ponder the questions it raises."
                                                —*The Women's Review of Books*

"It took the labors of Hercules to hoist Human Rights onto the platforms of international conferences and to make those rights as important as business and political criteria among nations in their dealings with one another. Over the years a considerable number of people have attempted to pressure the Soviets and other regimes toward greater toleration of dissidence, and one of the most effective has been Jeri Laber. This book is her personal story but it is also a concise history of the human rights epoch as she saw it from the end of World War II to the present."   —ARTHUR MILLER

"Laber's passion shines brightly in this memoir, as does her courage . . . Human rights activists in particular will find Laber's recollections insightful and inspiring."
                                                                —*Booklist*

"*The Courage of Strangers* details the courage of dissidents and writers, scientists and intellectuals, and not least the courage of an American woman to reach out beyond her sphere of safety. It is an inspirational story, as well as a useful introduction to Soviet and human rights studies." —*The Forward*

"[W]hen the governments in the East collapsed, it was often the friends of Jeri Laber, the outcasts of the Helsinki federation, who became the new leaders. . . . Jeri Laber certainly was the real thing." —*New York Law Journal*

"My friend Jeri Laber tells in this good book of risking her life as a spy with no connection whatsoever to any government. Her hatred for injustice sent her into countries with cruel governments, some of them American allies, to gather news of atrocities from victims, which she then told the whole world about. Much as we might wish otherwise, our own government could not, for reasons diplomatic or economic or military, or even ideological, engage in such compassionate espionage. A subtitle for the next printing might be: "The Privatization of National Honor and Common Decency."" —KURT VONNEGUT

The Courage of Strangers is a moving autobiographical account of Jeri Laber's journey from domestic life with its pleasures and trials to her public role as one of the founders of the Human Rights Watch. Beneath her cool in detailing the history of the Human Rights Movement, there is a moral passion which claims the readers attention on every page. Jeri Laber's story—of personal bravery (she would never claim it) and stunning public testimony—is compelling and beautifully told. —MAUREEN HOWARD

"[D]etails her often dangerous trips to Brezhnev's Soviet Union and East European nations and chronicles the events leading to the development of Helsinki Watch and Human Rights Watch. . . . Inspirational testimony to the value of a human rights organization that investigates and publicizes human rights violations with fairness and without regard to political ideology or US foreign policy." —*Library Journal*

"With a gift for storytelling, Laber weaves together passages that intrigue . . . with rare moments of glory. . . . The result is a thoughtful . . . but usually fast-paced, inside view of Eastern Europe during a cataclysmic era." —*Hope*

THE

COURAGE

OF

STRANGERS

Coming of Age with the Human Rights Movement

JERI LABER

With a Preface by Václav Havel

PublicAffairs
NEW YORK

For Charlie
We think the same thoughts,
we dream the same dreams.

Published in the United States by PublicAffairs™, a member of the Perseus Books Group.

Book Design by Jenny Dossin

LIBRARY OF CONGRESS CATALOGING-IN-PUBLICATION DATA
Laber, Jeri.
The courage of strangers: coming of age with the human rights movement / Jeri Laber; preface by Václav Havel.—1st ed.
p. cm.
Includes index.
ISBN 1-58648-288-2 (pbk.)
1. Laber, Jeri. 2. Women social reformers—United States—Biography. 3. Women human rights workers—United States—Biography. 4. Women human rights workers—United States. I. Title.
HQ1413.L33 A3 2002
303.48'4'092—dc21
[B]
2001060350

10 9 8 7 6 5 4 3 2 1

CONTENTS

PREFACE

I am pleased that readers all over the world will have the opportunity to read the memoirs of Jeri Laber, the well-known director of Helsinki Watch and my longtime friend.

Jeri, as executive director of the new American Helsinki Committee, first visited Prague in September 1979 to make some contacts within the Czech community of dissidents. Jeri visited Prague many other times and, therefore, became the focus of attention of repressive Czech agents. She was interrogated by the police repeatedly, the last time in October 1989, when she became one of the last foreign prisoners held for political reasons in the territory of Czechoslovakia.

In the era before November 1989, Jeri represented for Czechoslovak dissent not only hope but also a tie to the whole world, as well as a sign that the world knew and cared about us. I love to remember how we collaborated, at a time when we still could not imagine where our teamwork would lead us. Today I pay attention to human rights as president of the Czech Republic, but Jeri continues in her efforts to improve human rights throughout the world through the Helsinki Committee of Human Rights Watch.

I greatly appreciate Jeri's lifelong work. I am certain that the publication of her memoirs will contribute to a deeper knowledge by readers of that turbulent era in our nation's history.

VÁCLAV HAVEL

PROLOGUE

Prague, November 1988. I am alone, walking along a deserted, dimly lit street, looking around me in the hazy smog to see if I'm being followed. I know the way to Rita's apartment: I was there on my last human rights mission, less than a year ago.

For nine years now I have been traveling beyond closed borders for Helsinki Watch, the human rights organization I helped found. I've come to like traveling alone. I feel in control—of my schedule, of my conversations with dissidents, of the choices I make, of my own emotions.

There are times, however, when I wouldn't mind some company. Right now, for example, when I'm feeling nervous—not about street crime, which is almost nonexistent in a police state like Czechoslovakia, but about the police themselves: *Are they watching me? Will they arrest me? Will they find the money?* I have a history in Czechoslovakia. In 1983 I was arrested and expelled from the country for meeting with dissidents. Ever since, I've been suspect.

Just a few hours before, at the airport, I had a run-in with the state security police. My name must be on a computerized blacklist, for when I presented my travel documents, the officer in charge disappeared with them for thirty interminable minutes. He returned with some customs officials. Together they led me to a curtained booth, where they searched my suitcase thoroughly. They went through my handbag and my wallet, counting my money, turning the pages of my address book, examining every scrap of paper they came across. I was not surprised. This type of search has become routine for me whenever I enter Czechoslovakia. It is their way of saying they are watching me.

I always take precautions when I travel to such unwelcoming countries. I carefully code my address book before leaving the United States, so that only I can decipher the names and addresses of the people I plan to see. I weed out any papers that mention the words "Helsinki Watch": credit cards, airplane confirmations, business cards. I never bring in any literature that might be considered subversive. I've learned that I can take notes in a script so tiny it can't be read without a magnifying glass: I put them in my raincoat pocket, rolled into a little ball, when I pass through customs on my way home.

This time, however, I am breaking my own rules. Strapped to my waist under my sweater is a money belt containing $2,000, a small fortune on the Czech black market. It is a grant from Helsinki Watch that I am bringing to the new underground Helsinki Committee in Prague. I did not declare it on my customs form; if I did, I would have to explain, later, where and how I spent it. I was gambling that they would not inspect my bulging waistline—and I was right. That didn't stop my heart from pounding loudly, even after I had left the airport in a taxi headed for my hotel. I can't wait to get the money to Rita. She will know what to do with it.

Now, entering her apartment building, I am afraid. The staircase is so dark: I cannot find the light switch, and I've forgotten to bring the little flashlight I usually carry with me. I stumble on the stairs, light a match at each landing to read the names on the doors. Finally I see a brass plate that reads R. KLÍMOVÁ. I knock softly, the door opens, and Rita—short, stocky, a bundle of contained energy—greets me warmly but wordlessly. I enter the apartment without saying a word, taking my cues from her.

To my surprise there is a slight young woman standing in the living room. "Milena," Rita whispers, and I realize this is the daughter whom I had never met. I know Rita's son, Vladya, who is deeply involved in underground publishing. But up until now, Rita has kept Milena away from dissident activities to protect her, her two small children, and her job as an art historian.

Rita signals me with her eyes and hands: *Where is it?*

I lift my sweater, unstrap the money belt, and give it to her. She hands the belt to Milena without unzipping it or counting the bills, and Milena buries it at the bottom of a laundry basket full of clothes. Kissing her mother and giving me a little wave, she disappears down the dark stairs, the basket resting on her hip. Rita and I relax and begin to talk in the bugged apartment. No one listening in would know that Milena and I had even met.

That was November 1988. We did not know—we would never have dreamed—that a year later, communism would end in Czechoslovakia. There would be huge, peaceful demonstrations. Rita would become the English-language voice of the revolution, telling the outside world what was happening, interpreting for Václav Havel as he was rushed into power.

Back then we could not have imagined that Rita would make an amazing trajectory from dissident to diplomat, becoming the first ambassador to the United States from a new, post-Communist Czechoslovakia. Nor would I have guessed, some thirty-five years earlier when I began studying Russian literature at Columbia University, that I would some day be involved in events that would end the long reign of tyranny in Eastern Europe.

. . .

My story is a personal one, though it deals with some of the most dramatic events in modern history—the growth of dissent in the Soviet Union, the birth of the human rights movement, the fall of communism in Europe. I was a player in those events. I have a unique point of view.

How did my colleagues and I manage to build a human rights movement so significant that dictators and torturers throughout the world could not ignore us? How did I, an ordinary American, a private citizen with no ties to any government, find myself fighting oppression in many countries—the Soviet Union, Czechoslovakia, Poland, Hungary, Romania, Bulgaria, Albania, Yugoslavia, Turkey, Afghanistan?

Human rights work is not as glamorous or mysterious as it may seem from afar. It is depressing work, for we deal with human suffering on an almost unimaginable scale and must come to grips with the enormous evil in people as well as the miraculous good. It is frustrating work in which occasional small successes must compensate for the growth of repression in so much of the world. I was lucky to be involved in one of our most spectacular successes—the fall of communism in Europe. Though many other major factors contributed to that fall, the role of private citizens, hundreds of thousands of them eventually, was pivotal. This book attempts to answer some questions I am frequently asked: How *did* it happen? What role did your group play? And how did *you* become part of it all?

My life might very well have taken a different course. Born to conventional, well-to-do parents, I was raised to believe that my place was in the home. I resisted that notion from the start, yet I always assumed that no matter what interests I pursued, there would be a man—a father, a husband—to support and take care of me.

In 1978, when I was forty-six years old, my illusions were shattered. My father was sick and bankrupt, my husband had left me, my children were growing up and leaving home. I was a freelance writer and editor at the time, with a Russian-studies background and a commitment to human rights. But my marriage and family had always come first. Suddenly, I was on my own. My life, as I had known it, was over.

I looked inward, drawing upon my own interests and convictions, and was able to turn my passions into what eventually became my career. A whole new life opened before me. I became a founder of what is now Human Rights Watch, the largest human rights organization in the United States. I helped build an international citizens' movement—the International Helsinki Federation for Human Rights. I traveled to some of the most repressive countries in Europe. I learned about the courage of strangers. I met secretly with dissidents and torture victims and helped them in the fight to end repression in their countries. Many of these people had other lives before they took up the struggle for human rights. They did not know that they would be transformed by that struggle, that some of them—Andrei Sakharov, Václav Havel, Lech Wałęsa, others—would become respected leaders in their own countries.

My life changed, too. In my work to help others, I became free and independent myself. I learned to distinguish between naive idealism and harsh reality. I came to see the amorphous nature of good and evil in our world. And I reached the conclusion that—for me, at least—work, no matter how rewarding, cannot substitute for a meaningful personal life.

There is a message in my experience and in this book: that everyone has something to offer, that ordinary people, when they feel strongly enough, can do extraordinary things, and that it is never too late to start.

PART I

Rooted

1

If I were to trace my awakening to human rights abuses, I would start in the early 1970s, before the term "human rights" was commonly used. Or perhaps I would begin well before that, in the formative years of my childhood, when more than a million children, no different from me, were being gassed and cremated as part of a "final solution." Or maybe it all began before I was born, in legends of injustice and fear passed down through my family by ancestors I never knew, whose names I do not know.

Amorphous strands of memory and experience came together for me in December 1973. Nothing spectacular happened—it was just an article I read in a magazine, the *New Republic*, describing unthinkable acts of torture. The words came at me in a rush, shattering my complacency, shaking my belief in human decency and ultimately changing my life.

I learned from that article that torture was being used by governments in more than fifty countries throughout the world. I was stunned. I did not know, nor did most people at the time, that torture was so widespread and so brutal.

Though it now seems hard to believe, human rights abuses, as we think of them today, were not generally discussed or publicized at that time. Governments did not interfere in what was considered another government's internal affairs, journalists did not investigate such crimes, and ordinary people just didn't know about them. The words "human rights" did not come up in conversation.

Among other victims, the article described a young Greek girl with long black hair, a political prisoner, who sat motionless for hours in the corner of her cell, her large, dark eyes occasionally filling with tears. Witnesses said the girl had been kept naked on the prison roof for two nights. "The second night they pushed a wooden rod up her anus and another in her vagina and hung her with handcuffs from a hook on the wall, stark naked like that with the rods still in her, all night."

I was already forty-two at the time, married and the mother of three girls, including a teenager with long dark hair. It was my daughter's face I saw on that tearful Greek girl as I thought of her, constantly, in the weeks that followed.

I was obsessed by what I had read. I had to do something about it.

2

I was a working wife and mother in the early 1970s, too busy to take up causes except in the most superficial ways. The great movements of the 1960s—civil rights and the anti-Vietnam protests—had called out to me. I wanted to join them, but I had a husband, two young children, a new baby, and a part-time job. I had no time.

Back in college, I'd been politically active, the first woman ever to run for president of the Student Council at New York University. My party won, but I lost—a woman president, it appeared, was too much of a novelty in those days. Quite a few more years would pass before other women would succeed where I had failed.

I was in college in the early 1950s, a quiescent, apolitical time, the lull before the 1960s storm. Nonetheless, I was drawn to left-wing politics. I came under the spell of a graduate student in his early thirties, who became both my boyfriend and my mentor. Arthur was too much of a maverick to join the Communist Party, but he was sympathetic to communism, as he understood it. Every day we read the *Compass*, New York's left-wing newspaper in the early 1950s, and heatedly discussed its editorials. Arthur, who was from a working-class family (his mother cleaned toilets at LaGuardia Airport), refused to believe anything negative that people wrote or said about the Soviet Union. He was eloquent and impassioned, and I, who felt undeserving of my own easy, upper-middle-class life, saw virtue in a society that believed in distributing wealth according to needs.

Sidney Hook, NYU's distinguished philosopher known for his strong anti-Communist views, had taken a shine to me; he saw me as a promising student and asked me to serve as president of the student Philosophy Circle. He was upset one day to see me walking hand in hand with Arthur, whom he knew and considered a "fuzzy thinker." He took me aside after class. "That's a surprising friendship for someone like you," he remarked in an awkward, avuncular fashion. Then he thrust a book at me, *Czechoslovakia Enslaved.* "Read this," he said. "It will tell you the truth about communism." I dismissed the book as propaganda and put it aside without opening it. I would read it with interest many years later, when I was traveling regularly to Prague on human rights missions.

.   .   .

I constantly badgered my father during my college days. With Arthur prompting from afar, I spoiled many a Sunday dinner by asking loaded questions.

"Dad, how would you feel about selling that property next door to a Negro family?"

He would become defensive: "I don't care what you think," he would snap, looking up from the newspaper he often read at the table despite my mother's entreaties. "I'm not about to bring down real estate prices by selling to Negroes."

And we were off. I would keep the argument going for the rest of the meal. I never got him to agree with me, but at least I had his attention. Since childhood, I'd been trying to get him to take me seriously, but it was only when I began to challenge some of his basic values that I finally seemed to be getting through.

.   .   .

My father had made a remarkable journey in the United States. A Jewish child from Russia, he was eleven years old and threadbare when he and his family arrived in New York City in 1906. He started the L&P Electric Company in 1919 when he was twenty-four, initially to convert homes from gaslight to electricity. The company prospered. "We did neat work and kept our promises," was Dad's simple explanation for its success. Dad became a professional engineer and the chairman of the board of his company, which eventually had five divisions, the largest of which controlled the wholesale distribution of Fedders air conditioners in the Northeast. He employed well over 150 people and could always find a job there for talented, or needy, members of his family.

My father was born in 1895 in a town not far from Brest Litovsk in what is now Belarus but was then within the "Pale of Settlement." The Pale was a vast area controlled by the Russians, some 750,000 square miles, stretching from the Baltic Sea to the Black Sea and encompassing regions that today are in Russia, Poland, Lithuania, Belarus, and Ukraine. Created by the tsars to keep Jews under control, it was a huge ghetto in which the Jews led impoverished lives, denied the rights of other citizens and terrorized by murderous anti-Semitic attacks known as pogroms—bloodbaths that were instigated or tolerated by the authorities.

Dad's father made and sold cheese, using milk he bought from a wealthy landowner. He traveled back and forth between town and farm because Jews were not allowed to live in the countryside. My father's intelligence must have been apparent at an early age, for he was meant to be a rabbi and sent to study with a rabbi in Minsk.

Dad's mother, Leah, whom I was said to resemble, had a stern, strong face and a crippled body, the result of an ice-skating accident when she was a girl. She was willful and intimidating, the matriarch of a large family that included her seven younger brothers and their families, all of whom made their way to the United States in order to avoid the Russian army, which forcibly conscripted Jews for service as long as twenty-five years.

The brothers adapted to American life in widely different ways. Joe, one of my father's uncles, fair-haired and handsome, had been the first to make the crossing and had brought the others over one by one. It was his fiancée, Minnie, who met Dad's family at Ellis Island, after they passed through Immigration. Minnie wore a big hat and a long fur-trimmed tunic coat. "I will never forget the way she looked, tall and beautiful," my father told me. As they crossed the Williamsburg Bridge by tram, he caught a glimpse of the New York City skyline, "a sight never to be imagined," he later wrote in an unfinished account of his early life.

Joe established a successful machinery business and raised a family of blond, blue-eyed American children, at ease on the tennis court and the golf course. But my father's uncle, Markel, and his wife, Pesha Baile, never managed to learn English and spoke only Yiddish. They ran a tiny notions store in the Williamsburg section of Brooklyn and lived in a cramped tenement just above it. I would shrink from Pesha Baile when she tried to kiss me. With her loose black clothes, missing teeth, and unkempt gray hair, she looked like a witch out of my fairy tale books rather than what she was—a simple woman from the old country, out of place in a new world.

.   .   .

When Dad arrived in New York—a tall, shy eleven-year-old who spoke no English—he was put in first grade, where he towered self-consciously among his classmates and was the butt of their jokes. But with his keen intelligence and mechanical turn of mind—he could build anything, fix anything—he quickly moved ahead to become a classic American success story, leaving the religion and the old-world customs of his parents far behind.

My father became a staunch Republican. His politics were based on what was good for his business: He hated labor union leaders, Franklin Delano Roosevelt, Communists, and Democrats, in more or less that order. He had little sympathy for the poor. Hard work and honesty had gotten him where he was; anyone in America could do the same. *What about me?* I used to wonder. *I have everything I want, not through hard work, just because I'm his daughter.*

My mother was born in Philadelphia in 1904, one of six children whose parents had fled the pogroms in Vilnius, Lithuania. Her family moved to New York City when my mother was a child, to a poor section of the Bronx, where the two oldest sons found good jobs and helped support the others. Both young men, still in their twenties, died in the influenza epidemic of 1918. My mother's older sister, Rose, gave up an art scholarship to Cooper Union and went to work so that my mother and the youngest brother, Joe, could finish high school. Mom was musically and linguistically gifted, but college was out of the question for her. She worked for a short time as a French-to-English stenographer, then met and married my father when she was not yet twenty.

Mae and Lou Lidsky, Mom and Dad. I was proud of them. They were an attractive couple: she youthful, vivacious, fun-loving; he thoughtful, reserved, capable. Different in so many ways, they were nevertheless deeply devoted to each other. They never argued in my presence; I used to wonder if they argued at all.

.   .   .

In the 1930s, while the rest of the country was in a deep economic depression, Dad's company continued to grow; among other jobs, he signed a contract for more than half a million dollars with the Brooklyn Edison Company to carry out its changeover program from direct current to alternating current. We moved from a two-family house on a tree-lined street in Sunnyside, on the Brooklyn-Queens border, to a large new home that Dad designed and had built under his close supervision. It was in Jamaica Estates, a small enclave on the far outskirts of Queens.

Our new neighborhood was in the throes of social change. Its unpaved roads and many undeveloped acres, covered with huge, ancient oaks, were just within the New York City limits and would soon be made accessible by a new thoroughfare, Grand Central Parkway. Expensive new homes would transform what was mainly a blue-collar, Catholic community into a solidly upper-middle-class suburb. We were among the first of the new arrivals, and we were resented for being rich—and Jewish.

Dad named our house Triple Oaks, a pretension that never caught on. Most people referred to it as "the big house on the hill." A solidly crafted Tudor-style home, built of brick and stucco, it was one of the largest in the neighborhood. There were French doors on the landing of the imposing central staircase, leading out to a wrought-iron balcony that overlooked the sloping front lawn and the multi-trunked oak tree that had inspired Dad's choice of name. Back in 1936 it was a technological wonder, with central air-conditioning, a built-in room-to-room intercom system, garage doors that opened automatically, and, buried under the steep cobblestone driveway, wires that heated up to melt the snow.

I loved my home as if it were a living thing and missed it terribly when I went away in the summer. But I also felt embarrassed because my house was so much bigger and nicer than those of others. It set me apart from my friends at a time when I wanted to belong: Many of them lived in small houses or apartments in other parts of Jamaica.

Much later, when my horizons widened, I discovered there were people richer than we were. I had friends who lived in Manhattan, on Fifth Avenue and Park Avenue in large apartments with uniformed butlers, maids, and cooks who called them "Miss Barbara" or "Miss Alice." It was a relief to learn that we were far from the richest family around.

·   ·   ·

I worshiped my father. I loved his craggy face that became more handsome as he aged. He was strong and capable and made me feel safe; I knew he would always take care of me. But I was also a little afraid of him.

He was given to long, meditative silences that troubled me. He never told me what was on his mind. He didn't take me seriously. He saw me as a pretty, amusing little girl and wasn't really interested in what I had to say.

Dad never alluded to the mysterious place called Russia where he had spent his childhood, although he would occasionally mispronounce a word in a way that revealed something foreign. I asked him once about the faraway, snow-covered land with the onion-domed churches that I saw in the illustrations of a favorite book of Russian fairy tales. He seemed angry with me, as if I had stumbled on some secret. "I've never read any fairy tales," was all he would say. I felt he was hiding something, something bad, something frightening. It made Russia all the more intriguing to me.

Reclusive and austere by nature, Dad seemed embarrassed when I kissed him and took little note of my day-to-day life. He absented himself from most everyday family matters, except in extreme situations when my mother called on him for support. Then he weighed in sternly, always of course on her side.

Friends and family came to my father for advice about their jobs and homes. They were in awe of his knowledge and his financial success. But Dad was basically a very simple man. He spent all his free time working around our house, which he made into a showplace. Like his father before him, Dad had magic hands. He could fix anything—a broken zipper, the catch on a necklace, a faulty appliance. I loved the little cottage he built out back as a woodworking shop; it had shutters, window boxes, and a front porch. He spent every spare moment there by himself, working on his current project, whistling tunes he made up as he went along. When workmen were around, he would often take off his jacket, roll up his sleeves, and work alongside them, no conversation necessary to gain their grudging respect.

Dad was an intuitive gardener whose grounds won first prize each year in the Jamaica Estates Lawn and Garden Contest. I would follow him around in the garden, always asking to help. He gave me the boring jobs—weeding and raking leaves—but he did, finally, give me a patch to call my own, into which I transplanted wild flowers from the woods, surprising and delighting him with my success.

When I tried to enter Dad's shop, however, he shooed me away, saying I might get hurt. Not so with my younger brother, Bob: Bob was expected to work alongside Dad from an early age, holding long planks of wood as they went through the saw, hammering nails, learning the craft. Dad's mother and his sister Mary, as accomplished with needles as Dad was with tools, must have seen in me a familiar family aptitude and drive: They took me in hand and taught me *their* work, "women's work"—sewing, knitting, and crocheting. They applauded my nimble fingers and the intensity with which I applied myself.

Dad told me once, quite casually, how he had prevented a terrible accident by knocking a man off a ladder: "I was inspecting a factory where our company was going to do some work. I spotted him up there, his body all rigid, holding a hot wire. So I pushed him off the ladder, just in time." I was impressed that he could act so quickly and knew what to do. *He saved a man's life*. I was filled with awe.

My father was indeed exceptional, but I put him on much too high a pedestal. I dealt with his remoteness by idealizing his wisdom and strength. I became upset when he showed weakness—his nervousness, for example, before giving a speech at a testimonial dinner in his honor. I saw him cry only once, when his father died, and that too upset me. I didn't like to think of him as soft or vulnerable.

.   .   .

My mother always said we were a lucky family and I believed her. Now, however, I find it strange that I could accept her myth of our "happy family" when one of her three children, my beautiful, talented older sister, June, suffered from debilitating depression and other emotional problems that became more severe as she grew older. June tried to conform to Mom's expectations: She was a model child when she was young; her problems did not surface until adolescence. It was not until her first "nervous breakdown" when she was eighteen or nineteen that my parents sought help. If they were aware of her distress before then, they kept their worries from me and Bob. This was consistent with Dad's reserve and Mom's general tendency to discourage disturbing questions. She would brush aside troublesome thoughts and conversations and pretend that unhappiness did not exist.

My mother lived in an unreal world of her own making. She willed herself to be happy and denied or rejected any unpleasant things that came her way. I felt protected by her unfailing optimism. It drove my troubled sister away, but it gave me strength.

When my mother talked about how lucky we were, she was probably referring to the way we lived. My father had made more money than either of them had thought possible, and that enabled her to be carefree and self-indulgent. Dad, nine years older than Mom, pampered her, though he was quite puritanical when it came to his own pleasures. He spoiled her like a favored child, and she seemed to love it.

Mom was slender, with pale blue eyes that she proudly highlighted with a wardrobe that favored shades of blue and green. Her face was actually rather plain, but she had a flirtatious, feminine style that made her appear prettier than she really was. She loved to dress up, to sing and to play the piano, to travel. She was a natural dancer who kept up with all the latest steps and was constantly on the lookout for dance partners. Dad would not set foot on a dance floor.

Every morning, before beginning an active day, my mother would spend some leisurely time getting dressed. Her dressing room, the size of a small bedroom, had rose-colored carpeting, floor-to-ceiling mirrored cabinets, a dressing table with a built-in sink, and, hidden behind a mirror, a small combination safe for her jewelry.

I remember sitting and watching as she powdered, preened, and inspected her image from every angle. Something about the scene repelled me, even as it drew me in. I couldn't help being fascinated by the color-coordinated shoes and clothes, each in its own special place; by the many mirrors and the hidden safe. But my mother's absorption in herself and how she looked also seemed distasteful and embarrassing to me. She wasn't beautiful and mysterious like the vain queen who banished Snow White; she was just my mom. Why did she spend so much time at the mirror? Even at a young age, I felt that there should be more to life than buying clothes and dressing up in them.

Sometimes Mom would try to involve me. "Shall I wear my blue-and-white spectators or plain navy blue shoes?" she would ask. "Why don't you pick out the right pocketbook for this dress?" She was trying to teach me her taste in things; taste mattered a lot to her. My mother and Aunt Rose, her older sister and closest friend, bought most of their clothes at Saks Fifth Avenue. Mom wore heather tweed skirts and matching cashmere sweater sets, or simple, Chanel-type suits. Her "good" dishes were Wedgwood—plain white without a touch of trim; her sterling-silver flatware was graceful with only a small scallop at the bottom. Dad believed in buying the very best of everything, and Mom always opted for understatement. She seemed afraid to step out of line in any unexpected way.

Like Dad, Mom had a lot of energy that she focused mainly on our home. It was perfect in every detail—with the most up-to-date modern appliances, a full set of ceramic dishes used only for outdoor barbecues, a linen closet so overstocked that fifty years after they were purchased, I inherited dozens of pale pink Cannon towels in their original, unopened cellophane wrappings. Her dinner parties were legendary among her friends—she could seat and serve twenty-two with matching dishes and stemware, and the various courses came and went like actors in a well-directed play. Indeed, Mom often rehearsed the entire menu by trying it out on the family the week before.

On weekend mornings I would sleep the drugged sleep of an adolescent. From far away, grazing the edges of my dreams, I could hear the familiar sound of Dad's electric saw, harsh and strangely comforting, the music of my childhood. Birdsong and summer breezes would float through the open windows rippling the curtains, gently urging me awake. As the clock inched past noon, Mom would start banging pots and pans downstairs in the kitchen as if it were New Year's Eve. Sometimes she would walk briskly through my room on the pretext of airing something on the upstairs porch; she always let the screen door bang as she passed through. She couldn't stand indolence in her children. My brother remembers being tormented by her daily question: "What did you accomplish today?"

My mother, like most of the women in her set, seemed content to be a housewife. Still, she had a great reverence, almost hero-worship, for a woman she knew from high school who had become a well-known doctor. She wrote her fan letters, copies of which were among Mom's personal papers that I sorted after her death. I found them embarrassingly self-effacing and threw them away.

My mother's aspirations for me were predictable enough—to marry "well" and lead a comfortable, country-club life. But curiously enough, it was she who introduced me, when I was in my early thirties, to Betty Friedan's revolutionary work, *The Feminine Mystique*, which ushered in the women's liberation movement. "This is a book *you* really ought to read," she said, stressing the fact that it would be more meaningful to me than to her. She knew by then that I had rejected how she lived. I know it hurt her. Yet she also understood and even encouraged my desire to do more with my life than she had with hers.

3

Five years old and new in our neighborhood, I wandered across the road where a boy named Billy Kane was playing on his front lawn. He threw rocks at me and shouted: "Go away! I'm not allowed to play with Jews!" I was stunned. Until that moment, I had thought everyone was Jewish; it was a label, nothing more, since my parents were not at all religious. I ran home crying and was upset that my mother seemed so resigned about what had just happened to me. "Don't bother with him," she told me, "Go play with your sister." My parents did nothing to intervene, nor did they try to make friends with the Christian neighbors who surrounded them. They seemed long-suffering, accepting, as if this was what it meant to be Jewish. I wanted them to fight back.

I was a strong-willed child, quick to bridle at restrictions. When I was about seven, I was forbidden to play with Winona, a strange, sad little girl who lived at the foot of our hill with her shadowy mother and mean-spirited grandfather. My mother disapproved of them, probably because they were poor, and unconventional. "Why?" I kept asking Mom, but she remained silent. So I disobeyed her.

Winona was part American Indian. She had nut-brown skin, long, stringy hair that never looked washed, and a broken front tooth. She wore flimsy, tattered skirts that had once been her mother's. I found her mysterious, and touching. She was more of an outsider than I.

We made dates to meet secretly in a clearing in the woods. There we planted a woodland garden between the trunks of two fallen trees and buried a dead bird under a handmade wooden cross. I was terrified one day when a gaunt man in a wrinkled black suit suddenly emerged from behind a tree. "That's my dad," Winona assured me, as she rushed into his arms. Later she told me, "He can't come home no more 'cause he stole from my grampa." Winona's father showed up frequently after that, bringing us chewing gum and giving Winona notes and little presents for her mother. I felt sorry for him. I didn't believe he was a thief.

When Winona didn't come out to play for several days in a row, I gathered up my courage and rang the doorbell of her house, where I had been forbidden to go. Her grandfather answered and without a word set his dog on me, an ugly chow with a black tongue who growled viciously and snapped at the seat of my overalls as I raced back down the driveway. I never told my mother what had happened. Soon afterward, they moved away, disappearing without a word. Mom was glad to see them go. I was heartbroken but kept it to myself.

I was the only Jewish girl in my class until sixth grade, when Lois arrived. Lois and her family were newcomers to the Estates, where they had built a huge, rambling house. My mother encouraged our friendship. I can still hear her excitement, talking to my father and Aunt Rose: ". . . both so pretty—from the back you can't tell them apart—the same height, the same hair, even the same camel's hair coats."

My best friend, Dotty, a broad-shouldered, athletic girl who walked to school with me every day, was jealous of Lois. Dotty's family was poor and Irish Catholic: Her mother, whom I adored, was a seamstress with a worn, pretty face and the old-country habit of catching her breath mid-sentence in a way that always took me by surprise; she taught me to do a backstitch by hand that was as even as any done by machine.

Dotty formed a club, secretly named the "anti-Jew club." Lois and I were not allowed to join; for a long time we didn't know why. When Dotty later disbanded it, she told me casually: "My mother said it would look bad if someone from the newspapers found out." *Why didn't she tell her it was wrong?* I wondered. I felt betrayed, not just by Dotty but by her mother.

Lois later transferred to a private day school in Forest Hills. I pleaded with my father to let me go too, but he wouldn't hear of it. "The public schools are fine," he said. And so, once again, I was alone, the only Jew, good practice perhaps for those times in the future when I would be the only woman.

Christmas was a mortifying time for me. The neighborhood houses were lit up with wondrous decorations; only ours remained dark, a dreary advertisement that we were different. Once, at Dotty's house, I brushed against the Christmas tree and knocked off a shiny silver ball that shattered as it hit the floor. Overwhelmed by the tree's beauty, I had never before come close enough to see that the ornaments were made of glass. I was horrified at what I'd done.

When my parents finally gave in to my pleas and allowed me to join my friends singing carols on Christmas Eve, I hovered around the fringes, unhappy and uncomfortable with the words of the songs. Secretly, guiltily, I wished I had not been born Jewish. I didn't know about the millions of Jews in Europe being sent to their deaths. *I* worried about not belonging.

.   .   .

I was the naughty middle child, affectionately dubbed "Little Miss Mischief" by my father. June, five years older and better than perfect when she was young, was always held up to me as an example. Bob, five years younger, was an adorable little boy who could do no wrong. I got attention by misbehaving. I was also rebelling against my mother's frequent refrain: "Why can't you be more like June?"

She didn't know it was wrong to be constantly comparing us. She told me: "You're Dad's favorite," which put me on edge, for if he favored me one day, he might favor June the next. She encouraged a competition between us, then lectured me about the evils of jealousy. I was ashamed that I envied my sister and tried to hide it.

Competition was the norm at Public School 131. Each new teacher would ask me: "Are you June's sister?" and then say: "I hope you turn out to be as smart as she is." I almost did: June graduated first in her class; I graduated second in mine.

June had brought fame to the school by winning a citywide poetry contest when she was in seventh grade. Her poem, which was framed and hung on the wall of our family room, didn't rhyme; it was called "Thought" and was written in "free verse." I was impressed. *How does she know about such things?* I could, and still can, recite the poem from memory:

Thought is a winged creature
that may fly from you in a moment.
It is soft and may tread on your brain
with a velvety ease.

Thought is a creature held by chains
that haunts you day and night.
It tramples with many feet
weighted with heavy iron.
Thought is a beautiful thing
more lovely than an angel.
Thought is an ugly hissing dragon
bringing dread.
Thought may bring glimpses of the place
so secretly, beautifully hidden.
An eternal happiness.
A new world.
Thought and Belief will clasp hands;
they are lovely sisters.
Thought was made by God and
belief has put *that* thought into our souls.

I felt a little thrill each time I read the words "lovely sisters" in June's poem. I hoped she was thinking of herself and me when she wrote them. In my heart I knew she wasn't.

I tried to shine in my *own* way, by being as different from June as possible. Perhaps I sensed that her goody-goody behavior was not normal and wanted to distance myself from her problems. Perhaps I was responding to my mother's pressure to conform. But in the course of rejecting June as a model, I also turned away from much that was admirable about her: her scholarly interests and her creativity.

Instead, as a teenager, I embraced every fad that came along and made me feel normal. I wore white bobby socks and penny loafers, huge shirts filched from my father's closet, and rolled-up "dungarees," the proletarian blue jeans that our generation first made fashionable. My friends and I were at the Paramount Theater in New York City when the young Frank Sinatra serenaded a tumultuous crowd of swooning girls. I listened to popular music in my room, the volume turned way up. I had crushes on boys and wove elaborate fantasies about them.

At Jamaica High School, I became active in sports and student politics, part of an "in" crowd that disparaged serious work. I studied as little as possible and did well nonetheless, graduating among the top ten in a class of more than 400. My yearbook designation as "class politician" didn't please me; I would have preferred "best athlete." My passion for sports was a socially acceptable channel for my competitive instincts. Unlike June, who disdained physical activity, I was naturally athletic. I could excel without feeling guilty about competing with her.

As an adolescent, I fought constantly with my mother, who disapproved of the clothes I wore and the hours I kept. I felt guilty about upsetting her—I didn't want to hurt her, she seemed so vulnerable—but I also sensed that given my sister's increasingly strange behavior, Mom was secretly relieved to have the problems of a typical teenager on her hands.

June was becoming more and more distraught. She was moody and withdrawn, spending her days writing in her diaries behind the closed door of her room, screaming "Get out!" if I dared to walk in. She was an embarrassment to me in front of my friends: Her hair was wrong, her clothes were dowdy, and she was always disapproving of the things we said and did. I longed for an older sister with whom I could be close, a sister to learn from, to confide in, to be proud of. But the rare times we spent together were never quite right. I turned instead to my kid brother, Bob, who became my pal and sidekick. My parents marveled at the hours I spent teaching him to ride a bike and praised me for my patience. They didn't understand that I was doing it for myself: I was determined that *he* would be normal.

June was a freshman at Queens College when she really fell apart. She would burst into tears at the dinner table for no apparent reason and race to her room, slamming the door behind her. I could hear her in there, crying and shouting unintelligible words as my father tried to reason with her. I was thirteen when it began. No one told me what was going on. I tried to shut it out by going downstairs and calling one of my friends.

June's misery commanded Dad's attention. He spent countless hours, or so it seemed to me, shut up with her, trying to understand her problems, looking for ways to fix her as if he were coping with a malfunctioning machine. June was suffering, and Dad was, too. She got to him in a way I never could. I was jealous of his involvement with her, but even if it had been a matter of choice, I was not about to follow her and her demons down that unmarked road to madness.

I never tried to understand what was wrong with my sister, not until much later that is, when we were both young adults. Back then we went our separate ways, as we always had. She stayed in her room a lot; I acted as if she wasn't there at all. Now sometimes I wonder if she was just too deep, too original, too sensitive to stand up to our mother's demands, if the pressure on her to be like everyone else didn't drive her over the edge.

There was illness at the core of our family, serious illness, yet one would hardly have known it at the time. Mom remained cheerful, hiding June's problems from the world, from me and Bob, and, to a large extent, from herself. She turned her attention to me. I was—I *had* to be—the healthy one: pretty and vivacious like my mother, interested in clothes and boys like other girls my age. I could be smart, but not too brainy; competent, but not intimidating. I was on display—to show the outside world how normal and happy my family remained, despite some minor problems with my sister.

.   .   .

World War II brushed my life in the most glancing ways. My father was an air-raid warden and went out into the darkened streets during air-raid drills wearing a special helmet, looking important to my young eyes. In school we knitted blanket squares for our boys in the service and sang patriotic songs. One of my cousins had a husband in uniform. A friend's older brother was drafted into the army toward the end of the war and did not return.

In 1947, I read Anne Frank's diary and learned about the Holocaust. I was sixteen at the time, about the same age Anne was when she died. Like others who read Anne's moving work, I was profoundly affected by her story. It was my first glimpse into the depths of human depravity. Nothing in my life had prepared me for the possibility of such evil.

I used to study Anne's photograph for hours at a time. She had shiny dark hair and deep-set eyes, like mine. She could have been my sister. She could have been me.

It was an accident of geography that forced Anne Frank into a cramped hiding place where she was discovered and sent to Auschwitz, while I had spent the same years—the war years—attending school and going off to summer camp. Anne and I might have shared a common destiny—we were both Jewish, both children in the time of Hitler. Yet at sixteen her body was moldering in a mass grave in Bergen-Belsen, while I was just discovering the dark side of human nature.

Learning about the concentration camps changed my attitude toward being Jewish. Young and impressionable, I knew at last where I belonged—

not with my Catholic friends who taught me to genuflect before the statues of saints in their church, not with my parents who bore the burden of being Jewish with stoic dignity, but with the memory of Anne, who died merely because she was Jewish.

For years I had nightmares about the gas chambers. I would awake in terror, gasping for breath. I would not discuss my dreams with anyone. My childish fears would only trivialize what had happened to the millions of children who perished. I tried to console myself by clinging to the assurances of world leaders. "Never again," they said, "never again." I really believed them. In time, my nightmares went away, leaving only the dull ache of guilt.

.   .   .

Guilt was the secret companion that accompanied me through childhood: guilt that my family was richer than others, that I had escaped the Nazi death camps, that I was jealous of my sister—guilt that I felt so guilty. And when June broke down irretrievably, turning against her family, I felt doubly guilty, afraid that I had somehow driven her mad by my desire to win away my parents' love.

June eventually married and had two children, then succumbed to another, more serious breakdown. She was hospitalized for a year in a private psychiatric hospital on Long Island. Dad paid the bills, and Mom helped out with the children. But after her release, June broke off all relations—forever—with Mom and Dad and, soon afterward, with me and Bob. She and her family lived like recluses in a ramshackle house in Seacliff, Long Island. Mom and Dad, desperate, went there several times unannounced, but June refused to open the door to them. She disappeared from our lives. Sometimes it seemed as if she had never existed. Mom seldom mentioned her. It was Dad who kept wondering out loud: "What happened with June? What went wrong?"

What might have been a normal competition between sisters turned tragic—and left me afraid of my own power; for as June began to fade from the family scene, I became what I had secretly wished to be—the only daughter. An irrational sense of responsibility for June's illness stayed with me for years, as I unconsciously looked for ways to redeem myself for what I thought I had done.

.   .   .

My parents worked hard to find a good prep school and, later, college for my brother, but they were indifferent when I was ready for college. "A girl's education isn't that important," Dad told me; he actually said that too much education might make it hard for me to find a husband. His only stipulation was that I stay close to home. He said he didn't *trust* me enough to let me go away to school, and I thought better than to ask him what he meant. Left mostly to my own devices, I ended up commuting to New York University, a school I had never even visited before my first day of class, in January 1949.

At first, college seemed no more than a continuation of high school. I was crowned "freshman queen" in a beauty contest for incoming students and was profiled in the college newspaper. I made the girls' varsity basketball team. I was invited to join one of the best-known sororities and wore the sorority uniform: a white wool jacket with green Greek letters on the upper left pocket.

Then, in the summer of 1950, a college friend and I went to Europe on a crowded student ship, the aged Dutch *Volendam;* the owners had converted the staterooms to dormitories and charged a relatively cheap rate for the passage. The crossing took ten days, which were spent in constant partying around kegs of Dutch beer.

I was surprised that my parents had agreed to let me go. Perhaps they wanted to make up for their refusal to send me to an out-of-town college. Travel to Europe was not common in those days. It was mainly the very rich who crossed the Atlantic on luxury liners in a style few could afford. I was the first among my family and friends to travel abroad, although within a few years, people would begin traveling for pleasure by airplane. Less than a decade later, my parents and others like them, all dressed up for the plane ride, would take tourist trips to countries in Europe, Asia, South America, and Africa. But in 1950 crossing the ocean was still a fairly adventuresome thing to do.

Three months in Europe worked a profound change in me. Surrounded by art, music, and history, meeting Europeans of my own age, learning about our differences and similarities, I became aware of how little I knew and how much I wanted to learn. Europe was still recovering from a war that had left it with bombed-out cities and hundreds of thousands of refugees and displaced persons. The students I met were more serious, more scholarly than their American counterparts. They made me ashamed of the beer-drinking college boys from the *Volendam* whom I ran into on occasion in Paris and in Rome.

I returned to NYU in the fall, consumed by a new desire to study. Literature and philosophy became my main fields of interest. Both brought me in touch with Russian literature, with the works of Dostoyevsky and Tolstoy. I felt an immediate, mysterious affinity for these writers. They wrote about Russia, forbidden territory in my father's household. Perhaps that made them all the more appealing to me.

The world of ideas opened up for me, not just in class but among new friends with whom I became engaged in nonstop intellectual discussions. Many of them were part of Professor Sidney Hook's Philosophy Circle, an after-school discussion group that attracted some of the best minds in the university. The leftist views I shared at the time with Arthur, the politically persuasive graduate student who was then my boyfriend, were disparaged by most of the members of the Philosophy Circle, who shared Professor Hook's strong anticommunism. Our political arguments were stimulating and made me question my own beliefs. College life took on a new, bohemian character. My campus became Washington Square Park and certain Greenwich Village bars we frequented, like the Minetta Tavern and the San Remo, hangouts for writers, artists, and intellectuals who still lived in the Village in those days.

In my senior year, Professor Hook offered me a graduate fellowship in philosophy. I was flattered but did not accept. Philosophy seemed too abstract to become a lifelong pursuit. I was torn: I wanted to continue studying, but I also had a vague notion of "working with people."

One day in the cafeteria, I ran into Burt Rubin, whom I knew from my class on existentialism. Burt was a married army veteran with a mop of curly brown hair, a large nose, and thick, dark-rimmed glasses. Though bookish looking, he had the personality of a wild man and a touch of genius. We shared a passion for Dostoyevsky, but Burt's was so encompassing that he was fast becoming a Dostoyevsky character himself, right under my eyes. Burt smoked pot regularly, an unusual addiction in the 1950s, and he approached life with a manic intensity that was sometimes alarming. His emotional ecstasy over cosmic ideas—the nature of life, of God, of evil—was interspersed with colorful erotic fantasies that he shared with anyone who would listen.

Burt took me aside. "Look at this," he said excitedly, showing me the catalogue of the Russian Institute, a new program at Columbia University. "An entire course in Dostoyevsky, another in Tolstoy. Russian-language courses, so you can read them in the original. And a lot of other stuff on Russia and the Soviet Union. Doesn't this sound great?" It *was* great. It seemed custom designed for me. I could get my fill of Russian literature and also learn more about communism. We both decided to apply.

4

Dad was furious when I told him I wanted to study Russian. It was as if I was taunting him, bringing the past back into his life. He had put Russia far behind him, a nightmarish country of anti-Semitic pogroms.

"Are you crazy?" he exploded. "You and your cockamamie ideas! Why *Russian*? How will you use it? We have nothing to do with those people!" He had willed himself to forget every Russian word he once knew. "And what is there to learn about those Commies anyway?" he continued. "Who would want to teach that stuff but a bunch of Commies?" It did not cross his mind—and it barely crossed mine—that I might be seeking to understand my own origins by studying the country of his birth. Church Slavonic literature and Marxism-Leninism, polar points of the Russian Institute's fare, seemed equally unrelated to the Jewish shtetls where my great-grandparents, and their parents, had lived and died.

Back in 1952, I attributed my interest in Russia to my passion for nineteenth-century Russian literature. Tolstoy had introduced me to an evocative world of rural beauty, of jaded aristocrats facing extinction and spiritual serfs on the brink of freedom—a world of troikas and balls and musings on human dignity and destiny. Dostoyevsky had plunged me into dark questions about human suffering, the existence of God, and the relationship between good and evil. This was not the world of my father's family, the ghettoized Jews of the Pale. This was *Russia*, the Russia Dad hated. Yet I felt a strong connection to it, and to the critical outsiders who played such a major role in Russian literature. They called to me, perhaps because of their social consciousness and humanitarian ideals. Unlike my father, who denied his Russian roots as antithetical to his Jewish background, I sensed a spiritual community in being both Jewish and Russian.

Years later, when I began working with dissidents in Russia and Eastern Europe, I understood and identified with their role as outsiders. That there were many Jews among them seemed natural to me: Jews, as the longtime pariahs of the region, would be especially sensitive to abuse. My own long-standing attraction to Russia began to make sense. It seemed like destiny that I had ended up working against repression in the place where my ancestors had suffered.

The Russian Institute also intrigued me because of its courses on communism. I wanted to learn more about the ideology I found both appealing and suspect. My romance with Arthur, the left-wing graduate student, had ended painfully when he confessed that he was married. I was left with uneasy feelings about his credibility in general, including his politics, which I had found so compelling.

.   .   .

Dad always indulged me when it came to girlish things like buying prom dresses and giving parties, but he was less obliging when he considered my requests inappropriate. He refused to use his new Cadillac to give me driving lessons, for example. "Women don't need to drive," he declared with finality. When Bob turned sixteen, it was different: Dad brought home a used company car, and we both set about learning how to handle it.

Dad also believed that I should marry after college and not go on to graduate school. "Men don't want eggheads for wives," he warned me. My mother, who usually kept out of our arguments, agreed with him on that point. Dad didn't actually forbid me to go to Columbia—I was of age, having just turned twenty-one—but he did what he assumed would accomplish the same thing: He refused to pay.

Looking back on it now, I think Dad was probably worried that my left-leaning, antiestablishment views would get me into trouble. It was 1952, the height of the McCarthy era, and there was an anti-Communist witch-hunt going on the United States. He must have felt that studying Russian, an unusual thing to do at that time, would make me suspect. Soviet studies were then offered only at the graduate level in the United States, and only at two institutions—Columbia and Harvard. Despite my father's concerns, these programs were anything but hotbeds of communism. The student body was carefully screened. It was assumed that many would end up in the U.S. foreign service or the CIA.

Some of my favorite professors at NYU were victims of McCarthyism; they had been fired or were under scrutiny for their pro-Communist views. Although I felt like a coward and am ashamed of my behavior to this day, I did not become involved in their defense. Signing petitions supporting suspected Stalinists, combined with my interest in studying Russian, could easily have been construed as softness toward communism. I didn't want to jeopardize my chances of getting into the Russian Institute. I was thrilled when I was accepted. My father notwithstanding, I was determined to go.

.   .   .

I worked all summer, leading teenagers on bicycle trips through New England and the Pennsylvania Dutch country. My earnings, combined with other money I had saved over the years, were enough to pay the $400 it then cost for the first semester of graduate school and the $10 weekly rent for a depressing room in an old lady's apartment on 115th Street near Broadway. My goal was to win a scholarship for the remainder of the two-year program. The work was tough and competitive, and I studied feverishly that first semester to get the grades I needed. Burt was also after a scholarship, and we were both consumed by anxiety, his more openly expressed than mine. "Look at that guy," Burt would say, pointing to a fellow student. "He has a Ph.D. in geography and a master's in economics. How can we compete with *him*?"

Burt and I spoke every evening on the telephone, like schoolchildren, nervously comparing our answers to the Russian-language homework we were given daily. As a result, we both excelled in the language courses that were an important part of the first year's curriculum. I won a scholarship, as did Burt, but my sense of triumph soured when my adviser, Professor Ernest J. Simmons, after telling me the good news, remarked: "I don't know why we waste our money on you women. You get married right after school, have babies, and that's the end of it all." His words were especially hurtful, I think, because I was so uncertain myself. On the one hand, I considered getting a Ph.D. and teaching Russian literature; on the other, though only twenty-one at the time, I felt pressure from my parents to find a husband and start a family.

.   .   .

Dad needn't have worried about any Communist brainwashing at the Russian Institute. The "Commies" among the professors were *former* Communists, and no one, I soon learned, was more vehemently anti-Soviet than a former believer betrayed by the cause. It was fascinating to hear my professors talk about their experiences in Russia in the 1920s and early 1930s, when the Communist dream, still young, was already turning bad. This was as close as I thought I would ever get to Russia—not because of my father's antipathy but because Russia had declared itself and its satellites off-limits, closed to the outside world. The Iron Curtain, defined by guard towers and barbed wire, stretched more than 4,000 miles through the heart of Europe, following an irregular, unnatural path that separated "East" from "West."

The Soviet Union covered one-sixth of the earth's land mass, including the town where my father was born and my grandparents spent more than half their lives. Seen by many as the most threatening country in the world, it was forbidden territory to anyone who did not wholeheartedly embrace the Communist cause. Because we were thus deprived of first-hand research opportunities, our studies relied a lot on conjecture—reading between the lines, disproving official statistics, analyzing the placement of Soviet officials on the reviewing stand at the May Day parade—a rather mysterious science that was sometimes called "Kremlinology."

By the 1950s, with the Cold War at its peak, the only Americans left in Moscow were the small and isolated U.S. Embassy staff and a handful of U.S. newsmen, some of whom had married Russian women who could not get visas to leave. These journalists parsed their words carefully so they would not be censored or expelled; their uncritical news reports sometimes made them politically suspect in the United States. Indeed, the *New York Times* hired an American-based Soviet expert, Harry Schwartz, to write interpretive critiques of the unjudgmental articles sent by its long-time Moscow correspondent Harrison Salisbury. But Salisbury, when he eventually returned to New York, surprised us all with his hard-nosed interpretations of Soviet reality that won him a Pulitzer Prize.

.   .   .

I studied the Russian language intensively, with several hours of language classes every day. I found the language beautiful, lyrical. I loved to read Russian poetry and to hear it read aloud. I learned the words to Russian folk songs and listened to Russian music while I did my homework. I was caught up in the magic of Russia.

I also studied Communist ideology. Reading Marx, Lenin, Trotsky, and Stalin, I found it hard to understand how a political philosophy based on the pseudo-scientific premises of dialectical materialism could be superimposed on a culture as mystical and as complex as Russia's.

Our professors were intent on showing us how the Soviet experiment had failed, how the country's early revolutionary fervor had been dissipated by the terror unleashed by Stalin. We learned about the countless victims of Stalin's collectivization programs and purges, about an entire country possessed by fear. My father could not have come up with a better institution to dispel my naive views had he set out to create one himself.

I came to see that one of the things I valued most—the right to question authority—was impossible under Stalin. I learned that no government should be trusted when it evokes a blissful future to justify its repressive actions in the present. I found it impossible to believe that Soviet communism had produced the New Soviet Man, a creature willing to sacrifice personal freedoms—even to confess willingly to fabricated crimes against the state—in order to serve the Communist cause. I pored over officially published Soviet literature, trying to read between the lines, looking for signs of dissent. My master's thesis, on the concept of Socialist Realism, explored every small hint of disagreement that I could find in Soviet literary criticism.

.   .   .

The small student body at the Russian Institute was an elite group academically; quite a few were older than I was and already had advanced degrees in other fields. They were, on the whole, gearing up for careers in academia or the government. Some of them were already employed by the CIA, although this was never said outright; they had been sent to the institute "by the government" to develop an expertise on Russia.

I became part of a small, self-styled discussion group. We considered ourselves more politically astute than most of our classmates and held frequent meetings of what we jokingly referred to as our "secret cell." Some of us had had previous flirtations with left-wing thinking, but we were all by then strongly anti-Stalinist. We were condescending toward friends and public figures who remained sympathetic to the Soviet Union. We called them "fellow travelers"—people who discounted the gory details of Stalin's reign and refused to acknowledge the facts.

In March 1953, stunned by the news of Stalin's death, we called an emergency meeting of our little group to discuss the future:

- Who will replace Stalin?
- Will there be less repression?
- Will there be new purges?
- How will we even know what is going on when the very fact of Stalin's death was kept from the outside world for more than six hours?
- What went on during those six hours?

We were so very serious, as if the future of the Soviet Union lay solely in our hands.

.   .   .

I went to these meetings with Austin Laber, a second-year student at the Russian Institute whom I had met early on at a party to welcome new arrivals at the institute. Austin, my senior by six years, had finished law school before coming to Columbia and emanated self-confidence; he was one of those accomplished people who so intimidated my friend Burt. I found Austin smart, witty, and ambitious, and we were soon spending all our time together.

Austin had firm opinions about everything, from the books I should read—Freud, Marcuse, Harry Stack Sullivan—to the clothes he would have liked me to wear, including wide-brimmed hats, which didn't become me, and sexy nightgowns, which were not my style. I was taken with his strong personality and pleased that he and my father got along well from the start. I thought he was like my father, that he would take care of me and not let me down.

One day, visiting my parents in Jamaica, we watched Dad climb a shaky, twenty-five-foot extension ladder in his garden to change an outdoor spotlight high up in a tree. None of the younger men around—Austin, my brother Bob, some of my brother's friends—offered to do the job for him. "You're not so young any more," I admonished Dad when he was down again. "Why didn't you ask the gardener to do that?" "I don't like asking people to do things I wouldn't do myself," Dad replied.

"Your father's a great guy," Austin said later, looking back on the day. I was so pleased that he admired my father. It was then that I began to think about marrying Austin.

Austin had come to the Russian Institute after law school because the State Department had more or less promised him a job after graduation as its legal expert on Soviet affairs. But in 1952, while we were both still students, the first Republican president in twenty years, Dwight D. Eisenhower, was elected. The new people at the State Department sounded very much like my father when they asked Austin: "Why would we want a legal expert on the Soviet Union? We have nothing to do with those people." Austin joined a Wall Street law firm and became a specialist in tax law.

5

I was annoyed when I heard my mother's cheery voice on the phone. I had just started a new job, working in a tiny office where I had very little privacy. *Why is she calling me here? She knows she'll see me at dinner.* I had moved back home for the summer in order to plan my wedding. Austin and I were getting married in the fall.

My new job—as foreign editor of the *Current Digest of the Soviet Press*—began in July 1954, soon after I finished at the Russian Institute. Getting the job was a stroke of luck: It was one of very few jobs in the Russian field in New York City. The *Digest* published English translations of important articles from major Soviet newspapers and journals for an audience composed of scholars, journalists, and government officials. I had worked there part-time as a proofreader, in order to support my studies. Then, just as I was finishing at the institute, Priscilla Johnson, the *Digest*'s longtime foreign editor, left for a freelance writing career, and I was offered her job. Despite my limited Russian vocabulary, I could handle the selection and translation of articles: The Soviet press was so predictable in those days, so full of Communist Party jargon, that I knew what an article would say, almost word for word, on the basis of its headline.

Mom was apologetic. "I'm sorry to bother you at work, but a really important-looking letter just arrived for you. It's from [she was reading now] the Embassy of the Union of Soviet Socialist Republics in Washington, D.C. Do you want me to open it?" My mother had the curiosity of a young child when it came to unopened mail and packages. She often infuriated me with her unrestrained nosiness about such things. This time it was different. "Open it, please! Quickly!" I implored.

Some months earlier, I had learned that a group of students at the Russian Institute had decided to apply for visas to visit the Soviet Union. I asked to join them. There had been vague flutterings of change in the USSR since Stalin's death—a West European student group had been admitted there on tourist visas, as had an American lawyer traveling alone. It seemed worth trying. We applied for visas, not mentioning that we were students at the Russian Institute, which had been criticized several times in the Soviet press for its anticommunism.

Months had passed with no word, and I had pretty much forgotten the whole thing. Then suddenly there was the letter that my mother was reading to me over the phone, informing me that I had permission to travel in the Soviet Union for four weeks in the month of August. Three others from our larger group received similar letters—Gay Humphrey, Frank Randall, and Ted Curran. It was never clear why we four were singled out, and especially why I—the only one without an Anglo-Saxon surname—was among them. I had thought my Russian-sounding name would work against me: The Soviet government was wary of émigrés. Yet my Russian origins were clearly apparent to Soviet officials, for they added a female ending to the name on my visa, changing it from Lidsky to Lidskaya.

It was the third week of July. We had about a week to get ready if we were to be there in August. The timing could not have been worse for me—I had just started my new job, and Austin and I were planning an outdoor wedding at my parents' home in early September. But this was the opportunity of a lifetime. Everyone understood that.

Our wedding date was changed to October. Priscilla Johnson kindly offered to hold down my job while I was gone, and my boss agreed to a leave of absence. Our professors went to bat for us, convincing suspicious U.S. State Department officials that we were politically reliable. The U.S. Passport Office in record time removed the ban on travel to the USSR that then appeared in every U.S. passport. My father, suppressing his fears, gave me the $2,000 I needed for the trip.

.   .   .

American students traveling in the Soviet Union as tourists? It was unheard of. We might just as well have been going to the moon. I was caught up in a whirlwind of activity. Then, suddenly, we were off, four young people in their early twenties—two women and two men—about to travel some 7,000 miles within the Soviet Union, visiting Moscow, Leningrad, Tiflis (now Tbilisi), Tashkent, Bukhara, and Samarkand. Soviet officials would treat us like royalty. Western correspondents would follow us around to get our impressions. A picture of us talking with young Russians on a Moscow street corner would appear in the *New York Times* on August 17, 1954, accompanying an article by Harrison Salisbury with the headline: FOUR COLUMBIA STUDENTS TOUR SOVIET: EXPERTS' KNOWLEDGE OF LIFE IN RUSSIA AMAZES HOSTS.

We traveled from Helsinki in an empty Aeroflot plane sent expressly for us. A brief article in *Pravda,* the official Communist Party newspaper, described us as Russian Institute students, dispelling any illusions we may have had that our Russian studies backgrounds had slipped by unnoticed. We were given rooms of true turn-of-the-century splendor in Moscow's National Hotel. I was overwhelmed by mine—it was huge, perhaps some 400 square feet, with luxurious brocaded couches and armchairs, lamps with fringed silk shades, and a separate sleeping alcove that could be screened off from the room by dropping a heavy velvet curtain. I opened the French doors, stepped onto a balcony, and caught my breath in wonder. Spread out before me was a view I knew well from photographs but had never expected to see in person: the Kremlin, its towers topped by brightly lit red stars; the Lenin-Stalin tomb, with a long line of people waiting to enter; the enormous expanse of Red Square, and St. Basil's Cathedral with its multicolored onion domes. The streets were spotlessly clean and empty; almost no one owned a private car. Traffic was permitted in Red Square in those days, but only an occasional vehicle passed by.

We were in the hands of Intourist, the official and only Soviet tourist agency, known to work hand in hand with the KGB, the Soviet secret police. The small sum of $19 a day covered a first-class hotel room, a guide, a car and driver when we wanted one, and coupons for four meals a day in the hotel dining room. Because we never ate more than three and often only two meals a day in the hotel—where the food was good but the wait interminable—we were left at the end of our trip with many unused meal coupons, which the hotel staff obligingly allowed us to trade in for caviar. I returned from the trip with more than thirty tightly sealed jars of the finest Beluga caviar, most of which I hoarded, parceling it out discreetly on special occasions over the next few years.

Intourist planned a packed itinerary and kept a close eye on us during our travels. There were, of course, the obligatory propaganda sights: model collective farms and factories, Komsomol and Pioneer camps, and museums of the revolution. But that was just a small part of what we did. In Moscow, we saw the treasures in the Kremlin's Great Palace, visited the Tretyakov Art Museum, viewed the famous subway stations, went to a soccer game, and saw *Swan Lake* performed at the Stanislavsky Theater. In Leningrad, we wandered along the Nevsky Prospekt and the canals and visited the Winter Palace and the Hermitage Museum. It was apparent from the start that the government wanted our visit to be a success. Not all our requests were granted, but we were given some opportunities that were quite remarkable for people of our age and status.

Most astounding was a meeting that was arranged for me with Anatoly Surkov, head of the Soviet Writers Union. It was audacious of me to ask for it—I was emboldened by the cooperative attitude of our Intourist handlers and by my own eagerness to talk to Soviet experts about their literature, which I had been studying intensively for the previous two years.

As it turned out, the meeting, which lasted more than two hours and included Anatoly Safronov, a well-known Soviet writer, was memorable for me mainly as a lesson in humility. Fresh from graduate school, having just completed my thesis on Socialist Realism, I was able to astound my hosts with my knowledge of their subtle literary debates. "She knows a lot about our literature," Safronov remarked to Surkov, as I was holding forth. But in my attempts to impress them, I ended up doing more *talking* than listening. And by zeroing in immediately on sensitive issues, I put them on the defensive: They became guarded and circumspect. When I returned home and decided to write about the meeting, I found little in my notes that was interesting. I had wasted an exceptional opportunity by showing off rather than getting the writers to talk.

This experience would stay with me over the years. I learned to be low key when interviewing, even to appear stupid. When people are at ease, their words are often unconsciously revealing.

.   .   .

It is hard to describe what it meant to penetrate the Iron Curtain in 1954, how great the divide was between East and West. I had studied Soviet society as if it were Mars, never expecting to see it firsthand. And now I was face-to-face with Soviet people, the New Soviet Men of my thesis. Fearful of being punished for talking with Americans, shockingly ignorant of the outside world, full of misinformation and prejudice, they were at the same time eager, oh how desperately eager, to talk to us and to learn about life outside their limited sphere. Their sense of deprivation was almost tangible.

I felt as if I had traveled backward in time. The technological trappings of capitalist economies were nowhere to be seen. Moscow's streets were constantly swept by troops of women in white coats using primitive-looking brooms. Clerks in the stores used abacuses to tally up bills. New apartment houses, with laundry flapping in the courtyards, were already shabby and showing signs of decay. Some stood alongside ancient wooden cottages, dilapidated but still charming with their ornate, painted window frames, each intricately carved in a different Russian folk design.

There were pigs roaming the city streets in Tiflis, capital of the Georgian Republic, a lovely city surrounded by mountains. We visited Stalin's birthplace in the town of Gori, about sixty miles west of Tiflis, a tiny shack protected from the elements by an imposing marble pavilion. We were taken on a stunning drive along the Ordzhonikidze Highway and were left breathless by the hairpin turns and steep slopes of the legendary Kazbek Mountains.

In Tashkent, Bukhara, and Samarkand, cities in the Republic of Uzbekistan, we encountered blazing heat and bedbugs in the first-class hotel. The old adobe huts in Samarkand had not yet been crowded out by new Soviet architecture; life seemed almost the same as in Muslim countries just over the border. Donkeys and camels jostled us in the crowded streets, men sat aimlessly in the teahouses and veiled women shopped in the dusty bazaars. Famous mosques, designated as museums, were in disrepair: We picked up pieces of ancient mosaics, lying with refuse in the dirt around a mosque. Yet all of this had a Soviet cast as well: Loudspeakers blaring out Soviet news and propaganda were a constant reminder that this remote culture was part of the vast Soviet empire. The newscasts included frequent invectives against U.S. imperialists, which made us a bit uneasy as we wandered along the winding streets.

The differences in the way we dressed and talked attracted less attention in Uzbekistan and Georgia than it did in Moscow and Leningrad. The Central Asian and Caucasian people were so far removed from the Soviet center that some of them actually assumed we were Russians from

Moscow. Wherever we went, we were followed by large crowds, but in the provinces they seemed less suspicious, more open, when they discovered we were Americans. I still remember a young girl in Samarkand, reaching out to touch my arm, as if to check whether I was real.

In Moscow, it was another story. The four of us, two men and two women, all of us tall and thin even by U.S. standards, had clothes, shoes, haircuts, and a manner that immediately marked us as foreign. Within minutes of leaving our hotel each morning, we were surrounded by growing crowds of curious Muscovites who unceremoniously fired questions at us. *"Otkyda vui?"* (Where are you from?) was inevitably the opener. Afraid they might be frightened off if we said we were Americans, we postponed the ultimate shock of revelation by asking them to guess. Their guesses often began with outlying Soviet republics—Georgia, Kazakhstan, Ukraine—then went on to countries of Eastern Europe, such as Czechoslovakia or Poland. We were asked if we were from Mongolia, from China. When we finally said "America," our words were electrifying. A number of people nervously faded from the crowd, some of them to report us to the equally nervous police who would arrive sooner or later to break up the group and bring us to the local police station. There, despite our carefully prepared documents in English and Russian, they telephoned some higher authority to make sure our presence in Moscow was permitted. In the course of the month, we experienced sixteen such arrests.

Some of the crowd, usually students, remained until the police arrived, firing questions at us nonstop.

- Which is better, the Soviet Union or the United States?
- How much does a worker in America earn?
- Does everyone have a car?
- Do *you* have a car?
- Are Negroes allowed in universities?
- Have you ever seen a Negro lynched?
- Why is America so warlike?
- Are there any new Tarzan movies?
- Tell us about jazz.

They examined the contents of my pocketbook with fascination: the cigarettes, the ballpoint pens, the notepads, the cosmetics. We often made arrangements to meet again with those who seemed less timid—we wanted to see how average people thought and lived—but only a few showed up at such prearranged meetings, and we were never invited to a private home.

I was frustrated by our inability to connect with ordinary Soviet people. To see what was behind the facade, to find out what they were thinking—that was more important to me than all the sights we were seeing. I knew our guides were intentionally keeping us busy so that we would not have time to strike out on our own. My companions accepted our tightly knit schedule more happily than I, touring museums with notebooks at hand as though they were in Florence or Rome. At the end of the day, they were tired and ready to go to bed, wanting to be fresh for the next day's tour. I, on the other hand, wanted to see what Soviet nightlife was like. But I was afraid to stray too far from the hotel by myself: An American woman alone at night in Moscow could not walk about unobtrusively. On one occasion when the four of us had dinner in a Moscow restaurant, a Russian worker, egged on by his friends, came over and asked me to dance. When I told him I was from the United States, he looked stunned and quickly abandoned me, right in the middle of the dance floor.

On our arranged tour of Moscow State University, where we were hosted by our Russian counterparts—English-speaking students whose academic specialty was the United States—I met a young man who seemed taken with me and gave me his phone number. I tried later on several occasions to call him at the university, hoping that he might be able to give me an unofficial glimpse of student life, but he never returned my calls. I worried that I might have gotten him into trouble just by trying to reach him.

The people we *did* meet seemed happy, secure, and confident, just like the New Soviet Men and Women who were the subject of my master's thesis. But I had claimed such people could not really exist, except in an Orwellian world of mindless robots. I became confused. I did not want to believe that the interests of the collective could replace individualism, especially in a country like Russia that had such a rich, highly developed culture. "Things no longer seem black and white," I wrote in my diary, talking about Mila, one of our guides: "She is shy, but with a sense of placid calm. She *knows* she is right. It is frightening." On another occasion,

I wrote: "The Soviet Union has given its people a meaning and a purpose
. . . and the security that comes with it. They have replaced God with
Lenin and Stalin. They have replaced personal values with economic and
material ones. These people are healthy and happy, as long as they conform. They have all the answers and their purpose is to struggle for the
betterment of all." In a burst of youthful melodrama, I asked: "Are we
individualists the last remnants of a dying world? As Dostoyevsky said,
why wish a terrible freedom on people who have no desire for it, who fear
it and do not know what to do with it?"

.   .   .

Time magazine had sent us off with thirty-five rolls of color film. CBS
Television had given us a 35-millimeter movie camera and more than a
dozen reels of movie film. Our trip was a news event: We were to record
everything we saw. Many of our professors and colleagues were also
depending on our impressions to augment their understanding of the
USSR. No one knew at the time that as the post-Stalin era progressed, the
Soviet Union would guardedly open its borders to outsiders and even to
exchange students. Our trip was seen as an aberration. I felt a strong
responsibility to absorb everything and report back accurately. Looking
back on it now, that 1954 trip might be seen as the first of the many fact-
finding missions in my career. But at the time, it seemed like a once-in-a-
lifetime experience.

Now the trip was ending and I was in a hurry to get home: It was September 9th, I was getting married on October 3rd, and I did not even have
a wedding dress. I booked a plane ticket from Leningrad to New York via
Helsinki, scheduled to leave Leningrad the morning after my three companions left by train for Western Europe, where they planned to travel a
bit before returning home.

As the one responsible for taking photographs, I had all the Kodachrome film in my suitcase; the others took the movie film and camera.
When the customs officer at the Leningrad airport asked me if I had any
film, I readily answered "yes," having been assured by the U.S. Embassy in
Moscow that there was no longer a law against taking out unprocessed
film. Unfortunately, that news had not reached the Leningrad airport. The
customs officer informed me gravely that I was not allowed to take undeveloped film from the country. "We will process it for you," he assured
me. But Kodachrome film was relatively new and under copyright at that

time and could only be developed by special formula in a Kodak labora-tory. When I tried to explain, matters became much worse. Despite, or perhaps because of, the obvious technological gap between the Soviet Union and the West, Communist Party ideologues claimed that Russians had invented everything from the telephone to the shortwave radio and fostered great national pride in Soviet science. "Our Soviet scientists can process your film," he told me firmly, becoming increasingly intransigent. "We will develop it to be sure you have not broken any of our laws, and then we will send it to you." It was against Soviet law to photograph bridges, prisons, or military installations, and I had taken special care to avoid such subjects.

My plane was to leave in five minutes. I asked to phone the U.S. Embassy in Moscow (there was no consulate at that time in Leningrad), hoping that someone there would clarify the matter. But the call did not go through. I didn't know what to do. I was frantically sorting through my options. *If I stay here arguing with them, I will miss my plane. That would be terri-ble. I have to get home, I'm getting married. But I can't leave the film behind. It will be ruined. I'll disappoint everyone.*

Maybe I should stay and try to convince them? But I have no money left. I don't know anyone in Leningrad. How would I manage?

I was eager to see how my photos had turned out. I had stayed up late at night in my hotel rooms, reading about apertures and f-stops in the Leica handbook, trying to do as good a job as possible. We were count-ing on selling photos to magazines to make up some of the costs of the trip. *I can't just abandon the film.*

My mind was racing. The rolls of film that were visible in my open suit-case were only half of what I actually had. The rest were in another part of my suitcase, still covered by my clothes. "Here, take them," I said impetuously, throwing the film on the counter and slamming my suitcase shut. "I can't miss that plane," I wailed, running out through the departure gate with the remaining film still in my suitcase. The plane was sitting way out on the tarmac, waiting for me. But one of the younger officials, who spoke some English, was on to me. He ran after me, repeating: "Please, you have more film? Please, you have more film?" I ignored him, carry-ing on hysterically about my fear of missing the plane, an act that came all too easily to me at that overheated moment. He fell behind me, and I saw him talking at a telephone connection out on the field.

I boarded the half-full plane and collapsed into the first empty seat I saw, my heart pounding with fear and then with wild relief as I heard the engines start up. The plane sat still while the engines revved, then suddenly they died. The doors opened and in came the two customs officials, the younger one in the lead. "Bring your suitcase and come with us," he said, glaring at me with unconcealed hostility. They led me forward to the pilot's cockpit, drawing a curtain behind us. "Open the case," he ordered. I did, and they took the remaining film.

They could have arrested me. I had lied to a Soviet customs officer and had tried to smuggle film out of the country. But when the plane finally left for Helsinki, I was on it, without the film. I felt angry, mortified, and guilty, even more so when I arrived at Idlewild (now Kennedy) Airport in New York and was whisked through customs by some top brass from *Time* magazine who had somehow learned I was arriving and were there to pick up the film.

Austin and my parents were also there waiting for me. Dad, who usually kept his feelings to himself, could not contain a huge smile of relief when I entered the airport waiting room. I realized, perhaps for the first time, how terrifying his family's stories about the pogroms in Russia must have been. Even later on, when I began traveling to the region frequently, Dad was never at ease until I was home again.

·   ·   ·

I was ashamed of my behavior at the Leningrad airport. It was reckless. If I had been brave, I would have stayed behind with the film. I was convinced at the time that had I stayed there and argued it out with customs, demanding to see some higher authority who knew about the change in the law, I would ultimately have prevailed. Now, knowing the Soviet bureaucratic mentality far better than I did then, I doubt that there was anything I could have done. But back then I thought I had failed in my one opportunity to stand up to a dictatorial government. I didn't know I would have many more occasions to test my mettle against Communist police and officials.

The film, by the way, did arrive at my home, some six months later, in a box addressed to me in care of the U.S. Embassy in Moscow. It had been processed for black-and-white and was ruined. But my friends had brought out the movie film without difficulty. We showed it on CBS television and gave many interviews to the press. Gay and Ted wrote an article for the *Ladies Home Journal*. I traveled frequently over the next year or so to Washington and to various universities, showing the movie film and describing to rapt audiences what I had seen and done in the Soviet Union, a land beyond reach.

.   .   .

Austin and I were married as planned in a lavish, traditional, outdoor wedding at my parents' home. On the morning of our wedding day, I wandered around alone, the pampered bride, while everyone else was busy getting ready. The caterers were setting up in the kitchen under Mom's scrupulous eye. A seamstress from Bergdorf's was putting the finishing touches on my gown. An organ was set up on the back lawn and the organist was trying it out. Two huge tents were raised—one over the patio, the other over a graveled area that until a few weeks before had been the playground where, as a child, I had done daredevil stunts on the swings and slide.

I wanted a few moments alone with my father, to share some loving words with the man who would soon be giving me away. All my life, whenever I tried to talk to Dad, my mother seemed to get in the way, but on this day she was much too busy to pay attention to us. Dad had his own problems, however. His garden had passed its peak and there was not enough color for the guests. At the last minute, he had ordered fifty pots of chrysanthemums and he was now burying them in the ground so they would look natural. The "boy" who delivered them had been my classmate in grammar school. Even back then, while *my* life was so carefree, he delivered flowers after school for his father's small florist shop on Hillside Avenue. He seemed uncomfortable in my presence—as I was in his—on that cloudy Indian summer day of my wedding. Our eyes never met.

The sun came out just once that day, at the very moment that Austin and I were pronounced man and wife. We took this as a good omen. But a superstitious friend quietly discovered that the traditional glass, wrapped in a napkin and placed on the soggy earth, did not break when Austin stamped on it; he predicted that the marriage would not last and gave it six months. He was right about the marriage, but his timing was a bit off—by twenty-three years, to be precise.

.   .   .

Our first apartment was a one-bedroom, wood-paneled "parlor-floor-through" with three fireplaces in a brownstone building on West 103rd

Street, just off Riverside Drive. Austin liked the apartment but was ready to look elsewhere because it had only one small bedroom closet. "That's not a problem," I said, "we'll add another one." He looked at me as if I were crazy. This was before the "do-it-yourself" era, and people like us didn't use carpenters in a rental apartment. But I was my father's daughter: We made things work. Dad took some measurements, and a week later the closet was delivered in pieces by one of his company trucks. He had built it to match the existing closet, and he assembled it quickly in our bedroom when he next came to see us.

Ten months after our marriage, I was pregnant. I left my job at the *Current Digest* in May 1956, a week or two before Abby was born. I did *not* send a birth announcement to Professor Simmons, my Russian Institute adviser who had made gloomy predictions about my future passage from scholarship to motherhood. He may have been right, but—holding our lovely baby in my arms—I could not have cared less.

6

The USSR had emerged from World War II as a fearsome super-power. Communist governments, with Soviet support, gained power in much of postwar Europe—in East Germany, Poland, Hungary, Czechoslovakia, Bulgaria, Romania, and Albania. There were large Communist Parties in France and Italy. Communists took over in North Korea after the war and won China in 1949. By 1950, the USSR and the United States were fighting their first "surrogate war," with North and South Korea as the combatants.

The USSR encouraged and assisted revolutions in poor, developing countries where Communist propaganda had strong appeal. It seemed bent on world domination, if not by direct aggression then through subversion.

By the 1950s, the Communist threat was a major issue in the United States. The House Un-American Activities Committee and Senator Joseph McCarthy created an atmosphere of fear with their efforts to ferret out Communists in government and the arts. Although the U.S. Communist Party was tiny, it was considered very dangerous and its leaders were prosecuted under the Smith Act. Communists were accused of spying for the Soviet Union, most notably Julius and Ethel Rosenberg who, though found guilty, probably would not have been executed, as they were in 1953, if emotions had not been running so high.

Anticommunism in the United States fueled Stalin's paranoia. The United States became the external enemy he needed to justify harsh repression of any opposition at home. At the time of his death in 1953, a new purge was in the making—the "doctors' plot"—in which Jewish doctors were targeted as the victims. Although Stalin was ruthless, he had made himself seem so omnipotent that millions of his subjects grieved when he died, not knowing how the USSR would survive without him.

The Soviet Union remained a threat after Stalin's death, trumping the United States in the race to explore space. In 1957, it put the world's first satellite—*Sputnik*—into orbit. In 1961, it would send the world's first astronaut—Yuri Gagarin—into space. The USSR developed hydrogen bombs and nuclear warheads. It had the technology to attack the United States from afar. Americans, traditionally protected by two vast oceans, were vulnerable for the first time. If we took the initiative, as some suggested, and bombed the Soviet Union, we might be annihilated in turn. The U.S. government adopted the less radical strategy of containment: to hold the Soviet Union to its postwar borders and to fight the spread of communism elsewhere.

Yet the Soviet Union—the *real* Soviet Union, the one I saw when I traveled there in 1954—was a backward country. Consumer goods were scarce and primitive, technology for common people was nonexistent, housing facilities were shabby and overcrowded, new construction was already crumbling, elevators didn't work, tap water ran brown. Soviet resources were invested in heavy industry and the military at the expense of ordinary citizens. And even the vaunted Soviet military strength was not as great as it then seemed.

Western analysts were quick to condemn Soviet authorities for their crass disregard for the welfare of their people. But virtually no one asked the more probing question: Could it be that the USSR did not have the resources or the infrastructure to do both at the same time: to keep up its military might and meet the needs of its citizens?

·   ·   ·

Nikita Khrushchev, an erratic and blustery man who became Party leader in 1955, understood that the Soviet Union could not continue to exist in isolation. He began to seek economic relations and diplomatic contacts with the outside world. He was a coarse fellow who on one occasion scandalized the diplomatic community by angrily banging his shoe on the table at a session of the United Nations General Assembly. He must have been dismayed when he saw the streamlined modernity of New York; compared to Moscow, it was the world of the future. Yet he bragged to the West: "We'll bury you," referring to the Soviet Union's economic potential.

Khrushchev knew the Soviet Union was falling behind the rest of the advanced world in the production of electronics, automobiles, and ordinary consumer products. He planned major increases in services and goods. But he probably didn't fully grasp—no one did at the time—the inherent, deep-seated problems in the Soviet economy that would later emerge. The old saying about the Soviet economic system—that people pretended to work while the government pretended to pay them—was really a critique of its centralized command economy. It had no flexibility. It eliminated competition, both internal and international, thereby destroying any incentive to produce. It led to an unwieldy distribution system, overproduction, and waste, as well as low morale among workers.

The Soviet economic crisis would continue to deepen during the rule of Leonid Brezhnev, who would replace Khrushchev in 1964. But it was not until Mikhail Gorbachev's arrival in 1985 that there would be serious last-ditch efforts at economic reform. Westerners who traveled to the USSR during Brezhnev's long rule, myself included, would make fun of the Soviets' inefficiency—how no one functioned and nothing worked—but we continued to tremble before Soviet military might. The memory of the Soviet army's heroic victory over the Nazis at Stalingrad was always there in the back of our minds.

.   .   .

By 1958, five years after Stalin's death, student exchanges had begun between the United States and the USSR. Many of my friends at the Russian Institute, including those who had been denied visas when we all applied to visit in 1954, signed up for one-year language programs at the Moscow and Leningrad State Universities. There they were able to experience Soviet life in greater depth than had seemed imaginable to me just a few years before and to master the Russian language through daily use. Burt Rubin, with whom I had crammed during our Russian-language courses when we first entered the Russian Institute in 1952, spent 1959 in Leningrad, leaving his wife, Betty, and their daughters at home. When he finally returned to New York, he seemed more Russian than the émigré Russians he surrounded himself with in his Upper West Side apartment. He entertained them and us with vodka and *zakusky*—a table full of appetizers such as herring, boiled potatoes, sour cream, dill, and pickled beets—and impressed even his Russian friends with his flawless, unaccented Russian. My Russian—once on a par with his—was not good enough to keep up at his gatherings. I felt shy about using it and embarrassed when I wasn't understood.

Burt, it turned out, suffered from manic depression. Later, in the early 1970s, he would go back to the Soviet Union carrying many bottles of sleeping pills and there try to take his own life. Poor Burt spent many months in a Soviet psychiatric hospital, one of the dreaded institutions where political dissenters were sent. The doctors there were wonderful, according to Burt. He spent the rest of his short life—he died in his sleep when he was in his early fifties—searching for the Russian drug they had given him that had made him feel happy again.

Study in the USSR was not an option for me in the 1950s. I was married. I had responsibilities to my husband, a house to run, a baby, and another soon on the way. It would be outlandish even to think of leaving for a year in order to advance my career. The sacrifice that Burt and Betty made was extreme, but understandable in the case of a man. But what kind of woman would put her career ahead of her family and leave them for a whole year? No one that I knew. Certainly not me.

.   .   .

After Abby's birth in 1956, I stayed at home, learning to cope with a life that was very new to me. Caring for a baby, cooking for my family and friends, furnishing our brownstone apartment—all this was an exciting challenge, and I threw myself into it. It was easy, and fun. In those early days, Austin and I shared the cooking and housekeeping. He was more experienced than I, having lived on his own for some years.

Back in the 1950s, people like us, just starting out in life, could find nice apartments for relatively little money. Austin and I were also helped along by gifts from our parents. We shocked the older generation by painting our walls white and our ceilings brown (walls were always a real color in those days; ceilings were always white). We bought dark-brown carpeting, earth-toned fabrics and "Danish modern" furniture with a dull teak finish that we thought was a nice contrast to the burnished Victorian paneling on the walls. But before we even finished fixing up the apartment, I became pregnant again.

In 1958, we moved to a small, run-down, two-bedroom penthouse on Riverside Drive and 90th Street with a large, wraparound terrace. I scraped, spackled, and painted the apartment by myself, three coats on every wall. I planted my first rooftop garden, learning what sort of trees would prosper in the wooden planters that Dad built for us. I was getting ready for Pam, who was born in September 1958, an affectionate baby with big, round, dark eyes and lots of curly dark hair, a striking contrast to her sister Abby's sunny blond, blue-eyed charm. I made dresses for the girls—blue for Abby, red for Pam—and knitted blankets, hats, and sweaters for them. Like my father's, my hands were always busy.

.   .   .

At around this time, I was asked by two friends—Paul Willen and George Sherry, who had both belonged to our "secret cell" at the Russian Institute—to join them in a new, part-time venture: launching a newsletter called *Soviet Sphere*. It came at a good time for me—I was housebound and needed an intellectual challenge—but I was upset that they had excluded Austin, for reasons they never explained. I knew Austin was hurt. We were all at the institute together, and Paul and George were our friends. Somehow I managed to smooth things over so that eventually all four of us were involved. The project, as I recall, never got beyond the first issue.

Would Austin have felt the same chagrin had the situation been reversed? Probably not, nor would I have allowed myself to feel hurt. No matter that we both had the same academic credentials. He was the man. His interests—and his ego—came first.

In the early years of our marriage, Austin and I shared a consuming absorption in the Soviet Union, reading all the relevant publications and discussing them together. I began writing articles on Soviet affairs, and Austin would read and edit them. But the 1950s were an apolitical time: We gradually turned inward, more concerned with psychology than with politics. "Family togetherness" became our ideology, psychotherapy the answer to all problems. Our friends, who used to gather at our apartment for after-dinner dessert and heated political and philosophical discussions into the early hours of the morning, now arrived with strollers and car-cribs. Our bed, on which they always threw their coats, doubled as a resting place for sleeping infants. The topics of conversation also changed:

We might start with literature or world politics, but we invariably ended up with child raising and Dr. Spock. We all wanted large families—four children or more. Children were the common denominator that kept friends, and marriages, together.

Our involvement with our children disguised the fact that Austin and I were growing apart and beginning to disagree on many things. His political views were much more conservative than mine, and he became angry with me when I disagreed with him, especially in public. He was far more critical than I of our friends and family, and he often refused to see people whom I liked and enjoyed. We approached life in very different ways: I was cautious and orderly, perhaps to a fault. Austin was expansive and extravagant, always buying things and wanting to eat in expensive restaurants. He liked living on the edge: paying bills only when dunned, making risky investments, missing trains and planes because he insisted on showing up at the very last minute. At first I was under his sway: He was older than me, very opinionated, an indulged only child who flew into rages when he didn't get his way. Later I began to take issue with him, not only with his views but with the disparaging way he treated mine. It seemed we were always bickering.

There were good things, too, and they held us together. Austin was lively and adventuresome. At his urging, we explored New York City and rented vacation homes in London, Mexico, and other places where I would not on my own have thought to go. We lived well: We had no reason to save, because my father was there as a backup. Above all, there were our children, a challenge and a delight. Their love sustained me and made me happy. And so, like my mother, I looked mainly at the bright side of things. I wanted to believe I was happily married. I told myself I was.

Yet I was often restless. My marriage lacked the intimacy and tenderness I longed for, and I sometimes found myself looking at other men, wondering whether I would be happier with someone else. The marriages of some of our close friends began coming apart, but I never seriously considered that mine might end. I had been brought up to think marriage was forever.

I also worried about my career, that I would have no profession to return to once my children were older. Burt's fluency in Russian filled me with envy. How I would have loved to have had his language skills—and the experience of living in Russia for a whole year.

A few years after Stalin's death, there was a remarkable "thaw." It was launched by Khrushchev, who stunned the world with a "secret" speech in February 1956, delivered at the Twentieth Communist Party Congress in Moscow. Focusing on the most forbidden topics, Khrushchev exposed Stalin's "cult of personality" and openly discussed the crimes that had taken place at Stalin's orders. He described the climate of fear in which legions of people were arrested almost at random, many on the basis of anonymous accusations made to settle some everyday score. The Khrushchev government began to release political prisoners—hundreds of thousands who returned with corroborating tales of an enormous network of prisons and labor camps where inmates suffered from forced labor, brutal cold, torture, and starvation.

An estimated 50 to 60 million people had perished in one way or another at Stalin's hands, far more than under Hitler. Yet during Stalin's lifetime, that horrendous truth was not known, not believed, or not discussed by most people in the Soviet Union or by Stalin's apologists elsewhere. Five years before Khrushchev's secret speech, when a former Soviet labor camp inmate, a Pole named Gustaw Herling, published a memoir exposing the cruelty of the Soviet prison system, there were many who refused to believe his story. Herling's experience was eerily similar to that of Jan Karski, a Polish resistance fighter during World War II. Karski had brought the news of the Nazi death camps to Western leaders in London and Washington, only to find that they already knew but preferred *not* to know about the extermination of the Jews. It was a politically inconvenient topic.

When Khrushchev, one of Stalin's henchmen, gave the astounding details of Stalin's reign, the facts could not be denied. They reverberated widely, causing people in many parts of the world to reconsider their attitudes toward Soviet communism. Even my studies at the Russian Institute did not prepare me for the full extent of Stalin's bestiality. They certainly didn't prepare me for the spectacle of Nikita Khrushchev, the Party leader, acknowledging such abuses.

I puzzled over Khrushchev's motivation. He probably felt a need to bring the fresh air of truth to a society that was stifled by the stench of its own evil secrets. But he obviously did not anticipate the explosive ramifications of his speech. Instead of reflecting well on him for his daring, it raised questions about his own complicity in Stalin's crimes and about the role of other Soviet leaders as well. Soviet citizens who had believed in the Communist ideal were being told they were the victims of a demented tyrant's paranoia. Rather than see the Party as Stalin's *victim*, as Khrushchev had portrayed it, many people *blamed* the Party. They felt betrayed and angry.

There was open discontent in Eastern Europe in the aftermath of Khrushchev's speech, especially in Hungary, where thousands of angry demonstrators took to the streets in October 1956. Despite his talk of reform, Khrushchev did not hesitate to quash the Hungarian protesters. In November, he sent tanks and several hundred thousand troops to Budapest to subdue them. Thousands died, and nearly 200,000 more were forced to flee to the West. Imre Nagy, the reform-minded Communist acclaimed by the demonstrators, was later hanged, together with several hundred of his colleagues.

.   .   .

The thaw took its name from *The Thaw*, a 1954 novel by a veteran Soviet writer, Ilya Ehrenburg. Although it would seem very tame today, I found Ehrenburg's novel a marvel at the time. It showed a hidden side to Soviet life and ignored the dictates of Socialist Realism that life be shown as it should be rather than as it is. Just out of graduate school, I brought the book to the attention of the editors of the *New Republic* and asked to review it in their magazine, which I did (October 10, 1955), describing it as "the most important literary work published in post-Stalin Russia." There were soon more—Vladimir Dudintsev's *Not by Bread Alone*, Vera Panova's *The Seasons*, and Leonid Zorin's *Guests*, among others. I reviewed them, too, praising their boldness and candor. "Within the ranks of the Writers' Union," I wrote in *Problems of Communism* (January–February 1956), "an important battle seems to be raging between writers who demand greater freedom for Soviet literature and those who cling stubbornly to the precepts of Zhdanovism" (Andrei Zhdanov was Stalin's repressive cultural tsar).

In my 1954 master's thesis, I had tried to prove, on rather slight evidence, that Soviet writers were chafing under the restrictions of Socialist Realism. Now, just a few years later under a new Soviet leader, a group of Soviet writers were mounting a struggle against censorship and publishing works on hitherto forbidden topics, including the personal and ideological conflicts of ordinary people.

Many Soviet officials were violently opposed to such revelatory writings, and a backlash soon began. In 1957, Boris Pasternak provoked official fury by publishing *Doctor Zhivago* abroad. In 1958, when it was announced that he had been awarded the Nobel Prize for literature, a vituperative campaign forced him to refuse it. In 1960, a group of young people whose names were later to become familiar ones in the annals of dissent—Aleksandr Ginzburg, Yuri Galanskov, Edward Kuznetsov, Vladimir Osipov, and Vladimir Bukovsky—organized public readings of literature in Mayakovsky Square, but the readings were soon forbidden and many of the organizers arrested and sent to prison or mental hospitals. Later, in 1963, the poet Josef Brodsky, whose status as a writer was not officially recognized, was sentenced for "parasitism" (living off the work of others).

While trying to keep the lid on a boiling pot, Khrushchev at the same time was turning up the heat. He continued his anti-Stalin campaign, revealing further crimes at the Twenty-Second Communist Party Congress in 1961. In 1962, as if to prove his point, he permitted the publication of Aleksandr Solzhenitsyn's *One Day in the Life of Ivan Denisovich*. *Ivan Denisovich*, a small masterpiece of understatement and quite unlike most of Solzhenitsyn's other works, was the first officially published work to describe the unbearable daily struggle in a Soviet labor camp under Stalin. The book created a sensation, especially within the Soviet Union. It sparked a flood of prison literature from other former prisoners who wanted *their* stories to be heard. But Khrushchev barred their publication. He seemed worried that he had gone too far.

At a 1963 Kremlin meeting, Khrushchev shocked the liberal poet Andrei Voznesensky by publicly upbraiding him: "You want to challenge us? We'll grind you to dust. And we will turn to dust anyone who is an obstacle to the Communist Party. Now there will be no thaw, no melting, but instead a frost will descend. For people like you we will make a rock-solid frost."

.   .   .

Khrushchev's political zig-zagging ended in October 1964, when he was ousted from power. He was replaced by Leonid Brezhnev, stolid and sphinx-like, who did not hesitate to arrest dissenters and reassert authoritarian rule. A black cloud of repression descended over the Soviet empire.

It would hover menacingly throughout Brezhnev's eighteen-year rule and begin to dissipate only in 1982, with his death.

.   .   .

Khrushchev had been an erratic reformer at best. His constant vacillation from thaw to frost probably reflected his own uncertainties as well as the pressure he undoubtedly felt from his more conservative colleagues. Yet his courageous exposure of Stalin's atrocities left an important legacy. A generation of young Party officials who came of age under Khrushchev were strongly influenced by the thaw. One of these men was Mikhail Gorbachev, who would become Party leader many years later. I am convinced that his policies of glasnost (openness) and perestroika (rebuilding) would not have been possible had Khrushchev not laid the foundations.

7

Brezhnev's icy hand brought an end to the thaw. The signal event was the arrest of two respected Soviet writers—Andrei Sinyavsky and Yuli Daniel—who had dared to criticize the Soviet state in satirical fiction published abroad under pseudonyms. For more than five years, their works had appeared in the West while their identities had remained unknown. I, along with others who followed Soviet literature, began to speculate that their sophisticated stories and essays might have been written by a Soviet émigré, or even forged by a Western writer. But the Brezhnev government eventually unmasked the real authors, tried them, and in 1966 sentenced Sinyavsky to seven years of hard labor and Daniel to five. Their trial and sentencing, well covered in the Western press, was a great blow to those of us who had hoped that the Soviet Union was changing. I described the scene in the *New Republic* (March 19, 1966), where I reviewed Sinyavsky's writings:

> At their "open" trial, the courtroom doors were closed to sympathetic students and friends and to the foreign press; articles in the official Soviet press on the eve of the trial extolled the "democracy of Soviet justice" and then proceeded to castigate the accused in the most acrimonious terms; [the] case . . . was clearly prejudged by the court, by the state-controlled press and presumably by at least a segment of the Soviet public deprived of access to the offending works.

Sinyavsky's works, published abroad under the name "Abram Tertz," often verged on the surreal. One of his characters fantasizes that the rough drafts and finished versions of novels that were torn into bits and "conscientiously flushed down the drain every morning" were subsequently caught in a "special dragnet or sieve underneath each house" and painstakingly pieced together again for delivery to the Prosecutor's Office. He also predicted his own fate in the story "The Trial Begins." For me, his most moving work was an essay entitled "What Is Socialist Realism?" in which he expressed for an entire nation the spiritual tragedy of the failed Soviet experiment:

> So that prisons should vanish forever, we built new prisons. So that all frontiers should fall, we surrounded ourselves with a Chinese wall. So that work should become a rest and a pleasure, we introduced forced labor. So that not one drop of blood be shed any more, we killed and killed and killed.
>
> In the name of the Purpose, we turned to the means that our enemies used: we glorified Imperial Russia, we wrote lies in *Pravda* [Truth], we set a new Tsar on the now empty throne, we introduced officers' epaulets and tortures. . . . Sometimes we felt that only one final sacrifice was needed for the triumph of Communism—the renunciation of Communism.
>
> O Lord, O Lord; pardon us our sins!
>
> Finally it was created, our world, in the image and likeness of God. It is not yet Communism, but it is already quite close to Communism. And so we rise, stagger with weariness, encircle the earth with bloodshot eyes and do not find around us what we hoped to find.

The Sinyavsky-Daniel trial was a show of force, aimed at intimidating Soviet citizens. Instead, it served to mobilize political protest in the USSR. Demonstrations and appeals on behalf of the two writers brought activists together in what might be considered the start of the Soviet human rights movement. Samizdat (self-published) literature, both fiction and nonfiction, played an important role. It was hand typed by unsung heroes at great risk. Using carbon paper, they could turn out no more than a dozen copies at a time, yet lengthy books, as well as petitions and reports on arrests and persecution, were produced, hidden, and clandestinely circulated. The typists were sometimes turned in by suspicious neighbors who heard the constant clatter of the typewriter keys late at night. They were tried and sent away to prison, but new people always seemed to emerge to take their places.

Samizdat was produced throughout Eastern Europe as well. The Czechs became known for their individually bound and painstakingly illustrated samizdat books. The Romanian authorities tried to stamp out samizdat by requiring that the typeface of every typewriter be registered. In January 1968, four young Soviets—Aleksandr Ginzburg, Yuri Galanskov, Aleksei Dobrovolsky, and Vera Lashkova—were tried and sentenced for samizdat publishing, including the compilation of a "White Book" on the Sinyavsky-Daniel trial. But an underground publication, the *Chronicle of Current Events*, continued to appear, giving factual reports on arrests and persecutions and printing the texts of petitions and appeals. Arrests had taken place all through the 1950s as well, but people had no way of knowing about them. It was not until the mid-1960s that samizdat made such information available and united human rights activists.

. . .

In August 1968, Soviet-led troops invaded Czechoslovakia. They put an end to an exciting era of reform known as the Prague Spring and established a permanent military presence there. It was a stunning blow to the Czechs and Slovaks who supported Alexander Dubček, the reform leader who promised "socialism with a human face." I still remember where I was—vacationing in Northeast Harbor, Maine—when I saw the morning paper reporting the invasion. No other event in public life, except perhaps the assassination of John F. Kennedy, had filled me with such helpless pain. The Brezhnev Doctrine had been clearly demonstrated to all of Eastern Europe: The USSR would resort to force to maintain the allegiance of its satellites.

In Moscow seven unbelievably courageous people (*seven people!*) attempted to demonstrate in Red Square against the invasion of Czechoslovakia, only to be arrested on the spot. One of the seven, Larisa Bogoraz, caught my special attention when I read about her arrest and sentencing at that time. Larisa had been involved with two prominent dissidents: her first husband, the imprisoned writer Yuli Daniel of the 1966 Sinyavsky-Daniel trial, and Anatoly Marchenko, a young dissident writer, also in prison. I sensed real drama in her story and read everything I could find about this courageous woman, so many thousands of miles away. I never dreamed that we would someday meet.

.   .   .

Activists in Moscow began to form groups. The first, in 1969, was called the Initiative Group for the Defense of Human Rights. Then in 1970, the Committee for Human Rights was organized. The names of the members of these early groups now seem like a who's who among Soviet dissidents. The police set out to destroy them. Most of the group members were arrested and sent to prison or, in some cases, declared insane and put away in psychiatric hospitals, where they were administered debilitating drugs. By the early 1970s, human rights activity in the Soviet Union seemed at a virtual standstill.

.   .   .

I had begun working again in the early 1960s, three days a week as a writer and publicist in the New York office of the Institute for the Study of the USSR. The institute, an anti-Communist think tank based in Munich, Germany, published materials on the Soviet Union aimed mainly at the Third World in order to counter the Soviet propaganda that was then being distributed widely in underdeveloped countries. A number of my fellow workers at the institute were Russians, early émigrés from the Soviet Union. A few of them were, or claimed to be, members of the Russian nobility, and it was not uncommon to find a well-dressed prince running the duplicating machine or an elderly count stuffing envelopes. I found them interesting and amusing.

I looked forward to the office Christmas party each year, which always began with a gala Russian banquet, prepared by staff members and their spouses and spread out on a cloth-covered Ping-Pong table in the office recreation room. Many of the foods were new to me, but the tastes were enticingly familiar and reminded me of meals my grandmothers had made. There was caviar, both red and black; several kinds of *pirozhki* (light, flaky pastries filled with ground meat, cabbage, or mushrooms); *pelmeni* (boiled dumplings often served in a delicate broth); beef Stroganoff; hard-boiled eggs with anchovies and dill sauce and salad Olivier (made with diced chicken, potatoes, and dill pickles). Vodka flowed freely and there was no end to the toasting. No matter how late I stayed, the party was in full swing when I left, and the sight the next morning of broken bottles and overturned chairs testified to even wilder partying as the night went on.

I got recipes from my colleagues and began preparing Russian food at home. One of my specialties was a meat-filled cabbage and beet borscht that I often served as a main course with mushroom *pirozhki* on the side. I followed it with thin slices of *paskha*, the sumptuous Russian Easter dessert made with farmer cheese, butter, cream, sugar, almonds, and other sinful things. My love affair with Russia now extended to its cuisine.

I was glad to be working again, back in touch with what was happening in Russia, but I found it hard to be away from my children, even part-time. I always returned from work with little presents for each child, tangible testimony to my feelings of guilt. The job itself was heaven-sent, a little sinecure where I was encouraged to write whatever I wished for outside publication, using the organization's library and resources. It was as if I had a writing grant with no strings attached. And it came at the right time, when it was becoming increasingly difficult, if not impossible, for me to write at home. Our new baby, Emily, was born in 1965. I now had three children clamoring for my attention.

We moved just before Emily was born. The cooperative apartment we bought in an Arts and Crafts building on West 86th Street would be my home for the next thirty years. It was big, a turn-of-the-century sunny duplex penthouse with a two-story living room, lots of oak paneling, and four bedrooms—a rare find, a great New York apartment, but it needed lots of work. Over the next year, my father arrived every Saturday morning in his work clothes, tool kit in hand. He installed massive oak bookcases that he had prefabricated in his shop at home. He built us a new fireplace and mantel and painstakingly reassembled, with Austin's help, an intricate mahogany overmantel that we had impulsively bought at an auction in New Haven. I planted a garden on our large open rooftop. Over time, it became an urban oasis of tall trees, vines, and bushes, and I became known among my friends and neighbors for my green thumb.

.   .   .

The 1960s were extraordinary—a time of political, social, and sexual upheaval—but I did not become involved as I might have had I been single and a decade younger. I was in my thirties at the time, facing up to adult responsibilities. I was too settled to join the freedom brigades, too busy to march on Washington. I viewed the happenings in Woodstock with a mixture of regret and relief: regret that I was too old to be there, relief that my children were too young. I was a supporter, not a participant, although I was not immune—few were—to the forces that were "blowing in the wind."

My office sent me to conferences in Munich on two occasions in the early 1960s. It was not easy for me to leave the children behind (they stayed with my parents during the week and Austin on the weekend). Once there, however, I found it liberating to be on my own in Europe again and for a brief time to reclaim an independent life among respected scholars in the Soviet field who valued my views and my company.

After Emily was born, life became more complicated; nevertheless, I went back to my part-time job when she was about three months old. Our new apartment had a real dining room, where we gave frequent dinner parties, some of them for Austin's professional friends. It was a busy and demanding life, a grown-up life, and I took a childlike pride and pleasure in being able to make it work. Then, in 1966, my mother became ill with breast cancer and whatever remained of the child in me soon vanished.

.   .   .

Mom's ability to repress and deny extended even to her own death. At first we hid from her the fact that she had cancer. She asked no questions of the doctor or of us, and we took this to mean she did not want to know. Later, when she could no longer deny she was dying, she talked about it with Dad, even suggesting that after she died he might marry Ruth, a widowed neighbor and friend. "She's always admired you," Mom told him.

With me, she was remarkably cheerful. "I can't complain," she told me one day, some weeks before she died. "I've had a love affair with your father for more than forty years." I was sitting at her bedside at the time, on a brilliantly sunny fall day. The golden oaks outside her window cast long, flickering shadows on the pale white carpeting of her room. They seemed to be asking us to admire their dying burst of beauty.

My mother soon grew oblivious to the world outside. Her circle became very small, circumscribed by weakness and pain, admitting only the few who still mattered—Dad, me, Bob. I called June at her home on Long Island and told her that our mother was dying. She sounded vague and removed and flatly refused to come.

.   .   .

My mother was sixty-three when she died in October 1967. During her dreadful two-year illness, Dad stayed home from work and devoted himself entirely to her care. There was a brief remission, during which he took her on a bittersweet trip around the world. As her condition worsened, he took care of all her needs, for the first time in his life preparing meals and washing dishes. Mom told me that at night, when pain kept her from sleeping, they would lie awake, silent, holding hands. One evening she felt too weak to climb the stairs and he did not have the strength to carry her. They sat on the bottom step, arms around each other, weeping.

Their closeness touched me profoundly. It made me question my own marriage—how Austin would refuse my attentions when he was sick and how impatient he became with me when I was not feeling well.

I also came to realize how important my mother was to me. I had always adored my father and felt that she got in our way. I didn't understand it was *she* who created the bridge between us and interpreted him to me. I worshiped him because *she* did. She made me *his* favorite because I was *hers*. Without her, Dad seemed diminished. In a way I felt I was losing them both.

I had always taken my mother for granted. *Some day, there will be time. We will grow closer, I will understand her better, I will offer her more of myself.* Now that time would never come. It was only when my mother became sick and needy that I realized how much I loved her and needed her. Only after her death did I come to appreciate how her love had encouraged my sense of worth. *My dear Mom. I have now lived half my life without you, yet hardly a day passes that I don't think of you and mourn your absence.*

Not knowing whether she was sparing me or herself by her reluctance to discuss her impending death, I played by my mother's rules to the very end. But after she died, I agonized over our mutual deception, wondering if our final days together might have been closer and more loving had I encouraged her to discuss her feelings and fears. I was full of remorse that I had not given her enough love and respect when she was well. I felt devastated. Never before had I experienced a grief so deep and personal that I could not share it with anyone. Never before had I felt so alone.

.   .   .

My job with the Institute for the Study of the USSR came to an end in 1970 when it was revealed that Radio Liberty, its parent organization, was covertly funded by the CIA. There was no reason why the U.S. government should not compete with the Soviet Union's vast propaganda offensive, but instead of doing so openly, it had authorized the CIA to secretly fund and even set up anti-Communist organizations that were ostensibly private. Radio Liberty was one such group. It survived the scandal and continued to operate, openly funded by the government, but the New York office of the Institute for the Study of the USSR, where I worked, fell victim to the cost-cutting and restructuring that followed. I had been with the institute on a part-time basis for almost twelve years. I left on good terms with my employers: I had a stack of articles to my credit, and a huge Russian-language atlas of the world as a souvenir.

.   .   .

In 1973, Solzhenitsyn's masterpiece, *The Gulag Archipelago*, was published abroad and distributed at home in samizdat. It was a monumental work, a memorial to the millions who had perished under Stalin, ultimately published in three volumes and some 2,000 pages. The *Gulag* is a unique, exhaustive, nonfiction work that documents every aspect of the labor-camp network, building one detail upon another in what may be the lengthiest and most excoriating account of institutionalized terror in world literature. It shook the foundations of Soviet society and brought home to Soviet citizens and to all of us, more vividly than ever before, the full scope of Stalin's terror.

I had become something of an expert on the writings of Solzhenitsyn, whose various novels I reviewed. One of them, *August 1914*, had given me a hard time when I struggled to write about it for the *New Republic* in the fall of 1972. It was an important book, the first volume of what Solzhenitsyn considered "the chief artistic design of my life." As the deadline neared, with nothing on paper, I began to panic. Then one morning I awoke understanding the reason for my writer's block. I had assumed, along with other reviewers, that Colonel Vorotyntsev, the enlightened, Westernized officer whose actions bind the novel together, was Solzhenitsyn's spokesman and hero. But I was wrong: The character who spoke for Solzhenitsyn was the religious prophet he called "the Stargazer." Seen in this light, I understood that the novel, like Solzhenitsyn himself, was both religious and nationalistic, that Solzhenitsyn believed in "the vigorous, inexhaustible spiritual strength of Russia," which in turn depended upon "the cultivation of one's own soul."

Solzhenitsyn was not, as most people then believed, a Western-oriented democrat like the well-known dissident physicist Andrei Sakharov. To the contrary, he was a messianic prophet, a Russian nationalist with strongly conservative leanings. Different from each other as they were, Solzhenitsyn and Sakharov were both critical outsiders, part of a long Russian tradition. Solzhenitsyn even talked about the writer's role as "a second state," as the conscience of society.

For a time, Solzhenitsyn seemed to be courting martyrdom at the hands of Soviet leaders. "No one can bar the road to truth," he declared, "and to advance its cause I am prepared to accept even death." Instead he was forcibly expelled from the USSR in 1974.

I seemed to be the only one around who understood Solzhenitsyn's views. Just before he took up residence in the United States, I cautioned American readers that this courageous man was not the liberal democrat that his Western admirers expected. It was not a popular position to take. It was based solely on my reading of his writings, but I was convinced that I was right. I wrote two articles to that effect, cover stories in *Commentary* (May 1974) and in the *Columbia Journalism Review* (May–June 1974)). They were poorly received by some of my colleagues in the Soviet field, one of whom actually called me a "traitor." I was vindicated, however, by Solzhenitsyn himself when he arrived in the United States and immediately revealed himself to be, if anything, more of a nationalist and a reactionary than I had predicted.

I found myself in good company when Andrei Sakharov took issue with Solzhenitsyn in a essay that was smuggled to the *New York Review of Books* and appeared in the June 13, 1974, issue, a few weeks after my articles on Solzhenitsyn were published. Solzhenitsyn and Sakharov, each reacting against communism in his own way, seemed to be playing out an old dichotomy in Russian thinking between the Slavophiles and the Westernizers. Sakharov's article was remarkable, not for what it said about Solzhenitsyn but for its clear exposition of Sakharov's own Western-oriented beliefs:

> [Solzhenitsyn's] opinions are alien to me. I consider the democratic path of development the only possible one for any country. The servile, slavish spirit which existed in Russia for centuries, combined with a scorn for people of other countries, other races and other

beliefs, was in my view the greatest of misfortunes. Only under democratic conditions can one develop a national character capable of intelligent existence in a world becoming increasingly complex.

.   .   .

After going to an office three days a week for a dozen years, I found myself at loose ends. When the children were in school, my free time was unstructured, aside from the occasional book reviews and articles I would write. Actually, I had felt depressed and in limbo ever since my mother's death, which made me question the emptiness of my marriage and a lack of purpose in my life. I pursued a number of interests, looking for a creative outlet for my unhappy feelings. I took several courses on film at Columbia University. I studied photography at the School of Visual Arts. I learned to print my own photographs and set up a darkroom at home. I began writing a cookbook with Molly Finn, a close friend since the early days of my marriage: *Cooking for Carefree Weekends* would eventually be published by Simon & Schuster in 1974. And I became involved in fixing up a weekend home that Austin and I had bought in 1969 in Litchfield County, Connecticut.

It was an old farmhouse with some forty acres of land in a place called Judd's Bridge, overlooking a brook and a bucolic landscape where a neighbor's cattle meandered and grazed. I loved it the minute I saw it, sitting a bit awkwardly atop a steep rise, the unmown lawn full of mustard weed and cow vetch. And I loved what it added to my life: a connection with the passing seasons and with nature and a place to be alone with my children, especially during summers in the early 1970s when we spent unbroken time there, reading, swimming in the pool, going to the local movie house. I made my own pasta, baked bread, and put up preserves. I dried herbs and flowers. I transplanted wild flowers, as I had as a child. I planted my first perennial flower garden in the foundation of what was once a silo and spent countless hours weeding and staking it. Gardening is as close as I have ever come to religion. Working in the garden never ceases to fill me with wonder at the complexity of nature, the continuity of life and my own small place within it. Back then it helped me come to terms with my life and with my mother's death, perhaps as more conventional religion might for someone else.

Austin loved the house, too, but it did not bring us closer. If anything, it helped us arrange our lives so that we were apart a good deal of the time. I spent as much time as I could in the country while he was in the city, and we both seemed better off for it. On weekends, we filled the house with family and friends. When we were both in town, he worked late, seldom coming home for dinner, except when we had guests.

.   .   .

In a way, I was glad that Mom was not around to see what happened to her lucky family. Dad, who had neglected his business during the years of her illness, seemed unable to cope with the turmoil he found when he returned to work. An ugly struggle had begun between different branches of the family vying for who would control the business after he was gone. The company decided to become a publicly held corporation, offering shares to stockholders, only to find that its financial basis was not solid, and indeed was much shakier than anyone had known. A severe economic recession in 1974 drove the business into bankruptcy, and Dad, who had personally guaranteed several million-dollar bank loans, was left exposed to his creditors. He lost everything. For a while it looked as if the family home might go, too, but he managed to hang onto it because the owner-ship papers were in the name of his new wife, Ruth, the family friend he had married in 1969.

I had been raised with the expectation that I would inherit millions of dollars. I even had plans to someday establish a small foundation and fund good works. That dream was suddenly gone. Austin's work suffered as well, for the family business had been one of his major clients since 1960, when he had established a private law practice. As the company was col-lapsing, Austin and my father had a falling out over tactics and money, and their relationship was never good after that. Dad tried not to involve me in his anger toward my husband. Austin, however, demanded my loyalty and seemed unaware of how painful it was for me to take sides. Secretly, I blamed my husband for much of what had happened. I felt as if I were being pulled apart.

For the first time in our life together, Austin and I needed money and there was no one to turn to for help. I began to look for work. Since there were no jobs in New York in the Soviet field, I tried to find a job in pub-lishing, only to discover that the publishing industry was also feeling the recession. Nevertheless, some freelance editing work began to come my way from editors trying to compensate for diminished staffs. Because I had recently published a cookbook, I was asked to edit or ghostwrite a number of cookbooks, which I did for very slight pay. I also got a job reviewing restaurants for the Connecticut supplement of the *New York Times,* but that job was so logistically complicated that I quit after six harried months.

Then a more ambitious project came my way—a two-year contract to coedit a completely new revision of the venerable old *Fannie Farmer Cookbook,* the rights to which had recently been acquired by Knopf. I was delighted to get the job. It paid reasonably well, although there would be no royalties. I would be working with a highly respected editor, Judith Jones, a serene and gracious woman who had the intelligence and broad range to be editor to such disparate writers as John Updike and Julia Child. Through Judith, I was introduced into the rarefied world of food experts, including James Beard and Craig Claiborne, and became privy to much of the gossip around which that world turned.

I was the writing end of the collaboration; my coeditor, Marion Cunningham, reworked and tested the recipes. I plunged into the job with enthusiasm, but I soon found it tedious to come up with superlatives for rice pudding or broccoli in cheese custard, especially because Judith, with her uncompromising eye, was quick to spot any false note in my descriptions. Marion's total fixation on the project and her lack of interest in things I found important began to irritate me.

My two main interests at the time could not have been more different: cookbook writing, which I did mainly for pay, and writing about Soviet dissidents, whose fate meant everything to me. I felt slightly schizophrenic: One day I was agonizing over life-and-death matters in the Soviet Union; the next, Marion and I were making two white cakes (one with butter and one with vegetable shortening), which we brought to dinner at James Beard's home to see if he could tell the difference—and of course he could.

One morning I found a sickening article on the front page of the *New York Times:* a course-by-course description of Craig Claiborne's $4,000 dinner for two in Paris (he had won it in a television fund-raising auction). I found it obscene to spend that kind of money on a meal and considered writing a letter to the *Times* to say so. But when I arrived at Judith's office that day, I found my cookbook colleagues avidly discussing Mr. Claiborne's menu choices, savoring them with vicarious pleasure. I said nothing. Once again I was the outsider.

8

Marcos Arruda, a young Brazilian geologist, was arrested in São Paulo on May 11, 1970, on his way to meet a young lady, a painter named Marlene Soccas, who, it turned out, had been arrested several days before and violently tortured. Marcos was taken to OBAN (Brazilian security police) headquarters where he was kicked, clubbed with truncheons, head pounded on the floor, ears banged in the cupped "telephone" style. Stripped, he was bound tightly wrists-to-ankles with thick ropes and hung over a suspended bar upside down, wires from a camp telephone attached to his toe, leg, testicles, through which electroshock traveled with varying intensity for several hours while he was beaten all over with the palmatoria—a plaque full of holes which raises huge hematomas. When he fainted, water was poured over him on his "parrot swing" to augment the sensitivity, and the wire was applied to his face for terrible shocks in the eyes, nostrils, mouth, till one policeman remarked, "Look, he's giving off sparks. Put it in his ear now . . ." Smashing his testicles, burning him with cigarettes, putting a revolver in his mouth, threatening dreadful sexual abuse could not revive him to confess, and the tormentors left him, writhing uncontrollably, for the night. At dawn his tongue and eyelids were paralyzed, his face distorted with contractions and his leg stiffened like wood, the foot caught downward, toes black. No sole beating could budge it. Alarmed, they threw him into a van and sped him to a hospital where he was kept incommunicado for five months.

This—and much more along the same lines—is what I found myself reading on that day in December 1973 when I picked up the newly arrived December 8 issue of the *New Republic* and casually turned to an article called "Torture." It was written by the poet Rose Styron, whom I knew slightly. What did she mean by "torture"? A bad marriage? Raising teenage kids? Never did I expect to find what I did. I wanted to put the pages aside, but I felt compelled to read on.

> [Marcos] was then taken back to OB headquarters to "confess." A letter from Marlene reports that her captors said, "Get ready to see Frankenstein." "I saw a man . . . walking hesitantly, leaning on sticks; one eyelid half-closed, his mouth twisted, his stomach muscles twitching continuously, unable to form words . . ." "Encourage him to talk; if not the 'gestapo' will kill him." . . . "We did not speak, not because we were heroic, but simply because we had nothing to say."

Rose was unflinching. Her article went on to describe what had been done to Marlene. And to others, in many different countries: Greece, Brazil, Algeria, Turkey, India, South Africa, Northern Ireland, Indonesia, South Vietnam, Uruguay, the USSR, Spain, Poland, Czechoslovakia, and Argentina were some of the countries named. I knew about torture in the Soviet Union, of course, but I had never dreamed it was so widespread. "Torture is everywhere," the article declared.

I could not stop thinking about what I had read. I talked about it to anyone who would listen. My good friend Judy Crichton, through whom I had initially met Rose, suggested that I call her. "She's involved with an organization called Amnesty International," Judy told me. "That's where she got her information. If you want to *do* something, give Rose a call and find out more about Amnesty."

Rose and her husband, the writer William Styron, lived in Roxbury, Connecticut, not far from our country house. I called her, and we agreed to meet the following weekend at her home.

It was a lovely spring Sunday. I was acutely aware of the incongruity as we sat on the grass in the dappled shade of an old apple tree, discussing horrors that were almost impossible to comprehend. I had always tended to turn away from upsetting stories, sparing myself the details; I was, after all, my mother's daughter. Now, however, I had gone too far. Knowing just the little I did about these real-life nightmares, there was no turning back. I was involved.

Rose was about my age, with a radiant, freckled face and a halo of strawberry blond hair. She told me about Amnesty, then a little-known organization founded in 1960 in London. Its research bureau, also in London, collected and verified information about political prisoners. She explained that Amnesty organized groups in various countries to work for the release of political prisoners in countries other than their own. A typical group would adopt three political prisoners whose dossiers were sent from London, often with suggestions for helpful actions. "Amnesty uses public protests, private letters, pleas to government officials, money and publicity to get results," Rose explained. "Most often we use letter-writing campaigns." It was Amnesty's experience that a large number of letters, sent both to a prisoner and to the officials involved in his or her case, could help protect the prisoner from abuse, or even bring about release, because it showed that people in other countries knew, and cared.

Rose told me she belonged to an Amnesty group, one of the first to be established in the United States. "We meet up near Columbia University," she said. "Why don't you come to the next meeting?"

.   .   .

It was called the Riverside Group and had about a dozen members, many of them academics. We met in the apartment of Arthur Danto, a philosopher and art historian who lived near Columbia University. I knew only two people there: Rose and Barbara Sproul, a professor of religion at Hunter College. The group was very businesslike as it went through its list of prisoners, discussing actions that had been taken and others that might be tried. Coffee and cookies were served as we talked, but no one lingered after the meeting. This was not a social club, but a group of busy people giving valuable time to a cause in which they believed. I liked what I saw.

My Soviet studies background made me immediately welcome: There were two Soviet prisoners among the five for which the group was working, and I was asked to take charge of both cases. I agreed, though not without some misgivings. It seemed like a hopeless project to me. Soviet officials, unlike the leaders of some other countries, were notoriously inaccessible and intransigent. It was hard for me to believe that a campaign of letter writing, Amnesty's basic tool, would make a difference. I kept trying to think of other approaches.

One of the prisoners was a Ukrainian historian, Valentin Moroz, author of a samizdat prison memoir, *Report from the Beria Reserve*. He was near death from a hunger strike in Vladimir Prison, some 120 miles east of Moscow. The other was a thirty-two-year-old Russian activist, Vladimir Bukovsky, who had been in and out of prisons, labor camps, and psychiatric hospitals ever since he was twenty-one. The Soviet government was fond of calling dissidents madmen, sending them to psychiatric hospitals and forcing them to take mind-altering drugs. This was a brutal practice, especially in a country that declared itself medically advanced. Bukovsky had taken up the issue, collecting documentation and appealing to the International Psychiatric Association. As a result, he was condemned to such an institution himself.

We wrote to Soviet officials: to the minister of justice, to the minister of state security and to the commander of Vladimir Prison, where both Moroz and Bukovsky were then being held. We got others to write, using a chain-letter system whereby each person would ask three others to write letters about a particular prisoner and each of them, in turn, would ask three more to do the same.

In the fall of 1974, three or four months after I had joined the Riverside Group, I received some new information about Valentin Moroz. It included the following description of him written by a former fellow prisoner who had immigrated to Israel: "a gaunt figure . . . , sick and ghastly . . . The prison rags hung on him as if on a wire skeleton. Short, stubby hair on his dried scalp, and greenish, parchment-like skin, terrifying as that of a mummy, covered his high forehead and prominent cheekbones. And the eyes—no, I cannot convey what I saw in his eyes during this short encounter." It was heartbreaking to read this description of the prisoner who had become my responsibility.

I had an idea for publicizing his case. A few years before, the *New York Times* had introduced an op-ed page that published short essays by readers. I quickly wrote up the Moroz case, including the description I had just received. I ended with a plea for "articles and editorials throughout the world" to generate attention to his case. "The press has the power to promote, reveal, destroy," I wrote. "It might be able to save the life of Mr. Moroz, who symbolizes the agonies of countless others—and then save those others as well." I got up my nerve to call Harrison Salisbury, then editor of the op-ed page of the *Times,* whom I had met twenty years before, in 1954, when he was a correspondent in Moscow and I was a visiting student. He remembered me and liked what I sent him. It was published in the *Times* on November 9, 1974, under the heading "The 'Wire Skeleton' of Vladimir Prison."

Although it seems hard to believe this now, the facts that I revealed about Moroz and Vladimir Prison were new to most *New York Times* readers, and my article was seen as a shocking revelation. It was the first article on human rights to appear on the op-ed page and the first to use Amnesty International as a source. Amnesty members kept calling me that day to thank me. I also became an instant hero to the large Ukrainian communities in the United States and Canada. They reproduced my article in thousands of copies.

For a brief while I felt triumphant, especially when one of my new Ukrainian friends told me that as a result of my article, President Ford had put Moroz's case on the agenda at a meeting with Brezhnev. But Moroz remained in prison for five more years, until, in an odd kind of juxtaposition typical of that time, he became one of five Soviet prisoners of conscience to be exchanged for two Soviet spies held by the United States.

I continued writing about abuses, using Amnesty information as my source. I had found a successful formula: I began with a detailed description of a horrible form of torture, then explained where it was happening and the political context in which it occurred; I ended with a plea to show the offending government that the world was watching. The names and places were different, but the abuses were depressingly similar. I had no trouble getting articles published: "Torture and Death in Uruguay" (*New York Times*, March 10, 1976); "The Torturers" (*Washington Post*, September 25, 1976); "Philippines Torture" (*New York Times*, October 30, 1976); "Tortured Bodies and a Clear Conscience" (*Newsday*, November 9, 1976); "In Indonesia, a Writer's Plight" (*New York Times*, November 19, 1977). I began to be known for my graphic, upsetting articles. At the time, it was important merely to reveal what was happening because the facts of abuse were just not known.

In those early days of the human rights movement, our main strategy was to shame repressive leaders into changing their ways. We assumed that all governments wanted to be accepted in the family of civilized nations and that by publicizing information that was not generally known, we would bring the force of world opinion to bear on them. By shedding light on hidden atrocities, we would make governments sensitive to the image they projected to the outside world. Publicity was our primary tool.

When people asked me about Amnesty International back then, I would say that we worked for the release of prisoners of conscience, people jailed for what they said, wrote, or believed. I did not use the words "human rights" to describe our cause; it was not part of my everyday vocabulary and would have meant little to most people at that time.

To be sure, the notion of inalienable human rights is not a new one: It dates back to ancient Greece, though it is most frequently attributed to the seventeenth-century philosopher John Locke, whose concept of natural rights—the right to life, liberty, and property—was the basis for such stirring documents as the U.S. Declaration of Independence and the U.S. Constitution and Bill of Rights.

The Universal Declaration of Human Rights, adopted by the United Nations in 1948 in response to the genocide of World War II, contains thirty articles, a catalogue of political as well as economic and social rights. In my early years with Amnesty International, dealing with cases of torture and political imprisonment, I would frequently invoke articles in the Universal Declaration, especially those asserting that "no one should be subjected to torture and other cruel, inhuman or degrading treatment or punishment" and that "everyone has the right to freedom of thought, conscience and religion," to "freedom of peaceful assembly and association," and "to seek, receive and impart information and ideas through any media and regardless of frontiers."

The Universal Declaration would be augmented in time by a large and growing body of international human rights agreements, treaties, and institutions, many with the force of law. People would come to know of them. But back in the early 1970s, when I first became involved in human rights activity, the concept of human rights was mainly the province of legal and academic specialists.

．　　．　　．

On December 30, 1975, Vladimir Bukovsky's thirty-third birthday, our Amnesty group helped organize a "Free Bukovsky" vigil. Bukovsky, who had spent most of his adult life in prison, would be released a year later on December 18, 1976, as part of a prisoner exchange and deported to the

United States. My Amnesty colleagues and I would host a party for him in my apartment for some 200 guests who were eager to meet him and celebrate his freedom. In 1975, however, his case was virtually unknown in the West. Our vigil was an attempt to draw attention to his plight. We gathered outside the Soviet Consulate, a nondescript brick building near the corner of Third Avenue and 67th Street. No one in the consulate acknowledged our demonstration, except for a small figure we spotted on the building's roof, taking photographs of our group down below. I in turn began photographing him, hoping he would see my camera focused on him when he looked into his viewfinder.

Our group included some recent Soviet émigrés who had been exiled from the USSR for their human rights activities and some well-known Americans, whose presence, we hoped, would attract the press. I recognized several actors holding placards—Joel Grey, Tammy Grimes, Dustin Hoffman, Celeste Holm—and found myself walking alongside a tall, youthful-looking man in a sheep-lined trench coat, his freckled face red from the cold. He seemed lively and instantly friendly, confessing to me how thrilled he was to be walking behind Celeste Holm, whom he had worshiped when he was an adolescent and she the star of the Broadway musical *Oklahoma*. Extending his hand, he introduced himself: "I'm Bob Bernstein," and I knew at once who he was: Robert L. Bernstein, president of Random House, the only prominent businessman we knew of at that time who was really committed to the human rights cause.

Some months later, I received a call from Jill Kline inviting me and Austin to a dinner party. Jill was the wife of Ed Kline, an eccentric businessman and self-styled Soviet expert who was immensely knowledgeable about dissidence in the Soviet Union and for many years funded the publication of Soviet samizdat in English translation. I had known Kline when I worked at the Institute for the Study of the USSR and had recently met him again in a special group that Amnesty had organized in New York for members dealing with Soviet prisoners.

Because the party was on a Saturday night, I immediately declined. It had become our policy to refuse any invitations that would interfere with our weekends at our country house. "I'm so sorry," Jill said, "Bob and Helen Bernstein are coming, and we wanted you to meet them."

After I hung up, I began to reconsider. I really wanted to get to know Bob Bernstein. I knew we shared an interest in human rights, and I had an intuition, nothing more, that through this energetic man I might be able to transform my human rights work into something different, something new. *Austin wouldn't think twice about missing a weekend if something important to* _him_ *came up. But this is such a long shot. It's embarrassing even to tell him what I'm thinking.* I decided to go with my instincts. Austin, not quite understanding what I was about, reluctantly agreed to spend the weekend in the city. I called Jill back the next day to say we would come after all.

On the evening of the party, Austin annoyed me with his slowness in getting dressed. We left our apartment angry with each other and very late and couldn't find a cab. By the time we arrived at the Klines' party, more than a dozen people had assembled and the cocktail hour was almost over. I worried that I might not have an opportunity to talk to Mr. Bernstein after all.

But he recognized me as soon as we walked in. "I know you," he said when we were introduced. He remembered meeting me at the Bukovsky demonstration and had read my op-ed articles on human rights abuses. He immediately began generating ideas for other articles I might write. One, I remember, was about torture in Iran under the shah, and I had already written it.

At dinner, Austin mentioned I was editing the *Fannie Farmer Cookbook* for Knopf, a division of Random House. Bernstein seemed surprised and pleased. "Come see me the next time you're in the building," he told me. I called him before my next appointment at Random House. He suggested that we have lunch.

9

Lunch with the President of Random House was a bit daunting. I knew that a lot was riding on the impression I would make, that Bernstein would not have suggested our meeting if he didn't have some sort of collaboration in mind.

It was 1976, six years since I had worked in an office. Jeans and T-shirts had become my standard garb. I tried on every skirt and dress in my closet, only to find that they were hopelessly out of style. I ended up wearing a striped sweater and a short brown corduroy skirt that I had bought the year before when I began looking for work in publishing. The outfit had seemed more appropriate back then than it did at the French restaurant near Random House where Bernstein and I had lunch.

Bob Bernstein seemed oblivious to my casual attire, though our conversation was far from casual. He questioned me as if it were a job interview and was interested in many aspects of my life. He also talked a lot about himself, his family, and his work. He seemed eager to impress me even as I was being judged.

Bernstein had been making inquiries about me. He came right out and told me what people had said, clearly unconcerned about protecting their identities. "I understand you wrote some ill-advised articles about Solzhenitsyn," I remember him saying. I assumed he had been talking to Michael Scammell, a biographer of Solzhenitsyn and then the editor of the British magazine *Index on Censorship*. I knew Mike had disagreed with my take on Solzhenitsyn's essential conservatism. But when I began to explain my position on Solzhenitsyn and why it had irritated some of my colleagues, Bernstein quickly lost interest. He asked me about my family. "How old are your children?" "How much time are you willing to give to a job?" "What kind of salary would you want?" His attention span was disconcertingly short. He jumped from subject to subject, interspersing serious conversation with anecdotes about his three sons, whom he clearly adored.

One of the most appealing things about Bob Bernstein is his attachment to his family. As I came to know him better, I saw that it was his wife Helen and the boys who kept his flights of fancy grounded in reality and helped him define his relationships with others. I had been struck by something he said when I first talked with him at the Klines' dinner party. "There's only one situation in which I would justify the use of torture," Bob had volunteered out of nowhere, ". . . if my children were kidnapped and being held hostage. I would use anything, including torture, to find out where they were." It was a curious statement, intellectually untenable for a human rights advocate, but very human. I could see he had been wrestling with basic moral issues intrinsic to human rights work and had found his own breaking point.

Sidney Hook back at New York University had posed such questions theoretically in "Ethics 1" in order to stimulate our thinking. Now in my Amnesty work I was hearing about *real life* moral choices, the sort I hoped never to have to face myself. I learned about torture victims who had suffered unbearable pain in order not to implicate a parent, child, or friend— and about others who had broken under such pressure. I tried not to think about what I might do in such a situation. Not so with Bob Bernstein, whose feelings were closer to the surface than mine: He confessed his fears freely to me, someone he hardly knew at the time. I liked his openness.

Bernstein turned my head with the possibility that I might work for human rights in a paid, not volunteer, job. "I have an idea," he said to me halfway through our lunch, "but it may take some time to work it out." He explained that the Association of American Publishers (the AAP), had formed a committee—the International Freedom to Publish Committee—to work for free expression worldwide and that he was its chair. He said the staff person assigned to the committee, "a very nice person," had no real interest in human rights. "I'd like to see *you* in that job," he told me, "but it will take some doing."

.   .   .

Bob Bernstein was in his late fifties when we met. His hair had already darkened and was turning gray, but his densely freckled face and mercurial temperament spoke of the redhead he had been. As I soon came to know, he was given to sudden bursts of anger, tempered by sincere apologies once he calmed down. His occasional displays of arrogance were similarly undercut by his deep commitment to people in need. Over the years I would watch him develop from a nervous speaker to a funny and eloquent one, never more moving than when his fury was turned against those in power who were persecuting innocent people. His very real passion, and his ability to convey it almost at the drop of a hat, would help recruit many people to the human rights cause. I was impressed from the start by Bob Bernstein—by his originality, his imagination, and his access to influential people. I wanted to work with him. He had the drive and the power to get things done.

Bernstein told me about his visit to Moscow in 1971 with a group of American publishers. They were there to urge the Soviet government to sign the International Copyright Convention, which it did in 1973. Bernstein was shocked by the censorship he saw there. He was also dismayed by the rigidity of Soviet publishing officials. "They asked me to publish their books," he told me. "Then they told me which books I was allowed to publish."

Bernstein learned about Andrei Sakharov, the iconoclastic Soviet nuclear physicist. Sakharov, "the father of the Soviet hydrogen bomb," was the youngest scientist ever to be elected to the Soviet Academy of Sciences, in 1953 when he was thirty-two. He was given all the privileges of the Soviet elite: good housing, a car and driver, access to the best medical facilities, and so forth. But by the late 1950s, after pondering the moral implications of nuclear weapons, he came out against their testing, to the dismay of Soviet leaders. He continued to speak out—on environmental concerns and in defense of human rights victims. Eventually he was ostracized, stripped of most of his privileges, and continually harassed. Bernstein was enormously impressed by Sakharov's fearlessness and moral conviction. He met Sakharov in 1976 and became his friend and publisher.

In 1975, Sakharov had won the Nobel Peace Prize, but Soviet officials had refused to let him travel to Oslo to accept it. His wife, Elena Bonner, who was abroad for medical treatment at the time, ignored warnings by Soviet authorities and accepted the award for him in December. Bob and Helen Bernstein, together with Ed and Jill Kline, had gone with her to Oslo as moral support.

Instead of doing business with the Soviet Union like other American publishers, Bob Bernstein began publishing banned works by suppressed writers, which were smuggled out to him. His outrage put him at odds with many of his publishing colleagues at the AAP, who saw the Soviet Union as a vast, emerging book market, especially for medical and scientific texts. It was a conflict between business interests and human rights concerns, one that would be played out in many countries, and with much larger stakes, over the years.

The Association of American Publishers was tired of being harangued by Bernstein, but it couldn't ignore him—he headed the largest trade publishing house in the United States. So in April 1975, the AAP decided to form the International Freedom to Publish Committee as a separate entity under Bob Bernstein's chairmanship. The committee would take up human rights issues while other publishers did business. It was this group, a little more than a year old and with no clear direction, that Bernstein now wanted me to run.

.   .   .

The opportunity came faster than Bernstein had thought, thanks to the new U.S. president, Jimmy Carter. Carter declared his intent to rebuild the moral authority of the United States by making human rights a touchstone of U.S. foreign policy. I still remember hearing Carter talk about human rights in one of his televised preelection debates with Gerald Ford. *Is he talking about what we're doing?* I asked myself, incredulous. Within a short time, the words "human rights" seemed to be on everyone's lips. In 1977, Amnesty International would be the recipient of the Nobel Peace Prize.

Carter did not invent the notion of human rights as U.S. government policy: the U.S. Congress had already created a human rights office in the State Department and had passed laws to deny U.S. aid to countries that violated human rights. But Carter was the first president to promote the policy, elevating the head of the human rights office to assistant secretary of state for human rights and appointing a feisty advocate, Patricia Derian, to the position.

In early 1977, at Bernstein's suggestion, I called and was interviewed by Townsend Hoopes, then president of the Association of American Publishers, who was impressed by my Russian-studies background and by my many articles on human rights themes that I brought with me to the interview. He offered me a two-day-a-week job as a consultant to the AAP's International Freedom to Publish Committee, but when I asked for $10,000 as salary, a modest amount even then, he said that $10,000 was the committee's entire yearly budget and that I should work out my salary needs with Bob Bernstein.

I stifled my impulse to call Bernstein and report on the meeting with Hoopes. Bob Bernstein was a busy man with a lot on his mind. I thought it best to wait until I heard from *him,* after he had a chance to talk to Hoopes. I waited anxiously until his call finally came. I wanted that job more than anything.

But Bernstein was angry with me when we met—angry that I had not called him at once to report on my meeting with Hoopes. He also seemed angry about my salary request. He offered me $7,000 a year, saying he wanted to keep some money for committee activities. He told me pointedly, in a manner that seemed both paternal and patronizing, that I would be expected to work year-round and would not be able to take long summer vacations in the country. I was offended. *Does he think I'm some sort of trendy society lady who won't take the job seriously? Can't he see how committed I am? How responsible I am?* True, I was sad at the prospect of giving up the precious summer months I had been spending with my children in Connecticut. I had confessed my regrets to an Amnesty colleague who worked in publishing, not thinking it would go straight back to Bob Bernstein. I told him I couldn't do the job for $7,000 and left his office feeling humiliated by his attitude and betrayed by my Amnesty friend.

A few days later, Bernstein called to say he was stepping down as chair of the publishers' committee and planned to set up his own independent human rights group instead. "I'd like you to work on it with me," he said, with no trace of his previous anger. He told me that Winthrop Knowlton, the president of Harper & Row, would replace him as chair of the publishers' group. "Call Win about the AAP job," he said.

Win Knowlton, quick to describe himself as a quintessential WASP, had the clean-cut looks, crisp manner, and Republican connections of the corporate establishment. But he belied the stereotype with his sensitivity, his evocative writing skills, and his sentimental heart, especially when it came to human rights victims. He was deeply touched by a day he spent with dissident Russian writers in a country dacha outside Moscow and later wrote about it in the *Atlantic Monthly* (February 1978):

Oddly enough, I had thought that my publishing colleagues and I were the ones bringing freedom—a sense of how it really works—with us from America . . . I had not dreamed that I would bring back from Russia a deeper, truer sense of what freedom can be, the various simple, quiet freedoms I had seen during my day in the country, freedoms that are like stones, the small stones we pick up on the beach, that have been made to gleam by the terrible force of the elements.

Knowlton and I hit it off well. I could see he'd been giving some thought to his new responsibilities; he told me he wanted to expand the committee's work to other countries, in addition to the USSR. He suggested bringing speakers to the meetings to inform the committee members of human rights problems in various parts of the world. Then he asked about my salary. I hesitated for a moment, then told him the truth: that I had asked for $10,000 and Bernstein had offered me seven. I was glad I was open about it, for I could see that Knowlton was already privy to what I had told him. Then to my dismay, I heard myself saying that I could not take the job for less than $9,000.

"I'll be in touch with you soon," Win Knowlton promised me as I was leaving. I assumed he would talk to Bob Bernstein before making me an offer. I chastised myself all the way home for having suggested $9,000. In my eagerness to get the job, I had opened a negotiation: I would be asked to compromise at $8,000, not much better than the $7,000 I had refused from Bernstein. Knowlton called the next day: "The job is yours," he said crisply. "Ten thousand dollars." It was a great way to begin.

10

I was being paid for doing the work that so absorbed me. It seemed too good to be true. Later in 1977, when Bob Bernstein started his own group, the Fund for Free Expression, he asked me to be a consultant to the fund, working one day a week for $5,000 a year. The fund's original members, in addition to a number of publishers, included writers Kurt Vonnegut and John Hersey and journalists Anthony Lewis and Sidney Gruson of the *New York Times*. One of our first projects was to promote the British journal *Index on Censorship*, which published the works of censored writers worldwide.

I found myself working five days a week, not just the three for which I was being paid. I spent two days at my office at the Association of American Publishers and the rest of the week working for the Fund for Free Expression in a small room in the Random House building on 50th Street and Third Avenue. The room was buried within the education department at Random House and lined with shelves holding copies of *Index on Censorship*. We saw *Index* as a vehicle for getting our message out. I arranged for a test mailing and analyzed its results to determine whether a direct mail campaign would boost the journal's circulation.

Most days, before returning home, I would drop in on Bob Bernstein in his spacious office on the twelfth floor of Random House. It was the highlight of my day. Bernstein was always welcoming. When others came in to see him, he often included me in the discussions, giving me a taste of his publishing life. Actually, it usually worked the other way: The hapless visitor with a publishing matter on his mind would be treated to a summary of the human rights issues of the day, for that was what was on Bob's mind. Bob's vocal outrage mirrored my own deep-felt feelings, but he was much better at expressing himself. His diatribes seemed to irritate some of his publishing colleagues—they complained to me that Bob was too self-righteous—but I suspected that they were defensive because they didn't do human rights work themselves and that they saw Bernstein's appeals as a reproach.

It was a lot of fun spending time with Bob. There was a playful side to him: He kept up a constant stream of jokes and anecdotes and was given to pranks, usually lighthearted ones involving his friends and family, but sometimes deadly serious ones—against human rights abusers.

It was during one of our late afternoon sessions that Bernstein dreamed up a plan to pressure the shah of Iran and embarrass a number of prominent people. He showed me an invitation he had received to a dinner in New York in honor of the shah and his empress. The dinner was sponsored by many well-known New Yorkers, who saw it as a chic event and gave no thought to the shah's abysmal human rights practices. Bernstein suggested that we write to each of these people, telling them about human rights abuses under the shah and asking them to intervene with the shah on behalf of a specific Iranian writer whose case we had been working on in the AAP's Freedom to Publish Committee. I drafted a letter that a group of publishers signed. We sent it to their acquaintances who were sponsoring the dinner. Some were offended at the implied rebuke, but others were chagrined and apparently raised the issue. In any case, our efforts were successful. Within a few months, the writer Dr. Gholamhossein Sa'edi was allowed to leave Iran and visit our group in New York.

.   .   .

It was a heady, intoxicating time for all of us. We were caught up in the excitement of our cause, in our conviction that we could change the world. I spent all my time at human rights work—writing letters and articles exposing human rights abuses, recruiting others to join our cause, lobbying government officials in Washington to work for the release of specific prisoners. The work was urgent and important: I was trying to save lives. My friendships suffered, as did my family life. I put my work ahead of everything.

Following Win Knowlton's suggestion, I expanded the committee's focus from the USSR to three other countries that were gross violators of human rights—Iran, South Africa, and Argentina. Writers and publishers were among the victims in each of these countries, which made their cases especially relevant to our publishers' group.

Iran at the time was under the ruthless rule of the shah, whose regime was supported by the U.S. government. Tens of thousands of political prisoners were being held without charges in special prisons. Most of them had done nothing more than openly criticize the policies of the government. That was enough to warrant savage torture by the dreaded secret police, SAVAK.

One of my sources was Reza Baraheni, a bearded Iranian poet and professor who had recently immigrated to the United States. Baraheni had been arrested by SAVAK in 1973 because he criticized the shah's nationality policy. He was relentlessly tortured, with beatings that tore apart the soles of his feet and broke his fingers, threats to rape his wife and daughter, and a mock execution in which he expected to die. Baraheni told me about torture chambers with iron beds to which prisoners were tied and "roasted" and about whips, electric prods, and nail-plucking instruments. He described how people were hung and beaten with a club on the legs and tortured with electric prods on their chests and genitals. He described how victims were raped while hanging upside down.

It was my first experience interviewing a torture victim. Baraheni's words seemed to burn a hole right through my chest. I felt sick, a kind of nausea deep inside me in a place I didn't know existed. *Am I capable of dealing with this?* I felt almost panicky, wondering if I had the emotional strength to do the work I had chosen. *I have to stop reacting so personally. To get the details without absorbing the pain. Part of me, the feeling part, has to turn off. But do I want to become so hardened? What kind of person will that make me?* I was venturing into a dark underworld of inhuman malevolence and excruciating suffering, a world so far beyond ordinary human experience that it mocked the normal life I knew. I wasn't sure if I could handle it.

I became preoccupied with the torturers, with trying to understand how "ordinary" people could commit such atrocities. People who had been tortured often described their torturers as "family men" who left home each morning to do a job just like anyone else. I learned that the techniques and implements of torture were strikingly similar throughout the world and that torturers in various countries often insisted on being addressed as "doctor." I wrote about torture, over and over again, trying to comprehend the incomprehensible. In "The Torturers" (*Washington Post*, September 26, 1976), I wrote:

> These "doctors" venture forth each day to work in well-equipped torture chambers lined with modern acoustical tile and spattered with blood, vomit and urine. Their degrees are in rape, fingernail-plucking and whipping. They are engineers who manipulate wires that cause learned professors to bark like dogs and women to plead and laugh hysterically, no longer reluctant to betray their husbands ... A torturer's working day is long, his hours irregular. His involvement is total, immersed as he must be in the intimacy of his victim's flesh, blood, sweat, screams and tears. In order to debase another, he must also debase himself, for to torture without compunction requires the complete denial of his own humanity.

Many torture victims did not survive. Steve Biko, a thirty-year-old anti-apartheid activist in South Africa, was beaten, tortured and left alone in a Pretoria prison cell. He died in September 1977 while being transported, naked and handcuffed, to a hospital many miles from Pretoria. Donald Woods, an exiled newspaper editor who had written about Biko and who subsequently got in trouble with the South African police, came to one of our committee meetings and described the Biko case, and his own predicament, in detail.

.   .   .

In Argentina, the military junta that came to power in 1976 waged a "dirty war" that ultimately killed perhaps as many as 30,000 people and turned the verb "to disappear" into a dreaded noun—the "disappeared" *(desaparaecido)*. The slain were mainly young people suspected of left-wing sympathies. They were tortured, then murdered, their bodies disposed of without a trace. Many, it was revealed later, were pushed while still alive from airplanes over the sea.

One of the early victims in Argentina was Jacobo Timerman, the outspoken owner and editor of the Buenos Aires newspaper *La Opinion*, who angered the military by regularly publishing the names of the "disappeared." Timerman was kidnapped in 1977, when he was in his mid-fifties. He was imprisoned and tortured, and his newspaper was seized by the government. He was later released, but held under strict house arrest. As part of an international campaign on his behalf, our Freedom to Publish Committee persuaded Columbia University's School of Journalism to issue an invitation to Timerman. This recognition may have been instrumental in securing his release from house arrest in 1979, though he was then stripped of his citizenship and expelled from Argentina.

In 1981, Timerman was the keynote speaker at the Association of American Publishers' annual meeting in Florida, which I attended with him. A heavy-set man with a face that was alternately soft and pugnacious, he was a dynamic speaker with a keen, argumentative mind, always raising questions that challenged and disturbed, and equally provocative when he was off the podium, no matter what the topic might be. My good friend Toby Talbot translated Timerman's book about his experiences in prison. The Timermans and the Talbots had dinner at my home on an evening when a taped interview of Jacobo by Bill Moyers was coincidentally being aired on public television. We watched the program, teasing Jacobo about the way he turned the tables on his interviewer: "Let me ask *you* a question, Mr. Moyers," he said, and before you knew it, Timerman was interviewing Moyers.

Bob Bernstein befriended Timerman and published his moving book, *Prisoner Without a Name, Cell Without a Number* (Knopf, 1981), which included passages like the following:

> Of all the dramatic situations I witnessed in clandestine prisons, nothing can compare to those family groups who were tortured often together, sometimes separately but in view of one another, or in different cells, while one was aware of the other being tortured. The entire affective world, constructed over the years with utmost difficulty, collapses with a kick in the father's genitals, a smack on the mother's face, an obscene insult to the sister, or the sexual violation of a daughter. Suddenly an entire culture based on familial love, devotion, the capacity for mutual sacrifice collapses. Nothing is possible in such a universe, and that is precisely what the torturers know.

The Freedom to Publish Committee received some other visitors from Argentina—two women, founders of the Mothers of the Plaza de Mayo. Members of this group shared a heartbreaking experience—their children had disappeared. They held a silent protest vigil every Thursday in the Plaza de Mayo in Buenos Aires.

One of the women, Maria Antikoletz, had the same surname as my maternal grandmother, Annie Antikoletz. I mentioned this to her after her talk, and she told me that her husband's family was from Lithuania, as was my grandmother. Later, after she had returned to Buenos Aires, I found myself thinking about her—her name and her face remained in my mind, prodding some vestigial memory.

I called Aunt Rose, my mother's sister. She told me I had relatives in Argentina and that my mother's first cousin, Daniel Antikoletz, had been a lawyer and a prominent government official there. Maria Antikoletz's "disappeared" son, a lawyer named Daniel, was most likely his grandson—and my distant cousin. The many miles that separated the branches of my family seemed momentarily breached by this sad coincidence. It lent credence to a thought that crossed my mind frequently when I met or read about a human rights victim—that geography is destiny. Had I lived in another country, that victim could easily have been me.

.   .   .

Despite the dismal reports we received from different parts of the world, the Soviet Union continued to dominate our committee's attention, mainly because of its attitude toward literature. More than other dictators, the Soviet leaders knew, and feared, the power of the printed word. There were more writers in prison or internal exile there than in any other country in the world. These writers wrote about their travails in prison, and their books were smuggled to the West, works such as *My Testimony*, by Anatoly Marchenko; *Report from the Beria Reserve*, by Valentin Moroz; and *Prison Diaries*, by Edward Kuznetsov. These books, unlike Solzhenitsyn's *The Gulag Archipelago*, described the horrors of prison life *after* Stalin's death. Very little had changed.

.   .   .

Less than a year after I began work with the Freedom to Publish Committee, Win Knowlton asked me if I would like to work for Harper & Row. He was prepared to create a special position there for me, as a corporate public relations director. Among other things, I would be organizing special lectures and panels for the staff and the press on book-related intellectual and political themes. I would report directly to Win and Brooks Thomas, his second in command.

It was a job that could lead to an important managerial position, and it would have paid far more than what I was receiving. But I had no intention of leaving human rights work. Although I was good at publicizing the sufferings of individuals, I doubted I could summon similar passion for Harper & Row. Actually, I was a bit surprised that Win wanted to lure me away from work that we both found so important.

At about the same time, another job opening came to my attention, the directorship of the International League for Human Rights, a venerable organization founded by Roger Baldwin in 1941 and focusing mainly on the United Nations. Roberta Cohen, its excellent longtime director, was leaving to work on the staff of Patt Derian, President Carter's newly appointed assistant secretary of state for human rights. Roberta and I had worked well together on various projects, and she favored me as her successor. It was an opportunity to work full-time in a human rights organization, with a respectable salary and benefits. But when I went to the first interview, it did not feel right. The board members were stodgy and quarreled with each other in my presence. They seemed to lack the inventiveness and spontaneity that I valued in the members of the Freedom to Publish Committee and the Fund for Free Expression.

Bob Bernstein, who was on the league board, asked me if I wanted the job.

"If you do, I'll go to bat for you," he told me. "It will offer you a lot more security than you have now."

"But what about the work *we're* doing?" I asked.

"I'll just take my activities to the league," he promised.

But I knew it wouldn't work. Bernstein would not be happy catering to a board he hadn't created himself, and he would soon tire of the league's internal tensions. And so, I realized, would I. Moreover, I had misgivings about working full-time. I was working many hours because I wanted to, not because I had to, and therefore I felt free to take time off for personal reasons, when Emily was sick, for example, or a conference was scheduled with her teacher. I was one of the finalists for the league job when I decided to withdraw my application. I might not have been so cavalier about it had I been able to see a bit into the future.

In March 1978, after almost twenty-three years of marriage, Austin told me he was leaving. It was not an easy decision for him. It took courage and ruthless honesty to unilaterally end our marriage. In time, I came to think that what he did was right, that it gave us each a chance for new and happier lives and was probably better for the children as well. But at first, I was truly devastated.

The time for ending our marriage, in my view, had long since come and gone. I worried about what it would do to our children. I felt too immersed in family, friends, and a way of life to suddenly call an end to it all. There were too many people we would hurt, too many things we would destroy. I felt too old to begin all over again. I didn't know what I would do.

Like watching someone die after a lingering illness, the end of our marriage came not as a surprise but as a shock. Suddenly, everything had changed. I was overcome by a feeling of failure, humiliation, and just plain fear. I had always been taken care of—first by my father and then by Austin. Now, at the age of forty-six, I was virtually penniless and on my own. My strong, wise father, on whom I had always counted, could not help, financially or emotionally. He was recovering from a cancer operation that had cut a facial nerve, destroying his ruggedly handsome face and leaving him in permanent discomfort. In the past ten years he had lost his wife, his business, his money, his health, and his looks. Dad fell into a deep depression that lasted until he died, three years later.

It would be too facile to blame my divorce on my new career; our marriage was in trouble long before I became involved in human rights work. But my work may have accelerated the breakup, since I spent many evenings at meetings and my mind was often elsewhere. My work also brought me into contact with powerful and well-known people, and Austin, though not averse to mixing with people of celebrity and well able to hold his own in such company, did not seem to relish invitations that came to "Jeri Laber and her husband." He refused to attend Rose and Bill Styron's wedding anniversary party in Connecticut, just a few miles from our country home. "I don't know them and I'm not interested," he said. I went alone, emboldened by pique, and found myself holding forth to Lillian Hellman and some other well-known writers at my table who questioned me with intense interest about my human rights work. Although I didn't know it at the time, such solo performances were soon to become a way of life for me. I was on my own.

PART II

On My Own

(1977–1981)

11

There was a new human rights group in Moscow. It was formed in May 1976 by eleven Moscow intellectuals and led by Yuri Orlov, a diminutive physicist in his early fifties with curly red hair and an impish twinkle. They knew all too well they were tempting fate and would probably end up in prison. All previous human rights efforts in their country had led to arrests and sentences. But they went ahead anyway.

I was astounded by the courage of these people I did not know and was struck by the contrast. Here I was, helping to establish two human rights groups in the United States—the Freedom to Publish Committee and the Fund for Free Expression—with the encouragement and support of everyone I knew, including the U.S. government. Orlov and his friends had no such support. They had nothing to count on except the Helsinki accords, a new international agreement with no enforcement provisions that Moscow had signed less than a year before. They called their group the Public Group to Support Compliance with the Helsinki Accords, but it soon became known as the Moscow Helsinki Group.

. . .

The Helsinki accords, formally called the Final Act of the Conference on Security and Cooperation in Europe (CSCE), had been signed in Helsinki, Finland, on August 1, 1975. The agreement was the culmination of several years of meetings involving thirty-five nations: all of Europe (except Albania) and the United States and Canada. It was essentially a document of détente, drafted with the hope that nations East and West could cooperate economically and avoid nuclear war. Originally a Soviet idea, the drafting of the document reflected the Soviet Union's need for trade and stability, as well as its desire to legitimize its domination of Eastern Europe by getting the West to guarantee Europe's postwar borders.

The United States, skeptical of Soviet intentions, was lukewarm to the negotiations and a more or less passive participant. Certain West European countries—England, West Germany, the Netherlands—took a different approach: They pressed the Soviets to make human rights concessions, asking that there be free movement across the borders they were guaranteeing. Although the Soviets successfully fought off many of the attempts to insert human rights language in the document, they finally acquiesced to some of it in order to achieve their main goal—acknowledgment that Eastern Europe was in the Soviet sphere of influence. They had no intention, of course, of living up to any of their human rights commitments.

A large segment of public opinion in the United States distrusted the Soviets and opposed the Helsinki accords. Members of his own party attacked President Ford for signing them. The *Wall Street Journal* urged him not to go to Helsinki at all. Alexandr Solzhenitsyn, then living in Vermont, called it a "betrayal." There is historical irony in the Helsinki agreement that no one could have predicted at the time: Seen as a means of consolidating Soviet control, it would eventually become a vehicle for ending it.

The Soviets had made some startling concessions, on paper at least. They agreed to guarantee the free movement of people and ideas across international borders. They agreed to act "in conformity with" the 1948 United Nations Universal Declaration of Human Rights, thereby accepting by inference all the basic rights enshrined in that document, such as freedom of expression, religion, and association. They acknowledged linkage between the three main topics covered in the accords—arms control, trade, and human rights—and agreed that progress in one area would have to be accompanied by progress in the others. The Helsinki accords were thus unique among international agreements in asserting that the way in which a government treated its citizens would be a factor in signing trade and disarmament agreements.

.   .   .

When the full text of the accords appeared in *Pravda*, something unanticipated happened: Courageous individuals in Moscow were galvanized to form the Moscow Helsinki Group and to report on their government's behavior. They were acting in accordance with a provision of the accords that gave each individual the right "to know and act upon his rights." They were banking on the periodic Helsinki review conferences that would determine whether countries were living up to their commitments. With the first Helsinki Review Conference scheduled to begin the following year in Belgrade, they may have thought that their government would be constrained from punishing them.

The Helsinki Group in Moscow gave rise to others in the non-Russian republics of the USSR: in Ukraine and Lithuania in November 1976; in Georgia in January 1977; and in Armenia in April 1977. At about the same time, human rights groups focusing on the Helsinki accords were formed in Poland (the Workers Defense Committee, or KOR) and in Czechoslovakia (Charter 77). In Romania, an attempt to found a Helsinki group was immediately quashed and its potential leader, Paul Goma, driven into exile. The U.S. Congress created its own Helsinki Commission to monitor and report to Congress on human rights practices in the Helsinki countries; it was formed at the urging of Representative Millicent Fenwick, a Republican from New Jersey who had visited the Soviet Union in August 1975 and had met with Orlov and other Moscow dissidents.

.   .   .

In its first few months, members of the Moscow Helsinki Group compiled several thousand pages on human rights abuses in their country. Collecting information from victims and trusted observers, they laboriously copied and recopied it on manual typewriters, using carbon paper and praying that the police would not raid the typists' homes. An oft-told story from this period described a police raid on the home of an activist who was busy typing illegal samizdat literature. As they searched the apartment, finding nothing, the woman of the house stood at the stove, casually stirring a pot of borscht, into which she had dumped the incriminating documents.

The Moscow group addressed its reports to the heads of the thirty-five governments that had signed the Helsinki accords. It released them at press conferences attended only by foreign correspondents stationed in Moscow. Copies of the documents were also smuggled out to the West by sympathetic journalists and friends in foreign embassies. But the new group's efforts attracted little attention in the West—until the arrests began, nine months later.

Orlov was among the first to be taken, in February 1977. By the end of March, Aleksandr Ginzburg and Anatoly Shcharansky had been arrested, along with Oleksa Tikhy and Mykola Rudenko of the Ukrainian Helsinki Committee.

Orlov was sentenced to seven years in a strict-regimen labor camp to be followed by five years in internal exile. Shcharansky—charged with espionage—was sentenced to thirteen years of imprisonment and forced labor. Rudenko was sentenced to seven years in the camps and five years in internal exile. Ginzburg was sentenced to eleven years; Tikhy to fifteen. And these were just the first in a long line of arrests. The victims, ironically, had done nothing more than call attention to the persecution of others.

Seven members of the Moscow group were given visas to leave the USSR with the understanding that they would not be permitted to return. Ludmilla Alexeyeva, one of the group's founders, left for the United States. She was authorized to be the Moscow group's official representative abroad.

·   ·   ·

It was outrageous to see the Soviet Union arresting Helsinki activists on the eve of the first Helsinki Review Conference. Brezhnev wanted to be on a par with the other leaders who had signed the accords, yet he claimed that his behavior at home was *his* business and no one else's.

By October 1977, when the review conference convened in Belgrade, it was clear that Soviet leaders had no intention of honoring the commitments they had made in Helsinki. They were impervious to Jimmy Carter's human rights campaign. The conference itself, held in repressive Yugoslavia, was off-limits to the few human rights activists, émigrés from Eastern Europe, who tried to go there to lobby the delegates. The only delegate who spoke out forcefully was former Supreme Court justice Arthur Goldberg who, as leader of the U.S. delegation, had the title of ambassador. He shocked the assembled group, including some in his own delegation, by bluntly pointing to Soviet repression and naming seven of the many imprisoned dissidents. The meeting was a long, drawn-out affair, lasting six months; it set the pattern for two subsequent review conferences—in Madrid and Vienna–that would be even lengthier, each of them going on for close to three years. In time, these review conferences would begin to seem like semipermanent bodies for the expression of moral outrage. The Belgrade conference, the first in the series, ended with little more than an agreement to meet again—in Madrid in November 1980.

.   .   .

I met Ambassador Goldberg when I represented the Fund for Free Expression at a State Department briefing in Washington shortly before the Belgrade talks began. The briefing, for nongovernmental groups, was attended mainly by émigrés representing various nations and ethnic groups that had come under Soviet control—Lithuanians, Estonians, Latvians, Jews, Tatars, Czechs, and Poles. I attracted Ambassador Goldberg's attention as one of the very few who did not represent a specific interest group.

At his request, I wrote a briefing paper on problems of free expression in the Helsinki signatory countries. I focused particularly on the arrests of people like Yuri Orlov. I delivered the brief to the Waldorf Towers when Goldberg was in New York City a few weeks later. The ambassador's request, I assumed, was just one part of his efforts to build a constituency for the Helsinki process in the United States, where very few of his countrymen knew or cared about it. But my quick response set some extraordinary events in motion.

.   .   .

Goldberg returned from Belgrade discouraged. He had sought the limelight and was disappointed that no one seemed to appreciate how he had stood alone at the review conference, speaking out for human rights victims.

"What this country needs is its own Helsinki group," he told Bob Bernstein. Then he asked him: "Would you folks be willing to form one?"

"Not if I have to go out and raise more money," Bernstein replied. "I'm having enough trouble trying to keep the Fund for Free Expression afloat."

Goldberg spoke to McGeorge Bundy, then president of the Ford Foundation. On April 5, 1978, I found myself with Bernstein and a few others at a meeting with Bundy at the Ford Foundation. Bundy clearly liked the idea of a U.S. Helsinki Watch and seemed eager to push it through before his forthcoming retirement from the foundation. At his request, we drafted a proposal to set up a U.S. Helsinki Watch Committee as a project of the Fund for Free Expression.

In the summer of 1978, we received a small planning grant from the Ford Foundation. I was ready to start drawing up a plan at once, but Bob Bernstein, uncertain about how to proceed, held me back while he consulted with various people, trying to crystallize his own ideas. Finally, in the fall, he gave me the go-ahead. I met with dozens of people in the government and in the nonprofit sector to get their views on the feasibility of a U.S. Helsinki Watch and how it should function. I wrote a short report for the Ford Foundation on my meetings and our plans.

Meanwhile, Bernstein, who would be the chair of the new Helsinki Watch, began recruiting members. He had no trouble finding prominent people, including many he had never met before, willing to lend us their names. One of them was Orville Schell, who would become our vice chair. Schell, a former president of the New York Bar Association, was then in his early seventies, small and trim with silvery hair. He was a distinguished Wall Street lawyer with a brisk, businesslike manner whose human rights consciousness had been raised when he visited the Soviet Union on behalf of the Union of Councils for Soviet Jews. Orville's politics were surprisingly liberal and antiestablishment. He was deeply concerned about human rights abuses in many parts of the world, not just those he had learned about in Moscow.

In January 1979, we received a Ford Foundation grant of $400,000 for two years, which was to take us through the second Helsinki Review Conference in Madrid. With it, we established Helsinki Watch. It was exciting. It was intimidating. I could see how nervous Bob Bernstein was about it all, and that made me nervous, too. We weren't quite sure how to proceed.

12

On January 1, 1979, the clock began ticking. We had less than two years before the Madrid conference was to open—in November 1980. In that time we had to establish ourselves as a respected source of information. We had to document and dramatize human rights abuses in the Communist world and find ways to generate pressure for change. We needed an office, a director, a staff, and a concrete program of action. We had to be ready to play a significant role when the review conference opened, to make sure that human rights issues were at the forefront.

We had $400,000 to spend—at least we didn't have to worry about raising money. But having a big budget was not necessarily the best way to begin. We did not grow organically, as we should have and would have under other circumstances, adding staff as needed, seeking funds for specific projects as we went along. People in other organizations resented the ease with which we had received our funding; they were envious and criticized us as "elitist" and privileged. We felt enormous pressure to produce something, and in our hurry we made several false starts.

In a press release announcing Helsinki Watch, we explained ourselves as follows. We were responding to the call of the Moscow Helsinki Group for Helsinki committees to be established in all the countries that had signed the Helsinki accords. We would work for the release of imprisoned Helsinki monitors. We would criticize the U.S. government's shortcomings as well, and thus show by example how a Helsinki committee should and could function in an open society.

We were immediately attacked in the U.S. press: from the right, for daring to "equate" U.S. human rights practices with Communist abuses; from the left, for being an anti-Communist organization that pretended to be evenhanded.

Being criticized from both sides is not necessarily bad: To the contrary, it could indicate we were steering a correct middle course. But in fact, we *were* confused. The Helsinki groups in Eastern Europe focused only on *their own* governments, not on others. If we were truly a companion group, shouldn't we be monitoring the United States, thereby showing how it *could* be done? But our interest was mainly in what was happening over there, where citizens who spoke out were thrown into prison. In the United States, there was no such problem. There were myriad citizens groups already in place and functioning without pressure from the government. The American Civil Liberties Union (ACLU) and the National Association for the Advancement of Colored People (NAACP) were the largest and best known among hundreds of groups working for a variety of causes—prison reform, Native American rights, women's rights, children's rights, the rights of the disabled—the list goes on. We didn't want to duplicate their work, nor did we have the resources to do so. But we needed to be more familiar with it and with U.S. problems in general. We decided to look for a director with a U.S. civil liberties background, someone who might give our group some balance and provide the domestic expertise we lacked.

Bob Bernstein turned to Aryeh Neier for advice. Neier, who had just left his position as executive director of the ACLU, would have been an ideal candidate for the job, but he was not interested, not then at least. He chose instead to join the Helsinki Watch board and recommended David Fishlow, a colleague from the ACLU, for the position. Fishlow took the job assuming it would be mainly U.S. oriented. He did not initially comprehend how strong our international focus was, nor was he comfortable with it. He seemed wary of the Russian émigrés who provided us with information, many of whom saw America as the promised land and were conservative in their world outlook. Four months passed before Fishlow realized he was not the right person for the job. He left at the end of April.

Well into the first year of our two-year grant, we were without a director, without a program, and with barely a staff. We had taken an office, on 42nd Street between Second and Third Avenues; it was small, four rooms in all, but they faced south and were bright and sunny. I worked in one of them as director of the Fund for Free Expression, having moved my papers over from the Random House office I had previously occupied. While we searched for a new Helsinki Watch director, I involved the staff—a secretary and a public relations director—in the work of the fund.

.   .   .

We were busy at the time preparing a special book exhibit for the 1979 Moscow Book Fair that fall. The exhibit would appear under the auspices of the Association of American Publishers but was mainly being prepared by the Fund for Free Expression and a group of volunteers led by Sophie Silberberg, an energetic woman in her mid-sixties who had recently retired from a publishing career. We called the exhibit "America Through American Eyes." Designed to circumvent Soviet censorship, it contained only books published in the United States, chosen to illustrate American life in all its political, religious, and cultural diversity. We believed that the exhibit would illustrate by example the differences between Soviet and American people, not just in what we published but in how we lived.

The books were selected by a committee of writers, editors, and librarians headed by the easygoing Kurt Vonnegut. We compiled an English-Russian catalogue that described each book with a special eye on what it might mean to a Soviet reader. Thousands of catalogues were printed for us by the New York Times Foundation. They turned out to be the most sought-after items at the fair and would be clandestinely circulated in Moscow for many months after the book fair ended.

We were thrilled when John Updike, at Vonnegut's request, agreed to write an introduction to the catalogue. It arrived at our office one Monday morning. Sophie Silberberg asked me if I had read it. "No," I said, "I'm saving it to read on my way home." I was a fan of Updike's and looked forward to seeing what he had written.

"I'll be interested in what you think," was all Sophie said.

Some hours later, on the Broadway bus, I took out the manuscript and settled in to read it. To my dismay, I found it to be an anti-American diatribe, in no way suited to an upbeat American book display.

Updike began by contrasting the genuine love of books among Russians with the low tastes of American readers. He went on to lambaste American publishers for their commercialism and said that it was almost impossible to find good literature in a typical American bookstore. There was truth in much of what he said. But it could not have been more inappropriate. It was hardly the message we wanted our catalogue to convey.

I called Kurt Vonnegut first thing the next morning.

"Leave me out of this," Kurt declared. "John's my friend. He wrote this as a favor to me."

I then sent the piece to Bob Bernstein by messenger, without comment.

"This is unacceptable," Bob stormed over the phone an hour or so later.

"Yes," I agreed, "but how do we handle it with Updike?"

"Leave that to me," Bob said.

I was impressed by his dispatch in undertaking a delicate task. *He didn't get to be president of Random House for nothing.* But by the end of the day, the problem had come full circle and was in the hands of two women, one of them me. Bob Bernstein had passed the buck to Robert Gottlieb, then president of Knopf, the Random House imprint that published Updike. Gottlieb had passed the buck to Judith Jones, Updike's editor. Jones, my editor on the *Fannie Farmer Cookbook*, called *me*.

"Now," she said, "what are we going to do about Updike?"

In the end, it was Jones who spoke to Updike. I received a polite letter from him asking for his manuscript back. "After all," he wrote, "it isn't every day one gets censored by the Fund for Free Expression."

.   .   .

I was part of a search committee that began interviewing candidates for director of Helsinki Watch. We widened the search this time around to include people with a Soviet studies background. But the people we liked were disinclined to take the job. There was no guarantee that it would last more than two years, when our money would run out. There was no clear understanding of what the job would entail. A few applicants were concerned that Helsinki Watch might be too right-wing: There was a misguided perception among some American liberals that anyone who was actively anti-Soviet had to be reactionary.

This was not true, certainly not in our case. I had publicly criticized human rights policies in a variety of countries—Iran, Argentina, the Philippines, Indonesia—many of them with right-wing, anti-Communist governments that were friendly to the United States. My special interest in the Soviet Union came from my studies—it was where I could be most effective, the country I knew best. Bernstein's involvement came from his friendship with Sakharov and other Soviet dissidents; he, too, had a broad interest in problems in other countries, and on several occasions in his publishing career, he had courageously taken on the U.S. government as well. Others in our group were similarly committed, independent of politics of the right or the left.

We were all excited by the prospect of exploring new ground in which the old distinctions between right and left no longer seemed appropriate. We felt liberated from transient politics. We were creating a "new" ideology from precepts we believed had long been forgotten—a belief in the essential dignity of the human being, as defined in our own country's founding documents.

.   .   .

A young woman lawyer who applied for the Helsinki Watch position was appalled that our search committee was composed exclusively of men except for me. Over lunch one day, I tried my best to explain our all-white, all-male group that was not even conscious of the image it projected. I did not tell her that one member of the group had unabashedly declared to all of us that "the Helsinki job is not for a woman" and that he had refused to explain his thinking to me, he considered it so obvious. My assurances to her were not very convincing, I guess; she withdrew her application a few days after our lunch.

A small steering committee, the same eight men who functioned as our search committee, met in my office every Wednesday morning to discuss and develop a program. In addition to Bob Bernstein, Orville Schell, and Aryeh Neier, the group included Ed Kline, the businessman who published Soviet samizdat in English; Adrian DeWind and John Carey, both prominent New York lawyers; Jack Greenberg, who until recently had been the legal director of the NAACP Legal Defense Fund; and Bob McKay, former dean of the New York University Law School and head of the Aspen Institute's Justice Program. We agreed early on that Helsinki Watch would prepare a set of reports to be released at the opening of the Madrid Review Conference and that the reports would focus on abuses in the Soviet Union and Eastern Europe and also on problems in the United States.

Aryeh Neier was the most experienced member of the group when it came to nonprofit organizations. His forceful personality prevailed at those early meetings, especially because he was always willing to draft documents and press releases, which he did with incredible ease and speed.

I was not concerned that all the members of our steering committee were white professional men of about the same age. I felt special being part of their circle and never thought to press them to include more women. At times, however, I felt insecure. I wondered if I was being accepted for the wrong reasons—as the "token woman."

Looking back on it now, it seems odd that none of us questioned the lack of diversity in our inner sanctum, especially because the Ford Foundation, our only funder at the time, insisted that our board be well integrated, geographically and with regard to gender and race. Bob Bernstein had taken those concerns into consideration in compiling the letterhead board, which included a fair number of blacks and women. On a day-to-day basis, however, he chose to be with men like himself, and to my knowledge, even the civil libertarians among them, like Jack Greenberg and Aryeh Neier, did not question the composition of our little steering committee.

.   .   .

In May 1979, at my daughter Abby's graduation from Harvard, I ran into Win Knowlton, whose son was in Abby's class. Knowlton, no longer chair of the Freedom to Publish Committee, had joined the Helsinki Watch board. He took me aside. "Why don't you apply for the executive director's position?" he asked. "I'll back you. I think you'd be terrific."

If that thought had crossed my mind before, I had pushed it away. It would mean working full-time—more, actually, to make up for the time we had already lost. I had never considered full-time work when I was married, and now, as a single mother, it seemed wrong for other reasons. Although Abby and Pam were away at college, Emily, my youngest, had just turned fourteen and was bearing the brunt of the fallout from her parents' separation. I hated the thought of her coming home from school regularly to an empty house. In addition, my personal life was fraught with anxiety: over my sick father, a looming divorce, and the difficulties of adjusting to a single life after so many years of marriage. It was a terrible time in my life. How could I commit myself to a demanding full-time job?

But I was getting divorced. I would have to support myself. I knew little about money matters and had no idea of how much I would need to get by. I dimly suspected that sooner or later I would *have* to work full-time.

What I *did* know was that I wanted to keep working for human rights—more than anything else in the world. I didn't mind that it meant working for less money than I might get elsewhere or that the Helsinki Watch job was slated to end in less than two years. I'd manage somehow. What frightened me was the job itself. I had never run an organization, to say nothing of creating one. Could I do it? I decided to try.

On the morning of June 3, 1979, I sent a long, upbeat letter by messenger to Bob Bernstein. "I've been around from the beginning," I wrote. "I already know the people involved, I've struggled through the issues, been part of the consensus we've reached. Moreover, I know the kinds of demands made on the office and have probably given more thought to the specifics of staffing than anyone else. . . ." Describing how I would staff the organization and apportion its work, I filled three single-spaced pages and attached an organizational chart.

Bernstein called later in the day and asked me to meet him at the University Club after work. "I discussed your letter with Orville and a number of the others," he told me when we met. "You have a lot of fans. I got a very positive response." He sounded vaguely surprised by the reactions he had gotten, as if the people he questioned thought more highly of me than *he* did. "Of course," he continued, "you'll have to give up one of your other titles. I suggest you give up the Fund for Free Expression job and keep your job with the publishers. It has the most security." I agreed. "Well then," Bob said, "the job is yours. You'd better live up to their expectations." He said nothing about his own expectations. His lack of enthusiasm was deflating.

I suspected Bernstein's reserve had to do with Ed Kline, whose opinions he valued. It was Kline who was opposed to having a woman as Helsinki Watch director. Ed Kline and I had always had a good relationship—he admired my writings on the Soviet Union and believed they had done some good for the Soviet dissidents—but I was pretty sure he would not see me as an exception to his own rule. He must have told Bernstein he did not favor me for the job.

Ed Kline was not alone in his attitude toward women. Orville Schell, a few years later, reported on a mission to Central America that had been organized for him by Cynthia Brown, one of our most experienced and talented researcher-writers. "I went with Cindy Brown . . . a girl," he stated. (There was a spontaneous gasp around the table, mainly from the women.) When Bob McKay of the Aspen Institute was unable to make a meeting and suggested sending his colleague Alice Henkin in his stead, the group just assumed she was his secretary and said she should not come. (Henkin, a lawyer who succeeded McKay as director of the Aspen Institute, later became one of the most valued members of the Helsinki Watch board.)

I put up with all this because I was used to it. I accepted it. I was even part of it. I was of the same generation as the men who were running our organization. Their attitudes were familiar to me, similar to my father's, to Austin's, and to those of many of my male friends. Austin, for example, used to brag that he chose his secretaries by the shapeliness of their legs. It made me uncomfortable mainly for what it said about our relationship rather than because it was demeaning to the women involved. Despite my graduate degrees in Russian studies, despite the jobs I had held in the Soviet field, despite all the articles I had written and had published, Bob Bernstein believed he was taking a housewife straight into a demanding administrative position. Part of me believed it, too.

In the 1970s, very few women of my generation held managerial positions in professions traditionally considered men's. Many of my contemporaries did not work at all, while others were engaged in various artistic pursuits such as acting, painting, or writing, or they worked in "soft" professions as teachers or editors. In a way, entering a new career was easier for me than it might be for someone like me today: No one questioned why, well into my forties, I was not firmly set on a career track.

The Helsinki Watch executive committee often met at the Century Club, a private dining club that then excluded women as members and barred them from the public rooms. In order to include me in a meeting, the group rented a private wood-paneled meeting room on an upper floor; sometimes they teased me about the expense they had incurred just because of me. And I, I must admit, felt flattered to be given such special treatment. I liked it. Ultimately, it was a man—Jack Greenberg of the NAACP Legal Defense Fund—who refused to attend meetings at restricted clubs and sensitized the others to the issue.

Bob Bernstein continued to arrange meetings at such clubs whenever he could get away with it. "I know it's wrong, but it's so *nice* there," he would say. "The trouble with Bob is that he doesn't have any daughters," Aryeh Neier once remarked when I complained to him. It was an astute observation. Bob, the devoted father of three sons, put his stock in promising young men who were friends of, or could have been friends of, his boys. Actually, I did the same thing myself in reverse, building a staff almost exclusively of young women close in age to my daughters. But in my case, my staff helped open my eyes to women's issues. It was through them—and my daughters—that I gradually became sensitized to women's problems in the workplace and to my responsibilities as a model for younger women.

.   .   .

First, however, I had to conquer my own insecurities. I had reason to be insecure, for I was ill-prepared for the work I had taken on. Much of what I was called upon to do was new to me. I had never hired or fired anyone, and I knew nothing about educating and motivating a staff. I had no experience raising funds and no connections with potential donors. I had not done any public speaking and I was nervous about giving even the shortest report at committee meetings. I had little experience with radio and television interviews, and I had certainly never met with government officials to tell them what they were doing wrong. Rather than acknowledge my self-doubts, I hid them from my colleagues and sometimes even from myself. I tried to act as if it all came naturally to me.

I knew when to keep quiet (as a woman, I could get away with it) and I learned much by watching and listening. No one patronized me as they might a younger woman: I was in my late forties and commanded a certain amount of respect. And I *did* have qualities upon which I could draw. I was by nature well-organized and had honed my organizational skills as a mother and wife, managing the family's schedules and homes as well as a complicated social life. And I could write, and edit, with confidence.

Slowly, as I became more self-assured, I discovered that I could contribute a lot by virtue of being a woman. I used the skills I had acquired while my children were young, taking useful photos of the dissidents I met and opening my home to newly arrived émigrés—cooking and entertaining came easily to me. I could travel inconspicuously in repressive countries where the police saw little threat in a woman. I developed personal relationships with victims of human rights abuses. I could speak about them publicly with the kind of emotion that many men suppress in themselves. My reports on my human rights missions would become high points at our committee meetings.

.   .   .

Bob Bernstein was under pressure to find a director when he hired me. But I think he would have felt more comfortable, more eager to gamble on me, if I had been a man. It now seems ironic that the meeting at which Bernstein offered me the job took place at the plush University Club, in the only room where visiting women were then permitted.

13

Our plans for the Moscow Book Fair hit an unexpected snag when Bob Bernstein was barred from attending. It happened in the summer of 1979, a month or so before the fair was to open, when Bob already had his visa in hand. He had agreed to be interviewed by someone who claimed to be a Soviet journalist working for TASS (the Soviet press agency) in New York. Afterward, he worried that he may have been too outspoken in condemning Soviet repression. Sure enough, several days later, someone from the Soviet Embassy in Washington called Bernstein to say that his visa had been revoked. No reason was given. Bob was incensed.

Bernstein and I had legitimate reasons to attend the fair—he as the president of Random House, which was an exhibitor, and I as a staff member accompanying the Association of American Publishers' special exhibit, "America Through American Eyes." Once there, however, our main purpose would have been to meet clandestinely with the remaining members of the beleaguered Moscow Helsinki Group. We thought the book fair would provide a good cover for us. But the Soviets were on to Bob Bernstein.

Bernstein tried to persuade other American publishers to refuse to attend the fair without him. It would have been an impressive, and possibly successful, strategy, using the kind of language the Soviets understood. But none of the publishers, it turned out, were willing to participate in such a boycott. Some said it wouldn't work; others were afraid of losing their chance to explore a new book market. When Bernstein saw their reactions, he then suggested that *I* should refuse to go. That seemed pointless to me: My name meant nothing to the Soviets at that time; my absence would not be noticed by anyone. Moreover, I was the only one planning to go who had a specific human rights agenda and the only one who could be counted on to make an issue over the denial of Bob Bernstein's visa. I refused to stay home.

Of course, I was eager to go. It would be my first trip back to Russia since I was a student at the Russian Institute more than twenty years before. No country in the world was as intriguing to me. I had spent months planning the exhibit and brushing up on my Russian, even hiring a Russian language tutor at my own expense.

Bob Bernstein seemed disconcerted by my response. Until that time, we had agreed on virtually everything, and he had come to take my compliance for granted. The next time we met, he acknowledged our disagreement by remarking, with a touch of bemusement: "You know, you can be very aggressive." It was a cliché—the classic put-down of women who express independent views—but I let it pass. I left for Moscow as planned, in early September 1979.

.   .   .

Officially, I was there with the publishers' association, the AAP; no mention had been made in my visa application of my connection to the newly formed Helsinki Watch. But in fact I had a double mission in the USSR: one, for the publishers, to expose any censorship, publicize visa denials, and organize a dinner for dissident writers; the other, for Helsinki Watch, to make contact with the Moscow Helsinki Group. In the first instance, I had the tacit support of the American publishers visiting Moscow. When it came to the Helsinki Group, however, I was on my own. There were no rules to follow in any of these undertakings. I was improvising as I went along.

It was tense from the beginning. Books were being scrutinized and censored, and I was the only one keeping track. I needed to publicize the censorship and Bernstein's visa denial by getting the attention of the Western press. Fortunately, I had thought to send letters ahead to members of the U.S. press corps, informing them of my arrival date and alerting them to a potential story—censorship at the Moscow Book Fair. They all came looking for me to get the details.

It was easy to find me. We foreigners were housed in the Kosmos, a huge new tourist hotel with an "outer-space" motif, right across from the permanent exhibition grounds where the book fair would be held and quite far from the city center. There the police could keep a close eye on all of us. Like all hotels in Moscow, the Kosmos was closed to ordinary Russians; they would be stopped at the door and turned away if they dared to enter. Eager to set up our exhibits, we were forbidden to unpack our books until the censors went through the boxes and issued their stamp of approval.

I stayed behind at the fair on the evening the censors went to work, sitting inconspicuously in a corner and watching. In the space of a few hours, they went through hundreds of book cartons, instantly isolating books that might be offensive. As far as I could determine, they were looking for key words and subjects—anything dealing with the Soviet Union, of course, or written by writers on their "banned" lists, mainly Soviet émigrés. They also seemed to be looking for books that dealt with Hitler or with World War II, presumably to see if the accounts followed the Soviet line. A censor typically went through about three books a minute, separating the questionable books into a pile for further study.

Our "America Through American Eyes" exhibit contained 321 titles, many of which were critical of the United States—its economic policies, its foreign policies—as well as books that showed the racial and religious diversity of the American people. It was our intent to illustrate that Americans were free to express their thoughts and beliefs without persecution. It was also a good way to circumvent Soviet censorship, since our focus was on the United States and we were critical of the Soviet Union only by inference. And indeed, we *were* successful: Only one book was taken, a book of caricatures by David Levine that, we hadn't previously noticed, included a sketch of Leonid Brezhnev.

Books *were* taken from a number of other exhibits. I began to compile a list. I went from stand to stand, asking for titles. Some publishers, eager to stay on good terms with their Soviet hosts, were reluctant to acknowledge they had lost any books to the censors; others weren't sure, because some of their books, initially taken for review, were later returned. In addition, books had a way of disappearing during the night, and it was impossible to know whether they had been taken by the censors or pilfered by an eager reader. Each morning I confronted the book fair officials to complain about the latest seized books. It wasn't easy for me at first, given my tendency to please and compromise, but I found I could be a different person when it really mattered.

My list of more than thirty censored books became front-page news in the *New York Times* and scores of other Western newspapers. The press focused on the numbers, which changed day by day. I was constantly besieged by journalists asking me for the most recent list. Late each night in my hotel room, I painstakingly wrote out a dozen or more copies of the updated list of censored books to hand out to the press the following morning. (This was before laptop computers, which would not have been permitted in the Soviet Union anyway, and the police kept copying machines under lock and key.) When foreign journalists asked me to comment on the censorship, I always took the opportunity to deplore the denial of visas to certain people, Bob Bernstein in particular. The U.S. Embassy in Moscow was responsive to my protests and agreed to cancel a reception for Soviet publishers; it announced publicly that Bernstein's visa denial was the reason.

A few days into the trip, I caught sight of myself in a mirror and was shocked at how exhausted I looked. I was sleeping very little, operating on nervous energy, trying to accomplish everything I had set out to do. I was constantly aware that at any time I might run up against the secret police.

. . .

Several of us had brought along extra suitcases, full of down jackets and other warm clothing that we had been asked to bring by émigrés in the States for political prisoners and their families in the USSR. Now my colleagues were asking me what to do with these suitcases. It was my job to get them to the right people—the Moscow Helsinki Group.

I had called the dissident physicist Andrei Sakharov and his wife, Elena Bonner, when I first arrived in Moscow. They knew from foreign broadcasts that Bernstein had been barred from coming and they seemed to be expecting someone to call in his stead. They invited me at once to their apartment. Elena Bonner was a member of the Moscow Helsinki Group. She agreed to arrange a meeting for me with the group, but suggested that I wait until the very end of my visit. "You'll be under police surveillance once you meet with the Helsinki Group," she warned me. "Do your other work first; leave that until the end." Sipping a cup of tea in the Sakharov kitchen, I watched as Andrei and Elena eagerly examined the photographs

I had brought of their grandchildren who lived in Cambridge, Massachusetts. I also brought them a copy of the catalogue from the "America Through American Eyes" exhibit, and Andrei Sakharov read it, completely absorbed. "Only a society that is sure of itself can permit its people to criticize it," he remarked. That was exactly the message we wanted the catalogue to convey. I was thrilled to see that he got it so quickly, and impressed by his grasp of what we had in mind.

Sakharov was a most ordinary-looking man, balding, with thick-rimmed glasses and the pasty complexion and flaccid build of someone in poor health who spends his time indoors at sedentary, scholarly pursuits. On the five or six occasions that I was with him between our initial meeting in 1979 and his death ten years later, I found him pleasant but reserved, not given to the major pronouncements we all wanted to hear from him. I sensed that he was a kind man. I often felt his thoughts were elsewhere.

Elena Bonner was more open and feisty than her husband. She was a medical doctor who had known persecution from an early age: Her father was shot under Stalin, and her mother, to whom she was very attached, had spent many years as a political prisoner. With Bonner, as with many of the other Russian women dissidents I would come to know—Ludmilla Alexeyeva, Raya Orlova, Larisa Bogoraz, Sofiya Kalistratova, Malva Landa—first impressions were deceptive. These women, though about my age, reminded me of my grandmother. Overweight by Western standards, their hair was unstyled and they wore the kind of dresses I remembered my grandmother wearing—shapeless affairs, usually in a nondescript print. They looked like they would be most at home at the stove, ladling out cups of hot borscht. It took me some time to see that their disdain for "style" was a conscious statement, born both of necessity and of personal conviction. But I quickly learned that these were strong-willed, intellectual women of tremendous strength of character who ran interference for their men until, as was too often the case, they were arrested themselves, or left to stand on their own after their husbands were imprisoned or dead.

·   ·   ·

The foreign press in Moscow, under constant surveillance, worked collaboratively, rather than competitively. I was befriended by Anthony

Austin of the *New York Times* and Kevin Klose of the *Washington Post.* They brought me to the home of the writer Lev Kopelev and his outspoken wife, Raya Orlova. Lev, tall and barrel-chested, with a bushy white beard, kindly eyes, and a beaming smile, was an expert on German literature, a former political prisoner (the model for Lev Rubin in Solzhenitsyn's *The First Circle*) and the author of several books based on his prison experiences. Larger than life, he seemed to have stepped from a nineteenth-century Russian novel, a robust Leo Tolstoy, or maybe Father Frost himself, and his looks were as impressive to Russians as they were to foreigners. When I asked how he managed to get into the book fair without a ticket, Raya explained: "Lev used his beard."

The Kopelevs, both former Communists who had become disenchanted with the Party, lived in a modest apartment bursting with books, photographs, and people, where they ran an informal salon for the Moscow dissident intelligentsia and visiting foreigners. "Books are our gold," Lev told me, joyously receiving the few volumes I brought him. Raya, who hovered protectively over Lev, was lively and attractive and could have fit easily into New York literary life with her ceaseless intellectual energy, her involvement with people, and her nose for gossip. Her expertise was in American literature.

The Kopelevs, who had each been married before, had four daughters between them and, as Lev informed me, even more sons-in-law. "They divorce each other but they don't divorce us." I brought the Kopelevs a package from New York, gifts from Lev's daughter Maya, who was married to the human rights activist Pavel Litvinov. Pavel and Maya had been forced to emigrate about five years before because of Pavel's dissident activities. They lived in New York with their children. When I returned to the Kopelevs later that week, I found Lev and Raya huddled over a tape deck, listening to a tape recording that Maya had sent them. There were tears in Lev's eyes as he turned to me: "I'm hearing the voices of my grandchildren," he said. "And you know, Jeri, their Russian is worse than yours!"

.   .   .

Sitting side by side on a bed draped with a large spread and the overcoats of various visitors, Raya helped me plan an event that was bound to provoke the authorities: a private dinner hosted by the American publishers for Soviet writers, to be held in the Aragvi, a well-known Georgian restaurant in Moscow. The guests would include writers whose books were published in the West but banned in their own country. It was our view that such attention might help protect them by showing that they were known and respected abroad. Raya and I did all our planning in whispers. We wrote down the names of potential guests on a sheet of paper in my notebook, without mentioning them aloud. The Kopelev apartment, like hotel rooms, taxis, and just about every closed space we entered, was assumed to be bugged by the Soviet secret police, the KGB. Most of the writers we planned to invite were in disfavor. Their names had been expunged from reference books. They were "nonpersons" in the Soviet Union.

Almost as an afterthought, Raya suggested that I invite the writer Anatoly Marchenko, who had just finished serving a fifteen-year sentence, and his wife, Larisa Bogoraz, who had been with him in exile. "They are just back from exile," she whispered. "It would be very good to include them." Raya agreed to invite most of the writers on our list. I used a U.S. Embassy phone to call Yevgeny Yevtushenko, Andrei Voznesensky, and a few other establishment writers who accepted my invitation with enthusiasm.

Larry Hughes, the president of William Morrow Publishers, was then the head of our publishers' committee and would be the host of our dinner. He went with me to the Aragvi restaurant, where we met with the obsequious manager, anxious to please his foreign guests. With my halting Russian and a lot of amusing sign-language from Hughes, we managed to order a buffet-style meal for some sixty or more people. We did not, of course, tell him who our guests would be.

When we arrived at the Aragvi a few nights later, we found the restaurant surrounded by plainclothes police, who, while menacing, allowed everyone to enter. The room we had reserved was up a flight of stairs. I saw the manager on the landing, ashen-faced and almost paralyzed by fear, watching a stream of dissidents ascend—Andrei Sakharov, the Kopelevs, Roy Medvedev, Vladimir Voinovich, Vasily Aksyonov—some forty-five writers in all.

None of the establishment writers I had invited showed up. They had presumably heard the reception being scathingly denounced on the Moscow radio a few hours before it began. The police had provided inside information to the radio announcer, who focused on one of the invited guests, Anatoly Marchenko, whom he described as a recently released "criminal." All the noise, laughter, and high-spirited conversation could not still an undercurrent of tension, the depths of which we outsiders could barely fathom.

The Georgian-style buffet—caviar, cold chicken in walnut sauce, spicy eggplant dishes—was punctuated in the Russian fashion with many vodka toasts to international friendship and literary freedom. But I knew that for our Soviet guests, the decision to attend had not been made lightly. Although contacts with Western publishers might provide a sort of protection, the authorities could choose to be punitive.

Off in a corner, looking uncomfortable and out of place, were a shabbily dressed couple whom I knew at once must be Marchenko and his wife, Larisa Bogoraz. I went over to speak to them, but after the first few sentences, I found myself feeling awkward and at a loss for words.

Over the years I had read about Larisa Bogoraz and had come to think of her as a dramatic heroine, like the "Lara" in *Doctor Zhivago*. I was in awe of her courage—she was one of that tiny group that had had the nerve to demonstrate in Red Square in 1968 against the Soviet invasion of Czechoslovakia, and she had immediately been arrested for that defiant act. I was also intrigued by her love affair with Marchenko, which had triumphed over terrible obstacles. Reading between the lines, I knew the following: that Bogoraz, a linguist and intellectual, had worked courageously to defend her first husband, the writer Yuli Daniel, who was sentenced in the notorious 1966 Sinyavsky-Daniel trial and sent to a labor camp in Mordovia; that in the labor camp Daniel met Marchenko, an uneducated worker from Siberia, strong and handsome and still in his twenties, who was finishing a sentence of hard labor for attempting to cross the Soviet border into Iran; that Marchenko became politicized in the camps and was determined to expose the brutality he had suffered and witnessed there; that Daniel told Marchenko, on the eve of his release, to get in touch with Larisa, his former wife, in Moscow; that Larisa, ten years older than Marchenko, welcomed him into her Moscow circle of intellectuals and encouraged him to write his prison memoir, *My Testimony;* that they became lovers but were soon separated by their separate arrests, only to come together again in Siberian exile. They were married in 1971.

My idealization of their love story dissipated quickly when I saw their withdrawn manner, their worn clothes, missing teeth, and sallow complexions—testimony to the poverty and hardship they had experienced.

Their presence at the dinner was a warning to the other guests of a fate each was tempting. Indeed, the day after the dinner Raya asked for my notebook, turned quickly to the pages on which we had penned the guest list for the dinner, and blackened out the word "Marchenko" that she had written in my book. Even feisty Raya was afraid, afraid that Marchenko's name in her handwriting would be enough to incriminate her.

. . .

As Elena Bonner had suggested, I waited until after the dinner at the Aragvi restaurant to meet with the Moscow Helsinki Group. Actually, I waited until the day I was to leave Moscow: I took my bag with me to the meeting, so I could go straight to the airport afterward, before the police could pick up my trail. The meeting was in the Sakharovs' apartment. I went there alone: The American journalists who had accompanied me just about everywhere in Moscow found it too risky to be present at a Helsinki Group meeting.

A tall, lanky scientist—whose name I no longer recall—acted as my interpreter and drove me to the airport when the meeting was over. He was a Jewish refusenik (denied the right to emigrate); he had lost his job but managed to survive on clothes and money smuggled in from Jewish groups abroad.

The meeting began without ceremony. I told the group who I was and that we had recently formed the U.S. Helsinki Watch in response to what was happening to them. I assured them they were not alone, that we and others abroad were aware of the arrests and imprisonment of their members and were issuing protests. I suggested that we plan some joint actions, like issuing reports together and holding press conferences simultaneously at prearranged times.

And who were these Helsinki people with whom it was so dangerous to meet? Only about a dozen of them were left, mainly women, and elderly women at that. Oksana Meshko, seventy-five, and Malva Landa, sixty-two, had each defied bans on their travel to Moscow in order to meet me. Meshko, a Ukrainian activist, had spent eight years in prison, and Landa was being punished for helping distribute funds sent by Solzhenitsyn for political prisoners and their families. Sofiya Kalistratova, seventy-three, was an ailing retired lawyer who had defended many fellow dissidents. Naum Meiman, sixty-nine, was a former scientist and a refusenik.

These are the survivors, I thought. *The vigorous men who started the group—Orlov, Shcharansky, Slepak, Ginzburg, Grigorenko—are all imprisoned or exiled.*

There were also a few younger people. Ivan Kovalev and Tatiana Osipova were a married couple in their twenties, the son and daughter-in-law of Sergei Kovalev, an early activist who was serving a long prison term.

Although the room was bugged, they all spoke openly and without any sign of fear, describing the plight of their colleagues and their own persecution and harassment. I noticed that only one word caused them to pause and lower their voices to a whisper: That word was "Helsinki."

Irina Orlova, wife of the group's founder, Yuri Orlov, had been invited by the group to tell me about her husband. A slight woman in her mid-thirties with short-cropped hair and a nervous smile, she talked to me nonstop for more than an hour, describing her most recent "family visit" with Yuri Orlov at the Perm labor camp, a two-day train trip from Moscow. She found her red-haired husband had turned completely white and was weak from pain and numbness in his limbs. But his spirit, she assured me, was still strong.

Because the people in the room were mainly old and female, I assumed they were beyond the ominous reach of the KGB. Yet just a few months later, in January 1980, the Sakharovs would be exiled to Gorky, a city closed to outsiders. Elderly Oksana Meshko would be sentenced to a strict-regime prison camp and internal exile. Ivan and Tatiana, the son and daughter-in-law of the imprisoned Sergei Kovalev, would themselves be sent to prison. "Tanya-Vanya" we called them: They wanted to help Sergei but instead would experience his fate—backbreaking labor, miserable cold, a starvation diet.

I photographed each of the group members as we spoke in the Sakharovs' dark living room. Shooting without a flash, using only the light of a single lamp, I doubled the speed of the film and had it specially processed. The results were dramatic—black-and-white portraits of their strong and distinctive faces. The pictures subsequently appeared as a special feature in *Life* magazine in April 1980. I got a good response to the article and to several op-ed pieces I wrote based on my meeting with the Moscow Helsinki Group. Public interest seemed to be growing.

Helsinki Watch published a report listing the imprisoned Soviet Helsinki monitors. Initially called *Thirty-Nine Who Believed*, it was soon updated to include more than fifty activists in prison or exile. And that figure did not include the many others who had been forced to leave for the West.

.   .   .

As for the writers who attended our publishers' dinner in 1979, their situation also worsened. In March 1981, when Anatoly Marchenko was arrested for the sixth time in his forty-three years, I took stock of the others. Lev and Raya Kopelev, Vasily and Maya Aksyonov, and Vladimir and Irina Voinovich had been exiled to the West, stripped of their Soviet citizenship. Pyotr Yegides had settled in Paris. Georgi Vladimov suffered a heart attack shortly after interrogation by the KGB. Viktor Erofeyev, Vladimir Kornilov, Semyon Lipkin, Inna Lisnyanskaya, Yevgeny Popov, and Feliks Svetov had either resigned or been expelled from the Soviet Writers Union; without membership they could not be published or even mentioned in the press as writers. Yuri Druzhnikov, a refusenik writer, had no source of livelihood while he waited for a visa that did not come. Mykola Rudenko, Viktor Nekipelov and other Soviet writers who were already in prison or under house arrest at the time of our dinner remained there.

I was banned by the Soviet government from any further travel to the USSR.

14

When the second Helsinki Review Conference finally opened—in November 1980 in Madrid—the city became a circus, a very grim one. Activists from many countries flocked there. They held candlelight marches to honor the dead and imprisoned, and press conferences to discuss human rights. They pursued delegates from sympathetic countries, urging them to raise specific issues in the formal debates. It was a constantly changing show. Recent émigrés from the Soviet Union and Eastern Europe read out the names of their imprisoned colleagues. Others from the Baltics (Lithuania, Latvia, and Estonia), who had left in the 1940s when the Soviets took over their countries, marched in colorful, ethnic costumes. Afghan mujahedin in Muslim dress held press conferences to denounce the invasion of their country by Soviet armed forces. There were American Indians, criticizing U.S. policies toward Native Americans. Raoul Wallenberg's sister was there, demanding an accounting of what had happened to her brother, the Swedish diplomat who saved hundreds of Hungarian Jews during World War II, only to disappear into the Soviet gulag. Waif-like Avital Shcharansky often made headlines in her ceaseless campaign for the release of her husband, Anatoly. At any one time, there were several nongovernmental activities going on outside the conference hall. The international press was everywhere. We were busy arranging interviews, receptions, and press conferences for various victims of human rights abuse. Together with other organizations, we succeeded in making news of what might otherwise have been a dreary conference behind closed doors.

This was the kind of atmosphere Ambassador Goldberg had longed for in Belgrade: a sense of excitement and drama outside the meeting hall that brought human issues to life. Although lobbying by citizens' groups at the site of international governmental meetings is now quite common-place, to my knowledge it was in Madrid that the first major effort of this kind took place.

.   .   .

In the early days of Helsinki Watch, Bob Bernstein leaned heavily on our mutual friend Ed Kline. Just about every time I suggested something to Bob that involved the Soviet Union—a new report on the imprisoned monitors, lobbying specific government officials, whatever—he would say, "Ask Ed" or "Get Ed's okay."

Ed Kline was the quirky businessman and Soviet buff at whose home Bob and I had first really talked. How Kline ran his business was a mystery to me, for he devoted himself full-time to gathering information about the Soviet Union. He financed and edited the *Chronicle of Human Rights in the USSR*. He prided himself on being the first to know about arrests of dissidents, or releases, or exchanges. He had mysterious contacts every-where, including in the U.S. government, and he was on the phone con-stantly, pursuing rumors and facts.

Kline's only commitment—it verged on being an obsession—was to the group he referred to as "my dissidents"; they, in turn, were loyal to him and grateful for his ceaseless efforts and financial support. One of Kline's lasting contributions to our work was his suggestion that we hire as a part-time consultant Ludmilla Alexeyeva, a historian and the Moscow Helsinki Group's official representative abroad, a funny, gregarious woman then in her early fifties. Although totally dedicated to a depressing cause, Lyuda was always high-spirited and full of warmth: a hug from Lyuda really made me feel loved. Lyuda's involvement with the dissidents was charac-teristically personal. Her stories about them before their arrests brought them to life for me. These comrades-in-arms began as a group of friends, and they would always remain that for Lyuda. "When all your friends are going to Paris," Lyuda once said, "going to Paris is not such a big thing. . . . When all your friends are going to prison, going to prison is not such a big thing."

.   .   .

In the months before the Madrid conference opened, we followed the U.S. government's preparations, becoming part of an ongoing debate over tactics to use with the Soviets. The State Department on the whole opted for a low-key, nonconfrontational approach that would preserve U.S.- Soviet détente; the congressional Helsinki Commission, then headed by Congressman Dante Fascell (a Democrat from Florida), wanted the U.S. delegates to condemn human rights abuses by the Communist states. We favored Fascell's more aggressive approach.

Max Kampelman, a Washington lawyer who had led the preparatory talks and later became the head of the U.S. delegation, met with us on several occasions. Once, on the very day that we were meeting with Kampelman, a letter signed by Ed Kline and criticizing Kampelman for not being forceful enough at the preparatory talks was published in the *Wall Street Journal*. I didn't even know about the letter until Kampelman arrived, angry and upset. Nor do I know exactly what prompted Kline to write the letter, although I suspect he got caught up in some of the internal State Department disputes. It was awkward and embarrassing. We apologized to Kampelman and explained that Ed Kline's views did not reflect those of the committee as a whole, and after a while the meeting became amicable. But Bernstein was furious with Kline. Their relationship deteriorated after that, and Kline ultimately ceased being active on the Helsinki Watch board.

Even before the Kampelman episode, Aryeh Neier, one of the most active members of our board, seemed to be usurping Kline's place as Bernstein's most trustworthy consultant. Although Neier was not a Soviet expert, his knowledge about the world in general was prodigious. He was also experienced in raising funds and working with nonprofit organizations, whereas Kline was definitely not an organization man.

·   ·   ·

Ed Kline was wrong about Max Kampelman. He turned out to be a hard-hitting, skillful negotiator. He spoke out eloquently in Madrid on sensitive issues previously avoided by the diplomatic community and also used his excellent diplomatic skills to bring many of the NATO delegations along with him. In the first few months of the Madrid conference, the U.S. delegation publicized the names of sixty-five jailed Helsinki monitors and other imprisoned dissidents and condemned the Soviets for abusing many important human rights issues covered by the Helsinki accords, including family reunification, human contacts, cultural and religious rights, and freedom of information. There was plenty to protest, for one outrage followed another. The Soviet bloc countries arrested dissenters on the very eve of the conference and continued making arrests all during the drawn-out proceedings. They were, in effect, thumbing their noses at the commitments they made when they signed the Helsinki accords. More than fifty Soviet Helsinki monitors were in prison merely for trying to monitor their government's behavior. How wrong they had been in thinking the review conference would protect them.

We maintained a constant presence in Madrid, long after the other groups had gone home. We expected the conference to last about six months—as had been the case with the first review conference in Belgrade. Instead, the months would stretch into almost three years, with the conference ultimately ending in September 1983. Through it all, we continued to pressure the delegates. Our permanent representative in Madrid, an American named Marta Williams, organized press conferences for us when we visited and distributed our reports. In addition to documenting the arrests of Helsinki monitors in the USSR, Czechoslovakia, and Poland, we released nine reports on U.S. human rights compliance that helped establish our credibility as an evenhanded organization and deflected Soviet criticisms that we were focusing solely on them.

In the course of the lengthy Madrid meeting, our grant from the Ford Foundation was renewed, both in recognition of the work we were doing and because the Madrid conference had become the only forum in which East and West continued to meet. My wish had come true: Our work would continue indefinitely, even after the conference ended.

.   .   .

I traveled to the Madrid conference five times between its opening in November 1980 and its conclusion in September 1983. I could have, and probably should have, spent even more time in Madrid, but I was reluctant to be away from home, for my personal life was exceptionally demanding at that time and often in disarray. Austin and I were involved in acrimonious and emotionally exhausting divorce negotiations that put me under severe financial pressure. My father, already in bad health, was being treated for prostate cancer in Mt. Sinai Hospital, where I tried to visit him as often as possible. My children were off in different directions, each needing more attention than I was able to offer. Abby was teaching English at the University of Bologna in Italy, where she had gone in 1979 soon after graduating from college; I had managed only one brief visit there. Pam was finishing her studies at Barnard and living a few blocks away from me, but we still had trouble finding time to get together.

And then there was Emily, only thirteen when Austin and I separated and destined to spend her high-school years coming home to an empty house each day, waiting for me to return. I often let her down. Racing home in a taxi one winter evening, eager to see her before she left for her regular Wednesday-night visit with her father, I was too late. My taxi passed right by her as she bucked the Riverside Drive wind, heading toward Austin's apartment. Her book bag was strapped to her back; one hand held her violin case while the other pulled our little dog Duchess along on a leash. The wind whipped her hair across her face, frozen with grim determination and searing misery. I shall never forget her look at that moment, nor my anguish and guilt at the sight of her. *What have we done to our children, our family? What right do we have to inflict such pain on those we love the most?* Emily entered Yale too young, in 1981 when she was only sixteen. I missed her terribly and worried that I was not giving her the emotional support she needed.

When I wasn't worrying about my work or my divorce or my father or my children, I worried about everything else: about money and whether I would be able to support myself on my salary; about my friends, whom I no longer had time to see; about our dog Duchess, alone in the apartment all day. I worried also about spending the rest of my life alone. After twenty-three years of marriage, imperfect as they were, I found it hard to be single again. I thought it was too late to make a life with someone else, but it turned out I was wrong.

Charles Kuskin and I were both single in the early 1980s, bruised by failed marriages, needy, not used to living alone. We knew each other well: Our two families had been friends for many years. Although our shared backgrounds and experiences were a good basis for our new relationship, we had to contend with guilt and gossip. We were in forbidden territory, upsetting to our ex-spouses and confusing to our children and friends. Yet I never felt more certain of any relationship in my life—despite the many problems we had to work out.

Charlie's life, like mine, was in transition in more ways than one. After thirty years as a professional oboist, he had become a composer. He lived and worked on a fifty-foot Chris-Craft in the 79th Street Boat Basin, not far from my apartment. Down there, in the marina, the city seemed very far away. With Charlie, on the boat, I could escape momentarily from the pressures of my life and my work.

Charlie was full of contradictions. He adopted a macho, irreverent manner but was more sensitive and tender than any man I had known. One day he was happily drinking beer and shouting encouragement to the Knicks on TV; the next he was moved to tears at a performance of *The Magic Flute.* Different from each other as we were, we formed an emotional connection so strong and profound that the word "love" seemed inadequate to describe it. But my work kept getting in the way.

Charlie's youthful good looks, humor and charm were appealing to women: I could see that from the phone calls he received when I visited him on his boat. I didn't want to lose him to someone else, but I was often absent when he wanted to be with me, either working long hours at the office, or in Madrid, or later—worse still—in Eastern Europe, where I was out of reach, even by telephone. We missed each other terribly when we were apart. I tried to limit my travel, but my job made it hard for me to stay put.

.   .   .

During one of my visits to Madrid, I had a leisurely lunch with Orville Schell. I had never before spent time alone with him, and I had been somewhat intimidated by his rather clipped and businesslike manner. Our lunch turned out to be relaxed and surprisingly informal. We talked a little about the breakup of my marriage, and I confessed to him how heartbroken I was at the prospect of losing my weekend home in Connecticut. Orville told me about a treasured home in Martha's Vineyard he had turned over to his first wife when they divorced; it had recently come back into his life after she died and his children, the writers Jonathan and Orville, inherited the house. A house, he said, is just a house; it no longer meant as much to him as it once did.

Orville was then in his mid-seventies. He was married to a woman many years younger than he and was the father of two young sons— younger, I believe, than his grandchildren. He took great joy in his new family, walking the boys to school every morning and going on rough-and-ready camping trips with them. He was youthful in his bearing and outlook. I admired his vitality.

On another occasion, flying back from Madrid with Bob Bernstein, I again found myself talking about my divorce. Bob had taken a paternal interest in my problems when Austin and I first separated a few years before. He had advised me then to be tough and to get a tough lawyer. "Get as much as you can," he told me. "If you get too much, you can always give some back." But Austin himself was a tough lawyer, the very sort Bob had advised me to retain. As I described Austin's tactics, Bob became angry and frustrated. He reminded me then of my father, who thought he could fix people's lives as easily as he fixed their toasters and was confounded when he failed. After a long silence, Bob turned to me: "I hear you can hire a hit man for as little as $500," he said. I was stunned: He seemed so serious, I half expected him to offer me the money. I was also touched that he had gotten so involved. A minute later, we both burst out laughing: After all, we were supposed to be saving lives, not taking them.

Not long after, I gave up the war of attrition that my divorce had become. Anxious to get on with my life, I came up with a proposal that was so financially advantageous to Austin I knew he would not refuse it. When I told my lawyer what I was ready to do, she looked at me quizzically. "You realize what this means," she said. "You will have to work for the rest of your life." I had come so far in my own thinking that her remark took me aback. Of course I would work for the rest of my life. My work *was* my life. I could not imagine leaving it.

15

We hadn't figured on a Reagan presidency. Our work had begun during the Carter administration, when human rights issues were high on everyone's agenda. Patt Derian, Carter's assistant secretary of state for human rights, was outspoken and demanding, challenging foreign despots to change their behavior and others in the State Department to be more vociferous. Helsinki Watch could count on her for help and support. We had hopes for some real progress during Carter's second term.

But that second term was not to be. Reagan's victory in 1980 brought Carter's presidency to an abrupt end. And if Reagan had had his way, it would also have been the end of Carter's human rights policies.

In a sense, this was predictable—all new presidents want to make their own mark and not just carry out their predecessor's dreams, especially when the new president is from a different political party. But Reagan's attempt to cast aside the Carter human rights program was not just a sign of his independence: It reflected his own simplistic, black-and-white view of the world as either "Communist" or "democratic." It did not matter how a country treated its citizens or its enemies: If it was anti-Communist, it was our friend.

Reagan condemned the Soviet Union as an "evil empire" and encouraged U.S. involvement in anti-Communist struggles everywhere. His administration was ready to support all governments, no matter how repressive they were, if they were fighting against left-wing insurgents. In the case of left-wing governments such as those in Nicaragua and Angola, the U.S. aided, and even sponsored, right-wing insurgents.

Reagan found the theoretical justification for his policies in the writings

of Jeane Kirkpatrick, an academic whom he appointed ambassador to the
United Nations. Ms. Kirkpatrick's thesis, set forth in *Commentary* magazine
in September 1979, was as follows: "Although there is no instance of a
revolutionary 'socialist' or Communist society being democratized, right-
wing autocracies do sometimes evolve into democracies—given time, pro-
pitious economic, social, and political circumstances, talented leaders, and
a strong indigenous demand for representative government." In other
words, countries with left-wing totalitarian governments, such as the
Soviet Union and its satellites, were incapable of change from within
because the government controlled every aspect of society, whereas countries with right-wing authoritarian governments, like the military dictatorships that then prevailed in Central and South America, were capable of
internal change because their governments did not exercise total control
and there were other interest groups—businessmen, the church—that
could exert influence. Thus, it followed, the United States should support
authoritarian governments of the right and encourage them to become
more democratic but should oppose totalitarian governments of the left
because they were impervious to change.

Jimmy Carter had found it was not always practical to deny foreign aid
to countries that were human rights abusers. He was pragmatic and saw
the need to cooperate with certain governments despite their domestic
policies. He acknowledged this quite openly, saying that the Philippines,
for example, was of strategic importance to the United States and that we
would therefore support Manila, even though it abused human rights. But
the Reagan administration took pragmatism a step further: It distorted the
facts in order to prove that oppressive governments that were of strategic importance to the United States were not as bad as they really were,
or were "in transition to democracy" and thus deserved our support.

"Democracy" became the key word in Reagan's rhetoric, intended to
replace "human rights." But the nongovernmental human rights movement would have none of it. We were determined to keep human rights
the focus of U.S. policy, and with great effort we were largely successful.
Carter's contribution to U.S. political thought—the linking of human
rights concerns to U.S. foreign policy—might not have been his legacy
without the nongovernmental movement that kept it alive after he lost the
presidency.

Reagan appointed Ernest Lefever—a man who was on record for

wanting to repeal human rights legislation—to replace Patt Derian as the assistant secretary of state for human rights. Human rights organizations rallied and helped defeat Lefever at a tumultuous confirmation hearing before the Senate Foreign Relations Committee. A factor in his defeat was a well-timed appearance by the Argentinian newspaper publisher Jacobo Timerman, who had described his experiences as a former political prisoner and torture victim to a select group of senators at a dinner we hosted in Washington the night before. Lefever was finished once Timerman stood before the Senate committee. The hearings took place on my fiftieth birthday, May 19, 1981. I got home from Washington barely in time for the party my children were giving me.

. . .

When the Reagan administration turned its attention to Central and South America, supporting brutal military governments there, our Helsinki Watch board began considering the possibility of forming an Americas Watch to take issue with the U.S. government's policies in the region. I was all for it. I believed we would be more effective dealing with our own government than we were battling the Soviets. I knew that our work in the Helsinki countries would lend political credibility to an Americas Watch. I liked the idea of enlarging our scope to the non-Communist world: It would underscore the fact that we were neither right nor left in our orientation but solely concerned with protesting human rights abuses—wherever they occurred.

Bob Bernstein called one morning and asked me to come to his office later that day. Orville Schell was there when I arrived. I knew immediately that something was up: Bernstein often called on Schell for support when he was uncomfortable about something he was doing. "We're starting an Americas Watch," Bob told me. "Aryeh Neier will be launching it. He has agreed to join the staff on a full-time basis, with the title of vice chairman of both Helsinki Watch and the new Americas Watch. You will continue as executive director of Helsinki Watch, but Neier will be the chief executive officer to whom you will report."

It was awkward. Bernstein and Schell were assuring me that my position would continue as before while telling me at the same time that I now had a boss. I made it easy for them by accepting their news with grace. We parted on a cordial note, though the subtext was clear. On my way home,

I visualized Bernstein and Schell shaking hands, surprised and relieved that I had taken their announcement so well.

"You've been passed over," Charlie said that night over a late dinner on his boat. "Bob Bernstein was afraid you were going to make a scene; that's why Orville Schell was there."

"Yes," I agreed, "but it's not like being passed over for someone I don't respect. Aryeh Neier is a public figure. He's famous, the ACLU head who defended the right of Nazis to march through Skokie. He has experience, name recognition. And he's brilliant; he has a lot to offer us."

But although I barely admitted it to myself, I *was* concerned. I had gotten used to being independent. I didn't know what it would like working with, and for, Aryeh Neier.

.   .   .

When Neier first joined the staff, in the spring of 1981, he was admirably low-key. He did not interfere or even show much interest in the work I was doing but spent most of his time planning for Americas Watch—meeting key people in the field, raising money, and, I am sure, brushing up on his own knowledge of the region. His previous career had not prepared him for the international arena; he had a lot to learn. I think he welcomed the change and the new body of information to conquer. He seemed relaxed and chatty, in his element holding forth about his work at the ACLU to appreciative young members of our small staff.

The only real change I felt came from Bob Bernstein, who began to communicate with me only through Neier. I was busy at the time organizing an event at the New York Public Library, a "reception in exile," timed to coincide with the opening of the Third Moscow Book Fair in September 1981. The reception was Bernstein's idea: Both he and I had been blacklisted by the Soviets and could not get visas to go to Moscow for the book fair. Nor were there any dissident writers remaining there for us to see. Instead, we brought eighteen Soviet émigré writers from their various countries of exile to New York for a reception that included Russian food, an exhibit of banned books, and speeches by some of the exiles. Many of the writers we invited had been at our reception at the Aragvi restaurant in 1979 and had since been driven abroad.

Bob Bernstein was intensely interested in the preparations for the reception. Neier would come into my office, often several times a day, and say, almost sheepishly, "Bob wants to know how many people are coming," or "Bob asked me to find out if the speakers' program has been printed yet." I wanted to say, "Then why doesn't he call and ask me?" but I held my tongue. I knew Bob was trying to underline the fact that Neier was now in charge. I also knew Bob's behavior wouldn't last, that he would soon be back on the phone again, calling as he used to, full of questions and ideas.

The reception got advance publicity in an article that appeared on page one of the *New York Times*. This brought in a flood of ticket seekers, many more than the room at the library could accommodate. I was forced to say no to many last-minute callers. One request was on behalf of a financier named George Soros. Soros had not yet begun his philanthropic work; it was the first time I had heard his name. I was about to refuse him a ticket when the woman who requested it, Svetlana Stone of the New York Academy of Sciences, declared in a pointed way: "Mr. Soros is a very important man." "Anyway," she added, "he won't stay long. He only wants to meet two people: Vladimir Bukovsky and Bob Bernstein." Something told me it was prudent to say yes.

Our Book Fair Reception in Exile provoked a long diatribe in the major Soviet literary journal, *Literaturnaya Gazeta*. The author even maligned the site of the reception, pointing out that Bryant Park, just behind the library, was a hangout for drug addicts and criminals, which in fact it was in those days. This invective delighted us; it meant we were getting through to the Soviets, that our activities were having some effect.

.   .   .

I liked working with Neier. It was a relief to have another grown-up around. Our staff was young, mainly in their first jobs, and I had not realized how much I needed someone with whom I could consult and share responsibility on a day-to-day basis. And I thought I could learn a lot from watching Neier as an administrator.

Aryeh Neier was big and stocky, one of those men who carry their weight with ease and are surprisingly strong and well coordinated. He was proud that he never got sick—"I've never missed a day of work," he would brag—that he didn't wear glasses, that his short-cropped hair had no gray, and that he went without an overcoat in winter, except on the very coldest days. "I have subcutaneous protection," he once told me.

His reach was expansive. Where I used to worry about the expense of making long-distance calls to Washington, he was already talking about opening a Washington office—that is, after we moved our New York office to larger quarters so that we could expand our staff. He wanted us to be a large organization along the lines of the ACLU, and he was confident that he could raise the necessary funds. He was eager to merge with other human rights organizations, but only if we controlled everything.

Shortly after the event at the New York Public Library, Neier took me to lunch. He polished off his food quickly—I had barely begun to eat mine—then settled back for a discussion while sipping the one glass of red wine he allowed himself at lunch each day.

Neier asked me how I saw my work developing in the future and, before I could answer, proceeded to describe his own vision for Helsinki Watch. "I think it's time we do more than just collect information that comes to us through various channels," he said. "We should go out into the field ourselves, meet the dissidents, tell them who we are, get the information firsthand, find out what they are thinking and how we can cooperate." He paused. "There's only one person who can do all this, and that's you."

My heart sank. I realized that someone in my position should have been thrilled with the prospect of going abroad for human rights work. Indeed, part of me *was* excited at the notion and pleased that Neier trusted me to explore such untrodden territory. But a much stronger part resisted, though I knew Neier was right. Even if I could put aside my usual reluctance to leave Charlie and my children, I was consumed with worry about my father. He was back in the hospital and had entered the terminal stage of his illness. Strong, competent Dad who could bend the world to his will was fighting a battle he was destined to lose. *I have to be there for him, just as he has always been there for me. How can I leave him when he's dying?*

I said none of this to Aryeh Neier and agreed to begin planning a trip to the region. But instead, I procrastinated. Even when Aryeh began to prod me, I did not tell him about my father. In some foolish way I felt it was unprofessional to bring family matters into the workplace, an attitude Aryeh reinforced by his own disinclination to discuss anything personal. On the rare occasions when he mentioned his family, it was "my wife," or "my son"; although I had met them both, he never referred to them by name. He frowned on the office custom of celebrating each other's birthdays with a surprise cake and tried, unsuccessfully, to end it. And once when I explained that I would be coming in late the next day for personal reasons—I was excited that Abby would be visiting from Italy and thought to share that good news with him—he remarked dryly: "We all have personal lives."

.   .   .

I told Dad's doctor that I was contemplating a three- to four-week trip abroad. He encouraged me to go. "Your father's declining very slowly," he told me. "The chances are that nothing much will happen in the next month or so." Ruth, my stepmother, who was constantly at Dad's bedside, also urged me to go. Only Dad resisted.

Unlike my mother, who had faced her final illness without complaint and in remarkably good spirits, Dad was a cranky patient. He was not happy when I told him I was going away, but I knew it had nothing to do with his illness. He just didn't like the thought of me traveling in that part of the world. His attitude by now was familiar to me. He didn't expect me to change my plans, but he objected to them nonetheless.

And so, in the fall of 1981, I set off on a twenty-five-day trip to Czechoslovakia, Poland, Hungary, and Yugoslavia, winding up in Madrid to report my findings to delegates at the Helsinki Review Conference. Although I had stopped briefly in Prague and Warsaw on the way home from Moscow in 1979, this trip was seen as the first *real* mission in our organization's history. I am proud that I was the one to take it, as well as the many follow-up missions I made in those early years when I was the only one traveling for Helsinki Watch. By now I have gone on some sixty missions for Helsinki Watch and Human Rights Watch, and as time passes they have begun to merge in my memory. But the details of my 1981 trip to Eastern Europe—to a world that no longer exists—remain vivid in my mind.

16

Few people traveled to Eastern Europe in those days. It was a forbidding place, dreary and sad. And no one went there on human rights missions—the borders were closed to human rights investigators. Amnesty International, because it always notified governments in advance when it planned a visit, was effectively barred from sending delegations to the Communist world. But we had no qualms about being secretive. The goal was to get in. I could use any pretext that worked.

I applied for visas, listing the purpose of my trip as "tourism" and my occupation as "housewife." I began collecting the names of dissidents to see. I copied their addresses into a special address book, coding the information so that only I could decipher it, using "opish," a secret language that I had used with my friends as a child. *Opa Sopecropet Lopangopuopage.* Preparing for a possible police search, I removed my business cards, my office credit card, and everything else in my wallet that said "Helsinki Watch." I took these precautions to protect people I did not yet know, people already in serious trouble with the police who might be further compromised by meeting with *me*. No one told me what to do: I just used caution and common sense.

Today at Human Rights Watch we have training programs for people who go on missions. We teach them how to prepare in advance and what to do if they are followed or arrested. We train them in interviewing techniques and in taking testimony. We hold workshops where we act out hypothetical meetings with police and with hostile government officials. Anyone going on a first mission must be accompanied by someone with field experience.

But in 1981, there were no teachers, no procedures to follow. I was in uncharted territory. The tactics I chose to use were the beginnings of a methodology that would be adopted by our organization later on, when missions abroad became commonplace.

I got most of my information from émigrés in the United States and Western Europe. They warned me it would be like Russia: Telephones would be bugged and taxi drivers would report to the police. They cautioned me to leave nothing incriminating in my hotel rooms, which would also be bugged—and searched when I was out. They told me always to keep my notes on my person, to hide them when leaving the country, and to be discreet in what I wrote down in case my notebooks were confiscated.

My goal was to meet human rights activists in each country and find out how we could best help them. I knew that direct contacts with the dissidents would enable me to speak and write about them with authority. I didn't worry too much about my own safety: Being an American, I told myself, would protect me. I might be kicked out of a country, nothing worse. I knew, of course, that in the past, Communist police had chosen to make examples of certain Americans by framing them and throwing them in prison as spies. But that possibility seemed remote to me.

My main worry was that I might get other people in trouble by virtue of meeting with *me*. I knew that I had to be sensitive to people's feelings, to be sure they really wanted to risk talking to me, and to be careful of what I said.

I had lots of questions. How severe was the repression in each of the four countries I planned to visit? Who were the main human rights defenders in each place? What did they think about our idea of organizing an international human rights conference in 1982, and who would be the best person to represent them at such a meeting? Were there other joint actions we might undertake? Were there any contacts between dissidents in neighboring countries? And—the question of the moment—what was the effect of Poland's Solidarity movement on its Communist neighbors?

Solidarity, the independent trade union movement that was born in 1980 during strikes in Poland's Gdansk shipyards, had brought unprecedented free expression to Poland and had become an alternative voice within Polish society. No one knew whether its influence might extend elsewhere in the Eastern bloc. We didn't even know whether the people in neighboring countries knew about what was going on in Poland. Their governments, fearful of contagion, were trying to halt Solidarity's spread by suppressing any news about it.

17

Czechoslovakia, my first stop, was the most repressive of the countries I would visit. I had been in Prague briefly on my way home from Moscow in 1979 and had seen great tension there. Six activists, including the writer Václav Havel, Czechoslovakia's best-known dissident, had just been arrested, tried, and sentenced for being part of an organized group and for "subversion." Several of the people I had tried to meet in 1979 were under round-the-clock police surveillance in their homes.

Since my 1979 visit, there had been dozens of new arrests. Now, just as I was about to leave for Prague again, fourteen intellectuals had been detained and charged with maintaining illegal contacts with foreigners. Meeting with me, a foreigner, might put others in danger. I wondered if anyone would risk it. I did not want to get people in trouble by calling on them unannounced, yet there appeared to be no other way to approach them. Jan Vladislav, a writer and translator of children's books who had taken me around in 1979, making introductions when possible and steering me clear of places that were under surveillance, had since left for France. No one, I was told, would dare to be my guide this time around.

. . .

Abby called one morning from Italy, where she had been teaching English at the University of Bologna since her graduation from college a few years before. She was responding to a letter I had sent her describing my travel plans. "Mom?" Abby sounded excited. "How would you feel about me meeting you in Prague?" She had been reading a lot of Czech literature, she said, and was anxious to see the city. I said I would be thrilled to see her and have her company, but I warned her I would be too busy to do any sight-seeing. I was also worried about getting her into trouble, but she didn't seem concerned.

Abby, the eldest of my three daughters, was an inveterate traveler in those days. She used her free time under the relaxed Italian university schedule to explore Europe, including the East: She had discovered, almost a decade before other American tourists, that the Warsaw Pact countries were cheap and uncrowded, unspoiled by tourism, and among the few places in the world where American tourists were still a novelty. Although a history major in college, Abby seldom read a newspaper: History for her ended somewhere around the Renaissance. Prague, full of wonderful early architecture, was the kind of city she would adore. She arrived in Prague with a carefully annotated guidebook in hand.

We met on October 28 in the room I'd reserved at the Alcron Hotel and spent the first hour or so eagerly catching up on each other's news. It was great to see Abby, but my pleasure was tempered by a dull sense of anxiety that I could not dispel. This was not, after all, a pleasure trip. I was nervous about how it would go.

Abby was careful not to mention anything about my work or what I intended in Prague; I had briefed her in advance by phone before I left the United States. It was hard at first to become accustomed to the fact that someone might be listening to our every word. Occasionally one of us slipped, and the other would quickly put a warning finger to her lips. We felt equally constrained over lunch in the hotel café, where we immediately spotted a plainclothes police agent sprawled listlessly in a chair near our table, close enough to hear our conversation.

.　　.　　.

The Alcron, an untouched relic of Thirties-modern, had been the unofficial command post for Western journalists in August 1968 when Soviet-led Warsaw Pact troops invaded Czechoslovakia to put an end to the brief Prague Spring. It was assumed—and later proved—to be the most heavily bugged hotel in town. Over the years, however, it would become my favorite place to stay in Prague. I always knew what to expect: the excessively polite concierge behind the reception desk, the faded upholstery on the chairs, the luxurious down comforters on the beds, the delicious ham sandwiches in the café, the crippled violinist who serenaded a mostly empty dining room. I even felt a strange kind of comfort in seeing the same omnipresent police agent, looking bored and restless in the hotel lobby.

The Alcron was always half empty, its guests mainly members of Eastern bloc delegations or businessmen from other Warsaw Pact countries. Tourists in Czechoslovakia, especially from the West, were a rarity. Over time I came to wonder why Communist authorities weren't more suspicious of the many "tourist" trips I made to their countries in the 1980s. Why would a woman be traveling alone in such a dreary place, often at the most inclement time of year? The dissidents I came to know in Eastern Europe assured me that the police knew precisely who I was: "They're just watching you to see who you meet with and what you have to say." But I told myself the police were not that organized or that smart, that they probably didn't see much threat in a middle-aged woman like me. It made me more comfortable to think of them that way.

.   .   .

Abby and I left the hotel together, walking slowly and trying to look casual—the mother, dark hair flecked with gray, wearing a tweed coat and uncomfortable leather boots; the daughter, in jeans and sneakers, her light hair pulled back in a long ponytail. Once on the street, I told Abby my plan: that I had the names and addresses of people I intended to visit and hoped they would be willing to meet with me. I didn't urge her to come with me, though I secretly hoped she would. She must have sensed my anxiety; in any case, she didn't let me down.

We walked along the broad boulevard known as Wenceslas Square, pretending to be interested in the drab shop windows displaying Party literature, tins of food with monochromatic labels, and cheap costume jewelry. (Much of the jewelry, I later learned, was the product of forced prison labor under hazardous conditions.) Heading toward the National Museum at the top of the gently sloping street, we passed the statue of King Wenceslas, in front of which Jan Palach, a twenty-one-year-old student, had burned himself to death in 1969 to protest the Soviet invasion. Today that spot is decked with flowers and photos, a shrine of national pride, but it was unmarked and seemingly unnoticed on that gray day as we passed by.

We traveled the city on foot or by public transportation, always watching to see if we were being followed, never taking taxis or calling ahead by phone, hoping that people would be there when we rang their bells. We climbed dark staircases in one strange building after another, remaining absolutely silent so that no one would hear us speaking English. We lit matches to read the names on the front doors, signaling to each other in triumph when we found the one we were seeking. If no one was home, we repeated the procedure later that day, and the next, and the next. If someone was home and opened the door, we remained silent, handing the person a piece of paper on which I had written my name, U.S.A., and Helsinki Watch.

On a few occasions, we were invited in by people who talked freely to us about their problems and were willing to take the consequences. This made me a bit uneasy, for our open conversations, undoubtedly being recorded, could very well put *us* in jeopardy as well. But I kept my fears to myself, awed by the courage of these strangers.

Ivan Havel, Václav's brother, was one of the fourteen recently indicted intellectuals. He was allowed to remain at home pending the outcome of his trial. "Of course, they are eavesdropping on me," he told us, "but I don't care. I live my life normally. I have nothing to hide." Ivan, like many of the others we met, thought the increased repression in Czechoslovakia was a direct result of the success of Solidarity in Poland. "The authorities are nervous," he told us. "They don't want the same thing to happen here."

Small and unprepossessing, except for his winning smile, Ivan received us in the family apartment that had been divided in two: Ivan and his wife lived in one half; the other belonged to his brother, Václav, and Václav's wife, Olga. The apartment, overlooking the Vltava River, was in a substantial apartment house built in 1905 by the Havels' grandfather. We sat and talked in a large living room that had seen better days. Its most striking feature was a small round window, eccentrically placed to give a stunning bird's-eye view of Prague Castle. If someone had told us then that the castle would someday be home to Ivan's brother, we would have laughed in disbelief: Václav Havel was in prison, suffering from a succession of illnesses that would bring him close to death before he was finally released.

Ivan Havel wanted us to meet Kamila Bendová, the wife of an imprisoned dissident named Václav Benda, and with this in mind he walked us to her home, asking us to wait outside and warning us not to mention Helsinki Watch when we spoke to her. But Mrs. Bendová, it turned out, would not meet with us at all: Through Ivan, she explained that she worked in the scientific sector and was obliged to report any contacts with foreigners.

Jiřina Kynclová, the middle-aged wife of Karel Kyncl, an imprisoned journalist, was in her nightgown when she answered the door later that day. She did not ask us into her apartment, motioning to us to wait in the hall while she dressed. Then, at her insistence, we followed twenty paces behind her as she walked many blocks from her home, away from nosy neighbors. When we finally settled down in a little pub, she told us she was always afraid. She was just recovering from an operation and worried constantly about her husband's health in prison. Unlike most of the others I met, the Kyncls were prepared to emigrate if given the chance. Their son, a photographer, had already left for England, and they were estranged from their married daughter in Prague, whose ambitious husband frowned on an association that might damage his career. "I never see my grandson," she told us sadly, "although he lives just a few blocks away."

There was a furtive quality to many of our meetings: People turned up the volume of their radios and spoke with hushed voices, or chose to write their thoughts on paper rather than speak them aloud. Some insisted we talk outdoors, sitting on park benches in the cold, suddenly becoming silent when people passed by. We were told about activists who had recently been beaten and tortured during interrogations and of two murder victims, one of them a priest. Just before we arrived in Prague, a young woman dissident, Zina Freundová, had been sexually abused and savagely beaten in her apartment at 2 A.M. by three men who forced their way in. She ended up in the hospital with a concussion and believed her attackers were police agents trying to frighten her into emigrating, which she eventually did.

Despite the obvious tension, very few people refused to see us. I was touched by their eagerness to hear what I had to say. They were so isolated. They could not travel outside of Czechoslovakia, even to other Communist countries, or receive mail from abroad or foreign publications. Western radio stations were jammed and long-distance telephone calls were cut off.

Most of the people we met had been active in the 1960s, during the Prague Spring. They had helped liberalize politics and culture in Czechoslovakia and supported Alexander Dubček, the Party leader who preached "socialism with a human face." They had seen the movement crushed in August 1968 by Soviet tanks. They had been told in no uncertain terms that the Brezhnev Doctrine of obeisance to Moscow would prevail. And they had been forced to stand by while Dubček was replaced by Gustav Husák, the Soviet-backed Party boss who began the process called "normalization," backed up by the abnormal presence of Soviet troops and tanks, permanently stationed just outside of Prague.

Almost overnight, the Prague Spring activists became outsiders, an oppressed minority of some half-million people who lost their jobs, influence, and status and were ostracized in their own country. In 1977, nonetheless, 242 of them had the courage to sign Charter 77, an appeal to the Czechoslovak government to observe the human rights provisions of the Helsinki accords, including freedom of expression and other basic liberties. The charter was not a call to action and contained no political program. It merely asked that the government adhere to laws it had already approved and signed. Over the years, more than 1,000 people would add their names to the charter, though they were well aware of the likely consequences. Václav Havel explained early on that signing was "the right thing to do." For him it was simple: "There are certain causes worth suffering for."

The people we met, all charter signers, were special victims of the StB, the sadistic state security police. They told us they were watched, followed, and hounded. Most of them had lost their jobs and were forced to do menial work as janitors, window washers, and doormen. Their neighbors, they said, shunned them. Their writings were confiscated during repeated house searches. Many had had their passports and driver's licenses taken away and their telephones disconnected. In a policy of "guilt by association," their friends and relatives, their children, and their children's children were punished as well and, in what was perhaps the cruelest blow to a group composed mainly of intellectuals, their children were denied entrance to universities.

Yet there was a remarkable élan and cohesiveness within the group. They continued to report on human rights violations in Czechoslovakia and to organize a lively underground culture. They published literature independently, in hand-typed, hand-bound volumes. They gave private performances of unpublished plays in people's living rooms. Defrocked ministers and priests conducted church services in their homes. Professors held independent philosophy seminars in their apartments for students who had no access to or interest in the state universities.

The dissident group in Prague was close-knit: Shunned like lepers, they fell back on each other's company. It was like an exclusive club in which courage was the key to membership. Most of them had almost inadvertently crossed an invisible boundary that made them suspect. Protesting the arrest of a friend, signing a petition, reading an "illegal" book from the West—these were the "crimes" that made them dissidents. Many married and remarried within what they sometimes called "the ghetto." On one occasion, I would discover that the woman I had met on a previous trip as the wife of Ivan Havel had become the wife of the Havels' friend Jiří Dienstbier. My confusion amused them.

·   ·   ·

Abby and I called on Josef Danisz, a lawyer who had been briefly imprisoned for defending people accused of political crimes. Although we appeared without notice, he did not seem surprised to see us. He invited us into his small, dimly lit living room, where we sat on a lumpy, overstuffed couch. Clean-cut and boyish-looking, Danisz spoke little English. He called to his wife in another room to help. She joined us somewhat reluctantly, carrying a sleeping child in her arms. He introduced her as Anna Grušová.

Anna seemed very shy. She began to interpret for Josef, hesitantly at first; then, slowly warming to the conversation, she talked about herself as well. "I had no choice," she told us. "My family were all dissidents and so I, in a sense, was born into it." Her father, she explained, was Eduard Goldstücker, a former Communist official purged and jailed in the 1950s. Goldstücker, a Kafka expert, had been ambassador to Israel before his arrest. Later, during the Prague Spring, he was the outspoken head of the Writers Union. When the Soviets cracked down in 1968, he fled to England to escape yet another arrest. Anna told us she hadn't seen her parents in twelve years. Her first husband, the writer Jiří Gruša, also lived in exile, in Germany. Two teenage children from that marriage lived with Anna and Josef.

"I had no choice," Anna repeated, "but I know how difficult it has been for others, making a decision that they know will damage their children's lives and endanger their family and friends."

The Czechoslovak authorities would often strip people of their citizenship while they were out of the country. For this reason, many refused to go abroad on the rare occasions when they received such permission. "I worry about the cultural survival of my country," Ivan Havel had told us. "I think it's important to stay." Václav Havel had set a high standard by rejecting the option to emigrate, choosing to remain in prison instead. "It would be a fantastic thing to go somewhere for a year or two, or even ten," Anna Grušová confided to us. "But only with the feeling that you can come back. When Christmas comes, I will always want to be in Prague."

Anna was beautiful in a fragile way, with high cheekbones, luminous gray-green eyes, a delicate complexion, and dark hair that curled against her cheek in the style of the twenties. She seldom smiled. I was taken with her the moment I saw her. There was something familiar about her, as if we were related. I was touched by her shyness and the efforts she made to overcome it. I was impressed by her sensitivity and intelligence, and by the eloquence with which she expressed her views, in carefully chosen words and a fine, cultivated British accent. I sensed in her a profound sadness, much deeper than anything I had experienced.

Abby held the baby while Anna served tea. I could see that my daughter was taking it all in: the cozy room lined with overflowing bookshelves and our hosts—he, fair, self-assured, humorous; she, dark, self-effacing, serious. There was no trace of complaint as they described their situation, nor was there resignation. They were building a life together, trying to make it as normal as possible, despite constant harassment by the police.

Josef talked about the unusual circumstances of their marriage: "Anna and I were married eighteen months ago, just before I was about to go to prison for contempt of court. That's what happens to lawyers here. It was a real act of courage on *her* part, marrying a criminal like me." I caught Anna's fleeting smile.

"I never went to prison," he went on. "There was an amnesty. For some reason I was included, although the amnesty was not for political prisoners. It must have been a mistake." Danisz had lost his license to practice law in 1978; he was doing legal research in a law firm but was no longer admitted to the courts. "They call me in for questioning from time to time," he said, "and they periodically search the apartment without any warning."

"Have you *seen* Prague?" Anna asked suddenly, as we were taking our leave. "I would like to show it to you." I was touched by her suggestion.

We agreed to meet on Saturday morning under the clock in Old Town Square.

.   .   .

Saturday morning found us shivering in the misty, cobblestone square. Anna arrived late, breathless: "I am so sorry. It was difficult to find someone to take care of the baby." She was smartly dressed in a long jacket and straight skirt made of heavy wool in a bold plaid pattern. "Do you like it?" she said brightly, when I admired the fabric. "My parents sent the goods from London and I had it made here." The fog gradually burned off and the day turned fair and crisp, perfect for sight-seeing. "I can show you the castle and the famous churches and palaces, if that's what you want to see," she announced, "or I can show you *my* Prague." We chose the latter, of course.

We walked around for several hours, lingering especially in Malá Strana, below the castle, Anna's favorite part of town. She pointed out buildings that she loved, some tucked away on little side streets that we might not otherwise have found. At every turn we discovered unexpected architectural details, charming, whimsical, sometimes a bit grotesque. Anna joyfully pointed them out. I was struck by her passion for the beauty of the city in which she had experienced so much misery.

We ended up in the Slávia, a spacious but dingy coffeehouse in the Viennese style, a well-known hangout for writers and intellectuals. Anna was full of questions: How strong was the Solidarity movement in Poland? How did I feel about Israel? What was the U.S. doing in El Salvador? "I do not know what is happening in the world," she complained. "The only news we get is from *Rudé Právo* [the Communist Party daily]. The foreign radio stations are jammed, and the two Prague stations have only propaganda. The Voice of America sometimes gets through; as a joke, we call it 'Prague Three.'"

Anna ordered several of her favorite pastries and insisted that we try a bit of each. We sat there for a long time, sipping coffee, eating éclairs and talking about things that women all over the world discuss: husbands, children, clothes. For the first time since I arrived in Prague, I felt relaxed.

Then I ruined it all by commenting, more to Abby than to Anna: "This is the way it should be here. Three friends, at ease, talking, not looking over their shoulders to see who is watching." Anna lapsed into a very long silence. A heavy weight descended upon us, the burden of her thoughts. Then she spoke, softly, sadly: "When I first read Kafka at the age of twenty I hated him because his books were so cynical and negative. Now, however, I think of him often. At this very moment, for example, there are people somewhere whom I do not know who are deciding what will become of my life."

Anna was speaking figuratively, but her words were very close to the truth. The proportion of police to dissidents in Czechoslovakia was so great that specific security officers were assigned—sometimes exclusively—to a single dissident. A truly bizarre kind of intimacy often developed. A policeman would bait his quarry: "You seem to be having writer's block again," or allude to the intimate details of a domestic quarrel, or threaten blackmail over a clandestine love affair. Sometimes during interrogations the police would offer dissidents a way out—by informing, or by publicly renouncing their ideals. There were double agents everywhere, even within the charter movement, enough to surprise even the most cynical.

I did not see Anna again during that visit to Prague, but over the years we would become good friends. I valued her opinions and loved to quote her thoughtful comments in the articles I wrote. Her ideas were original and fresh. She was not one of the well-known dissidents who were used to being quoted by the Western journalists who occasionally visited.

Anna liked me, she said, because I was one of the few outsiders who understood "the mechanism of totalitarian power and how it works." "You can't really explain it," she said, "People either understand or they don't." I knew what she meant. In our office we often talked about people who "got it" and those who didn't. As late as the 1970s and even the 1980s, there were people who visited Communist countries and never fully grasped the dark side of the picture. My good friend, the writer Bob Crichton, an active proponent of civil liberties in the United States, went to the Soviet Union for a literary conference in the mid-1970s and returned full of enthusiasm, not just for the people he met but because he had seen no pornography, homelessness, or illiteracy. And as late as 1982, the writer Susan Sontag, at a Town Hall symposium in support of Polish Solidarity, confessed to a belated "discovery" that communism was as bad as fascism.

Anna thought I understood totalitarianism because I was Jewish, that

Jews have a "special sensitivity to repression." I suspected it had more to do with my studies at the Russian Institute. But I didn't argue the point with her. After all, what propelled me to the Russian Institute in the first place?

.   .   .

I had a long list of people to see in Prague. Abby and I did our best to find them, walking for miles, often in the rain, always checking to see if we were being followed. I took notes at all our meetings, using garbled initials to remind myself who the speakers were. It was then that I discovered that in order to keep my notes as inconspicuous as possible, I could write in a script so tiny I could only read it with a magnifying glass or by enlarging my notes in a copying machine after I returned home. Still, by the time I left Prague, I had filled a number of sheets in my notebook with tiny letters and was consumed with worry about how and where to hide them while going through customs. Ultimately, I decided to roll them up and keep them within reach in the pocket of my coat. I assumed customs officials were more likely to search my suitcase than my person.

As it turned out, my precautions were not necessary. We left Czechoslovakia without incident; Abby returned to Italy, and I went on to Poland. I planned to return to Prague as frequently as I could. The people I had met there were counting on me—to publicize their problems, to bring them information, to come back. I vowed never to let them down.

18

Warsaw in 1981 looked dreary and impoverished. Inflation was out of control; there were shortages of food, clothing, and many staples of everyday life. Yet there was a spirit of freedom in the air. I felt it in the way ordinary people spoke to me—openly critical of the government, totally without constraint. I saw a vibrant independent political life, with Solidarity buttons worn openly and proudly by almost everyone around. Solidarity was flourishing and the Polish government seemed paralyzed, unable to tame it. It had all happened in little more than a year.

In August 1980, following defiant workers' strikes in the Gdansk shipyards that spread throughout the country, the government had signed the Gdansk Agreement, accepting more than twenty of the strikers' demands, including the establishment of the Solidarity free trade union, with Lech Wałęsa at its head. It was an astonishing capitulation: By allowing an independent trade union movement to express the will of a growing segment of the population, the government, already more lenient than those of its Warsaw Pact neighbors, had lost any semblance of totalitarian control. The other so-called workers' states, especially the Soviet Union, felt threatened to their core by the existence of a workers' movement in Poland that *opposed* the state.

I had expected to be met at the airport by Zbigniew (Zbyszek) Romaszewski, head of the underground Polish Helsinki Committee, or by one of his colleagues. But no one was there when I arrived.

I took a taxi to my hotel. The driver, holding up a two-inch-thick wad of Polish zlotys, told me they were worthless and demanded to be paid in dollars. He explained that the only goods to be found were in the *Pewex* stores, hard-currency emporiums where Polish citizens were queuing up with their hoarded dollars. "We have rationing," he told me, "but what's the good? The food can't be found anywhere." The official exchange rate of thirty-three zlotys to a dollar was mocked by a black-market rate of 500 to a dollar. The U.S. dollar was the only currency that worked in Poland.

I immediately set out for the Warsaw Solidarity headquarters on Mokotówska Street. I was not prepared for the thrill of seeing the imposing building that Solidarity occupied. It was festooned with a huge Solidarity banner and bustling with several hundred mostly young, energetic and dedicated workers. I wandered from office to office, speaking to polite but preoccupied people. I was looking for members of KOR (the Polish acronym for Workers Defense Committee) whom I had met in 1979, during a brief stopover in Warsaw on my way home from the Moscow Book Fair. They were a small underground group at the time but had since become the intellectual backbone of Solidarity.

Eventually I was approached by Barbara Różycka, a Solidarity activist in her early forties; she explained in excellent English that none of the people I wished to see were in town. In a startling rundown, given the fact that as recently as a few months before, opposition figures were not allowed to leave the country, she told me that many were away at conferences abroad. Helena Łuczywo, who had taken me around in 1979, was at a meeting in Madrid. Mirosław Chojecki, head of the illegal underground publishing group called NOWA, who was free on appeal with a prison sentence still pending, was at the Frankfurt Book Fair. Zbyszek Romaszewski, my key contact in Warsaw, was in Radom, some fifty miles south of Warsaw, negotiating with the government; no one knew when he would return.

I had met Romaszewski briefly in 1979 at a hastily arranged meeting of KOR people in the home of Jacek Kuroń, one of the leading Polish activists. When I suggested the possibility of their forming a counterpart Helsinki Committee in Poland, Kuroń said, "Let's start one now," and turning to Romaszewski, assigned him the task. To my surprise and delight, the new committee immediately set to work, preparing what became a 182-page report on Poland's human rights record, compiled under the difficult conditions of search, seizure, and secrecy that existed in pre-Solidarity Poland. Helsinki Watch later released the report in English translation, calling it *Prologue to Gdansk*.

I invited Barbara to meet me for dinner at my hotel. She seemed intelligent and well informed and was the only one around who appeared to have time for me.

It was Friday afternoon. I wandered the gray streets, dismayed by the bleakness of the city, with its blank shop windows and long lines of grim-faced people waiting outside the virtually empty stores, eager to buy anything to get rid of their worthless money. I wondered whether there was any truth to the theory that the government was artificially creating the shortages in order to blame Solidarity and discredit it. At the suggestion of Polish friends back home, I had brought along a supply of such basic items as soap powder, shaving cream, coffee, toothpaste, and sanitary napkins. None of these were available at any price or in any currency.

Over dinner, Barbara told me that people were already grumbling about Solidarity. "The people are more radical than Solidarity," was the uneasy observation I heard both from her and others during my visit. Barbara, who told me that she came from a "good" Polish family, confessed she had no great love for Lech Wałęsa. "He's a charmer," she said, "but not a thinker." She told me Romaszewski would be back the next day and planned to see me on Saturday evening.

I awoke Saturday morning to rain and sleet. My only comfortable shoes were not waterproof; if I got them wet, they would not dry out in the cold, barely heated hotel room. Anyway, there was no place to go: It was a religious holiday and everything was closed. I had people to see on Sunday and Monday, and I expected to see Romaszewski that evening, but a long empty day in my hotel room loomed before me, an abrupt change from the nonstop pace I had kept in Prague.

Traveling light and expecting to be constantly busy, I had brought nothing with me to read, save a guidebook to Eastern Europe. Nor were there any English-language books or newspapers to be had. I had plenty to write about, but I was afraid to put my thoughts to paper: I would be passing through many more customs checks before I returned home. I thumbed through the guidebook disconsolately, my fingers cold and clumsy. I put on my coat, then eventually got under the bedcovers, trying to warm up.

My head was full of images of Prague. Something had happened to me there that I had not thought possible: I had fallen in love, not with a person but with a city, and a surprising city at that. I had seen some beautiful cities over the years—Paris, Venice, Rome—and I had brought home things to remember them by: a scarf and a bottle of green peppercorns from Paris; leather gloves and deep-green olive oil from Rome. I could remember how relaxed and elegant I felt, basking in the warm spring sun at a Paris café, nostalgically watching a young couple kissing near the Métro station. I could easily conjure up the mingled smells of coffee and chocolate in that little Italian bar in Rome where my reveries about living in Italy forever were interrupted by the sudden whistle of the espresso machine.

Prague was a city of broken dreams. There were no inviting places to eat, drink, and observe the passing scene. People on the streets were dressed well enough, but they seemed drab and unfriendly, introverted and brooding. The absence of competitive commerce meant no bright lights, no attractive window displays, no place to relax and enjoy the city.

Czechoslovakia had been used as a pawn in the infamous Munich Pact of 1938, in which the Allies abandoned the country to the Germans without a fight. An accidental benefit of this unconscionable deed was that Prague was not bombed during the war. Unlike other European capitals, its ancient architecture, some of it dating back to the ninth century, remained intact. After the war, when the Communists took over, new construction and development were modest by Western standards, and there was no attempt to prettify or exploit the city's intrinsic beauty. It remained pristine.

Some of my meetings in Prague had taken place in apartments in the old part of town, where the architectural styles—Romanesque, Gothic, Renaissance, Baroque—were a history lesson in themselves. Finding the apartments was always an adventure. Every small winding street held new surprises: gargoyles holding up a drainpipe, an elaborately carved front door, a little turret window looking down on a small square.

Here and there I had passed scaffolding, although no work seemed to be going on. *Like a beautiful, aging woman trying to rejuvenate herself. Prague does not need a facelift, it needs vitality, spirit.* The silent city seemed mysteriously empty to me, a lovely, lifeless museum. It filled me with a melancholy so strong I was close to tears.

Over time I would come to see that part of the mystique Prague held for me had to do with the people I met there. Anna Grušová, who showed me around Prague, was one of a number of people with whom I would form close friendships. This was quite remarkable, given the strained circumstances under which we met. The Czech dissidents maintained a relaxed style of ironic amusement, despite their dashed dreams. They tried to live as they had in the 1960s, when the scent of freedom permeated the air. I wondered whether I, in their place, could muster such quiet courage and humor. They were forced to make daily choices between good and evil, and when they spoke about principles, loyalty, and courage, their conversations were not abstract.

.   .   .

I'm not sure how much of this I understood at the time as I sat alone in that cold hotel room in Warsaw, wondering how to fill my time. Warsaw lacked Prague's architectural integrity; it had been rebuilt in the atrocious Stalinist style after heavy bombing during World War II. Nor, at that moment, did I feel any personal warmth: In Prague I was needed, sought after; in Warsaw, I felt in the way.

At lunch time I called room service and was sent an open-faced ham sandwich the size of a canapé and a tiny, watery cup of coffee. The bill was twelve dollars. I was still hungry, but embarrassed to order more.

For the first time since my trip started, I had time to think of home. I had been so busy, so consumed not only with the people I was meeting but with constant concerns about their safety and my own that my "real" life back home only entered my mind fleetingly. I suppressed worries that were just below the surface, especially about my father. Now I began to dwell on him. *Perhaps he's gotten worse. What if he's in pain and feels abandoned by me? What if he's miserable because I'm in Eastern Europe where he hates to see me go? Why am I sitting idle in this cold room in a strange city where no one could care less about me, when I could be at home with him? All my life I've wanted to show him how much I love him. Now, when he needs me, I'm not there.*

There was no point in trying to call home. Calls to the United States had to be ordered days in advance and required hours of waiting before they went through. I thought about Charlie and my children and felt pangs of loneliness and homesickness I hadn't experienced since childhood.

I had an early and unremarkable dinner in the hotel restaurant, stopping first at the reception desk to tell the clerk where I would be in case Romaszewski should call or come. I noticed that all the hotel employees were wearing Solidarity buttons. Another startling change was the presence of prostitutes soliciting openly in the hotel lobby.

After dinner I checked back with the reception desk and was handed a cablegram from the United States. It was from Ruth, my stepmother, whose perseverance and ingenuity would put many a human rights activist to shame. She had somehow gotten a cable through saying that Dad was OK, that they missed me and that I should take good care of myself and not worry. I brushed away tears of relief and gratitude.

Back in my room I got under the covers again and soon dozed off, dreaming of an earlier time in my life when my father was healthy and vigorous and my children were small. The dream ended abruptly—I bolted awake to the raucous ring of the telephone. It was Romaszewski from the hotel lobby. "Can I come up?" I looked at the clock: It was 10:30 P.M. "Of course," I said, hurrying to tidy myself and the rumpled bed.

Zbyszek Romaszewski, his wife, Zofia, and Barbara Różycka entered, hands and faces ruddy from the crisp night air. Zbyszek was tall and very thin, with an angular, pointy face. He had just returned from Radom; before that he had been at other meetings. "There is so much democracy in Poland, there's no time to work." He was joking, but I saw no humor in his face or in his bloodshot eyes, only great fatigue. He explained that most of the leaders of KOR, the group of intellectuals that included him, Jacek Kuroń, and Adam Michnik and had first taken up the workers' cause, were now involved in Solidarity, so much so that KOR had officially dissolved itself. The Helsinki Committee, which he headed, continued to work, preparing reports on human right abuses. He rattled off some particulars, as if by rote: Three people were in prison for political reasons, fifty to eighty union leaders had cases pending in court, and 150 more had been accused but not yet investigated. At least fifty Solidarity members had been beaten up in the streets in attacks they believed were police instigated. Activists continued to suffer from harassment, blackmail, forty-eight-hour arrests, and punitive searches and confiscations.

Zofia, her round, open face more relaxed than her husband's, spoke of discrimination against minorities and officially sanctioned anti-Semitism. "Don't be taken in by reports of a 'beautiful situation,'" she warned me. "In a country in crisis, all the ugly things come out." Zbyszek added: "The main work ahead is to change the laws. If the government shows more respect for human rights right now, it's through fear, not because of a change of attitude. The government can do anything, according to the law. There's even a rumor that they are building concentration camps to cope with our big movement."

My guests predicted a bitterly cold winter, fuel shortages, and power failures that would lead to riots and the imposition of martial law or, worse still, the use of Soviet forces to subdue the rioters. *There's no possible happy conclusion to their revolution,* I thought, *no way they can win. If Solidarity tries to take over the government, the Soviets will certainly step in. They've done it before—in Budapest, in Prague.*

But when I asked Zbyszek about attending an international human rights conference that we would organize in 1982, his response was optimistic. "Why not have it here in Warsaw?" he asked. "Why not?" I replied. "What a good test that would be."

Zbyszek asked me if I would send him copies of the constitutions of various Western countries. He and his colleagues were thinking ahead to a democratic Poland, but they were deprived of the most basic documents they needed to inform their plans.

It took some convincing to get them to accept the "care package" of coffee, soap, and other basics I had brought from home. "We are not starving," they assured me with pride. Zofia reciprocated by unfastening her Solidarity button and pinning it on my sweater. It was more elaborate than any other Solidarity button I had seen, and I still have it today.

It was around midnight when they left, but they were going on to yet another meeting. I turned on the television in time to see the end of a huge musical extravaganza from Moscow marking the November 7 anniversary of the Soviet revolution. Each intermission was marked by a Soviet-style commercial: a red flag bearing a picture of Lenin fluttering amid misty clouds.

Outside, a light snow was falling. The streets were quiet, empty. But a lot was happening out of sight. General Wojciech Jaruzelski and other military leaders, under severe pressure from the Soviets, were secretly making plans for the declaration of martial law a month later. On December 13, 1981, many thousands of Solidarity members throughout Poland would be seized at meetings and in their homes and imprisoned. The Solidarity trade union would be banned.

The human rights conference we talked about holding in Warsaw in 1982 would not take place. Zofia was arrested in July 1982. Zbyszek, who had gone into hiding at the time of the crackdown to work with the underground Radio Solidarity, was arrested in August and charged with treason, which carried a possible death sentence. He would be released two years later in a July 1984 amnesty, but we would have to wait until 1988 before an international human rights conference would finally be held in Poland.

19

Hungary seemed to be thriving when I arrived there, toward the end of my 1981 trip through Eastern Europe. Budapest's Old World charm, fine restaurants, and attractive well-stocked shops made it an appealing city for Western tourists, who liked to think of the Kádár government as being more liberal than others in the East. In truth, the government was interested in Western markets and technology and wanted to keep its Most Favored Nation (MFN) trading status with the United States, but it was wrong to confuse this friendliness toward the West with political liberty at home. People in the know sometimes called Hungary the "goulash archipelago," an arch reference to the perception that Hungarians had traded their political freedom for the creature comforts their Communist government was willing and able to provide.

I didn't expect to find dissidents in Budapest; my inquiries in New York had come to nothing. Shortly before I left for Eastern Europe, however, I had met a Hungarian philosopher in our office, a recent émigré in his thirties who had come to the office on a personal matter involving his green card. When I told him my purpose in visiting Budapest, he gave me the telephone number of a friend there.

Not knowing the rules, I played it safe, calling Ágnes Erdélyi from a street phone some distance from my hotel. I said I had regards for her from a friend in New York and that I would like to meet her. She sounded guarded and asked me to wait, then returned to the phone and invited me to her apartment. There was no warmth in her voice. I wondered what I was getting into.

There were three people waiting for me—Ágnes and her husband, Vilmos (Vili) Sós, and their friend Mária Kovács, whose husband, György Bence, joined us later. They were dissident intellectuals—Mária was a social historian, the others were philosophers—and appeared to be in their thirties. Vili, who seemed slightly older than the others, had a wry, sardonic smile and self-deprecating manner, as if he had seen everything and nothing mattered anymore. Ágnes was shy and serious, with an air of quiet competence. Mária Kovács, small and sultry, did most of the talking; she spoke the best English, for her father was a Hungarian diplomat and she had spent some of her early years as an embassy child in Washington. Curled up in a corner of the couch, she seemed haughty and supercilious at first, though her dark eyes flashed when she talked about the injustices of the regime.

All three of them, in fact, were cool to me initially. They were looking me over, not with fear, I thought, but with a mix of boredom and suspicion. Later, recalling that first meeting, Mária explained: "Lots of scholars and journalists were coming to see us. We were fed up. They kept lecturing us. Some of the people we met were really shocked, but they never did anything. You said you'd do something, and somehow I knew that you would. That's why I called Gyuri and told him it was worthwhile coming over to Ági's."

Gyuri was her husband, György Bence, who arrived at the apartment about an hour after I got there. He was short and round with a bushy black beard and lively eyes. Years later, at my home in New York, he told me he had lived with his grandparents during World War II, after his father was shipped to the front in a labor battalion and his mother was sent to a concentration camp. One day, he said, he was taken with his grandparents and several hundred other Hungarian Jews to the banks of the Danube, where Hungarian Nazis mowed them down with automatic weapons. Gyuri, then three years old, was found by the Budapest police wandering among the bodies. They took him to the local police station, where he was claimed by the family's former housekeeper, a Christian woman who sheltered him until his mother, who survived the camp, returned after the war.

.   .   .

When I was invited to stay for dinner, I knew that the group in Ágnes's apartment had warmed to me. I must have mentioned that I had written a few cookbooks: Years later, Mária told me how she had rushed into the kitchen to tell Ági: "She's O.K. She's a real person. She writes cookbooks!" When I seemed mystified, Mária explained: "That you had written cookbooks and restaurant reviews—now that was something exotic to us. It meant you were a well-rounded person, someone with common sense, and not just a proselytizer."

I liked them all and soon felt comfortable with them. The apartment, the books, and the way they dressed and spoke reminded me of my Upper West Side friends in New York. Their invitation to dinner was a welcome gesture of friendship and, as it turned out, of courage. By the second day of my visit, Mária reported she was being followed by four cars.

Their problems, which they described to me over dinner, were similar to those I had heard about in Prague; the main difference was that none of them worried about going to prison. Vili Sós had signed a petition in 1968 protesting the Soviet invasion of Czechoslovakia and as a consequence had not worked as a philosopher for thirteen years. He could not teach, do research, or publish. He believed his apartment and telephone were bugged. He had no passport, not even the red passport for travel to other East European countries. Gyuri Bence had been unemployed for ten years. He supported himself by doing freelance translations. Ágnes and Mária had research jobs, but no passports; they had gone to Gdansk during the Polish workers' strikes and had lost their red passports as well. But they were better off than one of their friends who had gone to Poland and met with a member of Solidarity; he was fired from his job when he returned.

My hosts were part of a small group, maybe several hundred in all, that called itself the Democratic Opposition. They seemed almost embarrassed to complain, knowing how much worse things were elsewhere in Eastern Europe. "It's hard to understand our forms of minor repression," Gyuri Bence explained. "They're not dramatic, as in Prague. But they deserve attention. The situation could get much worse in a moment."

The Democratic Opposition had a distinctly intellectual cast and included a disproportionate number of Jews. It was one of two dissident groupings in Hungary. The other, the Nationalist Opposition, was Christian and took a strong stand against the persecution of the large Hungarian minorities in Romania (some 2.5 million) and in Czechoslovakia (some 600,000). Their nationalist position had some guarded support among

Hungarian officials who were at the same time wary that such national-ism could turn into anti-Sovietism. There was not a lot of love lost between the two dissident groups. Bence and his friends suspected the nationalists of anti-Semitism, not without some justification.

Hungarian dissidents, it appeared, survived by avoiding direct con-frontation with their own government over *its* policies. "We are on a long rope," they explained to me. "Two things must never be questioned: the Soviet presence [in Hungary] and the supremacy of the Party." Both groups tended to focus on peripheral issues in *other* countries, such as the persecution of dissidents in Poland and Czechoslovakia and the plight of Hungarian minorities in Romania and Czechoslovakia. Their extensive samizdat literature was intellectual and philosophical in content, unlike samizdat in the USSR and Czechoslovakia, which dealt mainly with spe-cific human rights abuses in their own countries.

I spent an evening with György Konrád, Hungary's best-known con-temporary fiction writer, published in the United States as George Kon-rad. Konrád appeared to be about fifty. His clothes were rumpled and his manner unassuming; I found him engaging and warm. We talked for sev-eral hours, joined later by a young student named Judit who would some-day be Konrád's wife. Konrád told me how he had been arrested in Hungary in 1974 after an unpublished book he had coauthored was found during a search. He was held for only a week because of a concerted protest from writers in the West, where he was well known and where his writings, including his novel *The Case Worker*, were published. Konrád sub-sequently lived in New York, Berlin, and Paris, but had returned to Hun-gary in 1979. Although he was not punished for publishing abroad and remained a member of the Writers Union, his books went unpublished in Hungary and his name was not mentioned in the press.

Konrád wanted to know what I had seen and heard in Poland and Czechoslovakia. He hung on my every word. He said he felt close to the Democratic Opposition in Hungary but was also in touch with the nation-alists and was trying to bring the two groups closer to each other. He told me he had been one of four Jewish children in his village who managed to escape to Budapest and safety during the war while all the remaining Jews in the village were killed. He described the fury of the young Jewish men who were sent by the Nazis to work at the front and who returned to the village after the war to find their families murdered. "That's why so many

Jews became Communists after the war," he explained. "They saw the Communists as liberators." I commented on the large number of Jews among the current generation of dissidents in Eastern Europe and suggested that they had become disenchanted with the communism of their parents. He agreed.

A number of the dissidents I had met were children of privilege, born to parents from the Communist elite. Mária Kovács was an example, as was László Rajk, an architect in his early thirties who ran a "samizdat boutique" in his Budapest apartment. Rajk's father, also named László, had been an important Communist minister until he was betrayed by his best friend, János Kádár, then the interior minister. Kádár, who ultimately became the Party leader of Hungary, had promised the senior Rajk that he would go free if he agreed to confess to improbable crimes in a 1949 Stalinist show trial. Instead, Rajk was hanged. It seemed ironic to me that the father had lost his life in support of a lie, while the son was risking his freedom in search of the truth.

Mária told me that the young László, very tall and distinctive-looking with a square jaw, heavy brows, and strong features, was the image of his executed father and that older people, seeing him for the first time, momentarily turned pale; it was as if the famous Communist victim of Stalinism had returned from the dead.

.   .   .

On my last day in Budapest, I took Mária, Gyuri, and Ágnes to lunch at a well-known restaurant, famous for its foie gras. Two police agents followed us inside and sat, without eating, at the very next table, staring at us throughout our meal. They followed at a close distance when we left the restaurant. I was unnerved to see that when I said good-bye and turned into my hotel, at least one of them stayed on my tail.

Leaving Budapest several hours later, I was stopped at Passport Control by an airport official who looked at a list, made a phone call, and told me to wait while my suitcase was brought back from the airfield and into a curtained room. There four inspectors dumped the contents of my pocketbook on a table and went through my wallet, tossing papers around, counting my money, examining my traveler's checks, my credit cards, my carefully organized expense receipts, a letter I had started to write to my father and Ruth. They pulled things from my suitcase unceremoniously, scrutinizing my camera, a book in Russian by the Russian philosopher Berdayev that had been a good-bye present from Gyuri, and a huge map of Warsaw that they unfolded and studied in triumph. All of the "clever" places where I had at one time or another thought to hide my notes—tucked into the empty bottom of a dental floss container, wrapped in my dirty laundry, inserted between layers of a sanitary napkin—were the first places they looked. I was relieved that I had, as before, decided to keep my notes at my fingertips in the pockets of my coat; they did not look there. As I was cramming everything back into my suitcase, I realized that none of them knew much English. *They're not really trying to find anything incriminating. This search is punitive, a warning to me about my new friends.* The only thing they took was the map of Warsaw.

At one point in the search, they had seen some film in my bag and asked me if I had taken any pictures in Budapest. I had, of course, but I promptly and firmly said "No." Twenty-seven years had passed since my disastrous confrontation with customs officials in the Leningrad airport. This time I knew how to handle them.

I described my treatment at the Budapest airport in an op-ed article I wrote for the *New York Times*, "Hungarian Dissidents' Troubles," which appeared on December 22, 1981. My experiences came as a surprise to many Americans who had a benign view of the Hungarian government. They didn't understand that Kádár used a canny, devious governing style in order to maintain his liberal image.

"People are not punished the minute they do something like sign a petition," György Konrád had explained to me, "but some months later they may lose their jobs, ostensibly for incompetence, rather than for the real reason, disobedience. The dirty work is done by an administrator in response to government pressure rather than by the government itself."

·   ·   ·

Shortly after I returned from Budapest, I received a letter from my four new friends, telling me they were willing to risk "going public" if I could arrange for them to visit the United States. I went to Washington to see Elliott Abrams, then quite new in his job as assistant secretary of state for human rights, and I described their situation to him. Thanks to his intervention and to the Hungarian government's desire to accommodate the United States, Mária, Gyuri, Ágnes, and Vili received their passports in

1982. I arranged for them to be invited to New York University's Institute for the Humanities, to which George Soros had given money to support the stay of scholars from Eastern Europe. That was the start of an alternative academic career for the four Hungarian intellectuals. Their scholarly work in the United States sustained them through hard times and enabled them to resume their careers in Hungary once communism ended. It took so little effort on my part. It changed their lives.

20

The weight of repression seemed to be lightening as I followed my itinerary from Prague to Warsaw to Budapest to Belgrade. In Belgrade, it was almost like being in the West. Or so I thought until I actually arrived back in the West, at Frankfurt airport, where I emerged from black-and-white into Technicolor, like Dorothy entering the Land of Oz. The sparkling shops and food stores in the airport, the bustling activity of well-dressed people, and the noise—especially the noise—were dazzling to me after the silent, monotone gray of communism. Although that world of communism is haunting to remember in retrospect, at that moment in Frankfurt I was overwhelmed by a feeling of deep relief at being back in the West. I had done the job, it had all gone well, and I was free at last to talk and write about what I had heard and seen. The article I had been composing all along in my head could now be put on paper.

I wrote a long article on my trip for the *New York Times Magazine*; it was ultimately rejected, the editors explained, because the crackdown on Solidarity in Poland made my material obsolete. The article appeared instead in the *Village Voice* (December 23–29, 1981), under the headline "Eastern Europe: Dreams That Died." It surprised me with its prescience when I reread it recently. At a time when most people viewed the Communist bloc as an invincible monolith, I had written:

> The Soviet Union's East European empire is crumbling. The disintegration will not happen overnight, nor will it progress at the same speed in each country. Putting Poland in "quarantine" will not prevent contagion, for Poland is not the source of the disease, nor does it have

the cure. The upheaval in Poland is a virulent eruption of a deep-seated malady that has afflicted Eastern Europe for many years—a reaction to Soviet domination and its concomitant evils: the suppression of national aspirations, economic mismanagement, and political repression.

.　　　.　　　.

Before returning home, I had stopped briefly in Madrid for what we now call "advocacy," in this case using the information I had gathered to persuade the Western ambassadors to the review conference to be more forceful in condemning human rights abuses. Max Kampelman, the U.S. ambassador to the Madrid Review Conference, greeted me with an impressive show of confidence. Not yet knowing what I had to say, he had planned a luncheon for me to which he invited his counterparts, fourteen ambassadors from the NATO and neutral countries. They all showed up—such was the U.S. ambassador's clout—to hear me describe what I had seen and heard in Eastern Europe. To my surprise, much of what I reported appeared to be new and disturbing to my prestigious audience. I had to remind myself that human rights was just one relatively small part of their portfolios. I realized that many of them were focusing for the first time on the personal tragedies caused by human rights violations. Their response led me to believe that in the future they would raise human rights issues more vociferously with the Eastern bloc delegates to the conference. Kampelman was delighted with the way the luncheon had gone. I felt I had accomplished something important. I was more than ready to return home.

.　　　.　　　.

I had spent three and a half weeks in Eastern Europe. Except for those few days with Abby in Prague, I was completely alone. I dropped in on total strangers and convinced them I was a friend. I telephoned people from pay phones on the street and wondered if it was wise. I decided on my own what I thought of the people I met and whether I should believe what they told me. I took notes and worried about where to hide them. I was followed by police, not knowing their intentions. I was searched at the Budapest airport and thought I might be detained. Through it all, I felt calm and at ease, unaware of how tense I really was except at specific moments, for example when the lights suddenly went out in my Belgrade hotel room and I experienced real panic before I realized there had been a general power failure.

On gray, foggy mornings as I boarded the small planes that took me from country to country, I felt as if I were in a dream. I was usually the only woman on the plane. I felt invisible to the dour-faced men who never offered to help with my luggage or otherwise acknowledged my presence. I spent hours at a time in unbroken silence. I did not even write down my thoughts because I knew my writings could be taken from me at any time. Most difficult of all, I had no one to confide in—about anything—in all that time.

.   .   .

I was overcome when I saw Charlie waiting for me at Kennedy airport. How I had missed him! My words came tumbling out—what I had done, what I had seen—even as we walked to the parking lot. It wasn't until we were seated in his car that I realized he was unusually subdued. "I think we should go straight to Jamaica," he told me gently. "I spoke to your brother today. Your father's really bad."

A half hour later, I was at Dad's side. He lay in a hospital bed that had been brought into the master bedroom at the Jamaica house, with full-time nurses in attendance. The doctor's assurances that his condition would remain stable had proved wrong. I was appalled when I saw him.

Dad's breathing was hoarse and labored, and he could neither talk nor see me. "I'm back, Dad," I said over and over again. "I'm safe and sound. Nothing bad happened. I'm home." I could see he wanted to say something but couldn't. I took his hand, swollen beyond recognition, and pressed it gently. He held my hand for a long time, squeezing it again and again. I was in despair. *Dear Dad, please forgive me. Give me a chance to make it up to you. I'm here now and I'll be at your side until the end.*

Dad died that night. Everyone said he'd been waiting for me to return.

PART III

A Movement

Takes Shape

(1981–1985)

21

By 1981, President Reagan's war against the "evil empire" was being waged primarily in our own hemisphere. The administration saw Soviet encroachment behind every left-leaning government and every local insurgency in Central America. It applied the "domino theory," arguing that one country after another would fall under communism's sway, that we might have a succession of Cubas at our doorstep. El Salvador, Guatemala, and Nicaragua were key countries of U.S. concern. It was in these three countries that our newly created Americas Watch chose to take its first stands.

Over the years, the United States had armed and supported a series of murderous military regimes fighting local insurgencies in El Salvador and Guatemala. The governments of both countries used similar strategies: They killed or terrorized the peasant population in order to deprive the guerrillas of civilian support. These governments rivaled each other in brutality. Beatings, rapes, torture, mutilations, assassinations, and massacres were commonplace. The countryside was dotted with mutilated corpses, while terrified civilians were forced to take sides. U.S. involvement exacerbated and prolonged these struggles. When, in the 1990s, U.N.-brokered peace agreements finally brought an end to the warfare in both countries, the accounting was heartbreaking: some 70,000 victims in El Salvador and some 200,000 in Guatemala.

We were outraged by the Reagan administration's open support of regimes using such brutal tactics. We recoiled from a series of atrocities—the March 1980 assassination of San Salvador's Archbishop Oscar Arnulfo Romero in his church, the December 1980 cold-blooded murder of four

American churchwomen in El Salvador, the genocidal tactics employed by the Guatemalan military against indigenous Mayan Indians. The crowning touch came in December 1981, when the Salvadoran army massacred close to 1,000 people in the village of El Mozote and other hamlets in the surrounding countryside and the U.S. State Department denied that the massacre had taken place.

One of the most vocal proponents of the administration's policies was, ironically enough, its assistant secretary of state for human rights, Elliott Abrams, who tried to impugn the motives of domestic critics by implying that they were Communist sympathizers. The very same Abrams who had listened sympathetically to my account of the persecuted Hungarian intellectuals I met in Budapest in 1981—and who had subsequently used his leverage with their repressive Communist government to get them passports to travel abroad—seemed not to care very much about innocent victims accused of having left-wing sympathies. Abrams went to war with Americas Watch, in particular with Aryeh Neier, who headed it, and their exchanges of lengthy, vituperative letters soon filled the better part of a filing cabinet in our office. It angered me then, as it still does now, to think of the many hours Abrams spent in the course of his working day fighting human rights groups like ours—we should have been his constituency—rather than fighting abusive governments, as his predecessor, Patt Derian, had tried to do during the Carter years.

Americas Watch must have been particularly infuriating to Abrams because of its reputation for objectivity. It was, after all, a sister of Helsinki Watch, which had become known for its work in exposing Communist abuses.

Americas Watch reports on El Salvador were eagerly read by people in the United States who deplored the Reagan policies. U.S. public opinion had not been so polarized on a foreign policy issue since the Vietnam War. Responding to public protest, Congress passed legislation in December 1981 establishing periodic hearings on U.S. military and economic aid to El Salvador: The president was to certify at six-month intervals that the Salvadoran government was making progress in ending torture and murder and in curbing the armed forces. But the State Department used the hearings to justify increases in aid. It played down brutal practices in El Salvador by minimizing the number of dead and blaming reported killings on "right-wing death squads," supposedly independent of the government.

Americas Watch sent missions to the region and did its own research, testifying at the congressional hearings against the State Department's assertions of the Salvadoran government's "progress." We achieved some limited success in 1983 when the new U.S. ambassador to El Salvador, Thomas Pickering, acknowledged the link between the Salvadoran military and the death squad killings. In December 1983, Vice President Bush went to El Salvador, where he met with thirty-one top military officers and threatened to end U.S. military aid if the killings did not stop. The number of death squad assassinations dropped considerably after this ultimatum, although killings by the regular army continued. As late as May 1984, President Reagan was still attributing the violence in El Salvador to "a small, violent right wing" that was "not part of the government."

.   .   .

Americas Watch also documented abuses by both sides in Nicaragua, where the situation was reversed. There the Reagan administration called the left-leaning Sandinista government a "Communist reign of terror" and aided the Contras, Nicaraguan insurgents operating from bases in neighboring Honduras. Although the Contras waged terrorism along the border, kidnapping and torturing civilians, the administration called them "freedom fighters" in order to justify giving them financial support.

.   .   .

Our regular Wednesday morning meetings moved from my office to the spacious Random House conference room to accommodate our growing circle of board members and friends—professors, journalists, publishers, lawyers—who showed up regularly every Wednesday, sometimes bringing others who then became regulars as well. These open-by-invitation meetings—which continue to this day—then alternated between Helsinki Watch and Americas Watch. One week, Bernstein chaired a Helsinki Watch meeting in his inimitably free-wheeling style that loosely followed the agenda I had prepared but was peppered with his own thoughts and concerns. The next week, Schell chaired an Americas Watch meeting in his orderly, no-nonsense fashion, taking us through Neier's packed agenda with precision and soliciting input from others in the room.

Americas Watch was an instant success. Its reports, especially on El Salvador, were well covered in the press and were eagerly awaited by many outside our immediate circle who sought independent information as counterpoint to the U.S. government's propaganda. Americas Watch was able to send large delegations to Central America—it was geographically close and easy to arrange—and its representatives were allowed to travel openly as human rights activists. Governments in the region were eager to influence American public opinion, and their high officials often met with Americas Watch delegations to make their views known. The Wednesday-morning open meetings of Americas Watch were always packed and intense: People would pick up their morning newspaper, read about some new atrocity in Central America, and come to an Americas Watch meeting to discuss what we could do about it.

Meanwhile, attendance at the Helsinki Watch meetings was falling off; our members were getting tired of hearing the same old unchanging story of Soviet repression. I worried at times that Helsinki Watch would be eclipsed by its new sister. Although the reasons for the differences in our possibilities and effectiveness were quite obvious, I felt it was my responsibility to restore interest in our activities.

Aryeh Neier and I, running our related but very different "watch committees," had each found work that suited our personalities. Neier was pugnacious and confrontational, always seeking new targets and in his element taking on repressive governments and the U.S. government as well. I, on the other hand, did not relish confrontation. It came naturally to me to keep a low profile traveling incognito in Eastern Europe, and a deep-seated stubbornness and sense of responsibility kept me going there, time and again, in the absence of any tangible success.

Bob Bernstein set a good example for me. His dogged determination to take on the Soviets never seemed to waver. He was fond of repeating the comments of a Soviet official who once told him: "I know you American liberals. You go from one issue to another. You'll soon get tired of us." Bernstein was determined to prove him wrong. He never ran out of ideas. Some of them may have been impractical, but many were truly inspired.

At Bob's urging, we personalized the victims by publishing several booklets of short biographies and photos of imprisoned Helsinki monitors in the USSR and Czechoslovakia. We also produced a large wall calendar that highlighted the birth dates of the prisoners and gave their addresses in prison or labor camp, urging people to send them birthday greetings there. In 1982, Bob came up with the idea of a poster—a photograph of a decrepit, wasted Yuri Orlov surrounded by a red border with the slogan "Forgotten Man of the Year." Soon after we released it, we were contacted by a lawyer for *Time* magazine, which came close to suing us for using its format.

Aryeh Neier favored detailed, carefully researched, factually unassailable reports on human rights abuses. He dismissed Bernstein's ideas as "gimmicks" and did not agree with me that there was room for both approaches. Neier's main involvement was with Americas Watch, where it was essential that our reports be accurate: The State Department scrutinized them closely, disputing every detail. Americas Watch reporting set the high standard for which all the divisions of our organization would later become known. By the late 1980s, we would be running the equivalent of a medium-sized publishing house, turning out fifty or more reports each year, many of them book length.

At the first Americas Watch press conference, I was impressed to see how easily Neier took charge. He ran the conference, describing Americas Watch and the report on El Salvador that we were releasing. He fielded questions from journalists. Orville Schell, the chair of Americas Watch, sat with others in the audience and seemed unperturbed by his backseat role. At Helsinki Watch press conferences it was different. I always stepped back and let Bob Bernstein take over. Not having to speak publicly was a relief for me.

.   .   .

In 1982, we moved to new, larger offices in the Bar Building, next door to the Bar Association on West 44th Street. We shared the space with the Fund for Free Expression, the Lawyers Committee for Human Rights, and the Committee to Protect Journalists, all of us small organizations at that time. Aryeh Neier had plans to merge formally with the Lawyers Committee, but its director, Michael Posner, believing that his organization would be subsumed by the Watch Committees, chose to keep it independent, eventually leaving our offices for larger quarters elsewhere. I regularly worked late, until 8 P.M. at least, and Aryeh, who was the first to arrive in the morning, often worked late as well. "The Mom and Pop of human rights," Lawrence Weschler, the *New Yorker* writer, dubbed us when he arrived at the office after-hours one night and found the two of us hard at work in our adjoining offices.

Often, after the rest of the staff left, Aryeh would wander into my office for a chat. Our organization was then small enough that both of us could read and edit every report we issued, and we often discussed them, as well as the merits of the people on our staff and board. Mainly, however, Aryeh described his plans for expansion, which were already underway: Our Washington office would open in 1982 with Juan Mendez, an Argentine lawyer and former political prisoner, as the office director. Aryeh wanted to open more offices in the United States and overseas. There was no limit to his ambitions. I was impressed by his broad vision and his confidence, both in himself and, it seemed, in me. Talking with him in those early days was stimulating and helped build my own self-assurance.

One day, at the start of one of our open meetings at Random House, Bob Bernstein took me aside: "Orville was commenting the other day on how much you've grown in your job. He's very impressed with the work you're doing and how you handle yourself." "It's Aryeh," I found myself replying. "It's great working with him." I immediately regretted what I had said. I hated the self-effacing way in which I tended to receive compliments, deflecting to others the praise that I dearly wanted but found hard to accept. And the way Bob extended the compliment—attributing it to Orville while he distanced himself—was disappointing to me.

Orville was right. I had become a good administrator and worked well with members of the staff and board. And I was more relaxed when speaking publicly; at times I even looked forward to it, especially when I was just back from a mission. Yet these were not my most important strengths. None of my colleagues had seen me where it counted—in Eastern Europe with the dissidents who came to rely on me. My responsibility to them was the force that drove me and kept me going. Much as I tried, it was hard to convey to the people at home the true flavor of my work in the field.

· · ·

Bob Bernstein had entered my life at a critical time—when my father was dying and my marriage was ending. He had made it possible for me to build a new life—a meaningful life devoted to doing good—and a new persona as a professional woman with an increasingly visible public image. Although he was scarcely a decade older than I, I had made Bob into a father figure and, as with my real father, I sought his respect.

Like my father, Bob was powerful, the head of a big company, able to make things happen. I knew he liked me, as I liked him. I sensed correctly, even back then, that he would come through for me when I needed him. But I did not feel his full confidence in my work. I had yet to prove myself to him.

22

I was tidying up my desk one evening in early 1982, getting ready to meet Charlie for dinner on his boat, when Aryeh Neier walked into my office and settled himself down on the secondhand couch, not bothering to ask if it was a convenient time for me. He began one of the little speeches he was given to, and I groaned inwardly: *I will be late for dinner, once again.* But I knew there was no stopping Aryeh, short of downright rudeness, once he began. His speech started something like this: "When the Helsinki Watch was formed, the United States was in a period of détente with the Soviet Union. The Helsinki accords were just a few years old. Relations between the USSR and United States were more civilized than they are today . . . "

Neier always spoke slowly and distinctly, never stopping to search for a word. He didn't rush to get his points across as I tended to do when I was excited by a new idea. He laid out his thoughts systematically, like evidence in a courtroom, speaking in an uninflected monotone and telling me things I already knew. It often made me impatient, especially at moments like this when I was eager to leave.

Aryeh went on to discuss the disintegration of U.S.-Soviet relations and the exacerbation of Soviet brutality, giving obvious examples: the Soviet invasion of Afghanistan, the exile of Andrei Sakharov, the declaration of martial law in Poland, the forty-five Helsinki monitors then in prison in the USSR. "Therefore"—he was coming to the point now—"I think we should form an association with groups in Western Europe, in countries that have more leverage with the USSR than the United States now has. We should find out what groups are in existence and want to work with us. Where they don't exist, we should create them."

The idea was not new—we had been talking about forming an international organization for some time. But I had assumed that it would be a lengthy process, that Helsinki committees in Western Europe would form over time at their *own* initiative and that our role would be to set an example for them to follow. Now Neier was urging me to *make* it happen, and soon.

He had convinced the Rockefeller Foundation to give us the use of Bellagio, its elegant conference center on Lake Como in Italy. We would organize a meeting there of Helsinki groups, from both East and West, to take place in September of that year. I had eight months to find the right people to attend. It seemed daunting.

I knew the situation in Eastern Europe fairly well. I had good contacts among East European émigrés and, in my travels through Eastern Europe, I had already sounded out interest in an international meeting.

I knew much less about human rights groups in Western Europe, however. I spoke no West European languages and had few friends or contacts there. Yet in the months that followed, I would go from country to country seeking groups and individuals willing to work with us. I made my initial contacts through the East European émigrés I knew, mainly Czechs in Paris, Vienna, and London. They were in a good position to know West Europeans who were sympathetic to our cause. But it was up to me to ascertain the rest. Were the people they suggested motivated by genuine human rights concerns or were they doctrinaire anti-Communists? Would they be serious about forming a new committee and not just tempted by the prospect of a free week in Bellagio? Were they people who commanded respect in their own countries? Did they have the initiative and leadership abilities to form groups where none existed? Would they be able to raise the money to do so?

Between February and June 1982, I went to Geneva, Zurich, Paris, London, Madrid, Milan, Florence, Rome, Vienna, Innsbruck, and Amsterdam, while Neier helped out by going to Oslo, Stockholm, and Brussels. I found it was easy to make connections in countries where Helsinki groups already existed independent of us—in Norway, for example, and in the Netherlands, where I actually had to choose between three already existing Helsinki groups. Elsewhere, however, I found myself looking for a single individual, someone who would be interested in forming a national Helsinki committee or at least would give the project some thought.

To single out the *one right person* within a whole country—it seemed like a staggering task. It also went against my conviction that a national Helsinki committee would only be effective if it developed organically at its *own* pace, not at our instigation. Yet we were now committed to a September conference; I had to do the best I could.

In Milan, I met an engaging political activist whose views seemed right and who was eager to join us, only to discover, when I checked him out with others, that as a young man he had hijacked an airplane to make a political statement, an incident that continued to haunt him and to discredit him among his peers. I was disappointed, especially because I was unable to find anyone else in Italy who was both liberal and anti-Soviet and as interested in our project as he had seemed. I finally settled for an elderly professor in Rome who agreed to attend the Bellagio meeting but made it clear in advance that he was not an activist and would not be interested in forming a Helsinki group.

In Austria, I was put in touch with a young woman named Jana Stárek, energetic and well connected, a graduate student of Czech origins whose diplomat father had remained with his family in Vienna after the 1968 Soviet invasion at home. Jana set up meetings for me in Vienna with an extraordinary mix of lawyers, professors, politicians, and others, yet none of them seemed quite right to me. I left for home feeling very discouraged. I knew that Austria was a key country: As a neutral nation, it had some clout with the Soviet bloc, and Vienna's geographical position in the heart of East-Central Europe made it a logical place for the European office of the federation we hoped to create. It was essential to have a prominent Austrian at our September meeting.

Jana called me in New York a few weeks later: "Jeri, there's a Professor Pelinka at the University of Innsbruck. Everyone says he's great. I spoke to him on the phone and he's interested. But you'll have to go to Innsbruck to meet him. He's too busy to come to Vienna right now."

In June, I returned to Amsterdam to finalize plans with the Dutch group, then traveled to Innsbruck on a circuitous journey that ended with an evening train ride through the Bavarian Alps. I could feel my ears pop as the train climbed higher and higher, stopping at tiny hamlets along the way. There were no station announcements, nor was there a conductor to be seen on the almost empty train, and I began to worry I would miss my stop. The elderly couple in my compartment spoke only German and kept to themselves. I had read that the Austrian Nazis had been even more vicious to the Jews than their German counterparts. I found myself silently speculating about them: *These two would have been adults during World War II. Did they support the Nazis?* I remembered an account I had read by a death camp survivor—how at age sixteen he had stood at the window of a sealed cattle car transporting him to Auschwitz while Austrian teenagers threw stones at the passing train. As if sensing my thoughts, the couple got up and left the compartment, leaving me completely alone.

It was almost time for the train to arrive in Innsbruck. I made a quick trip to the bathroom at the end of the car. On my way back, I passed the closed glass door of a nearby compartment behind which a man stood silently, his pants open, exposing himself to me. I grabbed my suitcase and hurried to the other end of the car, where I stood nervously by the door, looking over my shoulder frequently until at last the Innsbruck station came into sight. I stumbled down onto the foggy platform, took a cab to my hotel, locked the door to my room, and collapsed into a deep, troubled sleep.

I awoke the next morning with a splitting headache. A warm, low-lying fog enveloped the city as I followed signs to the center, where I found a café and ordered coffee, sitting outdoors, my mood as gray as the fog. *How did I get myself into this mess, traveling all this way for one brief appointment late in the day? What a hapless project this is, combing whole countries for one person to start a movement.*

Gradually the fog burned off to reveal a spectacular sight: steep, snow-covered mountains rising almost perpendicularly at the city's edges, so close I could see the maneuvers of the skiers on the slopes above the town. As I sat there jacketless in a warm spring sun, my spirits lifted: This was as close as I might ever come to a day off. I decided to relax and spent the day exploring the city and its shops. I felt even better when, at 4 P.M., I met with Professor Anton Pelinka, who had both the stature and the interest I was seeking. He agreed without hesitation to join us in Bellagio.

.   .   .

The pieces were falling into place. By July, we had put together a disparate group from eighteen different countries, with varying degrees of commitment to what we were trying to accomplish. We had discovered only two like-minded, already functioning Helsinki groups in Western Europe—in Norway and in the Netherlands—and representatives from both these groups were planning to attend. In Canada, we found Irwin Cotler, an energetic law professor active in Anatoly Shcharansky's case, who was, in effect, a one-man committee. In France, there was Pierre Emmanuel, an elderly poet who had formed what appeared to be a non-functioning "Paris Helsinki Committee." There were observers from England, Sweden, Belgium, Italy and Finland, who were coming to listen and learn but were not necessarily committed to follow through. And there was Anton Pelinka, the professor from Innsbruck, who was committed to forming an Austrian group.

Three other participants were coming directly, though secretly, from repressive countries: Mümtaz Soysal, an Amnesty International activist from Turkey; Srdja Popović, a prominent Yugoslav lawyer active in human rights cases in Belgrade; and György Bence, one of the four Hungarian intellectuals I had befriended, who was trying out his newly acquired passport to the West, stopping first in Bellagio on his way to New York University. Finally, there were émigrés from Czechoslovakia, Poland, Romania, and the Soviet Union, representing dissidents who were not allowed to travel abroad for this or any other purpose.

The U.S. contingent, the largest, included me, Aryeh Neier, Bob Bernstein, and Orville Schell, plus two members of the Helsinki Watch staff: Catherine Fitzpatrick, our research director on the Soviet Union, and Elizabeth Wood, my assistant. George Soros, the financier and philanthropist, was now on our board and asked to attend as an observer. In those early days before he had set up a foundation, it was not uncommon for Soros to show up at meetings in various parts of the world. It was a convenient way for him to meet activists and find out how he could help them.

Orville Schell singled me out one Wednesday morning, right after our regular meeting at Random House: "I hope the people you've invited to this Bellagio meeting are of a high quality," he said. He must have been deciding whether it was worth his time and effort to go. I could see that my judgment was on the line, with Orville and with everyone else who would be attending. If the meeting didn't work out, it would be my fault. "Don't worry," I assured Orville. But I was actually quite nervous. I had made snap judgments about many of the people I invited. I couldn't really be sure how it would all turn out.

. . .

The summer of 1982 might just as well have been winter, as far as I was concerned—I never took a day off or found a moment to relax. There was too much happening.

Pam graduated from Barnard in June. Austin and I both attended the graduation ceremonies, but unlike Abby's graduation four years before when we were newly separated, we did not go together. I sat with Emily, pretending I didn't see him. He was with his new girlfriend, who wore a flowered dress and a wide-brimmed hat, the kind that Austin had always favored.

Our divorce became final later that summer. It was a relief at first to know that four years of costly, often bitter acrimony had come to an end. But it also forced me to confront a rather bleak financial picture. I had given up my rights to everything we owned, with the exception of the city apartment. Maintaining the apartment would take two-thirds of my salary, but I was determined to hang on to it if I could. The gleaming oak paneling and massive bookshelves in the two-story living room were my father's gift to me, a testimony to his love, measured in countless hours of painstaking carpentry work. I liked the dramatic effect it had on everyone who entered. I liked being known for having "that great apartment," even among people who had never been there. I liked the fact that my children considered it home. It was convenient to be able to put up foreign visitors and to give the annual office Christmas party. Keeping the apartment was an indulgence—my only indulgence, I told myself. I didn't allow myself to look too far into the future. I had no savings for retirement, nor was there an office pension plan at that time.

In August, Abby and her boyfriend came home from Italy for a month's visit, bringing with them two Italian friends. I asked her to help me by making some two-sided place cards to identify the Bellagio participants at the conference table and gave her a list of their names one morning at breakfast. When I returned from the office that evening, she and her friends were hard at work at the dining table, an encyclopedia open before them. They had gone to an art supply store and had bought paint, brushes, and poster board, and they were making oversized signs, each artistically lettered and decorated with large, colorfully painted flags of the participant's home country. It took them the better part of the next few weeks to complete several dozen cards. Aryeh seemed disconcerted when I showed him the finished product. "Isn't this overkill?" he asked disapprovingly. "Perhaps," I replied. Unconventional as they were, I was going to use them.

As September approached, I was in a state of anxiety, though I tried to appear calm and confident with my colleagues and staff. I had to deal with

the travel schedules of several dozen people. The logistics were complicated, as in the case of György Bence, the Hungarian philosopher making
his first trip to the West. I asked Abby, who planned to come up from Ferrara to help out at the meeting, to meet Bence in Milan and escort him to
Bellagio. I also had to prepare an agenda and a kit of background materials for each of the participants. I had to read and edit the papers I had
asked some of them to prepare. I needed to buy clothes, to find someone to water my terrace garden while I was gone, and to get Duchess to
New Haven, where she would spend a month hidden in Emily's dormi-
tory where the sign at the entrance said NO DOGS ALLOWED.

My relationship with Charlie was deteriorating fast: my frequent trips
and preoccupation with work had taken a toll. Charlie was no stranger to
the demands of travel; he had traveled extensively in many parts of the
world during his long career as a professional oboist. But he was now writing music, a solitary occupation. When he wasn't at the piano, it was natural for him to want to be with me. I, on the other hand, was in a
high-pressure, unpredictable job, where I had to be responsive to events
and to the needs of countless people. I was constantly on call and often
had to put our relationship on hold—just when we should have been
making up for lost time. By the time I left for Italy, in September 1982,
Charlie and I were barely speaking.

·   ·   ·

Very soon after we assembled in Bellagio, I knew the conference would
be a success. The Lake Como setting may have had something to do with
it: beautiful views, terraced gardens, comfortable rooms, excellent food,
and an attentive staff contributed to a pervading sense of well-being and
camaraderie. Abby's homemade place cards added a personal, informal
touch. But it was the participants themselves, especially those from repressive countries—the Soviet Union, Czechoslovakia, Poland, Hungary,
Romania, Yugoslavia, and Turkey—who gave the meeting its substance
and its soul.

Even I, who knew more than most about the problems they described,
was deeply moved by their accounts of life in a police state, about their
friends who were suffering in prison, about the horrors of torture, internal exile, and unexplained deaths during detention. It was fascinating to
see people from one oppressive country react with touching empathy to

the plight of people in another; for some, it was their first realization that their situation was not unique. The differences were also striking, as between Turkey and Hungary, for example: In Hungary, where freedom of expression was severely curtailed, there were virtually no political prisoners and no torture; in Turkey, where there was considerable freedom of expression, thousands of dissenters were in prison and most of them had been tortured. The abuses described in Turkey and Yugoslavia were especially surprising to people from the Soviet bloc who had always considered those countries "Western" and "free."

Mirosław Chojecki, representing Poland, made an appeal for the 4,000 or so Solidarity members then in detention. Chojecki was the dean of Polish underground publishing and was famous among Eastern European dissidents for inventing his own printer's ink because he was unable to buy it in Poland. He was also known for the ingenious way in which he concealed and moved printing presses all over Warsaw, right under the noses of the security police. In December 1981, when martial law was declared in Poland, Chojecki was in New York City seeking money for additional printing presses. With a warrant out for his arrest at home, Chojecki had no choice but to remain abroad and began working with a Solidarity support group in Paris.

Cathy Fitzpatrick, our Helsinki Watch expert on the Soviet Union, had come to Bellagio straight from a mission to Moscow and reported on the grim conditions she found there. Cathy spoke Russian fluently and knew how to dress like a Russian; with her broad, Slavic-looking face, she could meld easily into a Soviet crowd. During her recent mission, she had talked her way into a psychiatric hospital and interviewed a political prisoner there—by posing as his cousin from the provinces. It was a risky thing to do, and she got away with it. It's a good thing she didn't consult me; I would never have authorized it.

Mihnea Berindei, a Romanian historian, lived in exile in Paris. He gave what was perhaps the most exotic report of the day—exotic because it dealt with Romania, a country none of us had been allowed to visit and about which we knew very little. Romania, according to Berindei, was doubly cursed—with communism and with Nikolae Ceauşescu, its tyrannical leader. Repression was total, the economy was in shambles, underground dissent was nonexistent. Of Romania's 22 million people, he said, 1 million had filed requests to emigrate. He described some recent decrees in Romania: One passed in October 1981 stipulated prison sentences of six months to five years for stockpiling food; another passed in February 1982 required all farm animals to be registered with the authorities under penalty of confiscation, and still another, passed in January 1982, provided for children above the age of ten to be drafted to work in the fields. In July 1982, a law on "scientific alimentation" stipulated the exact amount of food allotted to each individual according to sex and kind of work performed. In an attempt to double the birthrate, Ceauşescu had declared abortions illegal: Women were subjected to routine gynecological checkups at their workplaces to make sure that pregnancies were not interrupted.

.   .   .

By the middle of the second day, we agreed to form an international Helsinki movement that would link groups in North America and Western Europe. Groups in repressive countries—the Soviet Union, Eastern Europe, and Turkey—could not join us officially, for fear of instant reprisals, but they would be represented by émigré observers authorized to speak on their behalf. Our new organization would be called the International Helsinki Federation for Human Rights. It would defend the rights of beleaguered Helsinki groups in the Soviet Union and Eastern Europe, encourage the formation of Helsinki groups in West European countries where none existed, and establish a coordinating office in Vienna. We set up a coordinating committee composed of representatives of the five existing Western groups and agreed that the committee would meet at the Helsinki Review Conference in Madrid in November, at which time we would formally announce our existence.

The atmosphere and outcome of the meeting could not have been better. Everyone praised me for the job I had done.

On the very day that the federation was established, we learned through the Voice of America that the Moscow Helsinki Committee, which had started the citizens' Helsinki movement, had decided to disband. The three remaining members, all elderly, were no longer able to withstand the constant police pressure. It seemed like destiny—our birth at the moment of their demise.

.   .   .

After the meeting, Abby and I traveled together in southern Italy for a few days; then she went back to Ferrara and I went on alone to Capri. I spent two days on Capri, listless amid all its beauty, feeling empty and very much alone. The triumph of the Bellagio meeting was still with me, but it did nothing to lessen a deep sadness. I missed Charlie terribly and wanted desperately to patch things up. I couldn't wait to get home.

23

There was an invitation waiting when I returned from Italy. It was to a conference in Romania, a country I had never expected to see. It was a rare opportunity and I immediately accepted. *Charlie will understand,* I assured myself as I got ready to leave. But I knew in my heart I was pushing things too far.

The conference, from October 8–10, 1982, had the official blessings of the Romanian dictator, Nikolae Ceauşescu. Indeed, it was to be held in one of Ceauşescu's favorite country retreats outside of Bucharest, a well-guarded complex built on the shores of Lake Snagov. It was like being invited for tea in Hitler's bunker.

The theme of the conference was "The Future of the Helsinki Process." Ceauşescu was sponsoring it as part of his grand campaign to make Bucharest the site of the next Helsinki Review Conference. The Romanian ruler's self-aggrandizement knew no limits. Having beaten his countrymen into miserable submission, he was now seeking the blessings of the international community by suggesting that Romania host a major international meeting.

Ceauşescu was a bit of a maverick within the Communist bloc, having demonstrated some independence from Soviet policies. Unlike other members of the Warsaw Pact, Romania recognized the state of Israel and had refused to contribute forces to the Warsaw Pact's invasion of Czechoslovakia. These divergencies from Soviet foreign policy attracted favorable attention from the United States and other Western countries, always eager to drive a wedge into the tightly knit Communist empire. The U.S. government rewarded Romania with Most Favored Nation (MFN) trading status, which gave it favorable tariff rates. Ceauşescu was proud of his so-called independence. Preposterous as it seemed, he was said to be after the Nobel Peace Prize.

I had considered Romania virtually impenetrable. Visas were not forthcoming, and tourists, when permitted, were closely monitored. Law No. 408 required Romanian citizens to report to the police within twenty-four hours any conversation with a foreigner. There was no organized dissent in Romania: Paul Goma, the Romanian writer who tried to organize a Helsinki committee, had been arrested and expelled from the country. All privately owned typewriters had to be registered with the police as if they were guns: As a result, Romania was one of the very few East European countries in which samizdat was nonexistent. It was said that one out of every four Romanians worked in some way for the Securitate, the secret police.

The meeting at Lake Snagov was being organized by a U.S. organization called the Institute for East-West Security Studies, which was funded in large part by a wealthy and well-meaning American businessman named Ira Wallach. The institute's founders believed they could improve East-West relations by arranging unofficial contacts and dialogue among leaders and opinion makers from East and West. They had managed in a relatively short time to gain the confidence and cooperation of some of the worst dictators in Europe. I had little sympathy for their approach and thought that the group was being exploited by its more unsavory members. For me, the conference served only one purpose—it was a way to get into Romania and have a look around.

.   .   .

Identified as the director of Helsinki Watch, I was surprised when I actually received a visa to attend. We had circulated a paper in Madrid in 1981 entitled "Bucharest Should Not Be the Site of the Next Helsinki Review Conference." I had also been critical of Romania at U.S. congressional hearings on the renewal of Romania's MFN status. Yet I not only received a visa but was given permission to enter Romania four days before the conference at Lake Snagov was to start.

But what would I do during those first four days? I had no contacts in Romania. There was no dissident movement. Anyone I spoke to there would have to report our conversation or break the law.

I called the few people I knew who might be helpful: Berindei, in Paris, who had spoken so eloquently about his repressed countrymen at the Bellagio conference; a Romanian émigré working for Radio Free Europe in Washington; some Hungarian activists in New York who had contacts among the Hungarian minority in Romania. A few days before I left, a man named Ovi Florea showed up unannounced at our office to ask for help for his brother, Mircea, who had begun a hunger strike in Bucharest on September 23 as part of his campaign to emigrate. I took his brother's address and promised I would visit him. Just before I left, Rose Styron called. When I mentioned I was going to Romania, she told me that Hannah Pakula, an American writer whose husband, Alan, had recently directed the movie *Sophie's Choice,* was in Bucharest doing research on the life of Queen Marie of Romania, the subject of a biography she was writing. "You'll probably be in the same hotel," Rose predicted.

.   .   .

It was late afternoon when I checked into the Intercontinental. I unpacked my bags and then, as I often did in Eastern Europe, went out for an aimless stroll, looking into shop windows and acting like a tourist. But my tourist posture, which didn't really seem natural anywhere in dismal Eastern Europe, was absurd in Romania; the shop windows were absolutely empty and the poorly dressed people on the streets seemed tight-lipped and forbidding. Bucharest had once been called the "little Paris of the East" because of its wide, tree-lined boulevards and elegant buildings. Now all was toned down, brushed over with drab gray, communism's signature color. Night fell early, and I could see immediately why someone had described Ceauşescu's Bucharest as a city lit by one light bulb. The streets were so dark I could not see ahead of me and found myself literally bumping into people as I walked. I retreated quickly to the hotel.

"Is there a Hannah Pakula registered here?" I asked the man at the reception desk, more out of curiosity than anything else. It was hard to imagine the wife of a Hollywood film director spending weeks in this forlorn place.

"Yes, he replied with alacrity, "she's in Room 732."

I thanked him and turned toward the elevator, but he was already dialing her number. "You'd better speak to her now," he said holding out the phone, unfazed by his own knowledge of her schedule. "They're going out to dinner in fifteen minutes."

Half an hour later, I was in a dark restaurant near the hotel with Hannah, a slender blond who was about my age but looked years younger, and Barbara Davis, her dark-haired, effervescent friend and traveling companion. They knew who I was and where I worked—they made that clear without my having to explain myself—and there was a tacit understanding that we would not talk about human rights or Helsinki Watch. Instead, we discussed Hannah's research in the National Archives on Queen Marie; Barbara, who had come along as company and support, was helping Hannah out in the archives. There wasn't much else to do, they told me, as they described their austere life in Bucharest. We talked about our children and about mutual friends back home. It was comforting to have unexpected, familiar company in a place where I was very much alone. But I knew I would not see them again in Bucharest, and probably shouldn't have been with them at all. I didn't want to get them in trouble or give the police any reason to disrupt their work. We were undoubtedly being watched, and there was no telling where my agenda would take me in the next few days.

.   .   .

I woke the next morning with a vague feeling of anxiety that was fast becoming familiar to me from previous trips. *What am I doing here in this strange city? I know no one. No one knows me. How do I get started?* I felt invisible, unrelated to anything around me. *I could disappear today and it would be weeks before anyone would miss me. If I didn't return home, no one would ever find out what had happened to me.*

The meager breakfast in the hotel—a stale pastry and some brown-colored hot water that passed for coffee—revealed how bad the food shortages in the country were. If this was all the best hotel in Bucharest could offer foreign guests—who would presumably receive preference over ordinary citizens—I could barely imagine the fare of the average Romanian. I headed off to the U.S. Embassy, where I had the name of a political officer who dealt with human rights. Although it was usually my practice to avoid the closely monitored American embassies in Eastern Europe so as not to attract attention to myself, I felt a need for a briefing. Perhaps he would suggest some people for me to see.

As I passed the entrance to the U.S. Consulate, not far from the embassy,

I saw a long line of people waiting to be admitted. They were seeking visas to emigrate. I also noticed a lot of uniformed police on the streets. There appeared to be one stationed on just about every street corner.

The political officer at the embassy knew who I was (following my usual practice, I had informed the State Department ahead of time about my visit). "There's no safe place to talk in the embassy," he told me at once. We communicated by writing things down on paper, much as I had done with the dissidents in Prague a year before. I showed him the name and address of the only seemingly solid contact I had—Mihai Botez, a mathematician whose work at the university permitted him to have contact with foreigners—and the embassy officer (I no longer remember his name) helped me find Botez's street—Alexander Donici—on the map I was carrying. "Be careful," he scribbled on my notepad. "You will be followed. Here's my card and my home number. If you get into trouble, call me."

.   .   .

I was in trouble immediately, for I could not find the street I was looking for, although it appeared clearly on my map. Someone stopped and asked if he could help me, and before I knew it, I had a crowd of people around me, all seeking to show me which way to go. One of them even enlisted the help of the policeman stationed on the corner. I stood at the center of all this attention, not knowing whether to laugh or cry. So much for my ability to move around unnoticed, for the reputation I was acquiring back at the office as an experienced "spy."

Eventually I ended up with one eager young man who offered to accompany me to the place I was seeking. When we reached the street, I thanked him, but he wanted to help me find the exact house. *Is he being helpful?* I wondered, *or is he snooping for the police?* It took some doing, but I finally got rid of him, then walked cautiously up and down the street for a while before stopping at the house in question.

Mr. Botez was not at home. I learned this from an elderly woman hanging laundry out in the yard. She might have been his mother, or his grandmother, or his landlady; I couldn't tell. Speaking in Russian, which she understood, I told her I was from the United States and where I was staying, thinking all the while how bizarre I must seem to her—a Russian-speaking American in Bucharest—and worrying that I might be getting Mr. Botez into deep trouble.

.   .   .

My next call was on a man whose case was one of the few known in the West. He had spoken out against the regime and had ended up spending some years in a psychiatric hospital, a common fate in Communist countries, where political dissidents were often treated as if they were insane. The street was completely empty as I approached his house, yet I knew that could be deceptive. *They might be watching his windows from a neighboring building. There could be cameras recording everyone who enters. His apartment is probably bugged.* I found him and his wife at home—they were both elderly and frail—and was pleased to see that she spoke some English. She told me they had been beaten up on several occasions when they tried to go to the U.S. Embassy in response to a letter of invitation they had received from an embassy officer. She asked me to explain this to the embassy, since they had no way of making contact. We spoke for a while, the woman interpreting for her husband, and I soon came to the sad conclusion that he was, in fact, mentally unbalanced. There was no way I could know whether it was the cause or the result of his treatment in the mental institution.

I was discouraged, yet determined to push on to at least one more place that day. I decided to look for Mircea Florea, the man who was on a hunger strike, whose brother I had met in New York.

I found his apartment without difficulty, but stopped short, uncertain, at the entrance. A black skull and crossbones, crudely drawn on a piece of white paper, was tacked to the door. *What does this mean? Is someone ill? Is the house under quarantine? Has someone died? Is this a warning to stay away? Written by the occupants? By neighbors? By the police?* Once again I realized how hopelessly unprepared I was for what I was doing. *What shall I do now? Well, there's no turning back.* I knocked on the door.

The Florea family—father, mother, son, and daughter—had first applied to emigrate five years before, in 1977. Their applications had been turned down on eighteen occasions since then. Both husband and wife had been fired from their jobs as a result. Now they had no way of supporting themselves, yet still they could not leave. They had sold all their belongings in order to buy food and were living in a house with hardly any furniture. We sat on cushions on the floor, facing their only table, which was laden with English grammars and textbooks. They spent their time studying English, convinced that they would get permission to leave. Mircea's brother in New York was working for them; they had faith in him. Although Mircea was on a hunger strike, he seemed healthy, lively, and optimistic, excited at the prospect of a new life in America. They loved trying out their English on me, and I had fun helping and correcting them. I promised to do what I could for them when I returned home. As I was leaving, I asked about the sign on the door—I had all but forgotten it—and was told that it was one of the children's drawings and had no special significance.

It was late in the day when I returned to the hotel. The phone in my room was ringing. It was Mihai Botez, who had been trying to reach me all day. He asked to see me first thing in the morning and said he had no problem about coming to the hotel. And with his arrival the next day, my mission began to take shape.

.   .   .

Botez was one of those rare characters one ran across occasionally in Communist countries. He seemed to operate with impunity, though he was outspoken in his criticism of "the leader," "the big one up there" (no one referred to Ceauşescu by name; someone might overhear, the word might be picked up by a listening device). He told me he had permission to meet with foreigners because of his work at the university. His English was excellent, he immediately understood my purpose in visiting Romania, and he was eager to help me. I wondered if I should be suspicious of him: He seemed too comfortable doing things that should have scared him to death. Yet I remembered others like him in other places: Andrei Amalrik, for instance, the Soviet dissident writer who was not arrested even after his controversial 1969 essay, "Will the Soviet Union Survive Until 1984?" was published in the West under his real name. There were questions at the time about Amalrik's integrity, reports that he was in league with the secret police. Such rumors continued until 1970, when Amalrik was arrested, convicted of anti-Soviet propaganda, and sentenced to three years in a labor camp. Some believed that the police on occasion tolerated such people in order to monitor their activities, see who they met with, and better understand the opposition. Others thought that the person in question might have had an unknown "protector" in high places. This unpredictability on the part of the police kept everyone confused and on their toes. I decided to follow my gut instinct that Botez was trustworthy.

Botez helped me find Dorin Tudoran, a tall, lanky poet then in his thir-ties. Tudoran was an excitable man who could not be held down. He had views and he expressed them, not only privately but at writers' meetings and in other public places. The police were eager to get rid of him and suggested that he and his family emigrate. But Tudoran wanted to stay: "Romania is my country. No one is going to force me out." I had a message for Dorin from the émigré Romanian writer Paul Goma, who lived in Paris: "Tell Tudoran that if he comes before January 1, he will get the job he's looking for." But Tudoran declined the offer: "Tell Goma if I go, they'll never let me back in." I was struck by the quixotic nature of the police: The family I had met the day before wanted desperately to leave and was refused; Tudoran was passionate in his desire to stay and was being encouraged to go.

Botez, Tudoran, and I had tea in a café in a Bucharest park, after which we walked under the trees in a light drizzle, talking about life in Romania. They told me that Ceauşescu was obsessed with paying off the country's foreign debt. He had cut off all imports and was exporting most of Romania's agricultural and industrial products, which was why food, medicines, and electricity were in such short supply. Bread and gas were rationed, and staples such as meat, coffee, and sugar were virtually unobtainable. Electric power was limited to about one hour a day: During some exceptionally cold winters in Europe, elderly Romanians had died from exposure in their own homes.

Romania was the first "cigarette economy" in Eastern Europe. I had been tipped off to bring several cartons of Kents with me, and I soon found out that a single pack could get me just about anything. People didn't smoke these American cigarettes but used them for barter. The taxi driver whom I paid with a pack of Kents would give my pack to the doctor who treated his son; the doctor would use it in turn to buy meat, and so forth. When I offered several packs of cigarettes to an ethnic Hungarian couple whose home I visited in Bucharest, they seemed insulted, as if I were offering them cash. I finally convinced them to take the cigarettes, not to barter them but to smoke them.

Botez told me about the monstrous "cult of personality" that Ceauşescu had built around himself, one that would make Stalin seem humble. He insisted that I visit the Museum of National History, three floors of which were devoted to the celebration of Ceauşescu's life and accomplishments. It was an unforgettable experience. There were paintings deifying the Ceauşescus, with angels singing in the heavens and a phalanx of Party apparatchiks positioned like saints around the royal couple. There were tapestries and rugs bearing their portraits. One floor was devoted to photographs of Ceauşescu's meetings with world leaders; every gift and trinket he received in his travels—a key to Chattanooga, Tennessee; a ten-gallon hat from Texas—was enshrined in a glass show-case. Nothing was too mundane.

The next day, I met with several members of Romania's large ethnic Hungarian minority, which numbered about 2.5 million of the country's 22 million people. Most of the ethnic Hungarians lived in the section of Romania known as Transylvania, which was once part of Hungary. I was told about forced assimilation practices and about ethnic Hungarians who were detained or persecuted for asserting their Hungarian identity.

I was always worried about getting people into trouble, but those I met seemed surprisingly unconcerned. When Friday came and I arrived at the designated meeting spot for the official bus that would take me and other conference participants to Lake Snagov, I was startled to see four people waiting there to say good-bye to me. They were standing side by side like an official send-off committee. Botez was there, together with the Hun-garian couple I had seen the day before. Dorin Tudoran was also waiting, and he presented me with a single rose. It was a snapshot of my activities in Bucharest, and it did not go unnoticed by the police.

.   .   .

The ambience at Lake Snagov bore no relation to the poverty in the rest of the country. The food was delicious, served in lavish portions; wine flowed freely, and the coffee was excellent. Each evening there was enter-tainment.

The group was diverse. It included people from the U.S. State Depart-ment and from the foreign ministries of Turkey, Romania, Austria, Yugoslavia, Spain, Canada, Germany, Greece, and France, as well as from think tanks in Moscow, Washington, Budapest, and elsewhere. The for-eign guests seemed complacent, apparently ignorant of the abominable conditions in the country that was hosting the conference. I was put off by the puffed-up pride of some of the Westerners who took obvious pleasure in brushing shoulders with important people from the East. But I kept my feelings to myself, trying to be pleasant and interesting, as my hosts expected me to be.

On the final day, there was a plenary session during which the various participants were encouraged to give their impressions of the conference. I could no longer ignore an unpleasant truth—that in three days of meetings supposedly focused on the Helsinki accords, the word "human rights" had not once been mentioned. I had a choice: I could let it pass—that would be the easy way, the expected way—or I could speak out. There was no one there to account to, only my own conscience. But I knew I would not be able to live easily with myself if I did not say something, and that this—the plenary session—was the only opportunity I would have to do so.

My heart began pounding loudly at the thought of what I was about to say. I forced myself to raise my hand and I was recognized by the chairman, Dr. Johan Jorgen Holst, director of the Norwegian Institute for International Affairs. My speech, as I remember it, went pretty much as follows:

> I think it is remarkable that at a conference devoted to the Helsinki process not a word has been said about human rights. Yet human rights are a basic component of the Helsinki accords. We all know that around this table there are people representing countries in which human rights monitors—members of Helsinki groups—are languishing in prisons under dreadful conditions. Unless these monitors are freed there can be no lasting peace and security between East and West.

The response was to ignore me. The chairman thanked me curtly and went on to the next speaker, who spoke about something totally unrelated to what I had just said. I could feel the blood rushing to my face, but I was still glad I had spoken out. Afterward, several of the participants, including the wife of Ira Wallach, the chairman of the institute, privately commended me for what I had said. "That took a lot of courage," Mrs. Wallach remarked approvingly. Someone from the U.S. State Department assured me that he had been raising human rights concerns quietly during his informal talks with Eastern bloc participants.

Then a major announcement was made: We were invited to meet with Ceaușescu himself the following day. I declined. I was due in Stockholm the next day and in Oslo two days after that—a one-day delay in my schedule would upset all my plans. At the time, I had no regrets about missing the audience with Ceauşescu, though now, in retrospect, I am sorry I never got to see the man in person.

.   .   .

I left Lake Snagov with several others on the morning of October 10. We were chauffeured to the airport, where we were met by several deferential aides who ushered us into an official visitors' lounge. There we were offered coffee and comfortable chairs while they took care of the exit formalities. Our spirits were high, as was often the case with Westerners who were about to pass through the Iron Curtain to the free and easy atmosphere of the West. Suddenly, one of the aides appeared and asked me to accompany him; he said there was a message for me. And indeed, there was. I was led into the office of the chief militia officer at the airport, a heavyset man in a brown uniform who rose behind his desk as I entered. We stood facing each other across the desk as he proceeded to lecture me, aided by a slight, thin-voiced interpreter who stood at his side.

"You entered Romania as a tourist several days before the conference at Lake Snagov," he announced. "We have received reports from Romanian citizens that while you were in Bucharest you spoke to people and broke our laws." He leaned forward, his hands on the desk, in an obvious attempt to intimidate me.

"I didn't know it was against the law to speak with Romanian citizens," I replied.

"It is if you discuss the sort of problems you discussed with them," he answered.

Although I often deplore my slowness in reacting to provocation, there are occasionally times when it is helpful. This was one of them: I held my own, for I had not yet begun to feel frightened. All the same, I knew better than to start arguing with him. I refrained from asking him exactly how he knew the content of my discussions with Romanians in Bucharest. I looked him straight in the eye as he told me, a cold smile on his face, that if I were to come back to Romania to talk to "discontented people about problems," I would not be welcome in his country. He referred several times to my attendance at the Lake Snagov conference, implying that had I not been a guest of the government they would not have waited this long to declare me persona non grata.

I could sense that he wasn't finished, that he had something more to say. And then it came, a clear and open threat: "The people you visited brought their problems on themselves," he said. "But if you choose to discuss their problems when you return to New York, they will have more problems."

.   .   .

I spent the next few days in Scandinavia, trying to help strengthen the international Helsinki movement we had launched in Bellagio. Gerald Nagler, a Stockholm businessman who had come to Bellagio to learn about the Helsinki movement, had put together a new Swedish Helsinki Committee in less than a month. Modeled after the U.S. Helsinki Watch, it had thirty members, prominent Swedes from many different professions. I attended the group's first meeting and told them about our work in the States. From Stockholm I went to Oslo, where I met with members of the Norwegian Helsinki Committee and discussed possible joint projects.

All the while, I was seething about what had happened to me in Romania. I was worried about the people I had met there: *Are they being punished for meeting with me?*

As soon as I got home, I went to Washington to see Elliott Abrams, assistant secretary of state for human rights. Despite his conflicts with Aryeh Neier and Americas Watch, Abrams and I had thus far maintained a good relationship, and he seemed proud of the help he had been to my dissident friends in Hungary. I told him about the threat at the airport and, at his request, gave him the names of the people I had seen in Bucharest. The State Department, through the U.S. Embassy in Bucharest, told Romanian authorities that it was following up on my visit and threatened to repeal Romania's MFN status if anything untoward happened to any of the people on my list. I also visited the Romanian ambassador to the United States and formally protested my treatment at the airport. I published an open letter to the Romanian ambassador in the *New York Times*. Then I wrote an op-ed article that appeared in the *Los Angeles Times* on December 15, 1982. I ended the article as follows:

Well, Mr. Militia Man (whose name I did not have the composure to ask), your program of intimidation has worked. I am not writing about the pathetically few visits that I was able to arrange in Bucharest, from which I learned nothing that hasn't already been well documented in the West. Instead I am writing about my meeting with you. It reveals more about the state of free expression in Romania than any report that I might have written about my conversations with your countrymen.

Soon afterward, perhaps as a result of my protests and the State Department's intervention, the Florea family received permission to emigrate. Mircea, arm in arm with his brother, Ovi, attended our annual office Christmas party in December.

For a while at least, my other contacts seemed to be all right. But being who they were, they did not cease their dissident activities. A year or so later, we began to receive reports that Botez was being harassed by the police. On one occasion he barely survived what was assumed to be a police-instigated assassination attempt when a car tried to run him down at a busy Bucharest intersection.

Dorin Tudoran also got in further trouble: At one point he was arrested and disappeared from sight. When he and his family finally left Romania for the United States in 1985, he told me that after my 1982 visit, he was called in for questioning by police who showed him a table full of enlarged photographs of him and me together—drinking tea in a café, walking in the park. There was even one of Dorin handing me a pale pink, long-stemmed rose.

24

The last thing I wanted to do when I returned from Romania was to go away again. I had so much to catch up on, at work, at home. Mainly I was afraid, afraid to tell Charlie that I was leaving once more, this time for Madrid. We had barely seen each other since August and were already pretty much estranged. I knew he would be angry, and he was.

"But it's a commitment," I explained. "I made it in Bellagio when we formed the International Helsinki Federation. We agreed to meet again in November, in Madrid. I didn't know I would be going to Romania in between."

"Don't talk to me about commitment." Charlie's voice was icy.

"Please try to understand," I went on. "I've spent the whole year trying to set up this group. I've put so much of my time and effort into it, I've involved everyone, people in the office, people in Europe, the foundations who gave us money for this. It's a major undertaking, it's my job. I have to follow through." He was silent.

"Look," I tried again. "These people are coming to Madrid from eight different countries, only because *I* told them it's important. They don't know the first thing about the Helsinki Review Conference, they don't know anyone. I have to be there, to show them how we lobby, to introduce them to people, to get them fired up. I have to prepare the press releases and bring them, I have to run a press conference there, I have to bring materials with me about the issues we want to raise. No one else can do this. Please, try to understand."

I told him about the work that was piling up on my desk, the dozens of phone calls I didn't have time to answer, the reports that were waiting for me to edit. I said I was out of touch with my children and felt awful about it, that I was way behind in paying my bills, that my house was a shambles.

"These are choices. You're making them," Charlie replied. "It's clear what comes first for you."

I began to cry. He softened, as he always did when I was upset. But I left him knowing things were not right.

When I called to say good-bye, Charlie wasn't home, or wasn't answering.

.   .   .

On November 9, at a press conference in Madrid, we announced the formation of the International Helsinki Federation for Human Rights—the IHF, as we had begun to call it. Three new national committees had formed since Bellagio—in Sweden, Austria, and Belgium; two of these, the Swedish and Austrian groups, were in neutral countries that had some leverage with the USSR. There were now eight national groups in the West, on paper at least. Four of them were merely one-person operations, but we didn't advertise that fact.

On November 10, we hosted a dinner for eight ambassadors to the review conference, one from each of the Western countries where we claimed to have Helsinki groups. The ambassadors found themselves in an unusual political combination involving both NATO and neutral countries, but it all went surprisingly well. They listened intently as I described my experiences in Romania and argued against having the next review conference there. They said they were willing to raise specific human rights cases during the conference and asked us to keep supplying them with information.

Just as the U.S. ambassador, Max Kampelman, took the lead among his peers, I found myself doing most of the talking on the nongovernmental side. Later, my colleagues praised me for my "professionalism." Seeing myself through their eyes, I realized, perhaps for the first time, that the human rights work we had begun, following our instincts and learning as we went along, had indeed become a new profession. I was at ease in my encounters with the diplomats in Madrid. I had the facts to back up my positions, I knew how to present them, I had firm ideas about what I wanted them to do. I realized that our International Helsinki Federation had a lot to learn before it could operate independently from me and my colleagues in New York. The IHF was a name, not an organization. So far it was only a facade, initiated and financed by Americans.

It was in Madrid that Gerald Nagler, head of the new Swedish Helsinki Committee, first spoke to me about an idea he was considering: He would leave his business in Stockholm and work on a voluntary, part-time basis as the executive director of our International Helsinki Federation. He was prepared to divide his time between Stockholm and Vienna, where we had decided to establish the IHF office. "What did I think of the idea?" he wanted to know.

Nagler was only in his early fifties at the time, but I was not surprised by his decision to retire; he did not seem happy or fulfilled working in the family jewelry business in Stockholm. His willingness to live in both Stockholm and Vienna also came as no surprise. Both he and his wife, Monica, had been born in Vienna, and Monica's family—her father and her married sister—lived there. Vienna was already a second home to them.

I was impressed by Nagler's eagerness to become involved and the speed with which he had put together the Swedish Helsinki Committee. But I had misgivings about a part-time, nonresident executive director, and a volunteer at that. Still, we had few other options. I talked it over with Aryeh Neier when I returned to New York, and we agreed to go along with Nagler's suggestion. The Vienna office was established the following year, in 1983, and Gerald Nagler became its director in early 1984.

.   .   .

It was mid-November when I returned from Madrid. I had been away in one or more foreign countries during just about every month of 1982. At last, I had no further plans to travel, at least for some months.

The holiday season was approaching, but it would be a dismal one for me. Charlie and I were not speaking. We had argued in the summer before I left for Bellagio. There were issues between us that we had to work out. But there was no time for anything when I returned from Bellagio, for I was suddenly off to Romania. And when I went to Madrid, right after Romania, it was the final straw. The time for reconciliation had come and gone.

I decided to have my living room painted. It was grimy from years of neglect, a visual testimony to the breakup of my marriage. The twenty-foot ceiling required the use of a special steel scaffold that I arranged to have delivered to my apartment. When the painters began setting it up early one morning, there was an accident: a piece of the metal structure fell backward, hitting me from behind. The blow was to my shoulders and head and did not really hurt me, eventually resolving into a small lump on the back of my head. But I was shaken up when it happened. After assuring the painters that I was all right, I made for my bedroom, where I lay down on the bed and surprised myself by bursting into tears. The shock had unleashed a torrent of unhappiness. I cried, not because I was hurt but because I was hurting.

The room they're painting is not a living room any more, it's an empty shell. The family that lived here, my family, is torn apart. This house was once a home, full of life—husband, children, grandparents, friends, everyone busy, lives converging, parties, celebrations. And I was at the center, holding everything together and being held together in turn. Weeping into my pillow, I forgot for the moment the endless bickering, the emptiness, the betrayals that characterized my marriage. I remembered instead the comfortable family life that sustained me and kept me in the marriage for so long. Now it was gone, and I had nothing to replace it. My hope for a new life—a life with Charlie—had ended as well.

.   .   .

But I did have something, something very important to me. At any moment I could conjure up a sea of faces—the faces of people I had met in my travels, and of others, political prisoners, whom I knew only through their photographs. These people were suffering, physically and emotionally, and they were counting on *me*. I felt that responsibility keenly. It gave purpose to my life.

Every day at work I sorted through papers describing horrible atrocities and the agonies of innocent people. At times it seemed more than I could bear. But I was not just standing by—I was doing something about it. I could not imagine a more meaningful way to spend my time.

There was yet another dimension to my work, the sense of belonging and commitment I felt whenever I entered my office. We had brought together so many exceptional people: the dedicated staff with whom I worked on a daily basis, and the caring people on our various boards to whom I reported when I returned from a trip. They had become a second family to me, a world I had helped create and nurture and to which I now belonged. How could I expect to have a rewarding personal life when my professional life was so full and so consuming? I had made my choice. It would have to sustain me.

.   .   .

When Pam and Emily came home for Thanksgiving, there were four Hungarian intellectuals at our dinner table. Halfway through the meal, the Naglers and their son, Niklas, arrived from Sweden, straight from the airport; they would be my houseguests while they were in New York. The conversation at dinner was a little stilted. Much as I wanted my daughters to be part of my new world, I could see they were not really comfortable with the foreign guests. I was sure they were thinking of past Thanksgivings—at my parents' home when our family was still together.

In mid-December I was invited to the birthday party of a close friend. Charlie knew her also, and assuming I would see him there, I felt apprehensive as I set out. The minute Charlie and I came face-to-face, however, the old magic took over and words were not necessary to bring us back together again, closer than ever before.

We had each learned a lot during our separation. It made us realize how much we meant to each other. It reinforced our love. But we had also come to value our separate interests, our separate friends, and, above all, our separate work. We had learned that we could each survive alone—without the props of a marriage and without, if necessary, each other. That did not weaken our relationship but made it stronger. Strong enough to withstand interruptions and absences, strong enough to accept that they were necessary.

We spent New Year's Eve on Charlie's boat, just the two of us. The marina never looked more fetching than it did on that crisp, cold night, the boats outlined by tiny holiday lights that blinked in concert with the spangled sky. We drank champagne as the boat rocked gently in the wake of passing ships.

I was planning another trip to Eastern Europe, but I wasn't worried about how to break that news to Charlie. We were beyond that argument, once and for all.

25

When Gerald Nagler asked to accompany me on a trip to Prague and Budapest in February 1983, it seemed like a good idea. Nagler was about to become the director of our International Helsinki Federation, and he had never been to Eastern Europe; he needed to learn the ropes. And I was happy to have his company. Traveling alone had its drawbacks: I often felt lonely, and unappreciated.

I planned the trip well, setting up meetings in advance. I didn't want to go from house to house without appointments as I had done before, perhaps calling unwanted attention to myself in the process. So I enlisted the help of the many East European émigrés I had come to know, asking them to let people know I was coming.

Nagler suggested we take his car—we would drive from Berlin to Prague and then on to Budapest—and I quickly agreed; I was eager to travel through the countryside and to see firsthand how small these countries really were, how close they were to each other in distance and appearance. Driving from one to another was like taking a trip through New England. I knew this intellectually, but it would be quite different to experience it on the ground.

What I didn't anticipate was the difficulty of crossing the various national borders by car, not just the borders between West and East but between East and East as well. We lost many precious hours—more than a full day of work, altogether—while our car and our belongings were meticulously searched at each of the six heavily fortified checkpoints that we passed through during our journey.

The border guards were on the lookout for ideas and people—the first to keep out, the second to keep in. They carefully inspected our passports and visas, scrutinizing them with furrowed brows as if they had never seen such documents before. They looked back and forth between my photograph and my face so many times that I began to wonder if they were holding the wrong passport. They inspected our suitcases, looked at our books and magazines, turned the pages of empty notebooks, and systematically pored through my address book, which I had carefully "coded." They searched the trunk of the car, removed the seats to look beneath them, and wheeled large mirrors under the chassis to be sure no one was concealed there. We spent an average of two hours at each border crossing.

.   .   .

We arrived in Prague late in the evening of February 24, planning to stay five days. I had been told to be at Josef Danisz's apartment at 10:30 the next morning, but Josef was not there when we arrived. It was his wife, Anna Grušová, who answered the door—Anna, who had taken me and Abby around Prague in 1981. Her smile was shy, as always, but her eyes lit up with pleasure at seeing me again. I was surprised at the depth of my own emotions as I hugged her.

Anna, in jeans and a loose T-shirt, looked pale and thin. She had been cleaning her house; I could see a vacuum cleaner in the middle of the hall behind her. It was a new apartment, larger than the one where I had previously visited her. They were still settling in, with cartons of books stacked against the walls waiting to be unpacked.

Anna's smile faded when she saw I was not alone. "Come into the kitchen," she said softly, in her formal English. "I will make some tea . . . real English tea. My parents sent it, it is the best in Prague." She apologized for Josef's absence: Something had come up, she didn't really know what, but she did not expect him back until late in the day.

When I asked her how things were, she seemed discouraged. "On the surface, everything looks calm," she said sadly, "but the pressure remains. We are called in for questioning all the time. People are tired and disappointed. Many have left." She told me that Jiří Gruša, her former husband who now lived in West Germany, had recently been stripped of his Czechoslovak citizenship and that their two children, who lived with Anna, were no longer permitted to visit him.

Gerald Nagler began firing questions at her: How many political prisoners are there in Czechoslovakia? How are they treated? Can their families visit them? Is there anti-Semitism? His voice was loud and his manner direct, unlike the quiet, elliptical way in which I instinctively conducted such conversations. I was taken aback. Expecting him to take his cues from me, I had neglected to warn him that Anna's apartment was undoubtedly bugged. Indeed, Anna obliquely confirmed as much when she told us that the apartment had previously belonged to dissident friends: "When we moved in, the systems were already in place," she said archly.

I could see Anna drawing further into herself with each question that she reluctantly answered. I couldn't tell whether she was nervous, as I was, that the conversation was being recorded in its unambiguous clarity, or whether it was just her natural reticence. I broke in by asking her to show us around the apartment, which she did with evident relief.

As we walked toward the bedroom, Anna told me in a whisper that Josef had set up a lot of meetings for me. She did not know all the details, but she showed me some of the highlights that Josef had scribbled on a piece of paper. Dinners were planned for three evenings with separate groups of people, all of whom I knew or was eager to meet. One was at the home of Eva Kantůrková, a writer who had recently been released from a year in prison without ever standing trial. Another was at the home of Anna Šabatová, whose husband and father were both in prison. The third dinner was at the apartment of Ivan Havel, Václav Havel's brother; Václav, who had been released from prison on medical grounds just a month before, might be well enough to attend. Anna linked her arm in mine: "It will be festive," she said, "a banquet. Josef has bought a goose."

As we were leaving, Anna reminded me of the sight-seeing tour Abby and I had taken with her in 1981. "Do you remember our visit to the Jewish cemetery? On a Saturday, when it was closed? Shall we try to visit it again, this time not on Saturday?"

"Why not do it now?" I suggested. We had nothing to do until her husband returned later in the day.

"I'll need a few hours to finish up here," she said, "I'll meet you at three."

We arranged to pick her up downstairs.

.   .   .

Driving back toward Wenceslas Square we spotted a restaurant, a typical workers' cafe, and decided to have an early lunch there. The food was cheap, the portions generous; the room was overheated and full of smoke. Over lunch, Gerald Nagler asked me what I thought of his interviewing technique. I think he must have sensed my discomfort, or Anna's. "Monica thinks I'm too direct," he remarked, referring to his wife, who did interviews for Swedish radio. I told him I tended to agree with Monica, especially because of the bugging devices. Gerald was listening intently. I could see he was eager to learn.

When we left the restaurant, I noticed a yellow police car marked "VB" ("Public Security") parked about twenty feet from our car. As we pulled out, the police car pulled up alongside us, motioning us to stop. Two policemen approached us and asked for "*dokumenty.*" They took our passports back to their car, where they remained for about fifteen minutes, checking with someone on the car telephone as we became increasingly uneasy. When they came back, however, they seemed friendly. They returned our passports and lightly chided us for having been illegally parked. We took the incident at face value and drove off.

Since we had some time to kill, I suggested we call on a few dissidents whose homes I could easily find. We made two stops, but no one was at home. As we were driving back toward Anna's house, our car was flagged down in the street by a solitary uniformed policeman who was standing directly in our path and seemed to have materialized from nowhere. He asked for our passports, then indicated that we should lock our car, leaving everything inside, and come with him. He motioned to a shabby, unmarked car that was parked at the side of the road with a rather seedy-looking man in the driver's seat. All of this was conveyed by gestures; he spoke no English, except one phrase—"It's okay"—with which he attempted to reassure us when we protested.

I took quick stock of the situation: In my bag were my notes from our talk with Anna and the names of some of the people she said we would meet. I had not thought to disguise this information yet, planning to do so later, before I left the country, in preparation for a possible search at the border. I made a split-second decision to leave my bag in the car, notes, money, papers and all, rather than call attention to it by bringing it with me. I did not know that they planned to take us away to a police station, but minutes later, we were ordered into their car by the driver, a plainclothes security policeman, and taken to the local precinct. During the several hours I spent at the police station, I was painfully aware that my bag was still in our car, open to inspection if they chose to force the locked doors.

We spent at least an hour in the waiting room of the police station, watching various people arrive and walk to a back room. It turned out they were all related to our case. There were two high-ranking officers in snappy military uniforms, two state security policemen in civilian clothes, and a woman interpreter in white pants and a red sweater, the last to arrive. We were then taken to the back room for what was more of a lecture than an interrogation. It was conducted by a rough-looking man in a leather jacket. Speaking through the interpreter, he told us: "You entered Czechoslovakia as tourists, but we know through our sources that you are making contact with dissidents and Charter people. We advise and recommend you to leave our country immediately or you will have great problems." He asked when we had arrived and from where, then said that we should be out of the country by 10 P.M. that evening. When I asked if we had any options, he became angry: "There are no options. Make no more visits to anyone, go straight to your hotel, pack and be across the border by 10 P.M. You are under control." The other plainclothesman, who had been silent until that moment—a tall man with a mustache, wearing a black trench coat—suddenly asked if we wanted to say anything. There was nothing to say. They drove us back to our car in silence.

It was the first time I had heard the words "under control," a phrase meaning constant police surveillance that was commonly used in Eastern Europe. Its meaning soon became clear enough when an unmarked yellow car containing three plainclothesmen followed our car at a close distance as we made our way back to the Alcron Hotel. They parked next to us outside the hotel and waited in the lobby as we went to our rooms and packed.

I called Jack Matlock, then the U.S. ambassador to Czechoslovakia, who had been a classmate of mine many years before at the Russian Institute at Columbia University. He greeted me warmly: "Jeri, I've been hoping for your call ever since I heard you were coming to Prague." I quickly explained what had happened and asked to see him. "Let me send a driver to lead you to the embassy," he offered. "It's not an easy place to find." When we left the hotel, it was in a curious three-car procession: At the head was the embassy car driven by a Czech driver who was undoubtedly in the employ of state security. Next came our Volvo, driven by Gerald Nagler. Bringing up the rear was the yellow sedan with three state security men.

Before leaving the hotel, I argued with the concierge in an attempt to get a refund for four unused nights that I had paid for in advance. "I am leaving against my wishes," I explained pointedly. "I don't think I should be held responsible for my room." The concierge, who knew me from previous visits, was proper and courteous, but firm in his refusal. Never as much as glancing at the security agents standing just a few feet away, he explained that I could get a refund only through my travel agent back in New York—which I eventually did.

Gerald Nagler, meanwhile, had applied himself to a still more practical pursuit—getting some food for us to eat during the long drive ahead. He went to the hotel dining room and persuaded the chef to pack up some of the elaborate open-faced sandwiches that were served at lunch and as appetizers at dinner. As the security men watched with dour hostility, we were presented with a large round tray of sandwiches festively wrapped in bright pink cellophane tied with curly, light pink ribbons.

.   .   .

Jack Matlock was apologetic. "Your experience is highly unusual," he told us, "but the Czechoslovak government has a right to expel anyone it wishes. They'll probably blacklist you in the future and deny you a visa. There's nothing the U.S. Embassy can do."

"Could someone find a way to tell our friends what happened?" I asked. "They are expecting to see us again, and I'm afraid I'll cause more trouble if I try to call them myself."

I kept thinking about all the preparations they had made, about the goose that Josef had bought. *What will they think when we don't show up? Will they be arrested because of me?*

I wrote Josef Danisz's name and address on a piece of paper and handed it to Matlock. Leaving the embassy together, we followed Matlock's car to the highway where he, heading home in another direction, pointed out the road to Austria. We had decided *not* to drive straight to Hungary, which was to be our next destination; we were afraid the Czech border guards would warn their Hungarian counterparts about us.

Instead, we headed for the Austrian border, about four hours away, still followed by the three men in the yellow car. It was 6:30 P.M. We had no time to lose if we were to meet their ultimatum.

.   .   .

Some forty miles out of Prague, we stopped at a gas station to fill up. The yellow car waited at a distance. As we left the pump, we decided to have a sandwich and, pulling over to the side, began to open the cellophane wrappings. The yellow car, which had started up when we did, was forced to stop again, now very close behind us. Trying to appear nonchalant, we made a show of sampling the delicious Prague ham, some pieces decorated with fancy swirls of Liptauer cheese, others with cutouts of pâté. *We'll show them we're not intimidated. Let them sit there watching us eat.* Our mock frivolity may have been too much for them. There was a sudden roar behind us, then an angry shriek of brakes as the yellow car turned sharply and raced away in the direction of Prague, quickly disappearing from sight.

.   .   .

We were alone on a dark, deserted highway. A full moon lit the snow-covered fields that bordered the road and gave a slight patina to the icy film that coated the blacktop surface. We passed through a small village, unchanged by time, quiet as a ghost town, with not a person in sight. Nagler had lapsed into uncharacteristic silence behind the wheel, drawing intermittently on his unlit pipe. I sensed he was blaming me—as an American—for our difficulties. "Swedes are welcome everywhere," he had told me proudly, only the day before, after the border guards had carefully searched *my* papers but not his. Now here he was, on the first day of his first mission to Czechoslovakia, expelled for visiting dissidents.

I, in turn, was blaming him, or, rather, my decision to travel there with him.

What went wrong? Was it the fact that I was with a man, a man who wore a business suit and looked important? It was a mistake—I had taken the easy way—driving around Prague in a foreign car. We should have mixed with the crowds on the subways and trams.

Or maybe it's because I planned the trip so thoroughly. Too many people knew I was coming. Too many meetings were arranged in advance. The police must have known something was up. It's all my fault. I was showing off, trying to impress Gerald Nagler with my efficiency.

I could no longer travel to the Soviet Union: My requests for visas were routinely denied. I was barred from travel in Romania. Now I was being expelled from Czechoslovakia, and the chances were I would not be allowed back in.

These were the unhappy thoughts that filled my mind as we sped toward the Austrian border.

.   .   .

The border at night appeared even more forbidding than it had by day. Two parallel lines of barbed wire and electrified fencing seemed etched in the snow, leading off into infinity, the lines becoming closer but never touching, like an art book illustration of perspective. Between the fences was a no-man's-land, heavily mined and periodically lit up by searchlights that restlessly scanned the area. We could see border patrols in white camouflage snow gear, guns slung over their shoulders, pacing the fields with police dogs. I saw two huge rabbits make a dash for it after the searchlight passed overhead.

The barriers that blocked our car from passing were made of iron so thick and heavy no car or truck could crash through. Two customs officials examined our car with surprising courtesy; one even smiled. The only car at the border, it took us just one hour to pass through the routine procedures. No special effort was made to inspect our papers.

Twenty minutes later we were in an Austrian village, the architectural sister of the Czech village we had passed through, but full of light and vitality. We sat in a café, drinking beer and eating goulash, hearing sounds that were suddenly dear to me: peals of laughter and high-spirited conversation that I had never heard in a public place in Prague. But my heart was heavy and my thoughts were back in Prague, in the dark, anachronistic beauty of its silent streets. I kept thinking of Anna Grušová, waiting in front of her building, all dressed up for some sight-seeing that would never take place.

.   .   .

I called Abby in Italy as soon as I reached Austria. I was smarting from my experience with the Czech police and knew she would understand, having been with me in Prague a few years before. I asked her to meet me in Vienna after I returned from Hungary; I would have a few free days, since my Prague visit had been cut short. She said she would try.

But when I got to Vienna, Abby was not there. I called her in Ferrara. "You know, Mom, I have a life, too," she explained, somewhat defensively. "I can't just drop everything and come running when it's convenient for you." She had a point, of course, but I felt doubly stricken—by my failure in Prague and by Abby's decision not to meet me. It was my first inkling that she felt secondary to my work and that she resented it. Over the next few years, I would learn that Pam and Emily often felt the same way.

From the time I was young, I had been determined to live a life different from my mother's. She never realized her intellectual or creative potential and was much too dependent on her children for emotional gratification, not just when we were little but when we were grown. I often felt responsible for my mother, that she lived her life vicariously, through me.

I wanted to be more than just my children's mother. I wanted to do something about the world they had inherited, to make it better—for them and for *their* children. I thought my daughters would appreciate my independence and my cause, that I would provide them with a positive image to follow as they set out on their *own* careers. And indeed, on one level, I had succeeded. I knew they had real respect for my work and were proud of me for what I was doing.

But my work also got in the way of many things they expected from me. I missed birthdays and births. I was not always around to help out when they had the flu, when the moving men came, when babies were sick, when relationships were breaking up. And even when I was there, my thoughts were often elsewhere: on the work I should have been doing or on some atrocity I just couldn't put out of my mind. Eventually, I came to see that my commitment to human rights work was for *me*, not for my children. And I sometimes wondered: *Would they have been happier with an old-fashioned mom?*

26

Looking up from my desk one day in the summer of 1983, I saw a young woman, visibly nervous, standing in the doorway. Our office was very small in those days: If the secretary who doubled as a receptionist happened to be away from her desk, people would walk right in. This visitor was dark-haired, slender and attractive, in her mid- to late twenties I guessed, about the age of my older daughters, Abby and Pam. She introduced herself as Nurşat Aygen and told me she was Turkish. She had come to see me about her sister, Gulşat, imprisoned in Turkey since March 1981.

Gulşat, she explained, was one of thousands of people arrested in the aftermath of a September 1980 military coup in Turkey. According to the Turkish government's own figures, in the seven months following the military takeover, 122,609 "suspected extremists" were arrested. Many of them were students, and very young.

Nurşat, who was the older sister, had graduated from Sweet Briar College in Virginia and was married to an American. She was afraid that if she returned to Turkey to take up her sister's cause, she would be arrested, too. Her information about Gulşat came from guarded telephone conversations with her mother in Istanbul and from information she received from Turkish friends.

This is what she knew: that Gulşat had been severely tortured by the police on several occasions after her arrest, subjected to beatings and electric shocks; that as a result, she was deaf in one ear and suffered from arthritis in her joints; that she was now in the eighth week of a hunger strike in Metris Military Prison and was reported to be on the verge of death.

Nurşat's voice was shrill, almost hysterical: "Please, you have to help her. She's my kid sister, only twenty-three years old—twenty-one when she was arrested. She's like an angel—blond, beautiful, talented. A medical student. She wanted to be a surgeon. She was never involved in politics or violence." Nurşat closed her eyes, trying to compose herself. "She was one of the best folk dancers in Turkey," she continued, "the youngest president of the National Folklore Association. Now she'll never dance again." She began to cry.

I asked about the charges. Gulşat, it appeared, was charged with belonging to an illegal organization and with advocating the violent overthrow of the government. The only evidence that the authorities had, according to her sister, was a confession extracted from Gulşat while she was being tortured. More than two years after her incarceration, her case had yet to be heard in court. "Aren't you doing anything about Turkey?" Nurşat demanded. "Don't you know what's going on there? Thousands of kids are in prison. Please," she begged, "see what you can find out about my sister."

.   .   .

As it happened, I was considering a mission to Turkey. Mümtaz Soysal, the Turkish professor of law who had talked about arrests and torture in Turkey at our Bellagio conference the previous fall, had been urging me to visit. "Come to Turkey," he kept saying. "I will show you what's happening there."

Turkey had signed the Helsinki accords; we had every reason to be looking into human rights problems there. But we were slow in doing so, partly because there was no significant Turkish constituency in the United States providing information to us and urging us to get involved and partly because we just didn't have the resources. My staff in 1983 consisted of three talented, overworked women: Cathy Fitzpatrick, who dealt with the Soviet Union and Yugoslavia; Joanna Weschler, a former Solidarity worker who followed Poland for us; and Janet Fleischman, my assistant, who was gamely trying to cover the rest of Eastern Europe. There was only one way to add Turkey to the list of countries we covered—if I did all the ongoing work myself. There was no one else to do it.

Nurşat and I ended up having sandwiches together in a coffee shop near my office. She was the first Turkish person I had met in New York. I thought she might be able to give me some information and some contacts. But it turned out she was not much help. She had been away from Turkey for some years, and her concern was mainly with her sister. Nurşat's conversation eventually degenerated into a litany of attacks against the U.S. government, which she held responsible for the terrible abuses in Turkey. Despite what I knew about U.S. government policies in the Americas, I did not want to believe that our government was knowingly supporting a regime engaged in the wholesale torture of students.

As soon as I got back to the office, I called the State Department's Bureau of Human Rights. My good relationship with the people there, based on our shared interest in exposing Communist repression, did not carry over to Turkey, I would soon learn. The State Department saw Turkey as a country to be courted, not criticized. One glance at a map told why. Turkey was poised at the crossroads between Europe and the Middle East, sharing boundaries with Greece, Bulgaria, the Soviet Union, Iran, Iraq, and Syria. Turkey was seen as the outermost military bulwark against communism, the ideal site for NATO military garrisons and electronic eavesdropping devices.

Back in the 1970s, Turkish society had been in a state of near anarchy, with as many as twenty to thirty political assassinations a day. Much of the terrorism had taken place on the campuses, where both left-wing and right-wing students packed revolvers in their book bags. In September 1980, the violence stopped when the Turkish military took over the government and established martial law.

Whether or not the U.S. government was behind the 1980 coup, as many alleged, the advent of a new military government in Turkey did much to allay the State Department's fears. Turkey's new military leaders were eager for Western support. They were fond of pointing out that Turkey was the only Muslim country looking westward, rather than eastward. They wanted to be considered part of Europe. Turkey became the third-largest recipient of U.S. military assistance. The U.S. government made it clear that it would stand behind the Turkish military, no matter what, and turned a blind eye to its excesses. I saw some potential in this close relationship: The State Department, if it wished, was in an excellent position to exert pressure on Turkey to improve its human rights practices.

I knew Judith Buncher, the officer in the Human Rights Bureau responsible for Turkey; she had been helpful to me before my visit to

Romania in 1982. I asked her if the State Department, through the U.S. Embassy in Ankara, might make some inquiries about Gülşat. "After all," I said, "her sister lives in the United States and is married to an American citizen."

About a week later, Judith called back.

"Your friend's sister is in a lot of trouble," she told me matter-of-factly. "She's been charged with a series of crimes, including the murder of a policeman, possession of a gun, carrying false identity papers, and being a member of Dev Sol [Revolutionary Left, a left-wing terrorist organization]. It looks like she's in for it."

"How do we know these charges are true?" I asked.

"We're not in a position to judge that, of course. But there will be a trial," was her reply.

"What about the allegations that she was tortured and forced to confess?" I responded.

"The authorities deny that," she said without expression, then added: "It does occur."

When I called Nurşat with the news, she did not seem surprised. She clearly had known how serious the charges were. I told her I was planning to go to Turkey and that I would see what I could find out while I was there.

.   .   .

On September 24, 1983, I arrived in Ankara and began the first of what would be many visits to Turkey. Roland Algrant, a member of the Helsinki Watch board who was born in Turkey, accompanied me during much of the trip. We were met at the airport by Mümtaz Soysal, whom I had not seen since the Bellagio meeting. I sensed that Soysal, a prominent professor and respected newspaper columnist, was in conflict between his wish to further his professional career and his abhorrence of the torture and abuse he saw around him. Over the years I would watch him grow closer to the Turkish government, and many years later, when he was Turkey's foreign minister and I had become expert on Turkey's human rights practices, it would be my role to ask him tough questions when he spoke at the Council on Foreign Relations in New York. But even as we debated, I attacking the Turkish government and he defending it, our eyes would meet in a shared secret—that it was Soysal who had first urged me

My childhood home: built like a fortress, it was my father's pride and joy.

My grandmother, Leah, the family matriarch. I was said to resemble her.

"Lovely sisters": June (left) and I are closer in this picture than we ever were in real life.

With Bob and June, 1945

My father at his happiest

My father and mother, 1958

The Crown

GENERAL STUDIES ✦ **SOCIAL COUNCIL**

VOLUME 1 NUMBER 2   COLUMBIA UNIVERSITY   DECEMBER 1954

COLUMBIA STUDENT VISITS U.S.S.R.

Iron Curtain Melts With Personal Contact

By Ann Palmer

Jeri Laber, a second year student at the Russian Institute studying for her Ph.D., took a one month trip to Russia this summer with three other students from Columbia. Attractive, and only 23, Jeri works at the office of the "Current Digest of the Soviet Press."

After studying at the Russian Institute for two years, Jeri and three other students decided that they would like to see for themselves the dynamics of Russian life. They applied for passports and visas and heard on August 2, 1954 that they would be allowed to spend thirty days in Russia. Within a few days they left by plane from New York City and seventeen hours later arrived in Helsinki where they were met by a special Soviet plane that took them to Moscow.

Arriving in Moscow they found they were free to look around at whatever they wanted. In fact the government, being short of guides, preferred to let them go alone and save guides for people who were less acquainted with the language and customs. Jeri and her three friends were, however, given a guided tour around Moscow University by twelve Russian students, some of whom could speak English. Most of the students Jeri met were studying the Humanities, but Jeri feels these students are not in the majority. What disturbed her about the American Literature majors at Moscow University was that very few of them had heard of Faulkner. Hemingway, on the other hand, enjoys general popularity. She was very delighted to meet a young man in Political Science, a Marxist Materialist, who had read a great deal of Hemingway.

During the tour, Jeri was confronted by a young Russian student who asked her the name of her Congressman and Representative, the names of their wives and how many children they had. Jeri, not being able to answer all these important questions, was amazed when the student rattled off the answers. Later she

About to depart for Russia are, left to right, Ted Curran, Gay Humphrey, Jeri Laber and Frank Randall.

found that he had spent the morning pouring over the Congressional Directory in an attempt to be impressive. Jeri's comment was, "I was impressed."

Near the end of the tour the American students were taken into a science lab. Here they were amazed to find a copy of the magazine "Photography" in prominent display. After carefully explaining that this magazine was not typical of American scientific publications, Jeri heard one Russian student say to his friend, "I told you we shouldn't have put that out." Another student sidled up to Jeri and told her with an amused expression that not quite all the labs were this well equipped. Jeri was surprised by this show of candid humor.

When we asked Jeri about youth activities in Russia, she first mentioned the Young Communist League to which 95% of the students belong

although membership was not obligatory. While she was in Moscow the League was having trouble with wayward members who had been impressed by American movies. The young men influenced by Tarzan movies were all growing their hair long. They were also adapting supposed customs of American culture in their dress, such as the zoot suit. The Young Communist League was campaigning for loyal members to try and persuade their erring friends to give up their foolish ways.

Jeri did not spend all her time in Moscow, but travelled around Russia to Leningrad, Tiflis, Tashkent, and Samarkand. She found that the uneducated lower class were very friendly and interested in the United States. The question that was most often asked her was, "How long did it take you to get here?" The most fascinating thing to these people was the short duration of the trip.

Penetrating the Iron Curtain, 1954

With my children in
Connecticut, 1970.
left to right: Emily,
Pam, Abby

Bob Bernstein, the day we met; Celeste Holm can be seen behind him on the picket line. December 1975.

Vladimir Bukovsky, Soviet political prisoner

Yuri Orlov, founder of the Moscow Helsinki Group, in the early 1970s, before his years in the gulag.

Our first office, 1981. I am second from the left; Aryeh Neier is third from the right; Sophie Silberberg is at the far right, front.

Elena Bonner and Andrei Sakharov studying the photos I brought them of their American grandchildren. Moscow, September 1979.

Andrei Sakharov was fascinated by our catalogue, "America Through American Eyes," Moscow, 1979.

The writer, Lev Kopelev. Moscow, 1979.

Raya Orlova, a pivotal figure among the Moscow intelligentsia, was banished from the USSR with her husband, Lev Kopelev, in 1980. Moscow, September 1979.

Larisa Bogoraz and Anatoly Marchenko.

Tatiana Osipova, youngest member of the Moscow Helsinki group, was sent to a labor camp in 1980 soon after I took this photo in Moscow, 1979.

Seen here enjoying a good joke with fellow dissident, Malva Landa *(left)*, Oksana Meshko *(right)* was sentenced soon afterward to a hard labor camp at age seventy-eight. Moscow, 1979.

Madrid conference, November 1980. Bob Bernstein at the podium; Orville Schell and I are on next.

Adam Luibroth

Ludmilla Alexeyeva, Madrid conference, November 1980.

Adam Luibroth

My friend, Anna Grušová, Prague, October 1981.

POLISH DISSIDENTS,
WARSAW, NOVEMBER 1981

Zbigniew Romaszewski.

Zofia Romaszewska.

Adam Michnik.

Jacek Kuroń.

Helena Luczywo.

HUNGARIAN DISSIDENTS,
BUDAPEST, NOVEMBER 1981

Mária Kovács.

György Bence.

Ágnes Erdélyi.

György Konrád.

László Rajk

From my notes: Crumpled into tiny balls and hidden in my coat pocket, the pages passed through customs.

Mihai Botez, dissident mathematician.

Dorin Tudoran, dissident poet.

Mircea Florea and his wife, on a hunger strike.

Dinner with the Turkish Peace Association defendants; Ali Taygun is at the left. Istanbul, September 1983.

Reha İsvan, in prison, greeting her husband Ahmet, the former mayor of Istanbul, on visitors' day. Metris Military Prison, 1985.

My search ends: Gulşat Aygen,
Istanbul, June 1987.

Susan Sontag and Kary
Schwarzenberg, among
others, in Budapest to
challenge the secret
police, October 1985.

Gerald Nagler *(left)* and
Kary Schwarzenberg,
Vienna, 1986.

Natan Sharansky, freed from prison, greets Elena Bonner at Random House, New York, May 12, 1986.

Yuri Orlov, in exile after seven years at hard labor. Siberia, USSR.

Wearing traditional dress, I interview Afghan refugees. Tribal area of North Waziristan, October 1986.

Weapons were kept hidden in this refugee camp, but these fighters would not pose without their AK–47s. Peshawar, 1986.

Anatoly Marchenko building his home during a rare period of freedom. He died in 1986 while on a hunger strike in prison.

Lev Timofeyev at our first meeting in Moscow, September 1987.

Strategy meeting before confronting the Russians, *from the left*: Larisa Bogoraz, Sergei Kovalev, Lev Timofeyev, me; standing: Irwin Cotler (Canada). Moscow, January 1988.

The Russian end of the table, with Fyodor Burlatsky at the center. Moscow, January 1988.

Andrei Sakharov's first visit to the U.S. *left to right:* Andrei Sakharov, Bob Bernstein, me, Aryeh Neier. Random House, New York, November 1988.

WARSAW, APRIL 1989

Lech Wałęsa (left), Kary Schwarzenberg (right), announcing our joint award.

Celebrating our human rights award. *left to right:* Kary Schwarzenberg, Frantisek Janouch, me, Adam Michnik. Warsaw, April 1989.

Václav Havel in the 1960s, during the Prague Spring.

Rita Klímová, Prague 1987.

Dignified and principled, Jiří Hájek triumphed over the worst moments in Czechoslovak history. Prague, March 1989.

Freed from detention. Prague, October 18, 1989.

"Now you know . . . ", Petr Uhl (left) and Jan Urban, talking about my arrest. Prague October 1989.

Greeting Václav Havel at our office, New York City, February 22, 1990.

Dmitrina Petrova, Bulgarian philosopher, tells me how she was roughed up by the police the previous day. Sofia, October 1989.

No tanks allowed. Jonathan Fanton outside the Estonian Parliament, Tallinn, January 1991.

Larisa Bogoraz, Moscow, September 1991

Charlie and his father, Lawrence Kuskin, Prince Edward Island, Canada, 1991

Starting a garden in the country, May 1994

Our house, upstate New York, 2000

to come to Turkey and had encouraged people he knew to meet with me and talk openly about their problems. It was Soysal who helped me forge the first links in a chain of connections that exposed me to the horrors just below the surface of Turkish society. I met professors, lawyers, scientists, artists, writers, and businessmen, all being hounded by the military regime. I had furtive encounters with young people who had been tortured in prison and with the families of political prisoners.

These people described torture techniques that seemed medieval in their barbarity. People were "crucified." They were given electric shocks to their genitals and other sensitive spots. They were sexually abused, immersed in freezing water, nearly suffocated, and brutally beaten. Some of the techniques had names: the "Palestine Hanger," during which a victim is suspended by the wrists, which are first tied behind the back, so that the arms are pulled from their sockets; and "Falaka," the savage beating of the soles of the feet until they swell, turn black, and sometimes burst.

I learned that of the more than 120,000 people who had been rounded up after the coup, an estimated 60,000 remained in prison. Under martial law, detainees could be held in police stations without charges for forty-five days and denied visits from their lawyers and families. Torture during such periods of detention had become routine.

I also learned that the Parliament had been dissolved, that the press, universities, courts, trade unions, and other formerly independent institutions had been taken over or severely repressed and that the country's largest ethnic minority—the Kurds—was being mercilessly persecuted.

.   .   .

On the surface, Turkey could not have been more different from the East European countries I frequented. Whereas East European dissidents, on the whole, looked favorably upon Americans and coveted both our freedom and our prosperity, the intellectuals I met in Turkey were mainly leftist and anti-American: Some of them told me they would sooner live in the Soviet Union than in the United States. Unlike many of my jaded American friends, these Turks were vitally interested in politics. We disagreed on many things, but our debates were lively, the kind of conversations I had not had since college.

Unlike the drab capitals of Eastern Europe, Istanbul was noisy, bustling, colorful. Bisected by many waterways—the Sea of Marmara, the

Golden Horn, the mighty Bosporus, it straddled two continents, with one part of the city in Europe, the other in Asia. I saw lively trading in the bazaars, breezy seafood restaurants along the Bosporus, and an outgoing atmosphere on the busy streets. The Turkish government's methods of surveillance were not as pervasive as those used in the Communist world. No visas were required to travel there at that time. I passed through customs with only a perfunctory search: They were looking for contraband, not subversive literature. Yet the people I met, mainly those whose leftist views were known, spoke to me only on the condition that I would not use their names. Under martial law, they could be sent to prison or even executed merely for criticizing Turkey to a foreigner.

.   .   .

Roland Algrant and I met with the entire political section of the U.S. Embassy in Ankara, seven people in all. I asked them about the hunger strikes that were then taking place in the prisons to protest inhumane treatment. According to what I had heard on the BBC, 1,600 people were on strike in several Istanbul prisons and three had died; these reports had been confirmed by people I met in Turkey, including relatives of the strikers. Yet the U.S. Embassy personnel dismissed the reports as "rumors." They did no firsthand research for fear of angering Turkish officials.

Some members of the embassy staff actually tried to rationalize the use of torture. "The Turks have always tortured," they said, as if in some way that justified it or at least explained why it was so hard to bring it to an end. I was angered by their attitude. It removed responsibility from the Turkish government, where I felt it rightfully belonged.

People at the embassy were aware of Gulşat Aygen's case. The State Department had asked them to make inquiries, and our Washington office, working with her sister, Nurşat, had enlisted the aid of Congressman Stephen Solarz and Senator Christopher Dodd, both of whom had asked the Turkish ambassador to the United States to intercede on Gulşat's behalf. But the U.S. Embassy staff had nothing new to tell me. No one had made an effort to contact Gulşat's relatives, to get independent information, or to verify the officially stated facts. I was dismayed by their indifference. *At least*, I reassured myself, *the Turkish government now knows that the U.S. government has some interest in Gulşat.*

.   .   .

I asked about Gulşat frequently, whenever I met anyone who might have some information about her. But her experiences, so dreadful for me to even contemplate, were familiar, even commonplace, to Turkish ears. "It's the young people who are suffering most," a lawyer told me. "Evidence given under torture should be thrown out by the court."

Instead, when a group of young men told the courtroom they had been tortured, they were beaten by soldiers in front of seven judges. When their lawyer shouted: "This is inhuman!" he was told to shut up or he would be beaten, too. The father of a young prisoner told me that when he went to Metris Prison to complain about the torture of his son, he was taken inside by the guards, who held him for ten days and tortured him with electric shocks. He had heard about Gulşat: "She was tortured, really bad . . . about three years ago." That was all he knew.

. . .

The U.S. Consulate had a surprise for us when we arrived in Istanbul: We would be allowed to observe the ongoing trial of the Turkish Peace Association, the first Americans to do so. The case was notorious because of the distinguished reputations of the twenty-six defendants, some of the most important political and intellectual figures in Turkey before the coup.

The Peace Association had been formed in 1977 to promote the peace and security provisions of the Helsinki accords. Its board included the president of the Istanbul Bar Association, the head of the Turkish Medical Association, the general secretary of the Turkish Writers Union, the wife of the mayor of Istanbul, a former diplomat and ambassador, several members of Parliament, prominent writers, journalists, and professors, and a well-known artist. These people had great prestige. Some of them had been sent by the previous government to represent it at international meetings.

After the 1980 coup, the Peace Association, like all independent organizations in Turkey, was banned by the military. Then, in February 1982, the members of its board were arrested and charged with "forming an organization aimed at achieving the domination of a social class over other social classes." In other words, they were being prosecuted for their supposedly pro-Communist views. And for formerly belonging to an organization that was perfectly legal at the time they were members. They had spent ten months in prison, but had recently been released to their homes and were now required to appear in court on the two days a week when their trial was in session.

The trial was being held in a courtroom within the Metris Military Prison complex, where security was very tight. We were told by the soldiers escorting us not to speak to the defendants who were entering the courthouse at just the same time we were. But they came right up to us, curious to know who we were and pleased to be receiving some outside attention. Many of them spoke English fluently. We were able to converse easily, even as the guards were trying to separate us. Someone asked if we would have dinner with them that evening. Algrant was leaving for New York that day, but I was staying on. I quickly accepted the invitation.

The courtroom was stark, its only decoration a bust of Atatürk, the founder of modern Turkey, whose likeness is ubiquitous throughout the country. Three military judges and the prosecutor presided from huge, red-leather-upholstered chairs. The prosecution had completed its case, and the defense was presenting its arguments.

The defendants, ranging in age from their thirties to their early seventies, were under orders to sit straight on backless benches, without crossing their legs. Eight soldiers stood at armed attention at the exits, as if they expected the bespectacled, scholarly looking gentlemen suddenly to revolt. I also sat on a backless bench in the gallery, and within a short time I could feel the physical strain.

My attention was drawn to Reha İsvan, the wife of the former mayor of Istanbul. She was the only woman in the group and had a strikingly dignified demeanor. With her straight-backed posture and proud, upturned chin, she seemed just short of defiant. A handsome woman then fifty-eight years old, with stylishly cut, straight gray hair, she wore a loose-jacketed suit and low-heeled, expensive-looking walking shoes. When we had talked briefly in the corridor before the trial began, I noticed she was wearing a brooch that perfectly matched my bracelet, a black-and-silver cloisonné piece by a relatively obscure Austrian designer I had discovered in Vienna about a year before. It was an odd coincidence. I could see that Reha had noticed it, too.

．　　　．　　　．

The dinner that evening was at the Bar Association, where a long table had been set up on an outdoor terrace. By the time I arrived, more than twenty people—defendants, spouses, and friends—had already begun a multicourse Turkish feast. In high spirits, they stood and applauded me and seated me in the middle, with the best English-speakers around me: Mahmut Dikerdem, Turkey's former ambassador to India, then in his seventies and suffering from various ailments; Ali Taygun, a theater director and playwright in his late thirties with perfect, colloquial English that he had picked up during his studies at the Yale School of Drama; and Reha İsvan, who told me that three generations of her family, twenty-six members in all, had graduated from American schools and that two of her children were then living and studying in the United States.

The male defendants had just spent ten months together in a communal prison cell, where they had become close. They had passed the time by giving each other lessons in their various areas of expertise. Although their public prominence protected them, on the whole, from being tortured, they were witness to the gross treatment of other, less prominent prisoners. "You can't believe what we have seen," Ali Taygun told me, describing the harsh abuse of other prisoners.

After a while I turned to Reha, who had been listening quietly. As the only woman in the group, I assumed her experience had been different. "I was in the women's prison at Metris," she explained, "in a cell with young political prisoners awaiting trial." I thought immediately of Gulşat as I listened to what Reha had to say.

"I have a guilty conscience," she told me, "for not being as militant as some of the young women in my cell. They were amazing, these young girls, the way they stood up to the guards." Reha shook her head from side to side, remembering them. "They would laugh as they described their torture. They made it into a joke, they made us cry with laughter at their descriptions of the torturers and the guards. But then, at night, I would hear them screaming and moaning in their sleep. They had nightmares. I told them they had to stop talking about torture after 7 P.M. so that they wouldn't have nightmares." She paused. "There was a very nice girl in my last ward. She and her husband were both taken in, in separate jeeps. A policeman whispered to her: 'Torture lasts just a short time, but guilt lasts much longer.' They raped her with a stick, in front of her husband. They had only been married for six months. Later, when her husband told the prosecutor, he responded: 'What did you expect us to do? Pat her cheek?'"

Reha also told me about a girl who was tortured before coming to Metris Prison. "They put her in a sack with a cat, then beat them both until the cat went wild and began attacking the girl."

I asked about Gulşat. "Of course I know Gulşat," Reha exclaimed. "She's brilliant, a lovely person. She was terribly tortured, in Mamak Prison, before coming to Metris. These girls have such spirit. The guards would stage raids on our cell. They would storm in, send the girls into the courtyard, then tear apart their things, ripping their underwear, grinding it underfoot, slashing their pillows open, leaving behind a mess of torn and dirtied clothes and feathers. But the girls would come back in singing, and cheerfully put everything back in order. They decorated the cell with pictures. They had 'parties,' making canapés from old beans, candles out of matches. They played chess and backgammon with bread crumbs. They did folk dances, with Gulşat leading them. It drove the soldiers crazy."

When I asked Reha whether Gulşat had been a terrorist, she seemed irritated. "I never asked. What difference does it make? She is a *child*. She is worth saving." She must have seen that I was discomfited by her response, for she at once became conciliatory: "If they accuse *me* of conspiring against the state, they can accuse anyone of anything."

.   .   .

Reha, I later learned, was a role model for the women who shared her cell, most of them young enough to be her daughters. Suffering from arthritis that had become worse from the prison dampness, she nevertheless kept up a disciplined program of exercises each day. She washed and set her hair as if she were going out visiting. "When they saw you," a former cell mate wrote in an open letter to the imprisoned Reha, "all the girls were ashamed of their dowdiness and tried to get themselves into shape. Everybody loved you. . . . I learned so many beautiful things from you . . . love, understanding, resistance, honor."

On visiting days, prisoners were separated from family members by two thick panes of glass. They talked to each other on telephones carefully monitored by the guards. Nevertheless, the girls were forced to strip naked before male guards who searched their body openings before and after family visits. Rather than subject themselves to such indignities, they refused all visits with relatives. But Reha did not refuse. Maintaining her proud demeanor, she stripped before mocking guards in order to see her family. I would later see a photograph of a beaming Reha embracing her husband during a rare "open visit" when the prisoners were actually allowed to mingle with their visitors. Her hair was long and loose, touching her shoulders, her smile was radiant and full of love.

.   .   .

I called Nurşat when I returned home to tell her what I had heard about her sister. In the next months we were successful in getting articles about Gulşat published in the *New York Times* and the *Washington Post*. Helsinki Watch also began a concerted campaign on behalf of the Peace Association. We helped organize Yale Drama School alumni to work for Ali Taygun. I sent information about the Peace Association to the editorial board of the *New York Times*; an editorial entitled "Bad Show—in Turkey" ultimately appeared in June 1984.

But the Peace Association defendants, who seemed so confident that they would be acquitted, did not fare well. In November 1983, less than two months after our dinner at the Bar Association, eighteen of the defendants, including Reha, were convicted and sent back to prison, with sentences as long as eight years.

.   .   .

When I heard that Elliott Abrams would be going to Turkey in July 1984, I saw a great opportunity. His would be the first official visit to Ankara by an assistant secretary of state for human rights. Given the close relationship between the United States and Turkey, and Abrams's specific human rights mandate, he would be in a position to do some good.

I wrote an article about Abrams's visit that appeared in the *New York Times* on July 13, 1984, while Abrams was in Ankara. Knowing the strategic importance of Turkey to the United States, I did not exhort Abrams to do what I knew he *wouldn't* do—criticize the Turkish government in public. Instead, I urged him to use "quiet diplomacy," the U.S. government's tactic of choice when dealing with "friendly" human rights abusers. I pointed out that Abrams had a choice to make: "He can discuss American geopolitical concerns . . . or he can exercise his special human rights mandate on behalf of many thousands of beleaguered Turkish citizens." I talked about political prisoners in Turkey and the merciless persecution of the Kurdish minority. Above all, I focused on the widespread use of torture.

Abrams's response, "The Myopia of Human Rights Advocates," came just one month later, on August 10, also on the op-ed page of the *Times*. It took my breath away. Not only did he offer an unabashed defense of Turkey's leaders, but he took the occasion to viciously and gratuitously attack the "ill-informed and self-righteous" human rights community in Europe and the United States for its "appalling shallowness of analysis" and its "shrill and uninformed criticisms of Turkey." He singled out the Council of Europe, Amnesty International, and Helsinki Watch, in our case misquoting from my article of a month before and referring to my "bizarre logic." Here's what he had to say about torture in Turkey: "The abhorrent practice was not unknown under prior Turkish governments, and one may wonder why so many human rights activists chose to make it an issue only after the military takeover of 1980 . . . they are concerned less with eliminating torture than with making a political point."

I was dismayed and angered by Abrams's attack on us and other groups. Among other things, it undercut any influence we might have had with Turkish authorities. He was telling them, in effect: "We don't take these people seriously, so you don't have to either."

I answered Abrams's attack in a long letter that appeared in the *Times* on August 16. I pointed out that Abrams had never found "shallow analysis" in Helsinki Watch's many reports on abuses in the Soviet bloc countries and that maybe *he* was the one with the "political agenda." I took issue with the only public speech that Abrams had made in Turkey: From it "one would never know that . . . at the moment he was speaking there were hunger strikes in the Turkish prisons protesting torture and inhuman conditions."

I also took Abrams to task for turning down a rare opportunity to visit Diyarbakır Prison in the Kurdish Southeast, which I described as "possibly the worst hell-hole on earth." His "indifference to human suffering," I said, was "inexcusable."

Diyarbakır Prison was notorious for the abuse of prisoners, mostly members of the Kurdish minority concentrated in the region. Four prisoners in Diyarbakır had burned themselves to death to protest prison conditions, and some 2,000 more were conducting a hunger strike in the prison at the time of Abrams's visit. Prisoners reported constant beatings and anal rape with truncheons. One former prisoner told me how his friend was forced to eat a rat. "The worst torture," he said, "is in the septic tanks where people are taken for punishment. Excrement is put on their faces; they are forced to drink urine. Many people die, many go crazy, almost all of them have TB." The Turkish government acknowledged the deaths of thirty-two people in the prison between 1981 and 1984; unofficial sources put the count at sixty-seven.

This was the prison that our secretary of state for human rights had declined to visit.

Had Abrams chosen to visit Diyarbakır Prison, he would not, of course, have seen the conditions I have just described. Prison officials would have cleaned up the portion of the prison that he was to be shown. But such inspections often have some lasting effects, aside from the clean blankets and TV sets that sometimes remain after the foreign visitors leave. Prison officials would have been put on notice that there was outside interest in their behavior and that their treatment of prisoners might be investigated again on subsequent occasions. Most important, the prisoners themselves would have known there were people in the outside world—representatives of the U.S. government, no less—who cared about what was happening to them.

Abrams was furious with me for what he described as my "ad hominem" (i.e., personal) attack. "Elliott won't take your calls anymore," a member of his staff told me. The grace period I had enjoyed with Abrams because of my work in Eastern Europe—and the very real help he had been to me in cases involving Hungary and Romania—came to an abrupt end.

.   .   .

I continued my work in Turkey, with Gulşat always on my mind. Her story became one of many Turkish nightmares that haunted me. There was Sevgi with her long, dark ponytail and huge brown eyes. Her two-year-old daughter, terrified, watched both her parents being horribly tortured over a seventy-two-day period in 1981. When Sevgi later tried to file a complaint about the torture, the police warned her not to make more trouble for herself: "Go home and take care of your daughter," they said.

There was the Kurdish lawyer Hüseyin Yıldırım, who was suspended from the ceiling by his arms and then by his legs, brutally beaten with a metal rod that broke his fingers, teeth, and jaw and led around Diyarbakır Prison by a cord attached to his penis. I met Mr. Yıldırım in Switzerland shortly after he escaped from Turkey. I shall never forget the torment I saw in his ravaged, once-handsome face.

Nor shall I forget a forty-year-old writer I met in Istanbul shortly after he was released from prison. A quiet, soft-spoken man, he told me he was suffering from nose and back injuries that occurred during torture and from continuous rectal bleeding that began after a truncheon was shoved into his anus. He had spent one and a half years in total isolation in a freezing cell where the walls were always wet. "I survived by growing a small piece of ivy which helped me psychologically," he told me. "I am not a pessimistic person. I tried to think of good things, things of beauty. The ivy grew to the height of one meter. Then, one day, they took it away. That upset me more than anything else that happened to me."

.   .   .

Government by the military in Turkey ended in 1983. It was followed by a succession of democratically elected parliaments in which the issue of torture was frequently raised. Each new government vowed to eliminate the practice, though to no avail. I continued to gather torture testimonies in Turkey, many more than we could publish.

In 1987, during a trip to eastern Turkey, I discovered that our ebullient young Turkish interpreter had a leftist political background and had spent a short time in prison when she was a student. She knew of Gulşat Aygen. They had never met, but they had friends in common and she had heard that Gulşat had been released from prison about six months before. I, too, had received word that Gulşat was free. It had come in a letter from Nurşat, with whom I had all but lost contact, thanking me formally, on behalf of her family, for my efforts on Gulşat's behalf. "Do you want to meet her?" my interpreter asked. "I think I can find her. Let me try, once we get back to Istanbul."

A week or so later, I met Gulşat in a cozy Istanbul restaurant she had suggested as a meeting place when I called her. She was blond and pretty, though in a plain, understated way. She resembled her sister, Nurşat, except for her coloring and her manner. Nurşat was nervous and high strung, whereas Gulşat seemed calm and relaxed and projected a sense of profound inner peace. Her English was excellent, her story as simple as it was chilling.

I am a leftist. My father was a man of books who taught us to have a mission. I wanted to work with the peasantry. I wanted to be a doctor in the east.

In 1981, a few months after the coup, the police came to the university where I was studying. They had a photograph that showed a blond woman holding a gun. They rounded up about five or six blond women, then decided that I was the girl in the photograph. They took a photograph of me to compare with the one that they had, then released it to the press saying that I was the guilty one. I was arrested and tortured several times [she gave the dates] with beatings and electric shocks. Now I am hard of hearing in one ear. I have arthritis. During my hunger strike, all my toenails fell off and now my blood cells don't reproduce properly.

They made me part of the Dev Sol case. Five and a half years later, my case was finally heard in court. An expert compared the pictures and told the judge that I was *not* the girl with the gun. On September 13, 1986, I was released.

Twenty-one years old when she was arrested, Gulşat was released at twenty-seven. Her youthful hopes and aspirations, her desire to become a doctor—all had abruptly ended because of mistaken identity, an irresponsible arrest, a confession exacted under torture, and the absence of any legal recourse for her or her anguished family. Even after her release, Gulşat could not be readmitted to the university until she was formally acquitted by the court, and her acquittal would not be official until all 1,250 defendants in the Dev Sol case were tried and judged. When we met, there were about 160 still waiting in prison to be brought to trial.

"You saved my life," Gulşat told me. "It was on the fifty-fifth day of my hunger strike. I was close to death when suddenly a doctor came and gave me injections. It happened just at the time that you made inquiries about me through the U.S. Embassy. I think they got scared that I might die and decided to save me. Three others did die. If you had delayed for a month, we wouldn't be talking here now. . . . When you are in prison, to hear that someone cares for you, it is the most important thing." Gülşat confessed that the hunger strike had been a mistake: "You should never use your body as a form of protest," she told me. But she had fasted for so long that it was physically impossible for her to resume eating in her wasted state. The medical intervention saved her.

"*You saved my life.*" What an amazing thing to be told, face-to-face, by someone I was meeting for the first time. I wasn't at all sure I deserved the credit, but it didn't really matter: The fact was—she was alive. I thought of Reha İsvan's words: "She is a child. She is worth saving."

.   .   .

I hesitated before asking Gülşat about her torture, not wanting to upset her. But she remained serene.

"I can talk about it without hatred," she replied. "I love people. If I am hurt, I can live with it, but I can't live without my belief in humanity."

Gülşat's eyes were shining with conviction: "When you believe in humanity, you must believe that your torturers are human, too. Once I was hanging from my wrists, blindfolded, naked, waiting for them to give another electric shock. I heard the head torturer complaining about a pain in his stomach. I suggested a pill that he could take, something I knew about from my studies, and later he came and thanked me. And he was the one who was torturing me! But he was also a human being who could feel a pain in his stomach. I think that when he was hurting me he was killing something human in himself."

"When I was in prison," Gülşat continued, "I saw soldiers under orders actually crying while they were beating us."

"But aren't you angry?" I asked, thinking of all those wasted years.

"I am angry, of course, because of what I lived through and what I saw people live through. And I am still scared. When I hear the sound of a car stopping in the night now, I wake right up. That was how they took me. We paid so much for being students in those times."

.   .   .

Gülşat married a doctor, but she herself never became the surgeon she once wished to be. "It's too hard for me to face people's pain," she told me. Instead, when she was finally readmitted to the university, she began studying linguistics. We would remain in touch over the years. In 1997, she would serve as my interpreter during a mission to Turkey, and in 1998, seventeen years after her arrest, I would receive an excited call from her, telling me that she had been offered full scholarships for graduate study in linguistics by Harvard University and by M.I.T.

27

When Jean-Paul Sartre, in the 1950s, described torture as "a plague infecting our whole era," he was not being overly alarmist. Fifty years later, at the start of a new century, torture, though condemned by most governments and international bodies, is still occurring in more than 150 countries throughout the world and is widespread in more than seventy. Its purposes are many: to extract information, to break the victim's will, to terrorize whole populations from voicing opposition to the ruling powers. Only a few governments today will openly admit they allow torture, but many condone it tacitly by looking the other way. Some of the techniques are virtually unchanged from medieval times; others reflect more sophisticated, modern technologies.

I have interviewed hundreds of torture victims in the course of my work. Many will never fully recover from the experience. The most devastated are those who broke under torture and incriminated others. Their physical, emotional, and spiritual pain defies description. They will never again be whole.

Other torture victims amaze me by their strength to resist and rebound. There is a remarkable similarity in what they have to say: "I could stand the pain because there was a part of me they couldn't touch." "They tortured my body, but not my soul." These comments helped me understand how they survived.

The Communist police in the Soviet Union and Eastern Europe were more insidious than their Turkish counterparts. In addition to the brutal forms of torture they used during interrogations and in the labor camps, they also perfected more subtle techniques that broke the will of society as a whole. They understood the dichotomy between body and soul that former torture victims describe. And they went for the soul.

They denied people their human dignity, forcing them to hide their thoughts, to pretend to agree with a system they despised. They created an environment in which no one could be trusted—pitting children against parents and friends against each other, breaking down the tiny threads that make up the fabric of civilized life. They crushed the spirit of entire societies, leaving a legacy of fear, distrust, and immorality that lingers to this day.

.   .   .

Taking testimony from torture victims is incredibly difficult. I learned to deal with it by closing off my feelings and willing myself not to imagine the details. Although we don't often discuss this at the office, I am sure my colleagues do the same. It is the only way we can do our work, but it nevertheless takes an unmeasurable toll, affecting our thoughts and dreams and forcing us to become tough in order to function.

I can still experience the horror and outrage I felt many years ago when I first read about torture—the case of the young Greek girl that led to my initial involvement in the human rights cause. Yet since that time I have thumbed through many hundreds of equally vile torture descriptions, calmly picking out those that I think will be most effective for an article or a report, discarding others that are either not graphic enough or too ghastly for the average reader. Sometimes, though, as I am matter-of-factly editing a report, inserting commas between sequential words like "beheaded, mutilated, and raped," the hideous nature of the material creeps up on me, taking me by surprise, and I am sick at heart. I find myself wondering: *What have I become?*

In 1993 I sat with two colleagues in a Zagreb restaurant after a long day of interviewing refugees from Bosnia. We were discussing a particularly gruesome story that had been recounted to us by several people that day: A male prisoner in a detention camp was allegedly forced by guards to bite off the testicles of another prisoner. "Was this physically possible?" "Did we interview anyone who actually saw it happen?" All at once, at just the same time, we stopped talking, each aware of a gross incongruity—three people discussing such a beastly atrocity, calmly, over dinner.

.   .   .

Trying to understand how someone could torture another human being, I followed the case of Sedat Caner, a former Turkish policeman, father of two, who, as a repentant torturer, gave a sensational interview to the Turkish magazine *Nokta* in 1986. Caner admitted to torturing nearly 200 people in seven years. "By the time my child was thirteen months old, I had tortured twenty-five people."

The article was illustrated with drawings of eleven different torture techniques he had employed, bearing names such as "Palestine Hanger," "Butcher's Hanger," "Septic Hole," and "Operating Table." Caner was involved in the torture of his own brother-in-law. "Torture was constantly on my mind," he said. "I could not get away from the stress of it. . . . At home I was like an unbalanced person who didn't know what he was doing. All my colleagues were in this situation. None of us wanted to work." Caner claimed he could not quit his job because he knew too much and would be killed. He compared it to working for the Mafia.

Other repentant torturers have similar things to say. Like the Uruguayan army officer who, back in 1976, smuggled some photographs of torture victims out of Uruguay in a letter that described his own revulsion for "all that I have the misery of witnessing and, worse still, of taking part in."

Not every torturer is born a monster. Many are ambitious young men, recruited as soldiers into elite forces and specially trained for the dirty work in which they then feel trapped. They are embarrassed or afraid to rebel, or convinced that their work is necessary to get information that will protect the state. But in the course of destroying other human beings, they are also destroying their own humanity. I often remember Gulşat's words: "I think that when he was hurting me he was killing something human in himself."

Torture is destructive to all of us—to the victims, to the torturers, to those who deny it is happening, and to those who are working to bring it to an end. It forces us to imagine things that should be unimaginable, to think thoughts that should be unthinkable, and to read words that should be unreadable. It forces us to acknowledge human evil and to question human good.

·   ·   ·

In 1974, a psychologist named Stanley Milgram conducted experiments at Yale in which he tried to prove that ordinary New Haven residents would follow orders to the point of administering life-threatening shocks to an innocent victim in the course of a supposed scientific experiment. Milgram's research on obedience to authority may have been flawed, but the results set me thinking about the complexity of human behavior— that people are not necessarily bad, or good, but that their actions may be influenced by the circumstances of the moment. Could it be that the same person might react differently at different times and in different situations, that heroic behavior does not necessarily mean that a person is "good" or, conversely, that people guilty of cruel behavior may not always be "bad"?

When Hannah Arendt's *Eichmann in Jerusalem* was published in 1963, I was upset by her observations on the banality of evil. Arendt suggested that Nazi leader Adolf Eichmann was remote from reality and lacked the imagination to understand the human consequences of his acts, "to realize what he was doing." She was impressed by the very ordinariness of the man, the fact that he was not the demonic incarnation of evil that one might have expected to find in an influential officer of the Third Reich.

I had grown up thinking of evil as the work of the few—monstrous, diabolical creatures who would eventually be brought to justice. I did not like to think of evil as inherent in ordinary people—my neighbors, my acquaintances, maybe even myself. Yet if in fact Arendt is right—and much of my experience in human rights work seems to reinforce her conclusions—then torturers, or potential torturers, may exist in every society.

I came to see that it is not enough to try to shame abusers or to lecture them about right and wrong. Society needs principles, but it also needs laws—to protect us from others and even from ourselves. It also needs strong and appropriate institutions to enforce those laws and to punish the transgressors.

28

A whole nation is dying. People should know!" This was the appeal of an Afghan resistance fighter I interviewed in 1984. His eyes burned with the fierce intensity of the mujahedin. Minutes later, they filled with tears as he began to tell me about the fate of two men from his ancestral village of Mata—brothers aged ninety and ninety-five. Old and blind, they stayed behind when the rest of the villagers fled a Soviet offensive. "They were very respected people. . . . The Russians came, tied dynamite to their backs and blew them up."

His was one of hundreds of interviews I conducted on the Afghan border during several visits I made there in the mid-1980s. I was investigating what for me was a new kind of abuse—war crimes, committed by Soviet armed forces against Afghan civilians. It was an underreported war, taking place behind sealed borders. No major newspaper was then covering it; it was considered too dangerous, too inaccessible. The few intrepid freelance journalists who managed to "go inside" Afghanistan had to enter the country illegally from Pakistan, usually with one of the resistance groups, and trek for many weeks over treacherous mountain terrain, dodging Soviet bombs, not sure how they would get out again.

On my first visit, in 1984, I was accompanied by Barnett Rubin, then an assistant professor of political science at Yale; he and I would later coauthor a book on Afghanistan, taking its title, *A Nation Is Dying,* from the testimony of that Afghan fighter. It wasn't necessary, we discovered, to go inside Afghanistan: There was an enormous amount of information waiting to be gathered in Pakistan, where there were more than 3 million Afghan refugees, an overwhelming exodus. And it was there on the

Afghan border—in Peshawar, the gateway to the Khyber Pass—that we spent two weeks interviewing refugees from every region and from every walk of life.

·   ·   ·

I also spent some time alone in the frontier town of Quetta, where camels competed with cars for transportation and the wilting heat of the day quickly faded into a cold night chill. I felt vulnerable there in my shabby ground-floor hotel room, with people conversing right outside my window. I got into bed fully dressed, a defense against the cold as well as any unexpected intrusions. As soon as I lay down, I was attacked by hordes of huge mosquitoes that appeared to have taken refuge in my room when the sun descended. I pulled the small, scratchy blanket over my head to still the frantic buzzing. It was impossible to sleep.

Wide awake, I thumbed through my notes from the day's interviews. Suddenly, I noticed the date—October 3, 1984—and realized that had I remained married to Austin, it would have been our thirtieth wedding anniversary. I was stunned by the weight of all those years, and feeling a need to acknowledge them, I wrote a letter to Austin by the light of the ceiling's single bulb. It was a short note, neither loving nor angry, just some musings on the passage of time and the unexpected turns our lives had taken—me in a forsaken hovel on the Afghan border, he now living in Key West, Florida, where he owned a luxurious hotel. I mailed the letter from Karachi the following day and wonder if he ever received it.

·   ·   ·

After my first trip to the Afghan region, I reported to a large, hushed audience in the Random House boardroom. I described some of the horrendous crimes Soviet forces had committed against helpless Afghan villagers: civilians burned alive, beheaded; bound men forced to lie down on the road to be crushed by Soviet tanks; grenades thrown into a locked room filled with women and children. I spoke of the impressive dignity of the refugees: Impoverished as they were, I never saw an Afghan begging. I wanted to move my audience as I had been moved, and I succeeded.

Aryeh Neier sat with downcast eyes during my recitation, his chubby, boyish face wearing its habitual frown. I found it disconcerting when I glanced his way, though I knew that his expression did not necessarily reflect what he was thinking. Afterward, looking slightly uncomfortable, he muttered to me: "You do that very well." It was a rare compliment. Bob Bernstein, on the other hand, was very generous with his praise: Over a dinner that night, he described my report on Afghanistan in glowing terms to Robert Silvers, editor of the *New York Review of Books*. Silvers called me the next day and asked me to write what would be the first of many articles for the *New York Review*.

Peshawar, in Pakistan's Northwest Frontier Province, was the base for my Afghan missions. It was different from any place I'd been before. Always a center of smuggling and intrigue, its noisy jumble of cultures and causes was heightened by the influx of Afghan refugees—the women covered from head to toe in ghostlike burqas; the men in turbans and baggy pants, automatic weapons slung over their shoulders. There were tiny shops displaying colorful goods that had been brought across the mountains by Afghan traders—Uzbek and Turkmen rugs and fabrics, nomad dresses, embroidered caps, tarnished jewelry with lapis lazuli stones—all speaking of an ancient life in Afghanistan that was being pounded into dust by the Soviets. While trying to convey this flavor in my article for the *New York Review*, I was wary of making the article sound like a travelogue. I knew that many people saw travel as a "perk" of human rights work. I wanted to explain how stressful our missions were.

Bob Bernstein was interested in all the tiny details of my trips. Talking one day in his office, he asked me about my accommodations in Peshawar. I described my room in Green's Hotel as small and claustrophobic, with one small window that was completely painted over so that it admitted no light and could not be opened. The only air in the room arrived in periodic bursts through a grill high up on the wall: I had no way of adjusting the temperature. There was no bottled water in the hotel; I brushed my teeth with 7-Up.

"How could you stand it?" Bob asked.

"Fortunately, I didn't spend much time in my room."

"What was the service like?" Bob wanted to know.

"Well, the bed was usually made up, but not *every* day. And there was a huge dead water bug on the bathroom floor when I arrived. I checked every night: No one ever swept it up."

Bob was appalled. "Why did you stay there? Wasn't there a better hotel?"

"We wanted to be at Green's," I explained, "because it was centrally located and not fancy. It's the kind of place where Afghan refugees could seek us out. And they did. By the second week, there were people waiting outside our rooms in the morning, wanting to tell us their stories."

"Also," I continued, "the restaurant in Green's Hotel was a real meeting place—for everyone interested in the Afghan war. Journalists and photographers. People working for humanitarian agencies. Anyone new in town. We went from table to table, talking to people, finding out what they knew."

Bob was completely absorbed. Then I told him that soon after we returned home, a bomb went off in the restaurant at Green's Hotel; miraculously, no one was hurt.

"These trips are really hard," Bob commented, more to himself than to me.

And yet, hard as they were, the missions I took were also invigorating. They allowed me to become completely immersed in the substance of my work, free of the many demands at the office and able to devote myself wholeheartedly to a single project. My trips brought me together with exceptional people and gave me access to their homes and to their life stories. They inspired my writing. They spoiled me for ordinary travel.

.   .   .

I'm not quite sure when it happened, but Bob Bernstein's attitude toward me changed. I would often hear him telling others about my "courage"—how I was kicked out of Prague or searched in Budapest. Although he tended to exaggerate the dangers I faced and the nature of my experiences, there was a note of pride and admiration in his accounts that pleased me no end. Our friendship deepened, based not only on shared interests but on mutual respect.

My relationship with Aryeh Neier, on the other hand, had not progressed as I had expected at the start, when I foresaw a promising professional partnership. Despite my efforts over the years to get to know him, to be his friend, he had become, if anything, more remote and overbearing, absorbed mainly, it seemed, in building a human rights empire. "That's how he is," I told myself, trying not to take it personally. But at times I couldn't help feeling he resented my independence and my growing prominence in the human rights field.

.   .   .

I was working longer hours than ever, often buying take-out food on my way home at 9 or 10 P.M., eating it alone in my kitchen while continuing to edit an article or report. Sometimes I dozed off at the kitchen table, awakening in the early morning hours, almost too tired to get myself upstairs. But I never complained. Everyone in our office was working very hard. And the people we were trying to help had lives much more difficult than ours. I always felt lucky to be doing human rights work, to have turned my passion into a profession. Sometimes it seemed too good to be true.

In 1985, together with Americas Watch, we formed Asia Watch; we now had three regional divisions and plans to create two more—for Africa and for the Middle East.

Our mandate was also expanding. At Neier's initiative, we began to investigate abuses by insurgent forces, initially in Central American countries. Before this, human rights groups, including ours, had focused only on violations by governments, applying the provisions of international treaties that such governments had signed. But this often produced a skewed, and seemingly biased, view of the internal armed conflicts in the region. By applying international humanitarian law—more commonly called the "laws of war"—as embodied in the 1949 Geneva Conventions and the Additional Protocols of 1977, we were able to monitor both sides in internal armed conflicts with more objective conclusions. Some purists in Amnesty International and other organizations initially saw our use of international humanitarian law as too big a stretch, but in time our approach would become the norm in human rights work. It was the first of a number of such creative departures that Aryeh Neier initiated and promoted.

In 1985, Helsinki Watch, the oldest and largest of the three watch committees, was in its sixth year. We were monitoring nine repressive countries by that time and had also begun reporting on human rights compliance in the United States, in such areas as race, women's rights, and the criminal justice system. I was no longer the only one going on missions for Helsinki Watch—members of the staff, board members, and various consultants participated in the more than fifteen missions I organized during 1985 alone. I testified in Congress about abuses in Romania, calling for an end to Romania's MFN status. I testified about torture in Turkey. During 1985, we published several reports each on Czechoslovakia, Poland, and Romania, a report on Afghanistan, and reports on Canada and the

United States. I made only three trips abroad that year, spending most of my time writing articles, testifying, organizing missions for others, and editing and publicizing our various reports.

.   .   .

In the summer of 1985, I took a few weeks of vacation. Abby was moving back to the States after almost seven years in Italy. She and her boyfriend planned to settle in North Andover, Massachusetts, where they both had found teaching jobs. But first they wanted to get married and have a big wedding party—more than 100 people—in my apartment, the family home. Austin wanted no part of our party and decided to give his own for Abby instead, a catered affair under a tent at the Connecticut house. So I was on my own.

I told Abby I couldn't afford anything too elaborate. "We can do it ourselves," she urged. "It'll be great, more personal, like the big parties you used to give." I agreed, knowing I would need help to carry it off. My family and friends—people I had neglected because of my work—responded with enthusiasm.

Julie Pratt brought a huge platter of shrimp. My stepmother, Ruth, prepared a dozen filet mignons. Molly Finn made sauce béarnaise for the beef and the poached salmon. Toby Talbot brought her wonderful anchovy potato salad. My neighbors gave me the use of their kitchen and refrigerator. Linda Asher lent me tablecloths and napkins for the candlelit tables I set up on the outdoor terrace. Judy Crichton brought the bread and put up out-of-town guests in her home. Abby and I made spinach soufflés and a big salad. Pam and Emily made an elaborate, three-tiered wedding cake for their sister, decorated with fresh flowers. And Charlie helped me in innumerable ways—planning, fetching, and playing host to all the guests and to the in-laws we were meeting for the first time.

The weather was beautiful and the dancing lasted well into the night. It was like the old days, but without any stress. I was happy. I still had a life apart from work. Much had changed for me, but I had my friends, I had my family, I had Charlie.

Abby was already a mother when she was married: Zeke, born in Bologna, was about eight months old when they returned to the States, and she was pregnant with Sarah. I had a married daughter, a grandchild, and another on the way. But I had little time to contemplate these milestones. I was measuring the passing years by political anniversaries and review conferences.

.   .   .

The tenth anniversary of the Helsinki Final Act was approaching. Many saw it as a time to take stock: What had the Helsinki accords accomplished? What had Helsinki Watch accomplished?

A group of Soviet émigrés led by Aleksandr Ginzburg and Vladimir Bukovsky issued a call to abandon the Helsinki Final Act. They said it was a useless document that had been violated from its inception and brought nothing but misery to the Helsinki monitors who tried to act on it. In a scathing article, *New York Times* columnist William Safire took up the call. He referred to groups like Helsinki Watch as "cottage industries" that had grown up around the Helsinki accords and were keeping them alive for their own purposes.

Responding to these attacks in an op-ed article that appeared in the *Times* on August 1, 1985, the tenth anniversary, I pointed out that "the accords have provided a rallying point for people struggling for freedom and peace." "I have seen the Helsinki spirit at work," I wrote, "in meetings with activists in Moscow, Prague, Warsaw, Budapest, Bucharest, Belgrade, and Istanbul. Voices may lower but eyes light up when the word 'Helsinki' is mentioned. To these people, 'Helsinki' means hope."

I was invited to debate Safire on television, on the *Today* show, a scary proposition given Safire's way with words and his reputation as a sharp-tongued debater. On the show, however, I found him benign and almost avuncular. I was more passionate about my position than he appeared to be about his, and I made a convincing case for continuing the Helsinki process. All the speaking and testifying that I had been doing was paying off. My nervousness vanished once I was on the air. I felt a new and welcome sense of ease and authority.

29

Sometimes, however, I found myself wondering if our work was doing any good. I knew we were important to the small groups of dissidents in the Soviet Union and Eastern Europe—we were publicizing their arrests, speaking out on their behalf, and visiting them, when possible. But was that enough?

In 1985, three years after Brezhnev's death, the Cold War was still seething. Our reports, testimonies, and articles seemed to have no effect. The only sign we had that the Soviets even knew of our existence was the fact that some of us were denied visas to travel there. In Turkey, we at least had an ongoing dialogue with the authorities; in the Soviet Union and its satellites, we were ignored.

Three years before, in Bellagio in 1982, we had created a new international organization—the International Helsinki Federation for Human Rights. We had hoped that the federation, with groups in Western Europe, would have greater leverage with Soviet leaders than our U.S. group seemed to have. But the federation thus far had been nothing but a burden. The excitement and high hopes that attended its birth had faded as we began to face reality. It was difficult to create new groups in other countries and to raise funds in Europe, where charitable contributions were generally not tax-deductible and where there were few foundations. And it was hard to convince the existing groups to conform to a common mold.

By 1985, there were nine West European Helsinki committees on the federation's masthead, but only four—in Norway, the Netherlands, Switzerland, and Sweden—were in fact committees, and of these only two actually had enough funds to set up an office. The other "committees" consisted of one or two individuals with no institutional backup. Our headquarters in Vienna had a two-person staff and a part-time, nonresident director, Gerald Nagler. It was supported by money I had helped raise from donors in the United States—the Ford Foundation and the J. Roderick MacArthur Foundation—and from a small European foundation in the Netherlands.

The Vienna staff lacked experience and needed guidance on a daily basis. They turned to me, across the ocean, for advice. I found myself spending many hours on the phone with Vienna—helping to compile mailing lists, editing newsletters, planning meetings, drafting agendas, providing background materials, and, all too often, settling tearful disputes. The staff even asked *me* for permission to close the office on an Austrian national holiday.

At least four times a year, I traveled to Europe on federation matters. I was constantly trying to recruit new members and to shore up existing groups. The International Helsinki Federation may have looked good on paper, but it was a facade, a "Potemkin village" propped up by me and my colleagues at Helsinki Watch in New York. I sometimes wondered if it was worth all the effort.

.   .   .

The federation needed a chairman, preferably a prominent Austrian, since Vienna was our base. Gerald Nagler suggested Karl Johannes von Schwarzenberg. Having no suggestions of my own, I agreed to his choice. Karl, or Kary as he was called, became the chair of the International Helsinki Federation in 1985, and I became the vice chair.

Our new chairman seemed like a strange and somewhat worrisome choice. Schwarzenberg was a Bohemian prince, the titular head of an aristocratic family that once had vast land holdings in Czechoslovakia. The Schwarzenbergs were as well known throughout Eastern Europe as, say, the Rockefellers are in the United States. The family's castles and palaces had been confiscated by the Communists, forcing them to leave Czechoslovakia in 1948, when Karl was a boy.

I thought it was inappropriate for our nonpartisan citizens' group dealing mainly with Eastern Europe to be headed by a well-known émigré from Czechoslovakia, and a dispossessed prince at that. I was afraid it would raise questions about our motivation and our objectivity. I remembered the virulent anticommunism of the Russian émigrés with whom I had worked in New York in the 1960s: They could never forgive the Soviets for depriving them of their homes, their money, their homeland. But Kary Schwarzenberg, I would discover, was different. He had no love for communism but was equally concerned with human rights abuses in non-Communist countries—in Turkey, for example, and in South Africa.

Kary was in his late forties when I met him, tall and erect, with short-cropped black hair, a square jaw, and a dark, well-trimmed mustache. His heavy eyebrows curled sharply upward, giving him a perpetually quizzical, ironic expression. He had rosy cheeks and a curiously delicate complexion that reminded me of the faces of certain men I had met who had spent a long time in prison—not a young face but a face unmarked by time, the face of someone for whom real life has been put on hold. The image was apt, for Kary, as an exile, lived in limbo, suspended as it were between two worlds: Communist Czechoslovakia, the land of his birth, and capitalist Austria, just a few hours from Prague, where he was an entrepreneur and a well-known socialite. Kary and his family lived in one wing of the huge Palais Schwarzenberg in the heart of Vienna. Kary had turned the central portion of the Palais into Vienna's most luxurious hotel, and he kept a close eye on every aspect of its operation.

At our first few meetings, Kary seemed distant and bored. When he spoke, it required deep concentration to make out his soft-spoken, slightly garbled English. With my parochial American outlook, I failed initially to see how smart and cultivated he was or to appreciate his tactful reserve and his innate diplomatic skills. It turned out he was very much the man for the job. Later, when the International Helsinki Federation finally found its way, we were fortunate to have Kary at our helm.

. . .

A unique opportunity was on the horizon. The Helsinki signatory countries were going to hold a Cultural Forum in Hungary in the fall of 1985, the first such East-West event to take place in a Warsaw Pact country. The possibilities were instantly intriguing. I saw a way to get the International Helsinki Federation involved.

The Hungarian government was eager for the cultural meeting, which would bring delegations from thirty-five countries to Budapest. The city was being fixed up in anticipation: There were new hotels under construction and a pedestrian walk had been built in the city center among shops displaying attractive goods from the West.

In March 1985, I took the short train trip from Vienna to Budapest with Gerald Nagler and several others from our Vienna office. We met with Hungarian writers and intellectuals and developed a plan for a counterconference, which we kept secret so as not to tip off the police. We were going to test the Hungarian government's assurances that private citizens could meet freely in Budapest during the official meeting. It was a perfect project for our Vienna office, strategically placed a few hours from Budapest.

.   .   .

On October 15, 1985, when the official Helsinki Cultural Forum opened in Hungary, more than fifty people from thirteen countries assembled unofficially at the Duna Hotel in downtown Budapest. The unofficial group—a group that our federation had quietly invited—included writers and philosophers from abroad, like Danilo Kiš, Hans Magnus Enzensberger, Timothy Garton Ash, Alain Finkielkraut, Jiří Gruša, Susan Sontag, Rose Styron, and Amos Oz, as well as independent Hungarian writers and thinkers like György Konrád, György Bence, and Sándor Csoóri.

We planned to hold our own meetings in the hotel's conference room, which we had reserved for the purpose. But a few hours before our program was to begin, the Hungarian government bowed to pressure, or potential pressure, from the Soviet delegates to the forum and tried to stop our meeting. We were told that the conference room was closed "for repairs." I hurried to a nearby hotel, where I booked another conference room without any difficulty, only to be called by the manager less than an hour later and told that "water leaks" made the room unusable. By then some seventy-five would-be participants were cheerfully milling about in our hotel lobby, waiting for our periodic announcements about what was happening.

A group of us then went to the Foreign Ministry to protest. There, a deputy minister tried out his charm by asking Susan Sontag for her autograph, then told us that our meeting "could disturb the atmosphere and work of the [official] forum" and that we could not meet in a *public* place.

His stress on the word "public" led us to believe that we might be able to meet in private surroundings. And that is exactly what we did.

The Hungarian intellectuals who were to be our guests became, instead, our hosts. Graciously, without complaining about the risks involved, they found a large private apartment and stocked it with refreshments for the 150 or more people who good-naturedly crowded together there over the next few days, sitting on the floor of a room that quickly filled with smoke and dynamic conversation. Despite an obvious police presence on the street outside, no effort was made to break up the meeting. Our discussions—covering topics such as ethnic identity, censorship, the writer under repression and in exile, and the future of European culture in a politically divided Europe—were charged with the excitement of breaking new ground. During those few days in Budapest, the Helsinki spirit was alive and flourishing.

The old joke—that a Hungarian is the one who enters a revolving door behind you and comes out in front—did not apply to my Hungarian friends but seemed apt when it came to their government. Hungarian officials had played it both ways. Neither the Soviet nor the American delegates could protest: We had been forbidden to meet and we were meeting.

.   .   .

Arriving in Budapest in a bright red Porsche convertible, Kary Schwarzenberg, our new chair, had made quite a stir. My Hungarian friends recognized the Schwarzenberg name immediately and, curious, gathered around his flashy car. The business card he handed out had just one word engraved on it: "Schwarzenberg." Some of the Hungarians, I believe, keep it to this day.

I had been surprised by Kary's decision to join us there. I thought it might be awkward, even embarrassing, to explain this prince-as-chairman to the bearded Hungarian intellectuals in the Democratic Opposition, and indeed, they were initially skeptical. But Kary attended all the meetings, casually dressed and sitting on the floor with the rest of us. Seeing his intense interest in the discussions and in *them,* their amusement soon changed to respect.

I came to see that Kary's erudition—his knowledge of Central Europe's political, religious, and cultural history, its art and architecture, its geography and folklore—was truly impressive. He was very much at home among East Europeans, both dissidents and officials, and he could make himself understood throughout the region by using a self-invented East European "Esperanto." He had a credibility that most Western human rights activists lacked.

.   .   .

It was in Budapest that the International Helsinki Federation came into its own. All my hard work was finally paying off. The tactics we used at the Cultural Forum—testing and pushing the limits of official tolerance— became our strategy, and we went on to use it whenever and wherever possible.

We organized, or tried to organize, citizens' conferences in countries where such meetings had never been allowed. We met, or tried to meet, with beleaguered East European Helsinki committees in public places in their own countries. We brought, or tried to bring, our dissident colleagues to meetings we set up with their country's officials. We were not always successful, but we kept on trying, trying to expand the realm of the possible.

Ours were small steps, seemingly futile when set against the monolithic power of the Communist states. But we found encouragement in some new talk about openness. It was coming from the most improbable of all places—Moscow.

PART IV

New Thinking,
New Tactics

(1985–1988)

30

Mikhail Gorbachev came to power on March 11, 1985. At fifty-four, he was the youngest Soviet leader since Stalin and a refreshing change from the three dreary old men who died in office immediately before him: Brezhnev, in November 1982 at the age of seventy-six; Andropov, in February 1984 at seventy; and Chernenko, in March 1985 at seventy-four. Gorbachev remained his country's leader through some turbulent times, until a fateful day—December 25, 1991—when, incredible as it still seems, the Soviet Union ceased to exist.

Gorbachev was intriguing from the start. Unlike his remote and secretive predecessors, he was energetic and outgoing, seeking out ordinary people and engaging them in discussion, his wife, Raisa, often at his side. He looked different, more like a Western politician than a Soviet dictator. Yet despite all this, he was a committed Communist Party member who had worked his way up through the ranks. I did not expect much from him.

.   .   .

Gorbachev said he would introduce "new thinking." His goal was ambitious: to bring the Soviet Union out of its long lethargy and reshape its economy along modern lines. His policy of perestroika (rebuilding) was announced soon after he took office. He launched a tough campaign against alcoholism, limiting the sale and consumption of vodka, and promoted a system of performance-linked salaries and bonuses. Both measures were designed to make Soviet workers more productive but did little to endear Gorbachev to those bureaucrats and workers who had become dissolute and lazy under the country's moribund economic system. In July 1985, Gorbachev moved Foreign Minister Andrei Gromyko, a hard-liner who had survived many a Kremlin power struggle, to the ceremonial position of president. Then he appointed a new foreign minister, Eduard Shevardnadze, who was more in the Gorbachev mold.

.   .   .

At first we saw no easing of human rights abuses. The title of Bob Bernstein's article in the *New York Times* on July 8, 1985, said it all: "Under Gorbachev, the Old Repression." Bernstein called attention to the plight of Anatoly Shcharansky and Yuri Orlov, both serving out their terms, the first in prison, the second in exile. He wrote about Andrei Sakharov, still banished to Gorky, who was then on a hunger strike protesting the denial of a visa to his wife, Elena Bonner, who needed medical treatment abroad.

Bernstein also called for "Soviet respect for the human mind," an appeal that was more prescient than we knew at the time. For Gorbachev, it turned out, understood what his predecessors had failed to grasp: that a country's greatest resource is the genius of the human mind and that people cannot work creatively in an atmosphere of suspicion and fear. And with this realization came his policy of glasnost (openness) and a gradual easing of repression.

.   .   .

The first signal came in October 1985, when Elena Bonner, after more than five years in exile with her husband, Andrei Sakharov, was given permission to leave Gorky for heart surgery in Boston. Then, in February 1986, Anatoly Shcharansky was released from prison in exchange for a U.S.-held spy. He was reunited with his wife, Avital, in Germany, and they went straight to Israel, where he renamed himself Natan Sharansky.

Sharansky was short, chubby, and funny, a computer scientist, a human rights activist, and a Jewish refusenik. After Avital left Russia for Israel, right after their marriage in 1974, he had set out to get himself expelled so that he could join her there. He became prominent in dissident activities and used his excellent English to show foreigners—Bob Bernstein had been one of them—the dark side of Soviet life. He thought the KGB would be eager to see him leave; instead, they arrested him.

Sharansky's case was well known in the West, thanks to a strong citizens' movement for Jewish emigration and to Avital's tireless campaigning. We saw his release as an isolated gesture to appease world opinion. It turned out to be the harbinger of a series of groundbreaking events that made 1986 a turning point in Soviet human rights practices.

.   .   .

On May 12, 1986, the tenth anniversary of the founding of the Moscow Helsinki Group, the Random House boardroom was packed with people, a standing-room-only crowd. They were there to see three of the Moscow group's founding members: Elena Bonner, physically frail from a six-bypass heart operation, but emotionally strong as ever; Natan Sharansky, whose buoyancy and irresistible smile belied the 403 days he had spent in punishment cells and 200 days on hunger strikes during his nine years in the gulag; and Ludmilla Alexeyeva, Helsinki Watch's vivacious consultant and the group's longtime representative abroad, whose ingenuous face registered a gamut of happy emotions, ranging from excitement to pure joy. It was the first time they had all been together since Sharansky's arrest nine years before, in 1977.

There was a lively press conference, during which the three kept interrupting each other—"just like back in the Moscow group," Lyuda said, laughing. Sharansky praised Yuri Orlov for starting the Moscow Helsinki Group:

> It was, of course, a great task, and I don't know of any other person in the Soviet Union at that time, and maybe even now, who could have organized people from such different directions, with such different interests. You see, there were Zionists, and monarchists, Russians and Ukrainians and Belorussians, and even Eurocommunists, I'd say, people of absolutely different views. There were those who wanted to leave, like myself or Vitaly Rubin, and those who were concerned about the situation in Soviet prisons and camps, and those who were concerned mainly about religious freedoms. But all of us were united by the Helsinki Group.

Elena Bonner explained that her own position in the group was initially symbolic: "I have to say, in the beginning, I think I joined the group only formally. I even said right at the outset that I wouldn't do any work. But I gave my name so that people would not think that Sakharov was against the group. Then it happened some people were arrested, some left . . . I was forced to become fairly active . . . and it reached the point where I held the annual political prisoners' day [press conference], on October 31, 1983, all by myself."

Lyuda Alexeyeva, quick to spot a good press opportunity, used the occasion to appeal for the thirty-six members of Helsinki groups who were then imprisoned. She pointed out that "for each ethnic, national or religious group there are such groups speaking out here in the free world . . . [but] when we come to the human rights activists—who themselves defend everyone else—it turns out there's nobody to defend *them*. Like Yuri Orlov, and others."

Seeing the three together, teasing each other in familiar ways, talking about their shared experiences and the sorry fate of their colleagues, I could sense what their circle must have been like at the start of it all— intellectual, idealistic, and iconoclastic. I found it hard to fathom the incredible courage they mustered to meet the tragedies that followed. I wondered, not for the first time, if I would have had the strength to do what they had done.

Sharansky and Bonner were not optimistic about Gorbachev. Sharansky, after all, had been just one of some 800 or more known Soviet political prisoners; the rest remained behind bars. Bonner's reprieve was temporary: She would soon rejoin Andrei Sakharov in isolation. I wrote an article for the *New York Times* to mark the Moscow group's anniversary, focusing as always on Yuri Orlov. The imprisoned founder of the group had finished his seven-year sentence in a labor camp in February 1984 and was serving five additional years in Siberia, in a dismal place in Yakutia, working as a security guard at a construction site. Recalling Irina Orlova's description of her husband and a recent photograph I had seen, I reported that his curly red hair had turned white and that his face was ravaged and haggard. I wrote that he was forced to live in "a manmade hell of physical cruelty and broken dreams."

.   .   .

I had not taken any vacation time in the eight years since Helsinki Watch began, except for exceptional events—the birth of a grandchild, a daughter's wedding. I felt too involved, too indispensable to be away from the office for "frivolous" reasons. In any case, I had no one to vacation with. Charlie was more self-denying than I when it came to taking time off: The erratic work life of a freelancer did not, in his view, include formal vacations. We spent much of our time together working under the same roof, on his boat or in my apartment. But eventually we wanted something more than weekend work-dates.

In the summer of 1986, Charlie and I flew to the West Coast, where we rented a car and spent two weeks driving along the Pacific shore from Big Sur to Seattle, stopping to see his son Nicholas in San Francisco and his daughter Julia in Seattle. My friends at work teased me: They found it hard to believe that I, who had been in just about every country in Europe and then some, had never been to California or the West. I loved the West. I loved being with Charlie, away from New York. We drove and drove, stopping to swim in the gray sea, sleeping in motels we found along the way, toting a bottle of scotch we had bought in Mendocino. The fog came in and we couldn't see the ocean. And it didn't matter a bit.

We had discovered vacations. From 1987 on, we would spend three or four weeks together each summer, in a beachfront cottage on Prince Edward Island in Canada—without television, without newspapers, only a radio tuned to Canadian music and news. We set up house there, took long walks along the cliffs, picked bouquets of wild lupine, and prepared shellfish dinners for ourselves and for friends from New York who came to see us. It became an escape, one that I longed for during the rest of the year, counting the months and then the days.

Yet even up there, on a windswept cliff overlooking the Gulf of St. Lawrence, certain people were never far from my mind. I sent postcards with innocuous messages to my dissident friends in Eastern Europe and the Soviet Union, hoping that cards from a remote tourist spot might get by the censors. It was a way of keeping in touch. I never knew how many actually reached their destinations, though occasionally I would receive something in return. Once a card from Jiří Dienstbier arrived from Prague: "Merry Christmas, Happy New Year, and thank you for taking an interest in our lives."

.   .   .

When I returned to the office after my trip to the West, some of the staff were grumbling. They had been working overtime to turn out reports, trying to meet Aryeh Neier's urgent deadlines. "I don't mind working hard when there's a reason," one of them told me. "But this was so arbitrary, there was no real need to get them out so fast. It ruined my summer." For the first time, I found myself questioning Neier's seemingly insatiable need for what he called "product." Our staff was dedicated and responsible; it seemed unnecessary, even insulting, to drive them so hard. I often encouraged *my* staff to take time off. I worried they would burn themselves out.

Neier let it be known that he spent every Sunday in the office, thus making Sunday an unofficial workday for those who sought his favor. On Mondays he would tell me in tones of great significance who had been in the office the day before. It never seemed to occur to him that some were there mainly to impress him and that others, myself included, found it more congenial and more productive to do their weekend work at home. Years later, after Neier had left the organization, I watched the Sunday attendance rate drop precipitately—with no lessening of "product."

.   .   .

The fall of 1986 brought more changes from Moscow. For the first time, Soviet diplomats began talking openly about humanitarian issues and seemed to acknowledge a link between human rights and international security. They became aggressive on the subject, attacking the United States and other Western countries for *their* human rights practices, a dialogue we welcomed. The Soviet government opened a Department on Humanitarian and Cultural Affairs that appeared to be its answer to the U.S. State Department's Human Rights Bureau.

Most important of all, Gorbachev and Reagan were meeting. Their second summit meeting was scheduled for October 1986 in Reykjavik, Iceland. In early September, the State Department organized a pre-summit meeting in Washington to brief and hear from nongovernmental organizations. Although I didn't take such meetings very seriously—they were mainly public relations gestures by the State Department—I nevertheless decided to attend.

The meeting was opened by Rozanne Ridgway, assistant secretary of state for European affairs and the highest-ranking official present. Roz Ridgway and I had met on a few occasions before—first when she came to address the Helsinki Watch board in New York and later when I visited her in her office in East Berlin just after she had become the U.S. ambassador there. She was a tall, imposing woman with a strong, intelligent face. We had developed an instant friendship based mainly on an unexpressed sense of affinity—we were professional women of about the same age, making our way in a man's world. Then Ridgway was promoted to assistant secretary of state for Europe: She was the top adviser to the secretary of state on the countries covered by the Helsinki accords.

Halfway through the meeting, Roz signaled to me to meet her outside. She led me to a comfortable couch where we could talk and told me she would be accompanying Reagan to Iceland. "We have the issue of Jewish emigration at the top of our list," she assured me. I was dismayed by her statement, although the misunderstanding was not unique: Many people confused Helsinki Watch's goals with those of the influential and well-funded Union of Councils for Soviet Jews, perhaps because several members of the Moscow Helsinki Group—Sharansky, Meiman, and Slepak—were also refuseniks who had been denied the right to leave for Israel.

"You've got it wrong," I told Roz. "Helsinki Watch isn't working for Jewish emigration. We support the right to emigrate, of course, but our main goal is to make the Soviet Union a better place for *everyone*, so that people will want to *stay*. We want them to release their political prisoners."

Roz was listening closely. "Who, for example?" she asked me.

"Yuri Orlov," I instantly replied, telling her who he was and why his case was so important to us.

Roz took out a piece of paper and wrote something down.

.   .   .

The call came through at the end of September, when I was away on a mission. "Tell Jeri she's got her man," Ridgway announced to my incredulous assistant. She went on to say that Orlov would be arriving in the United States in about a week and that the State Department wanted us to take care of him.

Orlov's release was part of a pre-summit exchange agreement in which a Soviet spy arrested in the United States would be traded for an American journalist, Nicholas Daniloff, who had been framed and held by the KGB. Reagan, who considered Daniloff a hostage, not a spy, wanted to add someone else to the bargain. Roz Ridgway, fortunately, had just the right name.

Soviet foreign minister Eduard Shevardnadze announced at a press conference that they had agreed "to release some person called Orlov." They stripped him of his Soviet citizenship before expelling him.

.   .   .

I was in a remote place on the Afghan border at the time of Roz Ridgway's call, traveling in the Tribal Agency of North Waziristan. It was my second trip to the Afghan region, a place I found both exotic and dangerous. The tribal areas, between Pakistan and Afghanistan, are usually off-limits to outsiders. Although nominally under Pakistan's control, they are run by local chieftains who employ their own rules and punishments. Having gained the confidence of Ahmed Zeb, the chief protocol officer of Pakistan's Refugee Agency for the Northwest Frontier Province, and also of the UNHCR (United Nations High Commissioner for Refugees), I was able to hitch a ride from Peshawar to the tribal areas on a four-passenger UNHCR helicopter. As we flew over the bleak, barren mountains, an extension of the Hindu Kush range that stretches on into Afghanistan, I thought of the bruised legs and swollen feet of a little girl I had met the day before in Peshawar. She had crossed these mountains on foot in a refugee caravan, carrying her few possessions on her back.

From the air I could see thousands of dark refugee tents that seemed to meld into the landscape, a monochromatic patchwork broken by wandering donkeys and camels and occasional flashes of brilliant red, the floral fabrics favored by Afghan women. We landed in Miram-Shah, just a few miles from the border, where I met up with Mr. Zeb. We then traveled with an interpreter and a photographer to the camps, our car protected from bandits and land mines by a truckload of armed Pakistani guards that led the way. I wanted to interview some of the hundreds of thousands of Afghan refugees who had recently come across the border.

I was led to an open field and was dismayed by what I saw. A huge tent had been set up to protect me from the sun. I was to sit there behind a long, imposing table, like a judge, taking testimonies from a crowd of several hundred highly emotional Afghan men who were milling in front of the tent. It went against all our rules: Interviews were supposed to be private, one-on-one. Testimonies given so publicly and heatedly might very well be exaggerated or changed in some way to please the crowd. There would be no opportunity for follow-up.

I had no choice but to go along. I listened to a number of different group testimonies by angry, excited men until I felt I could bring the hearings to a polite close. Then I wandered through the camp with only my interpreter, speaking to people individually, hearing what each one had to say.

As a woman, I was able to interview Afghan women, who were not allowed to talk to male outsiders. Disgruntled male relatives hovered just outside the tents monitoring our conversations, afraid I might try to photograph the women, which they did not permit. They seemed unable to comprehend why anyone would want to hear a woman's opinion, and some of the women, I noticed, seemed equally mystified. I kept moving from tent to tent, squatting and taking notes. I was completely caught up in the moment and could think of nothing else.

Back in Peshawar a few days later, I visited several schools for orphans. The testimonies of these child victims, I thought, would be fresh and especially moving to readers back home. Instead, I was appalled to find that young boys were being trained to hate and, eventually, to fight a "holy war against the infidels." One after another, in exactly the same words, they told me that their goal was jihad. When I asked five small boys in a refugee camp to pose together for a photograph, the men in charge asked me to wait; they fetched their Kalashnikovs and gave them to the children, who then struck a militant pose. "This is the generation that will fight and free Afghanistan," one of the men predicted. I suspect that many of those children have grown up to be part of the Taliban.

.   .   .

One morning over breakfast in my Peshawar hotel, I spotted a small item in the English-language newspaper announcing Yuri Orlov's imminent release. This was what we had been working for all these years, yet it seemed so out of context in those surroundings that it took a minute for me to absorb the news. Then I rushed to the phone to call my office and learned that yes, indeed, the report was accurate: Orlov would be arriving in New York in just a few days. Later, in an interview with the *Christian Science Monitor* on November 6, Roz Ridgway said: "One of the nicest phone calls I was ever able to make was to call Helsinki Watch in New York and tell the staff there that Yuri Orlov would be leaving the Soviet Union and could they help us in receiving him in the United States."

My first impulse was to abandon everything and rush home to be there when Orlov arrived. Instead, I stayed on in Peshawar to finish my work. I had come too far, and was too invested in what I was doing, to cut short my mission. I was the only one of our staff in Peshawar. There were plenty of people in New York to welcome Orlov.

On October 6, the day Orlov left Moscow for New York, I interviewed Mariam Kakar, the wife of Professor Hasan Kakar, Afghanistan's most prominent political prisoner. She had crossed the border into Pakistan in disguise, wrapped in a large shawl, her face dirtied, traveling some 150 miles from Kabul, the Afghan capital, to meet me. Removing her head scarf and shaking out her dark hair, she told me about her most recent visit with her husband, who was being held under miserable conditions in Pol-e Charki Prison in Kabul. After I wrote down all the details, we discussed whether publicity in the United States would be helpful. Her husband had told her he wanted such publicity, but she was afraid the Afghan puppet regime would use it to link him to the CIA. I told her about an interview I had conducted in Moscow in 1979—with Irina Orlova, Yuri's wife, who had told me about *her* visit to her husband in Perm Labor Camp. Like the Afghan professor we were now discussing, Orlov was virtually unknown at that time. But a campaign on his behalf was mounted in the United States, by us and by others. When I told Mrs. Kakar that Orlov was now free, she smiled for the first time, a trace of hope in her eyes.

31

Yuri Orlov arrived at Kennedy airport, welcomed by a mob of reporters, émigré friends, and representatives of various organizations, including ours. Everyone was competing for the attention of a tired and confused man, self-conscious before the cameras because his teeth had rotted away in prison. It was far too soon for him to know where he would live, what he would do, whether he would resume his work as a physicist or continue his human rights activism.

Orlov was very much his own man. I met him in New York soon after I had returned from Peshawar, at a small dinner hosted by Bob Bernstein in an Upper East Side restaurant. Orlov had been out of Russia for just a few weeks; he spoke with the help of an interpreter. He was tiny, almost elflike, but taut and wiry from his years at hard labor. His hair had indeed turned white, but he had a youthful twinkle in his eyes and an impish smile that had become presentable, thanks to Bob Bernstein's family dentist, who had treated him free of charge. I liked him at once; it was impossible not to—he was so bright and interested in everything and humorous about himself and the vagaries of his life.

Bob Bernstein had brought along a friend who was visiting from Johannesburg, and much of our conversation that night was about the struggle against apartheid in South Africa. I was disappointed because I wanted to hear what Orlov had to say about the Soviet Union. But I was also impressed by Orlov's rapt interest in South Africa and his genuine concern about the South African government's repression of the leftist African National Congress. He was a true human rights advocate: He didn't seem to care where the abuses were occurring or whether they were the work of left-wing or right-wing governments. Soon afterward, Orlov asked us to prepare two photographs for him—one of his friend Anatoly Marchenko, then on a hunger strike in Chistopol Prison, and one of Nelson Mandela, then detained on Robin's Island in South Africa: "One from the right in a left country; one from the left in a right country." He was prepared to campaign for them both.

And campaign he did, in Washington and during a monthlong odyssey to various European capitals, meeting with presidents and prime ministers, as well as with local support groups. Helsinki Watch paid for and helped arrange his trip. Cathy Fitzpatrick, our research director on the Soviet Union, accompanied him on his travels and served as his interpreter.

.   .   .

I saw Orlov's release as a goodwill gesture, timed to impress the one international forum that the Soviets seemed to care about—the Helsinki Review Conference. The third such conference was due to open in Vienna a month after Orlov's release, in November 1986. Poland, the pariah of the second review conference, did a complete about-face by releasing almost all of its political prisoners just before the third conference opened—a conciliatory move that overshadowed that of the Soviets. By releasing all the Solidarity activists, the Polish government was tacitly acknowledging that the attempt to crush Solidarity had failed.

Czechoslovakia was a different story. On the eve of the conference, the Czech police arrested seven members of an independent cultural organization known as the Jazz Section. Members of the Jazz Section had gone to Budapest in 1985 for the Cultural Forum, and the authorities were probably worried that they would attempt to lobby the delegates in Vienna as well.

.   .   .

I traveled to Vienna with Yuri and Irina Orlov, arriving a few days before the opening. Yuri was very animated on the plane, interested in everything he saw, commenting, sometimes ironically, on the differences, and similarities, between the West and Moscow. Irina, on the other hand, seemed to have shrunk since her arrival in the West. Eighteen years younger than Yuri, who was in his early sixties at the time, she curled up in the plane seat like a child, her face pinched and gloomy, her eyes vacant.

I thought I understood her unhappiness. She had been given five days' notice to leave Moscow forever, barely time to say good-bye to her family and friends and to give away her possessions, her books, and her photographs, for she was allowed to bring only one suitcase with her for the rest of her life. She did not complain or bargain for more time, for fear of upsetting the delicate arrangements surrounding Yuri's release.

I tried to speak to Irina in my rusty Russian, but she answered in monosyllables and I could not get through. What I did not know at the time was that she had left her heart in Moscow as well—with Sasha Barabanov, one of Yuri's close friends. Irina returned to Moscow soon afterward, and she and Yuri agreed to a long-distance divorce. I expected Yuri to be devastated, but he appeared to take it in stride. "Better [she should leave me for] a friend than an enemy," he commented. He joked with me about the red tape impeding his divorce. "Other émigrés are worried about family reunification, but my problem is how to arrange family de-unification." In early 1987, when Yuri began work in physics at Cornell University, he met Sidney Siskin, a funny, forthright, Brooklyn-born woman in her early forties, a lecturer in the humanities, who offered to teach him English. They were married as soon as Yuri's divorce came through.

.   .   .

Vienna in November 1986 was teeming with journalists from the United States and all over Europe, there for the opening of the review conference. More than fifty nongovernmental groups, including our International Helsinki Federation, mounted impressive displays in a building across from the meeting hall, with photographs and publications dramatizing human rights issues. There were symposiums, speeches, and press conferences, all the activities we had come to expect from the previous conference in Madrid. In Vienna, however, there was something new in the air, a current of anticipation, even excitement. No one knew exactly what to expect from the Gorbachev contingent.

On opening day, shortly before the conference was to start, I was walking in the corridor with several Soviet émigrés. One of them was Ayshe Seytmuratova, an angular, formidable-looking woman with an olive complexion, almond eyes, and high cheekbones. Ayshe was a Crimean Tatar, a former political prisoner who had immigrated to New York in 1978 and worked tirelessly for the rights of her people. Stalin had ruthlessly deported the Tatars from the Crimea to Central Asia in 1944, forcing 283,000 of them into sealed cattle cars without food or water. Close to half of them did not emerge alive. A Helsinki Watch publication, "The Punished Peoples," dealt with the Crimean Tatars' struggle to return to their homeland, as had many of the documents of the Moscow Helsinki Group.

Suddenly, walking toward us, we saw Eduard Shevardnadze, the Soviet foreign minister. He was tall and distinguished-looking, immediately recognizable by his silvery white hair. His manner was totally unlike that of other Soviet diplomats. He was walking slowly, and *smiling*, and the people who surrounded him were not security agents pushing their way through, but a crowd of Western journalists with whom he was bantering.

Although we tried to restrain her, Ayshe broke through the crowd and threw herself at Shevardnadze, making an impassioned plea in Russian for the Crimean Tatars. Shevardnadze did not seem startled, nor did he brush her off. He stopped and listened to her, a serious look on his face, and said that he would see what could be done. Speechless, we watched him walk on.

.   .   .

A thunderbolt struck when the conference opened. Shevardnadze proposed that there be a human rights meeting—a Helsinki "conference on the human dimension"—and that it be held in Moscow. The proposal met with stunned silence from both the Western and East European delegations. Even the Soviet delegates seemed taken by surprise. The Canadian ambassador to the review conference later compared it to "Hitler suggesting in 1938 that Berlin should host a conference on the welfare of the Jews." And an Austrian newspaper likened it to "a debate in the fox den about raising chickens."

Exactly what did the Soviet government have in mind? How could there be a human rights conference in Moscow when hundreds of political prisoners remained in labor camps and internal exile? When Marchenko was on a hunger strike and Sakharov was banished to Gorky? When dissident leaders like Orlov and Sharansky were stripped of their Soviet citizenship and prevented from returning home? When Western radio stations were being jammed? When Western human rights activists—like Cathy Fitzpatrick, Bob Bernstein, and me—were consistently denied visas and would not be able to attend?

Would the international press be allowed open entry? Would Soviet citizens have access to the delegates? Would people be allowed to lobby the delegates freely, as they had in Madrid and Vienna? The Soviet representatives were studiously vague on these questions.

The Shevardnadze proposal would remain an open and controversial issue throughout the drawn-out Vienna conference ("conference" seems like a misnomer for a meeting that would remain in session for two and a half years, until January 1989, and begin to feel like a permanent institution). Western delegates debated the Shevardnadze proposal to the very end. They differed on how to assess Gorbachev's "new thinking." They didn't know whether support of the Soviet proposal would encourage or discourage further reform.

The United Kingdom and Canada were outraged by Shevardnadze's audacity. Margaret Thatcher, in particular, was categorically opposed to any human rights conference in Moscow. Although there was some dispute within the U.S. government, the prevailing view was to use the possibility of such a conference as leverage to effect human rights changes and to set forth some strong preconditions.

Helsinki Watch was in agreement with the U.S. government's approach. We were also in agreement on the preconditions—releasing all political prisoners, allowing free emigration, and ending the jamming of foreign radio stations. As for the conference itself, we insisted that émigrés and foreign human rights activists be allowed to attend, that the press should have open access, and that Soviet citizens should be able to lobby the delegates. Setting these conditions was, in my view, tantamount to rejecting the Soviet proposal. I could not imagine the Soviet Union complying with them. The first condition alone—an amnesty for all political prisoners—seemed next to impossible.

And indeed, for a while, the Soviets appeared to have had second thoughts about the matter and seemed inclined to let it drop. There were rumors that hard-liners like Politburo member Yegor Ligachev and KGB chief Viktor Chebrikov were opposed to the whole idea.

The U.S. delegation, led by Warren Zimmermann, worked in close cooperation with Helsinki Watch, directly and through our Vienna-based International Helsinki Federation. Zimmermann was a career diplomat, unlike Arthur Goldberg and Max Kampelman, the political appointees who had preceded him at previous review conferences. I had expected a cautious approach from Zimmermann—he was a State Department officer working his way up through the ranks, not a political figure eager for publicity. Although low-key and self-effacing, Zimmermann turned out to be the most forceful and eloquent of them all, mainly because he cared so deeply. His speeches at the conference, citing the most minute details of persecution, were extraordinarily moving to many of the delegates.

I can see Warren Zimmermann now, at a reception given by our International Helsinki Federation for all the Western ambassadors to the conference. Tall and stooped in his disarmingly deferential manner, completely oblivious to his peers and other "important" people in the room, he is sitting in a corner with Lyuda Alexeyeva, intently absorbed in what she is telling him about the many Soviet victims still behind bars.

Despite Shevardnadze's grandstanding on opening day, despite the new accessibility of Soviet diplomats, the Soviet delegation was as intransigent as ever behind the closed doors of the conference. In response to Zimmermann's eloquent pleas—for Sakharov and Marchenko in particular—the Soviet delegates attacked the West for *its* human rights violations, citing homelessness and unemployment, trying to shift the emphasis from political rights to economic rights.

. . .

On December 8, 1986, Anatoly Marchenko died of a cerebral hemorrhage. He had made good on his pledge to die in prison if the Soviet Union did not release its political prisoners. That he had sent this pledge in a smuggled-out letter addressed specifically to the delegates at the Vienna conference made it all the more poignant when they heard the news. On December 12, when Warren Zimmermann asked the conference to agree to one minute of silence in memory of Marchenko, the Soviet delegates walked out. They were followed by the Bulgarians, East Germans, and some of the Czechs and Slovaks. The Poles and Hungarians remained in their seats in a surprising show of independence.

I had met Marchenko just once, at our 1979 publishers' dinner in Moscow, where he and his wife, Larisa Bogoraz, shabbily dressed and just back from exile, stood on the sidelines looking sad and ill at ease. He was a true hero to the human rights movement, dearly loved by his friends among the Moscow dissidents. They had high respect for his proletarian background, for his courage and strength of character, and for his many years in the gulag—he spent twenty of his forty-eight years in prison and labor camps.

That Marchenko died on the eve of major reforms in the Soviet Union makes his tragedy all the more terrible. But his sacrifice itself may have been the catalyst for the remarkable things that followed. It was certainly a factor.

.   .   .

On December 15, 1986, a week after Marchenko's death, workmen appeared at the Sakharov home-in-exile to install a telephone. The next day, a call came through—from the general secretary himself, Mikhail Gorbachev—informing the Sakharovs that their exile was over, that they were free to return to Moscow. The timing suggests a connection to Marchenko's death, since Sakharov and Marchenko were known to be friends. Moreover, Sakharov's health was failing. If he, the best-known human rights figure in the Soviet Union and probably the world, were to die in forced exile, it would make a mockery of the new image the Soviet Union was trying to project.

In addition, it was Sakharov's protest against the Soviet war in Afghanistan that had precipitated his exile in the first place, and Gorbachev may already have been contemplating the withdrawal of Soviet troops from Afghanistan, which would be completed in the early months of 1989. Why should the Soviet Union continue to punish Sakharov when the war he opposed had turned into a military disaster costing his country billions of rubles and leaving some 15,000 Soviet soldiers dead? Not to mention the brutal deaths of countless Afghans, the five million forced to flee to neighboring countries, the destruction of their homes and villages, and the decimation of the centuries-old infrastructure that made their land habitable.

.   .   .

At a January 1987 plenum of the Communist Party Central Committee, Gorbachev further developed his concepts of glasnost and perestroika. Despite the opposition of Party conservatives, the plenum agreed to multiple candidates and secret ballots in local Party elections. A series of other astonishing actions and announcements followed.

Several hundred political prisoners were released in January, with more releases continuing throughout the year: By the end of 1987, about half of the known political prisoners would be free. Among the first to see freedom were the prisoners whose cases we had been pushing. It appeared the Soviets had been paying attention after all.

The Soviet government also stopped jamming the major Western radio stations. They began allowing more people to emigrate. They claimed that the criminal code was being revised, especially the articles used to punish dissent.

Gorbachev called for a reexamination of the Stalin era. There must be no blank pages in our history or literature, he said. Like Khrushchev before him, he unleashed a torrent of suppressed information, soul-searching, and recrimination. Unlike Khrushchev, he did not try to stop it.

Stalin's enemies—Bukharin, Zinoviev, even to some extent Trotsky—were posthumously rehabilitated. An independent association called Memorial was allowed to form, initially to build a monument to the 20 million people who had died under Stalin's rule. Memorial later went on to become a human rights organization with branches throughout the USSR. Tens of thousands of other citizens' groups formed almost overnight, everything from gardening groups and parents' associations to mothers of Soviet soldiers and advocates for the handicapped and disabled. After years of repression, people were organizing, speaking out, demanding rights that they did not plan to relinquish.

.   .   .

Gorbachev announced another, equally startling change of policy—that the countries of the Warsaw Pact were free to develop in their own ways and that the number of Soviet troops in Eastern Europe would be reduced. He was, in effect, renouncing the Brezhnev Doctrine, which had been used to justify the Soviet-led invasion of Hungary and Czechoslovakia and the threat of such intervention in Poland. With the possibility of Soviet military backup no longer on the horizon, Communist governments in Eastern Europe were suddenly much weaker, more vulnerable to domestic opposition.

.   .   .

Gorbachev believed so firmly in communism that he thought it possible to change it from within. He did not seem to understand that he was unleashing forces that would ultimately be impossible to control.

32

Eager to see how Gorbachev's "hands off" policy was working in Eastern Europe and how it would affect our work there, I went to Warsaw and Prague in the fall of 1987. For the first time since the Communists took over in the aftermath of World War II, these countries were free to develop in their own ways, without fear of a Soviet invasion to set things right. I wondered if Gorbachev, when he said that "unity [in Eastern Europe] does not mean identity and uniformity," may have been tacitly acknowledging the very real differences that already existed within the bloc. I planned to write about my findings, and subsequently did: "Different Strokes in the Eastern Bloc" would appear in the *New York Times* on November 23, 1987, and later in the *International Herald Tribune*.

Both Poland and Czechoslovakia had long-established opposition movements—Solidarity in Poland and Charter 77 in Czechoslovakia. Back in the early 1980s, dissidents from both movements had braved similar dangers to meet clandestinely in the mountains at their mutual border. Now, however, their governments had gone off in very different directions.

Poland, after the government's unsuccessful efforts to crush Solidarity, was once again the freest country in the region, thanks to its active and independent Roman Catholic Church and a population known for its irreverent, irrepressible spirit. Unlike Hungary and Czechoslovakia, Communist Poland had never been invaded by Soviet troops, although the threat of such an invasion lay behind the Polish government's crackdown in December 1981.

The Czechoslovak government, far more repressive than the Polish one, was put in power after the successful crushing of the Prague Spring. It was not about to let the spirit of the 1960s resurface. It exercised tight control over the population as a whole, arresting, isolating, or ostracizing dissidents.

.   .   .

I had been told to arrive at the Warsaw airport wearing a white scarf and carrying a copy of the *International Herald Tribune* and that the person meeting me would be carrying a copy of *Elle*. Passing through customs, I was momentarily dismayed to see how many women were wearing white scarves and carrying newspapers. Then, through a glass window, I saw someone waving to me. It was a young Pole named Kris, whom I had met in New York not long before, and he was indeed carrying a copy of *Elle*. *But why? We already know and trust each other . . . I guess that's Polish humor. They like playing "cops and robbers," even when they don't have to.*

Helena Łuczywo, a longtime human rights activist whom I knew from my earliest visits to Poland, set up appointments for me and served as my constant companion and interpreter. (We never paid interpreters in those days; the activists just assumed that task, for our visits were very important to them.) Over the course of several days, Helena and I met with twenty-three different people, some more than once, representing a cross section of the dissident Polish intellectual and political elite. I was impressed with Helena's extensive contacts. She was smart and dedicated, and it came as no surprise to me some years later when she became the editor of *Gazeta Wyborcza* and made it the largest and most successful newspaper in post-Communist Eastern Europe.

"Something is changing," Helena told me. "You feel it in the air. I feel like I'm in the middle of a suspense story." The turning point had been in September 1986, when the Jaruzelski government released all its political prisoners. Now, a year after those releases, the government was engaged in a number of far-reaching economic reforms. It was promising the partial introduction of market economics, private and cooperative ownership, and worker self-management. The government was also talking about democratization and allowing considerable free discussion in the official press. People like my friend Kris were getting passports to travel abroad. The government was, in effect, cutting the ground out from under Solidarity by adopting, or promising to adopt, many of the economic and social policies advocated by the union.

The main topic of discussion at the time of my visit was Solidarity's future role—whether it should allow itself to be co-opted by the government or refuse to cooperate, no matter what. Some of the leading intellectuals in Solidarity—Adam Michnik, Jacek Kuroń, Jan Lityński—were arguing among themselves on this point, unable to agree. I could see they were confused and wary, but also flushed with the excitement of success.

Debates on the future of Solidarity were complicated by the fact that market reforms, which would most likely entail the closing of unproductive factories and lead to unemployment, were not necessarily in the immediate interests of workers. Was Solidarity exclusively a trade union representing workers, or was it rather a political and social force? Had it outlived its usefulness, now that divisions were appearing within its ranks?

Most of the people I met in Poland were so involved in their own affairs, they hardly mentioned Gorbachev. When I asked about his reforms, I was frequently reminded that the Soviet changes were "from above," whereas the initiative for reform in Poland came from below. "We're ten years ahead of the Russians," an activist lawyer told me impatiently. "Our reforms are because of Solidarity, not Gorbachev." He thought a moment, then added, "Some believe Gorbachev is because of Solidarity."

When I tried this out on Adam Michnik, Solidarity's boyish and unpredictable intellectual leader, he laughed. "Gorbachev is because of *Reagan*," he declared. Michnik read the Soviet press daily and was intrigued by superpower politics. "Reagan is the first American president that the Russians really fear," he continued. "The paradox is that *I* know it and Reagan doesn't." Michnik approved of Reagan's tough approach to the Soviets but hoped that he would also be open to the changes that were occurring under Gorbachev. "He should be tough, but also flexible," Michnik advised. *Of course Reagan is tough on the Soviets,* I thought. *He's proud of it. But can he be flexible, as Michnik suggests? Is there any reason why he should be?*

. . .

Czechoslovakia's leaders had a very different take on Gorbachev's assurances of noninterference. They saw it as license to continue their repressive policies unimpeded. At the time of my 1987 visit, they had begun to talk about "Czechoslovakia's special path."

I had discovered that I could still get visas to visit Czechoslovakia, despite my expulsion from that country in 1983. I was routinely stopped at the airport whenever I arrived in Prague, however, and subjected to a thorough search. I assumed the police were telling me that I was suspect and warning me that I would be watched.

Arriving in Prague on a crisp fall day in 1987, I soon saw that little had changed. People were being arrested while I was there, many of them young and not well known in the West. There were three house searches of Charter 77 dissident leaders that week, during which their writings, books, and typewriters were taken away. I happened to call on one of them—the philosopher and mathematician Václav Benda—the morning after his house had been searched. The apartment was in complete disarray: Books were scattered everywhere, the desk and floor were covered with papers, even the furniture seemed askew. Benda himself was not at home when I arrived: He was at the police station, trying to get a certified list of everything that had been taken. Benda's wife, Kamila, whose job prohibited her from meeting with foreigners and who had refused to see me for that reason back in 1981, was too upset to care about such technicalities. "This is our tenth house search in ten years," she told me. "When my husband was in prison and I was alone with young children, it was very upsetting. Now they are older and we have had some practice." She laughed disdainfully.

The Charter 77 activists were profoundly disappointed that the Soviet reforms had passed them by. They told me that Gorbachev's speeches were being censored in their country's official press. Their hopes had been dashed by Gorbachev's state visit to Czechoslovakia earlier that year, in April. It did not result in any positive changes or calls for increased freedom. Gorbachev had ignored requests from the Chartists to meet with him. The only sign that he may have been uncomfortable with what he saw in Prague was that he had cut his visit short by one day.

"If you expect to find any changes here as in the Soviet Union, you won't," my friend Anna Grušová told me gravely. "We are very skeptical about these new freedoms in the Soviet Union. We had the same experience nineteen years ago, in '68. . . . Anyway, it will not last long in the Soviet Union. They are just loosening the screws. The forces they are letting loose will be too frightening to them." After a moment, she added, "You can't expect anything from the Russians. They have never known freedom."

Anna and I were sitting side by side on a bench in a small park at the foot of a steep, wooded bank. On the quiet street above and behind us, I had noticed through the leafless trees two men, strolling aimlessly. I was afraid they were watching us, and although I knew it was unwise, I could not stop myself from turning around frequently to see if they were still there. Anna did not seem aware of the men or of my discomfort.

Anna looked pale, thinner than before, with dark circles under her eyes. I noticed that three of her fingernails were black and fuzzy. "It's a fungus infection," she explained self-consciously when she saw me looking at them. I shook off an irrational notion that something bad was eating away at her from within. She exuded such deep sorrow.

Anna and her husband, Josef, had separated. I was worried for her. "Are you able to support yourself at your present job?" I asked. Anna worked in an office, processing invoices and checking inventory, using an antiquated accounting system that she described as being fifty years behind the computerized West.

"Oh!" she exclaimed with a start at my inadvertent reminder. "I have to get back to work right now. I really should not have come here at all. They watch my hours. They think they have done me a favor by hiring me. . . . I suppose they have." Her voice trailed off.

"Why don't you look for another job?" I asked. "You have so many talents. You're so smart. You could use your English."

"No," she said, "the time has passed for me to make a new career. I will stick to this work until I get my pension. Nothing will ever change here."

Anna did not expect anything from Gorbachev. Soviet leaders came and went, and Czechoslovakia remained forever locked in the big bear's deadly embrace.

.   .   .

My contact in Prague had agreed to set up a meeting for me with the three current spokespersons for Charter 77. "Try to find a secure place," I had asked. Two days later I was given an address and an apartment number and told to be there at 8 p.m. that night. I didn't know whose apartment it was. It was in a part of Prague that was not familiar to me.

Setting out on foot, I found the building without difficulty. I climbed a dark staircase and rang the apartment bell. The door opened immediately. A flood of light spilled out into the shadowy hallway, framing a short, stocky, round-faced woman with thick, reddish hair, an engaging smile, and a decidedly New York accent. "You're Jeri. Hi! I'm Rita. C'mon in." *Well, I'm not the only American in Prague.* Curious, and somewhat relieved, I followed her into the living room where the three spokespersons were waiting. Rita immediately began to interpret for us, so quickly and effortlessly that it was as if we were all speaking the same language. I was impressed by her excellent Czech.

The three Charter representatives, one woman and two men, told me about themselves, their work, and specific human rights cases they were worried about. I took careful notes. Yet as we talked, with Rita confidently interpreting, I was able to carry on a separate conversation with Rita, sotto voce. I asked her, "Is this apartment bugged?" "How openly can I speak?" I didn't ask her about herself, although I wanted to. I became increasingly curious about her as the evening progressed.

At about 11 P.M., a tall, dark-haired young man entered the room and began talking quietly to Rita in Czech. She introduced him as her son, Vlaďya, and apologized for the fact that he spoke no English. It was only then that it dawned on me that Rita was not an American with perfect Czech, but a Czech who spoke classic New Yorkese. And then it all came together for me. She must be Rita Klímová, a woman I had heard about in my Amnesty group many years before. I had been given her name when I first visited Prague but never managed to make contact with her. Before the evening was over, Rita and I had discovered several mutual friends and I had heard the outlines of her life's story.

Rita's parents, both journalists, were early Communists; for a few years in the 1930s, her father was the editor of the Communist Party daily, *Rudé Právo.* One of the fortunate Jewish families to escape the Nazi occupation of Czechoslovakia, they lived out the war years with relatives in New York. Rita and I were the same age. Like me, she had spent her formative years, from eight to fifteen, as a typical New York "bobby-soxer." We may very well have rubbed shoulders at the Paramount Theater, listening to Frank Sinatra. "It was the time of my life," she told me wistfully.

After the war, Rita grudgingly returned to Prague with her family. She completed her doctorate and became a professor of economics at Charles University. She married, had two children, and was divorced in 1966; her former husband, Zdeněk Mlynář, had been a prominent member of the Dubček government and had immigrated to Vienna after the Russians invaded in 1968. Rita's second marriage to Zdeněk Klíma in 1978 ended with his death from a heart attack two years later. Her children, Vlaďya and his older sister, Milena, were both married, and Rita had several grandchildren. "I lost my university job in 1970 for 'incorrect political thinking,'" she told me. "Since then, I've stayed away from politics. I was busy raising my children. And I want to stay clean so I can go back to America . . . just once, for a visit."

.   .   .

Not long after our meeting, Rita made her long-anticipated six-week visit to New York. She walked the streets of Washington Heights, where she had once lived, looked up relatives on Long Island, and saw friends in Manhattan. She ate hot dogs and hamburgers and found them as good as she had remembered. I took her to the Broadway musical *A Chorus Line*. Other friends took her to St. John the Divine for the Blessing of the Animals. We window-shopped along Fifth Avenue. She found bargains on the Lower East Side. She loved it all. Everything about New York was thrilling to her.

Rita and I got to know each other well. She liked to gossip with me about the Czech dissidents, and her insights gave them depth and dimension. She helped us with our reports on Czechoslovakia. She spoke at a Helsinki Watch meeting one morning, where I had to assure the audience that she was really Czech. It was not just that her English was so fast and fluent but that her accent and gestures were almost a caricature of "Noo Yawk." I found it very lovable, especially because her friends in Prague told me that her speech in Czech was elegant and intellectual.

Rita and I kept up contact by telephone after she returned to Prague. Thanks to her fluency, we could speak cryptically. (She referred to Václav Havel, for example, as "my grandson's [Václav's] namesake.") She quickly became a key contact person in Prague, not just for me but for foreign journalists and other Western visitors. And I began to worry about her safety. She was playing the kind of role that Sharansky had played in Moscow, and I warned her, telling her how he had ended up in prison. Rita was not daunted. "I have my pension, my children are grown, I've had my trip to America. What do I have to lose?" She shrugged, like a true New Yorker.

33

By 1987, independent organizations were springing up throughout the Communist region. Among the most active were groups led by young people who had seized upon the two issues that would be hard to discredit: peace and the environment. Peace was traditionally espoused by all Communist governments through officially sponsored peace associations; the environment had become an undeniable issue since the May 1986 nuclear disaster in Chernobyl, which put Belorussia and Eastern Europe in the path of contamination. Although the new groups were promoting the "right" issues, the authorities distrusted them because they were independent—and because they sought contacts with like-minded groups in the West.

When the police began harassing and arresting the young activists, Helsinki Watch tried to defend them. They were part of "civil society," citizens joining together to take responsibility for the quality of their lives. We take such groups for granted in the West, but they had always been forbidden in Communist societies.

.   .   .

Cathy Fitzpatrick and Janet Fleischman—researchers on the Helsinki Watch staff—established contact with members of the new groups and attended some of their meetings. In May 1987, Janet went to Prague, where the peace movement was still quite small, and then to a seminar in Warsaw, sponsored by Freedom and Peace, a new, vibrant organization in Poland. It was the first solo mission for Janet, who had begun work as my assistant in 1983, right after she finished college, and had worked her way up to the position of researcher on Eastern Europe. Bright and outgoing, she had been eager to go into the field for some time and this seemed like an appropriate first venture. The new groups were mainly composed of young people, and Janet was more at home with them than I would have been. A new generation was coming of age—in Eastern Europe and in our office.

.   .   .

Like Janet, Cathy attended an independent peace seminar, this one in Yugoslavia, and she also met with peace activists in the Soviet Union and Hungary. A board member, Stanley Engelstein, went to East Germany where he met with peace and environmental groups. These trips culminated in a book-length report, "From Below: Independent Peace and Environmental Movements in Eastern Europe and the USSR," dealing with six countries: Czechoslovakia, East Germany, Hungary, Poland, the USSR, and Yugoslavia.

One of the peace activists mentioned in the report was Aleksandr (Sasha) Shatravka, a Soviet worker in his mid-thirties who had served more than four years of a five-year prison sentence for circulating a peace petition in his workplace in Siberia. In 1986, when the Gorbachev reforms began, Shatravka had been hastily released and exiled from his country. He arrived in New York in July wearing shabby clothes, his prison haircut not yet grown in. Cathy Fitzpatrick helped him get settled, as she often did with new arrivals. When the Lawyers Committee for Human Rights told me they wanted to honor Shatravka, among others, at their black-tie annual dinner at the Waldorf Astoria Hotel, I asked Cathy if she thought she could coax him into a suit for the occasion. It was a lot to ask—of him and of her—since he had put his trust in Cathy and might understandably feel exploited by being trotted out at a fund-raising dinner benefiting an organization he knew nothing about.

On the night of the dinner, I stood at the top of a graceful winding staircase as Cathy ascended, holding the arm of an elegant young man. It was Sasha, wearing a dinner jacket, black tie and all; he stood erect and handsome, his prisoner's haircut suddenly seeming stylishly short. He didn't take his eyes off Cathy. A year or so later, when Cathy came into my office and shyly announced she was getting married, I asked "Sasha?" She seemed surprised that I had guessed.

34

I first realized that Orville Schell was sick sometime in 1986 when he began missing the Wednesday morning Americas Watch meetings, a number of them in a row. Orville, as chair of Americas Watch, had always run those meetings with great élan. The unusual starting time, 8:50 A.M., was geared to Orville's routine of dropping his small sons off at school at the start of the day.

After a series of absences, Orville appeared one Wednesday morning, looking wan and peaked. His mind seemed to be elsewhere as he chaired the meeting, and at one point he lost his way in the agenda. That was the last time I saw him. Soon afterward he was hospitalized.

Orville died in June 1987. He was seventy-eight years old. The Orville H. Schell Jr. Center for International Human Rights at Yale Law School, which trains human rights professionals, was established in his name, as was an Orville Schell fellowship for our organization.

. . .

It was sad that Orville was not there to see our phenomenal growth over the next few years. Almost overnight we became a large organization with a multimillion-dollar budget, thanks mainly to the nonstop fundraising efforts of Bob Bernstein and Aryeh Neier. Bernstein and Neier complemented each other in their pursuit of funds, Bernstein with his uninhibited passion for our cause and Neier with his lucid explanations of our policies and practices. Our main funders were foundations, but we also began to attract significant donations from wealthy individuals. The human rights cause was really catching on. Just a dozen years before, it would have taken me some time to explain what we were about; now, when a taxi driver asked me what I did, all I had to say was "human rights work" and he would nod approvingly. And on two occasions the driver turned out to be an East European refugee who insisted that I ride free of charge.

In 1987, we moved to large offices, a whole floor on Fifth Avenue, right across from the New York Public Library. Helsinki Watch, Americas Watch, and Asia Watch were in full operation, and, with the help of a five-year grant from the MacArthur Foundation, an Africa Watch and Middle East Watch were under way. In 1988, we would create a new, overarching structure—Human Rights Watch—to oversee the regional watch committees, with Aryeh Neier as its executive director and Bob Bernstein as its chair. By 1989, ten years after we started in a four-room office on East 42nd Street with an annual budget of $200,000 and only a vague notion of what we were doing, our program would be worldwide and our budget of $4,400,000 would be quickly growing.

.   .   .

It was hard to keep up with our own growth; much of the time we didn't even try. Today we have a program department that helps plan the year's work and does the final editing of all reports and press releases. There's a legal department that scrutinizes our publications for accuracy and consistency, a communications department that edits articles and, together with our advocacy crew, makes strategic decisions as to when and where a report, release, or article should appear.

Back in the 1980s, however, we had neither the staff nor the structure for such multifaceted attempts at coordination. I filled all those roles for Helsinki Watch, making up the rules as I went along. I instituted routines, like weekly and annual staff meetings, that later became standard policy for the organization as a whole. I read, edited, and signed off on all our publications. I sent people on missions and planned missions for myself. I wrote articles and decided on my own where they should be published. I gave interviews on radio and television. I was in constant contact with the Vienna office of our International Helsinki Federation and helped in planning its programs. I had grown into my role as an executive and I liked it. I felt confident and independent running my own show. And I was doing so at an extraordinary time when both the region and our tactics were changing.

After almost a decade of hitting our heads against a brick wall, the leaders of the monolithic Soviet state were beginning to falter. They were responding—to *our* prisoner lists, *our* recommendations. We saw an opportunity to become active players in the Soviet Union and Eastern Europe and began seeking direct contacts with formerly unapproachable officials. We, and the Helsinki committees in Western Europe that we had organized, were virtually the only Western human rights groups that had been consistently involved in the region. Now everyone was turning to us—seeking our information and asking us for direction.

35

For eight years I had been denied access to the Soviet Union. In 1987, with Moscow campaigning to host a human rights conference, I decided to test its new openness by applying for a visa. I asked to visit the Moscow Book Fair in September. Bob Bernstein had received his visa without delay. I fully expected the same with mine.

Instead, I was turned down. I was bitterly disappointed. In order to do my job properly, I had to understand what was happening in the Soviet Union under Gorbachev. It was not enough to read accounts by others. I wanted to see for myself.

Publishers I knew sent telegrams to Soviet officials and to the State Department protesting my visa refusal. Roland Algrant, then chairman of the Freedom to Publish Committee, took the protest one step further. "I'm not going if you don't go," he told me . . . and he really meant it. He sent a telegram to the Soviet Embassy saying as much. "It was a great empty threat," Algrant later recalled. But the Soviets didn't see it that way. They may not have recognized his name, but he was, after all, the *chairman*. They called him and announced a "reconsideration"—my visa had been approved after all. Nicholas Veliotes, then president of the Association of American Publishers, later told me that concern over my visa denial had gone so high in the State Department that President Reagan had held up one of his speeches pending the outcome.

.   .   .

Many American publishers, intrigued by what was happening in the Soviet Union, decided to go to the book fair this time around. Some of them brought their wives. I brought along what was then a state-of-the-art Toshiba laptop computer, a $4,000 contribution from George Soros intended for a new human rights group in Moscow that I planned to check out. It was not illegal for me to bring a computer into the Soviet Union, as long as I registered it upon my arrival and brought it back out with me. But maybe I could sneak it through and leave it there; it was worth a try. On the spur of the moment, while waiting on the arrivals line in the Moscow airport, I explained the situation to one of my publisher colleagues, a woman who had not been to the Soviet Union before. She offered to carry it in with her hand luggage—and it went by unnoticed. It was a good move on my part because I was stopped at Passport Control and asked to wait for a half hour while they checked my papers, looked over my bags, and made sure that my visa had actually been approved.

I was struck by the change. In 1979, we had smuggled in down coats and warm gloves for prisoners. Now I was bringing in technology for ex-prisoners. It would be the first personal computer in dissident circles, and probably one of very few in the country as a whole. I wondered if anyone would know how to use it. It had been programmed in the Russian language, and I had memorized the start-up commands to pass on to the new owners.

.   .   .

Books were still being censored at the book fair, about forty altogether, from various countries. Twenty of them were Russian-language books published in the United States by Ardis Press, mainly novels by Soviet writers forced into exile, such as Vladimir Voinovich, Lev Kopelev, and Vasily Aksyonov. But the Western press was not much interested in censorship this time around; there was so much else to cover. The book fair officials, the same dour functionaries that I had accosted over censorship in 1979, were now conciliatory, saying how glad they were that my visa had come through and hinting they had interceded for me. They asked me not to make a fuss over books that were taken. One of them assured me, "Things will be different at the next fair."

Nevertheless, we posted a sign at our exhibit booth that read:

In the spirit of glasnost, we would like it known that twenty books have been confiscated by censors from the exhibit of an American publisher. We protest this action and any such action anywhere as contrary to the spirit and purpose of an international book fair.

The next morning the sign was missing from the locked office where we kept our things overnight. We made a new sign, larger and more conspicuous. Eventually that sign also disappeared.

.   .   .

I was eager to meet Lev Timofeyev, a journalist and economist who had been released from prison earlier that year, in February 1987, and had formed a human rights group called the Glasnost Press Club. As soon as I could arrange it, I went to his apartment in a huge housing complex on the outskirts of Moscow. I brought Bob Bernstein with me. It was the first time we had traveled together on a mission. Bob knew I had smuggled in a computer, but he was surprised when he learned that it was in the taxi with us. Later he would tell "the computer story" to friends back home, embellishing it, as is his way:

"I was in a taxi in Moscow with Jeri Laber, on our way to see a dissident named Lev Timofeyev. I said to Jeri: 'What's this I hear about you smuggling in a computer?' and Jeri said, 'It's right there under your feet—and *you're* going to carry it to Timofeyev.'"

Lev Timofeyev impressed me as a man with a strong sense of himself. In his early fifties, he was casually dressed, wearing slippers and a woolly brown sweater that seemed like an extension of his shaggy beard. His talk was expansive and jovial, in the Russian way, but the dark, brooding look in his eyes that I caught from time to time made me think that he would be quick to take offense. Although we had every reason to think that our conversation was being listened in on, Lev did not take any precautions. We spoke without constraint—no lowered voices, no scribbled messages, even when names were mentioned, or criticisms leveled, or plans for future activities were being discussed.

"It's not an organization, it's an open idea, a discussion group," Lev said, describing the Glasnost Press Club, his new organization. "We meet regularly and we invite the press." I was looking for a Russian group that would be a good affiliate for our International Helsinki Federation. The Glasnost Press Club seemed a likely prospect, especially when I learned from Lev that the Press Club, like us, had focused its attention on Shevardnadze's proposal for a human rights conference in Moscow and had set preconditions very similar to ours.

"A society that forgets that people are still in prison cannot claim to be moving toward democracy," Lev told us. He was concerned that some of the recently released prisoners were not allowed to live in Moscow and still did not have all their legal rights. He also complained that former political prisoners like himself were not being given a role by the government in the process of reform.

As we were leaving, I silently handed the computer to Lev, who later passed it on to Sergei Grigoryants, the editor of a new human rights magazine called *Glasnost*. Before I left Moscow I gave the start-up commands to a young man, somebody's son, who was puzzling over the machine. In the months that followed, we would receive smuggled out requests for cables and computer software. Known as "the first human rights computer," it would be used to publish *Glasnost* magazine for a year before it was seized by the police during a house search in 1988.

.　　.　　.

The highlight of the week was a reception we held for Soviet writers, quite unlike the one we had hosted back in 1979. Those Soviet writers who had been courageous enough to attend our 1979 dinner had to brave a cordon of secret police surrounding the restaurant in order to join American publishers in toasts to free expression. This time, no one was afraid to come. Long buffet tables in the Praga Restaurant were heaped with food and many bottles of Georgian wine. About 150 people attended. Most of them had received personal invitations, hand delivered a week in advance by Eliza Klose, the wife of a former *Washington Post* correspondent, whom I had hired to help organize the event, which she did quite openly and successfully.

The guests included prominent Soviet publishing officials and establishment writers, as well as members of the Soviet dissident intelligentsia. A number of the dissident writers, only a few months before, had been in labor camps or Siberian exile because of their writings. There were touching reunions between old friends, some of them emotionally or physically battered from their time in prison. There was also talk of those who were missing—writers who had been stripped of their citizenship and forcibly exiled abroad, and, of course, Anatoly Marchenko, who had died in prison less than a year before.

As one of several American hosts at the dinner, I found myself doing a balancing act between Party officials, who were going out of their way to be friendly to me, and the dissidents, who kept to themselves. I made a special effort to be attentive to some of the recently released prisoners who seemed uncomfortable rubbing shoulders with publishing bureaucrats. But other dissident writers, I noticed, were taking great pleasure in discussing their books with American publishers under the eyes of officials who had consistently ignored their work.

I ended that evening in the restaurant at the National Hotel, where in 1954, as an intrepid student in my early twenties, I had occupied an elegant suite. Bob Bernstein had asked me to join him and a few friends there. One of them was John Le Carré, a Knopf author. He was just beginning research for his book *The Russia House,* in which the Moscow Book Fair would figure prominently and one of the Russian villains would disparagingly refer to "the so-called Helsinki Watch."

.   .   .

A Russian Book Fair official whom I knew from before, an unpleasant man who had always followed the Party line, had become something of a joker now that humor was encouraged. "That was quite a party you had last night," he remarked the day after our reception. "On the one hand, there were writers just back from prison; on the other hand, there were people like me . . . maybe just about to go to prison."

Although we considered the dinner a success, some of our guests were skeptical. One, an unemployed literary critic, said the whole thing was a charade, demonstrating glasnost for the benefit of foreigners and the West. "Everything's changed and nothing's changed," he told me. "People who try to demonstrate are still being arrested and beaten." As if to underline his point, I found a classic KGB calling card when I returned to my room that night—a cigarette butt ground out on the carpet in the middle of the floor.

.   .   .

I left Moscow unimpressed. A lot more would have to happen before I would recommend a Moscow human rights conference. Gorbachev was a reformer, to be sure, but he had serious opposition within the Party and within society as a whole. Gorbachev was also limited by his own allegiance to the Party; his reforms were aimed at saving, not eliminating,

Soviet power. His perestroika was a policy of modernization imposed and controlled from above. It did not require democracy to succeed. It could even become a pretext for a crackdown. Lev Timofeyev had warned us about this: "Every historical theory ends in a river of blood," he said. "We know it all too well."

36

Gerald Nagler called me from Vienna one day in late September 1987, not long after my return from Moscow. He had some astounding news. "Jeri? You won't believe this. The Soviet government has invited us to Moscow! They want us to send a delegation—to talk about human rights. Early next year, in January."

Some months before, Gerald had proposed such a visit to Yuri Kashlev, the Soviet ambassador to the Vienna Review Conference, but I had not expected much to come of it. I was wrong. The news of the invitation to the International Helsinki Federation came from Kashlev himself at a September 22, 1987, press conference in Vienna.

Soviet leaders discussing human rights with a delegation of nongovernmental groups? A delegation that included Helsinki Watch, one of its harshest critics? For eight years they had ignored us and kept us from entering their country. Now they were willing to meet with us at an official level. It was astonishing. It took me back to another "first" in my experience, to that time, a year after Stalin's death, when Soviet officials offered visas to me and three other Russian Institute students to visit their closed country.

The Soviets were changing their behavior because of the human rights conference they wanted so badly. They had singled us out—the International Helsinki Federation—probably because of our high level of activity in Vienna. Western delegates to the Vienna Review Conference would be watching our visit closely. Our experience in Moscow might very well influence the Western vote in Vienna on the proposal for a Moscow conference.

After five years of hard work, our efforts to establish an independent Helsinki movement had finally paid off. Gerald Nagler and the staff had proposed the visit to Moscow and successfully lobbied for it with Soviet delegates in Vienna. Kary Schwarzenberg, as the federation's chair, had lent his prestige to the campaign; he often used the elegant Palais Schwarzenberg to entertain diplomats and engage them in discussion.

In the fall of 1987, the federation made an important decision: to invite a Soviet group—Timofeyev's Glasnost Press Club—to become a member. It would be our first member ever from a Warsaw Pact country. The Press Club agreed to join the federation in October, one month *after* the Soviets had invited us to Moscow. Although the timing was purely coincidental, Soviet officials would later charge that our federation had tricked them by not revealing that we had Russian members. We did not foresee this as a problem when we voted in the Glasnost Press Club. It turned out to be crucial once we were in Moscow.

·   ·   ·

I called Charlie right away to tell him about the invitation to Moscow. My travels were no longer a threat to our relationship. To the contrary, Charlie had become my closest confidant and was truly involved in my work. He always met me when I returned from a mission and heard my first impressions. He helped me clarify my thoughts and added his own insights. He read the articles I wrote and made helpful suggestions.

But we kept our professional lives quite separate. Charlie didn't attend my office functions, nor did I mix with the musicians, composers, and lyricists with whom he spent his time. Charlie lived in a world completely different from mine—some of his friends were his neighbors at the Boat Basin, an eccentric and interesting lot.

Living on a boat year round was not easy, especially on bitter winter days when the water pipes froze and the heating system went awry. Charlie didn't seem to mind those hardships. It was an unconventional life, a bohemian life, closer to the lives of the dissident artists and intellectuals I knew in Eastern Europe than to those of the wealthy board members in New York with whom I often socialized—the "gray suits," as the young members of our staff called them behind their backs.

I liked having a foot in both worlds, an alternate life that none of my colleagues at work even suspected. On sunny weekends I would throw on some old clothes and bring my work down to the boat, where I sat on the back deck, editing. Looking up occasionally to watch the gulls circling overhead or a huge barge moving by, I felt as far from the pace of New York City as I would in a harbor in Maine.

But I sometimes worried that I was losing Charlie, not to another woman but to a way of life that was attractive, original, and aggressively single. Would he ever want to trade that life for a more conventional life with me? I was in no position to suggest it at that juncture, yet I felt we were each becoming increasingly wedded to our very separate worlds.

.   .   .

In December 1987, a Gorbachev-Reagan summit meeting took place in Washington. Bob Bernstein and I were among some 100 guests invited by Secretary of State George Shultz to a ceremonial State Department luncheon in honor of the Gorbachevs. We entered the elegant State Department dining room and joined a long line of people waiting to shake hands with the Soviet leader.

As I approached Gorbachev on the receiving line, I prepared a few Russian sentences in my head, but at the last moment, I lost my nerve, afraid that he would answer me in Russian and I would not understand what he said. I was impressed by Gorbachev's firm handshake and the way his politician's eyes looked deeply into mine, as if we were the only two people in the room. I wondered if he looked at everyone that way or if he was focusing on my connection with Helsinki Watch. Perhaps he was thinking: "So you are the woman who has been writing all those nasty articles about me and my country."

After the luncheon, I went to see a member of Gorbachev's entourage: Professor Fyodor Burlatsky, a former Khrushchev speechwriter and an adviser to Gorbachev. He was the chairman of a new, government-endorsed human rights group, the Public Commission on Humanitarian Problems and Human Rights. We had arranged to meet at his hotel, where we carried on a pleasant enough, if somewhat vague, conversation. He told me his group was very new and included many prominent cultural figures. He said he didn't know anything about political prisoners in the USSR but would be interested to see our lists. I arranged to have them dropped off at his hotel the following day.

I found Burlatsky a bit sleazy. Perhaps it was the tasteless way in which he boasted about his accomplishments. Would he be helpful to us? Visitors to the Soviet Union traditionally needed an invitation from a counterpart group: the Academy of Sciences invited foreign scientists, the Writers Union invited foreign writers. Burlatsky's human rights group might be a source of future invitations to Helsinki Watch.

.   .   .

While I was with Burlatsky, Bob Bernstein was at the Soviet Embassy with a small group of American publishers invited to meet with Gorbachev. When we met at the D.C. airport on our way back to New York, I could see immediately that Bob was upset. He told me he had asked Gorbachev a simple question about his human rights plans. "Nothing provocative," Bob assured me, "but Gorbachev became red in the face, furious. He said he was sick and tired of being asked such questions and that Americans should look after their own human rights problems instead." I was shocked. Gorbachev's explosion seemed so out of character, especially at a time when he should have been on his best behavior.

We traveled back to New York in silence, lost in our own thoughts. Bob, I suspected, was mortified at having unwittingly disrupted a meeting of his publishing colleagues, many of whom already considered Bob a troublemaker. I felt deeply disturbed by Gorbachev's behavior. *Was this the real Gorbachev?* Despite the skeptical public posture I had taken toward the Soviet leader, I had secretly hoped he would turn out to be a genuine reformer. I must have been counting on him more than I acknowledged, even to myself. Now I didn't know what to think.

In a few weeks we would be in Moscow, meeting with top officials. Maybe then we would understand what was happening.

37

Soon after we began our meetings in Moscow, I realized we were getting a new Party line. Too many people were using exactly the same words. "We want cooperation, not confrontation" was the repeated refrain. It was a more promising line than the tired jargon of the past, but it was coming from the same officials who had been part of the Brezhnev chorus and had once sung a very different tune. I didn't believe them.

We were an international citizens' human rights group, in Moscow at the Soviet government's invitation. Our visit was important. It was covered by television and newspapers in our home countries. Delegates to the Helsinki Review Conference were watching with interest from Vienna: Our experience would influence their vote on the Soviet proposal to host a major human rights conference in Moscow.

Were the Soviet leaders sincere? Or were we just being used to further their own goals? Did they really believe that concern for human rights could be legislated from above and implemented by Party hacks who had spent their lives repressing basic freedoms?

Our delegation was composed of twenty-one private citizens from ten Western countries—Austria, Canada, Denmark, England, Germany, the Netherlands, Norway, Sweden, Switzerland, and the United States. Schwarzenberg, chairman of the International Helsinki Federation, was our leader; Bernstein, Fitzpatrick, and I were the U.S. representatives. We spent a freezing, snowy week in Moscow—from January 24 to 31, 1988—meeting face-to-face with many of the authorities who bore ultimate responsibility for the human rights abuses we deplored.

I doubt that the officials we met were told exactly what to say to us when we appealed for the release of political prisoners or for changes in the Criminal Code. They were old pros, used to catching the prevailing wind: Their pat phrases were taken from what Gorbachev and others in power were saying. Part of the "new thinking" was to speak candidly about past mistakes and the need for perestroika. "We lived through a period of stagnation," Leonid G. Sizev, the first deputy minister of the interior, told us in what was a recurring theme. "We can't solve all of our problems at one time."

Our hosts had clearly been instructed to be polite: They listened to our concerns, accepted our list of 360 political prisoners, promised to look into the matters we raised, and had no intention of following through. They sidestepped our repeated requests to visit some of the thirteen Helsinki group members who were then imprisoned in the Perm 36-1 Labor Camp in the Ural Mountains.

I didn't want our group to become docile pawns in a manipulative Kremlin game. We had to confront our hosts, to push them beyond their own limits and see what they would do. We had to challenge their glib assurances by putting them to some sort of test.

.   .   .

The issue quickly presented itself when members of our new Moscow affiliate—the Glasnost Press Club—asked to be included in our delegation on Wednesday morning, when we were scheduled to meet with the newly created—and officially sanctioned—Soviet human rights group; this was the group led by Professor Fyodor Burlatsky, the man I had met in Washington at the time of the Reagan-Gorbachev summit. Burlatsky's group, the only Soviet human rights organization that the government recognized, was what we call a "GONGO," which stands for "government-organized nongovernmental organization." The very notion of creating such a group was insulting, especially to the *real* human rights activists in the Soviet Union who had gone to prison for their activities and were now being treated as if they didn't exist.

The Glasnost Press Club had risked the possibility of arrest in becoming our affiliate. We had a responsibility to them; we had to show they were respected members of our group by bringing them with us to the Burlatsky meeting. There was also a larger issue—forcing the Soviet government to recognize them and other independent citizens' groups as a legitimate part of Soviet society.

But first I had to convince the members of our own delegation, many of whom were opposed to doing anything that would upset our Soviet hosts. There were people in our delegation I had not met before, parliamentarians and former ministers in Western governments, prestigious people who served on the boards of national Helsinki committees but were not that familiar with our tactics of confrontation. They had jumped at the opportunity to visit Moscow at an intriguing time but were less interested in the dissidents than they were in meeting Gorbachev. They knew that our chances for a Gorbachev meeting would evaporate if we were too assertive.

Confrontation was what I wanted. Hundreds of political prisoners were dying from backbreaking work in subzero temperatures while our hosts complained about how difficult it was to "solve all our problems right away." Why should we be commiserating with those "overworked" Soviet officials when their "problems" were flesh-and-blood human beings whose lives were at stake?

I hoped that our more timid delegation members would change their minds once they had actually met and talked with the Press Club's three representatives—Lev Timofeyev, Larisa Bogoraz, and Sergei Kovalev. All three had impressive backgrounds. Timofeyev, an economist and former political prisoner, was the bearded leader of the group and its spokesman. Larisa Bogoraz, the respected widow of Anatoly Marchenko, bore her hardships with a humbling dignity and stature. Sergei Kovalev, who was Sakharov's close friend and a pioneer in human rights activism, had spent ten years in prison and exile, sentenced several years before the Moscow Helsinki Group had even formed.

.   .   .

At 4 P.M. on January 25, our first full day in Moscow, we held a private meeting with the Glasnost Press Club members in Lev Timofeyev's apartment. Much to my disappointment, only thirteen of the twenty-one members of our delegation showed up. Lev had assembled a group of Soviet activists representing a variety of organizations. They told us about their activities and plans and about three separate demonstrations they would be attempting in Moscow during our visit. If there was a unifying theme to their expositions, it was their wish to create a second political force in the country, composed of "independent minds and institutions in society."

Father Yuri Edelstein, a dissident Orthodox priest with a bristly white beard, a long black cassock, and an improbable name, arrived late to the meeting. All conversation stopped when he announced to the group: "There's a car parked downstairs recording everything we are saying here. As I went by, I could hear all your voices from behind the curtains on the car windows. . . . And now," he added, "they hear *me* reporting this to you."

Within minutes of his announcement, the phone rang. It was the police, asking Lev pointed questions about his job and his wife's job, and suggesting that he go to the police station right away. Lev said he was busy and refused to go. He was calm enough while talking to the police but seemed pale and a bit shaken after he hung up the phone. Our group remained silent, taking it all in. I was shocked that the police would be so heavy-handed in front of foreigners, especially a group like ours that the government was eager to impress. Bob Bernstein kept his sense of humor. "I should have gone to Barbados," he whispered to me.

· · ·

That evening, after dinner at the hotel, we held an impromptu meeting of our delegation. I wanted everyone to agree that the Glasnost Press Club should be included in our pending meeting with the Burlatsky group. But many in the delegation seemed more opposed to it than ever. They didn't want to offend our hosts by bringing along people who were not on our initial list. They didn't want to spoil our chances of meeting with Gorbachev. "I can't believe we're talking about *manners*," I exclaimed at one point, exasperated. "Since when do the Soviets care about manners? They eavesdrop, they read people's mail, they arrest them for no reason at all. Let's remember the real issue here. It's getting recognition for a human rights group."

Someone suggested a compromise: We would make a formal request to our official hosts for the Press Club to be included in our meeting with Burlatsky; if they said it was OK, we would bring them. I went along with it. I had no choice.

The next day we met with our official hosts, the Soviet Commission on Security and Cooperation in Europe, and after a tedious forty-five-minute introduction by Mr. Tolkunov, who was officiating, we got down to business. When we raised the issue of the Glasnost Press Club, Tolkunov, caught off guard, became nervous and confused: "I know very little about them. . . . Quite frankly, we can not recognize the Press Club yet as a member of your federation. We have to think it over. They have to learn the procedures." He assured us, however, that the building where we would meet on Wednesday was "open to the public" and that "anyone can enter and take part." I hoped our delegation members would be reassured by his last statement. The rest of the day was packed with meetings, and we had no chance to confer among ourselves.

.   .   .

On Wednesday morning, Lev Timofeyev, Larisa Bogoraz, and Sergei Kovalev, dressed in their best clothes, were waiting for us in the hotel lobby. They planned to travel with us to the Burlatsky meeting. I was delighted to see them there. No one in our group would have the nerve to send them away.

But I didn't count on Labanov, a sour-looking police agent assigned as our "guide" and minder. He spotted them at once.

"He says we can't get on the bus," Lev told me.

Furious, I confronted Labanov. "They are part of our delegation," I insisted.

"*Nel'zya!* [It is forbidden]," he snapped.

Rather than start a conflict of wills, I looked him in the eye and said soberly: "Are you prepared to take full responsibility for this decision?" A shadow passed over his face and he dropped his eyes; it was as if I had struck a blow to his bureaucratic heart. He turned and headed for the telephone. By the time he rejoined us, Lev, Larisa, and Sergei were already seated on the bus.

Labanov's counterparts were waiting for us at the meeting place. They immediately tried to usher our Russian friends into the visitors' gallery and away from the long conference table, around which the Burlatsky group was already seated. About twenty journalists and several Western TV crews were milling about. We insisted that the Russians be allowed to sit with us at the table. Face-to-face with the police, our group seemed pretty much united.

I recognized Burlatsky at the head of the table, his dyed black hair slicked down for the television cameras. I headed straight to him, as the press, sensing a confrontation, turned the bright lights on us. Someone shoved a microphone between us just as I began to speak. "Please intervene, Mr. Burlatsky," I said in English. "They are trying to prevent our Russian members from sitting with us at the table." Burlatsky slowly took in the scene—the lights, the cameras, the microphone, the eager faces of the press. "Let them sit," he said magisterially, extending his hand in a magnanimous gesture.

.   .   .

For many of us, the success of the meeting, which would go on for five hours, hinged solely on whether Timofeyev, the designated speaker for the three, would be allowed to take the floor. We assumed, correctly, that Burlatsky had no intention of letting him speak. The atmosphere was incredibly charged, even more than one can glean from the taped transcript of the meeting, which was subsequently printed in the *New York Review of Books*. As Burlatsky and his colleagues droned on, introducing themselves and describing the work of their committee, we were planning our strategy, frantically passing notes back and forth to each other at our end of the table. Lev sat at my left, rigid, controlled, looking uncomfortable in his three-piece tweed suit. He had probably been awake a good part of the previous night preparing the remarks that he now wanted to deliver.

Kary Schwarzenberg, seated at my right, was ill at ease. Fully in sympathy with what we were attempting, he was at the same time the chairman of our delegation and bore the ultimate responsibility for our actions. Kary was by nature nonconfrontational. I understood: At an earlier time in my life, I was the one who was always conciliatory, trying to smooth things over. Suddenly Kary was summoned from the table by the KGB people who were watching us from the sidelines. When he returned, he told me the police had threatened to cancel the rest of our visit. I still have a note in my handwriting that I passed around at that point: "They have threatened Kary—if Lev speaks—We can't back off now."

When Burlatsky called on Irwin Cotler of the Canadian Helsinki Committee, Cotler asked that Timofeyev be given the floor in his stead. Burlatsky became incensed. "What are we up to? What do we want? A scandal, a confrontation? A show?" He said that he did not know the group and that "it is our prerogative to meet with those we invite." He then called upon one of *his* colleagues, who made a long and boring speech.

Kary Schwarzenberg, the next speaker, returned to Burlatsky's outburst, assuring him that we did not want a "show." He spoke softly and politely, as was his way. "We know the members of the Press Club. They are very knowledgeable and sincere persons who have suffered a lot."

Burlatsky heard him out, then quickly passed the floor to his own colleague, Mr. Nazarov. His intentions were clear: to ignore our requests and keep calling on other people. We looked at each other in dismay. *What now?* Nazarov had already taken the microphone.

Suddenly I heard myself shouting: "Point of order, Mr. Chairman." Burlatsky turned to me, startled, and I began to speak.

"I believe our chairman has made a request for the Glasnost Press Club to make a short presentation of their activities," I said. "They are members of our organization and they are part of us. I must say that I am surprised to hear that you do not know them. Last month they organized a seminar that was discussed in the press all over the world. But if you indeed do not know them, then I believe that this is an excellent opportunity to become acquainted with them."

Burlatsky then made an appeal to manners, pointing out that the group was not on our initial list of members. "It is not exactly polite to settle the matter by force," he said. "It is like forcing a bride on us in a marriage we do not want."

There were a few more exchanges, then Burlatsky, quoting Mao Zedong, pronounced: "The sky will remain clear, the birds will go on flying, the fish will keep swimming in the river if Timofeyev speaks." Then, sarcastically: "Let the cameras roll—everyone on Timofeyev."

Timofeyev did not disappoint. He was dignified and eloquent. He talked about the human rights movement in the Soviet Union, "groups that have been in existence ever since the Helsinki accords were signed." He gave the Burlatsky commission a list of political prisoners and a fifty-page report prepared by his group. He said that he regretted the reaction they had received: "Our task should be to recapture a common definition of words like 'freedom,' 'rights,' 'love,' and others expressing human values. Without a common ground, freedom and disarmament will not be possible."

.   .   .

Sergei Kovalev, who had sat silently during the Burlatsky meeting, had a negative take on it all when we saw him and Sakharov at dinner the following evening. "Our officials will capitalize on how well it all worked out, how willing they are to meet with us," he said. "But they are not honest, not acting in good faith."

A few days later, when Bernstein and I met privately with Burlatsky, he began by trying to establish how liberal he was: He told us that, as a Khrushchev man, he had lost jobs three times in his career for political reasons. Then he went on to advise us: "If you want to have *real* influence, you must deal with *our* group, not the Glasnost Press Club. Here we have really *famous* people." He was chiding us for consorting with former prisoners.

Burlatsky may have been a "liberal" in the Soviet context but he had apparently absorbed the values of the Communist elite. He looked down on *zeks,* former political prisoners like Kovalev; they were tainted, in his eyes, by the indignities they had suffered in the camps. It is one thing to lose your job for being aligned with someone who falls out of favor; it is another to go to prison for acting on your ideals. Despite temporary setbacks, Burlatsky had moved ahead in the system, while people like Kovalev were marginalized.

All this was apparent to me at the time, but I remained eager to develop a working relationship with his commission nonetheless. I wanted to prod them to do some real work. At the very least, I wanted their help in enabling us to send our own fact-finding missions to the USSR. When I suggested that his group meet with Helsinki Watch in New York, he was quick to agree, but suggested that we meet halfway.

"Where?" I asked.

"How about Paris?" he replied, "sometime in the spring."

.   .   .

We approached the Paris meeting, in May 1988, with cautious optimism. We wanted to do some serious negotiating with the Russians and to get them to follow through on our requests. We thought that once they were outside their country, they would be more relaxed, more open to our concerns. In addition to staff members and several lawyers on our board, we brought along Lyuda Alexeyeva, our consultant who had represented the Moscow Helsinki Group abroad for more than a decade.

But the Russians were mainly on a jaunt to Paris. At our meetings each day, they were aggressive: They kept trying to shift the conversation to prisoners in the United States, raising obscure cases they knew and cared little about. At night it was different. Having arrived in Paris with almost no spending money—there were limits on the amount of hard currency that could be taken out of the Soviet Union—they were happy to have us host them night after night at good French restaurants, where they shamelessly gorged themselves, ordering the most expensive wines and dishes on the menu.

Lyuda Alexeyeva was in tears at the end of one such evening. "They aren't what they claim to be," she lamented. "They're the same old Soviet bureaucrats. They have no interest in human rights." I could see how they patronized Lyuda, who was their antithesis in every way. Despite her many years in the United States, Lyuda remained very much a Russian in her appearance, concerns, and ties to her homeland, whereas they, many of them traveling abroad for the first time, put on Western airs.

At our very last encounter, Burlatsky reprimanded us: Our delegation, it appeared, was not "high level enough" for theirs, which included a "famous writer" (Vladimir Dudintsev, not exactly a household name) and other members of the Soviet establishment. "Next time," he said, "you should bring your *famous* people." He was referring, I suppose, to Arthur Miller and other luminaries whose names he had seen on our letterhead.

· · ·

Did we gain anything from our association with the Burlatsky commission? Very little, it turned out. Burlatsky and his colleagues, ineffectual figures in a period of transition, soon faded into obscurity. It was Sergei Kovalev, the former *zek* they disdained, who would take up where Burlatsky had failed. Kovalev would become a member of Parliament in 1990, chairman of the first presidential human rights committee, and, in 1993, Russia's first human rights ombudsman.

38

Our trip to Moscow had unexpected consequences elsewhere in the Soviet bloc. East European authorities, taking their lead from Moscow, felt obliged to meet with us. Like the Soviets, they set up GON-GOs, official human rights groups that would be our hosts. I seldom traveled alone and incognito in the late 1980s. Most of my trips were with others from the International Helsinki Federation; we traveled openly and requested meetings with the heads of various ministries.

But we refused to be co-opted by them for their own propaganda purposes. Turning Gorbachev's slogan on its head, we sought confrontation, not cooperation. We were constantly thinking up ways to push the limits of official tolerance and to be a bridge between the dissidents and their governments.

Our triumph in Moscow—when we forced the Burlatsky commission to accept our dissident colleagues—was part of a new strategy. It was a risky strategy, for we were prepared to be arrested for what we were doing. Together with local human rights groups, we organized meetings, seminars, and conferences on forbidden topics. Like free people in a free society, we held them openly in public places, daring the government to stop us.

Our new approach was actually not so new. I could trace it back to 1979, to the dinner for dissident writers that we had held in Moscow under KGB eyes, and to the unofficial cultural meeting we had organized in Budapest in 1985. But our efforts to confront the authorities were now accelerating rapidly. In 1988, we had a real triumph when we joined

Zbyszek Romaszewski and other Polish activists in organizing an international human rights meeting in Cracow: It was larger and more freewheeling than anything previously seen in the Communist bloc, with 1,100 participants, including 240 foreigners. The police did nothing to prevent it.

.   .   .

In November 1988, Czech dissidents announced a human rights seminar in Prague. They were trying to copy the Polish conference in Cracow, though on a much smaller scale. Twenty foreigners arrived, only to learn the police had arrested thirty-eight potential Czech participants in their homes the night before. Václav Havel, who had not stayed at home the previous night, showed up at the appointed time, but he had barely managed to open the meeting when the police arrived and arrested him unceremoniously on the spot. The seminar never took place. The Western participants spent the next few days issuing protests that were ignored, while the arrested Czechs and Slovaks were held in detention for four days.

.   .   .

I arrived in Prague a few days after the failed seminar and went straight to Rita Klímová's apartment. It was a tense time for me, the time I illegally carried in a large sum of money to give to the newly formed, underground Helsinki Committee. Rita was its secretary. I was counting on her to take the money off my hands, which she did expeditiously, burying it at the bottom of her daughter's laundry basket, which was quickly removed from the premises.

I asked Rita to set up a meeting for me with Václav Havel. It would be my first meeting with the playwright who was Czechoslovakia's best-known dissident. Havel had either been in prison during my visits to Prague or at his country house in Hrádeček, where he sought solitude in order to write. I didn't want to disturb him without good reason.

In 1988, I had a reason. Human Rights Watch was planning a tribute to human rights monitors worldwide, and Havel was our choice to represent Czechoslovakia. I knew Havel would not come to New York. He had turned down other invitations to go abroad, convinced that he would not be allowed to return home. But I hoped to persuade him to write a few words that I would read aloud at the event. As it turned out, Havel had a better plan.

.   .   .

We met at his favorite haunt in Prague, a small restaurant with red tablecloths, facing the Vltava River at the foot of the embankment outside his apartment building. Havel, whose English was not that good, had persuaded Rita to come along to interpret. She was somewhat intimidated by Havel at that first meeting, which was the beginning of their friendship. Later, he called on her frequently to interpret during his meetings with English speakers. She became his voice to the English-speaking world.

We spent several hours at Havel's regular table as various friends of his came and went. One of them was Jáchym Topol, a young man in his early twenties, who, it turned out, was Havel's choice to represent him at the Human Rights Watch event. Jáchym, who spoke some English but had never traveled outside of Czechoslovakia, had long blond hair and a sulky, 1960s "counterculture" charm. He was a writer, the son of Josef Topol, a poet and playwright who was one of Havel's closest friends. Havel, who had no children of his own, seemed to see Jáchym as a surrogate son. He was enchanted by his own inspiration in picking a young Czech "beatnik" to represent him at our New York tribute. Havel has a gift for ironic casting that he would later have good opportunities to employ.

The counterculture had great appeal for Havel and others of his generation who lived with vibrant memories of the 1960s, the time of the Prague Spring. His choice of Jáchym as his representative may also have reflected his belief that a new generation would lead Czechoslovakia out of the abyss.

Jáchym was by far the youngest of the "monitors" we honored in New York that December. He was enthralled at first sight when he entered our office—"so many beautiful young women, all working for human rights!"—and his offbeat manner endeared him to our staff. But not to Kary Schwarzenberg, who happened to be in New York at that time. Kary, trained in the ways of the Czech nobility, was not charmed by Jáchym's casual style. I spotted Kary and Jáchym one day in a restaurant near our office, seated at a table in a far corner, deeply absorbed in conversation. Later, Jáchym told me that Kary had lectured him on his dress and manners and presented him with several shirts and ties from Brooks Brothers that he was instructed to wear.

.   .   .

Although Havel was small, soft-spoken, and unassuming, there was an air of authority about him as well. I was aware of it from our very first meeting, in the restaurant down at the river. We spoke about the failed seminar and his subsequent four-day arrest. He said that the seminar would remain "indefinitely open" until it could meet without pressure. He seemed triumphant that he had managed to open the meeting before he was seized by the police: "I pissed over them," was his proud remark.

Havel asked me to attend a rock concert with him that evening. Although the authorities had recently tolerated two rock concerts in Prague, that evening's concert had strong political undertones. At midnight, a group called Midnight was to perform, and its members planned to preface their performance with an appeal on behalf of a rock hero, Ivan Jirous, a poet and art critic who was then in prison facing trial for having authored a political petition. The police had warned the group not to talk about Jirous. Everyone was expecting a showdown. Havel told me where the concert would be held, and we agreed to meet there at an appropriate time.

It was a cold, smoggy night. The taxi driver seemed unhappy about my destination and was eager to drop me off as soon as possible in the dark street where a crowd was milling about, waiting for the doors of the hall to open. I spotted Havel and his entourage, a group that included his brother, Ivan, Ivan's wife, Daša, and several others I knew. Havel was with a pretty woman, someone I had met during my very first visit to Prague. The rest of the crowd seemed considerably younger than the Havel contingent—there were many young men in their twenties with long, untrimmed beards and shoulder-length hair, gaunt, Christ-like figures in worn blue jeans. Havel seemed to be on friendly terms with many of them. He was treated with casual familiarity mixed with respect—for his writings, I assumed, and for his political courage.

I would never have survived the crush to get into the hall if Havel had not put his arm around me and escorted me in. Once inside, however, I lost him to the crowd, which danced in the smoky, strobe-lit, chairless auditorium, moving wildly to the beat, the singing, and the relentless noise.

It was a throwback to the 1960s, a time I also remembered fondly, but I felt awkward standing there, my foot tapping, without a partner. I met someone I knew from the U.S. Embassy and was grateful when he offered me a ride back to my hotel. When I left, at about 11:30 P.M., Havel was still dancing in the crowd. I never found out whether the controversial midnight appeal was made for Ivan Jirous. Some months later, however, I was an observer at Mr. Jirous's trial.

. . .

The day after the concert, I made another new acquaintance in Prague—Jan Urban, a newcomer to the dissident movement who had signed Charter 77 less than a year before. I asked him why he had decided to sign at that late date, knowing he would be targeted by the police. "I thought it over before I went to Moscow," he told me. "I expected to be arrested when I returned."

Jan had managed to attend the Glasnost Press Club's unofficial seminar in Moscow in December 1987. He had been a celebrity there, it was so rare that a Czech dissident could travel abroad.

We talked in Urban's simply and tastefully furnished apartment on Thunovská Street, in the shadow of Prague Castle. He was thirty-seven at the time, clean-cut and good-looking, the father of two young girls. His English was perfect and his manner sincere and appealing. He told me his father had been the Czechoslovak ambassador to Finland but had fallen into disfavor. He had died of a heart attack earlier that year after two upsetting interrogations by the secret police. Jan, who used to teach history, now worked as a bricklayer.

"After all these years of being under water, it was wonderful to speak openly and to see that these people thought like me," Jan told me, describing his reaction to the Moscow dissidents. The Russian organizers, afraid that Jan would be arrested when he returned home, brought him to meet Andrei Sakharov while in Moscow. Sakharov subsequently let it be known that Urban was his friend and made a point of phoning Urban in Prague on several occasions after his return. Only a year after his own release from house arrest in Gorky, Sakharov had the moral authority to protect others, even in another country. Jan told me that recently, during an interrogation, one of the security men growled at him: "If you didn't have your Sakharov!"

"I don't know if you fully understand the importance of this one particular man," Jan told me, "not only for the Soviet Union, but for Czechoslovakia. The regime here would smash him in a second if he were Czech."

39

O n New Year's Eve, at the close of 1988, I gave a big party in my apartment to celebrate Pam's marriage to Miguel Cerdera, whom she had met two years before in southern Spain. We served tapas and a Spanish-style buffet, prepared by Pam and Miguel themselves. The house was lit by many candles, and I blanketed the high ceiling of the living room with silver-spangled helium-filled balloons. The next day, with the balloons half-descended, I relaxed amid the postparty chaos. It was New Year's Day, the culmination of an eventful year. I thought back on all that had happened in 1988.

A new era of détente had begun as the United States and the USSR agreed to substantial reductions of their nuclear arsenals. Gorbachev and Reagan had become friends. In May 1988, during a Moscow summit, Reagan, in a remarkable about-face, announced that the Soviet Union, which he had earlier christened the "evil empire," had changed. Many credited Reagan with that change, a much too simple explanation. Gorbachev was being driven by many forces, including the Soviet Union's economic crisis and the attendant need to cut back on military spending.

One of Reagan's finest moments had occurred during the Moscow summit in May, when, standing under a statue of Lenin, he gave a stirring speech at Moscow State University about democracy and freedom: "Democracy is one of the most powerful movements of our age. . . . Freedom is the recognition that no single person, no single authority or government has a monopoly on the truth, but that every individual life is infinitely precious, that every one of us put in this world has been put there for a reason and has something to offer."

He referred to the new freedom in the air, to the "accelerated rhythm of hope, when the accumulated spiritual energies of a long silence yearn to break free."

.   .   .

In June, Gorbachev had called a special All-Union Communist Party Conference, the first since 1941. He appeared to have triumphed over his foes in the Party when the participants in the conference, who were elected outside the usual bureaucratic structures, supported his call for Party democratization and the rule of law in the Soviet Union and endorsed a complete overhaul of the Soviet system.

.   .   .

In November, Andrei Sakharov had been given permission to travel abroad for the first time. He was the guest of honor at a special Helsinki Watch meeting in New York on November 11, where he spoke for about two hours, giving his views on Gorbachev's reforms and describing the unrest among Soviet nationalities. Sakharov warned against Gorbachev's "unlimited power" and cautioned us against overvaluing his accomplishments. Like many thoughtful Russians at that time, he was upset by the "Gorby-mania" he saw in the West and pointed out that Gorbachev was more popular in the United States than he was at home. His advice to Reagan echoed words I had heard before—from Adam Michnik in Warsaw: "Be firm and principled, but flexible." "Firm but flexible" was, in fact, a good description of Reagan's approach to Gorbachev.

.   .   .

As the year was drawing to a close, columnist and former executive editor of the *New York Times* Abe Rosenthal, known for his strong anti-Communist stands, had been invited to visit Perm 35, a labor camp in the heart of the snow-covered Ural Mountains, about 900 miles or so east of Moscow, where some of the last remaining political prisoners were being held. No Westerner had been given this opportunity before. Rosenthal called Helsinki Watch for information, and Cathy Fitzpatrick and I went to his office to brief him. Impressed with Cathy's encyclopedic knowledge of political prisoners in the USSR, Rosenthal arranged to have her accompany him on the trip, which took place in December. As with most such "breakthroughs," the Soviets carefully controlled their American visitors, never allowing them to speak privately with any of the prisoners. Only one prisoner, consigned to the infirmary to keep him quiet, managed to shout a few words of complaint to them through a barred window. Nevertheless, the visit was important and set the stage for future prison visits by foreign experts. And a year or so later, the prisoners in question would all be free.

I was spellbound by Cathy's report when she returned from the heart of Russia, her description of the long drive from Perm to the labor camp, of the barren wilderness, the snow-swept landscape, the horse-drawn sleighs. This was the Russia that had captivated me as a child, unchanged over centuries. It was the Russia where my grandmother, a young girl skating on a frozen pond, had broken her hip and disfigured her body. The Russia of Pushkin, Tolstoy, and Nabokov that had called out to me so movingly. Mother Russia—beautiful, mysterious, cruel, sad.

.   .   .

By the end of 1988, 600 political prisoners on our lists had been released. The remaining 140 were people who had been convicted under nonpolitical articles of the Criminal Code, and the Soviets had agreed to examine these cases individually in bilateral talks with U.S. officials.

During 1988, more than 80,000 people of all nationalities had been allowed to emigrate, as compared to 2,000 in 1986. The jamming of all radio stations, including Radio Liberty and Radio Free Europe, had ended. Gorbachev had announced that he would reduce Soviet forces in Eastern Europe by 500,000 troops and 10,000 tanks. He had also promised to withdraw all Soviet troops from Afghanistan by February 15, 1989.

Reforms we had demanded as conditions for the Moscow human rights conference—the release of political prisoners, free emigration, and an end to the jamming of foreign radio stations—had actually come to pass.

.   .   .

Speaking for Helsinki Watch and the International Helsinki Federation, I wrote an article that appeared in the November 16, 1988, issue of the *International Herald Tribune*. In it I endorsed the proposal to hold a human rights conference in Moscow: "A Moscow human rights conference would . . . give the Soviet people a forum for discussing their government's past, present and future human rights practices. It would allow an infusion of Western ideas and values, including the concept that respect for human rights cannot merely be legislated from above but requires the active participation and vigilance of private citizens."

.   .   .

On January 15, 1989, the Helsinki Review Conference in Vienna finally ended, after more than two years of continuous meetings. As part of its Concluding Document, the thirty-five participating nations, impressed by the changes in the USSR and looking ahead to still more, agreed to hold a human rights conference in Moscow. They scheduled it for September 1991.

PART V

Beyond Our

Wildest Dreams

(1989–1991)

40

Within one monumental year—1989—Communist rule in Eastern Europe ended. It collapsed in six countries—Poland, Hungary, East Germany, Bulgaria, Czechoslovakia, and Romania—like a mockery of the domino theory that had guided U.S. foreign policy for so many years. Instead of countries successively falling under the *sway* of communism, as the U.S. government had feared would happen in Asia and Latin America, the countries of Eastern Europe fell *away* from communism, one by one.

Events in Eastern Europe also disproved the "Kirkpatrick doctrine" that the Reagan administration had so eagerly embraced—the belief that totalitarian Communist governments were impervious to peaceful change. Repressive systems that were considered immutable capitulated with hardly a struggle in the face of popular revolutions that were, with the exception of Romania, astonishingly peaceful.

There is poetic irony in the fact that the downfall of East European communism was brought about by the very masses whose interests the Communists purported to serve but whose allegiance they were unable to win. Ordinary people, hundreds of thousands of them, rose up in huge demonstrations against their Soviet-imposed rulers, and the former dissidents, who had felt so isolated, were catapulted into leadership. Emboldened by Gorbachev's "new thinking" and his assurances that the Soviet Union would not interfere in their internal politics, the countries of Eastern Europe held multiparty elections and, in another irony of the era, quickly outdistanced the Soviet Union in their reforms.

It was a stirring time, but also a sad one for some, an occasion for anger and bitterness. People were forced to acknowledge that the sacrifices and

deprivations they had lived with for so many years were for nothing, that
the Communist movement itself had been a failure. Their disillusionment
was expressed in a sardonic joke that made the rounds in 1989.

Question: What is communism?
Answer: The longest and most difficult path from capitalism to capitalism.

.   .   .

Not surprisingly, it was in Poland that the dramatic events of 1989 first
played out. After eight weeks of roundtable talks between Solidarity and
the government, the parties agreed in early April to hold a controlled, prearranged election in June. Solidarity would be allowed 35 percent of the
seats in the lower house of the Parliament. The upper house of Parliament, known as the Senate, would be restored and the senators would be
freely elected. The heated debates I had witnessed in Poland in the fall of
1987—whether Solidarity should stand alone or agree to work with the
government—had been resolved in favor of cooperation, for Solidarity
was agreeing to participate in elections that the Communist government
would control. Adam Michnik and Helena Łuczywo, the principled editors of the underground newspaper *Tygodnik Mazowsze,* also made an
arrangement with the government: They would be the editors of a new,
legal newspaper, *Gazeta Wyborcza,* even though it would be subject to government censorship. Helena was quoted in the *New York Times* on April
21: "You give up something to get something. It's a calculation."

As it turned out, it was an astute calculation. With *Gazeta Wyborcza* promoting the Solidarity slate, Solidarity swept the June elections, claiming
99 of the 100 seats in the Senate as well as its guaranteed 35 percent of
the lower house. Even more telling, almost none of the unopposed Communist candidates received the 50 percent necessary to be elected in the
first round of balloting. It was a complete triumph for Solidarity. By
August, there would be a Solidarity prime minister, Tadeusz Mazowiecki,
the first non-Communist government leader in Eastern Europe since the
Communists took over.

.   .   .

I went to Poland in April 1989 for a meeting of our International
Helsinki Federation. Planning a meeting in Warsaw was part of our new

strategy of confrontation: Would the Polish government allow us to meet there? By the time the meeting date came around, however, the barriers we had been planning to push had already collapsed. We were greeted with fanfare at the airport by members of the no-longer-underground Polish Helsinki Committee, who had prepared banners and badges for the participants and had set up appointments for us with important government officials.

The meeting turned into an open celebration when the Council of Europe announced that its 1989 Human Rights Prize would have two recipients: Lech Wałęsa and the International Helsinki Federation. Wałęsa and other Solidarity luminaries joined us at a festive Saturday night dinner at which we toasted each other and the success of the international Helsinki movement.

I was especially touched by Adam Michnik's speech at the dinner: "You supported us when we were in prison; I won't forget that." I knew he was referring to the U.S. Helsinki Watch—we had sent observers to his trial—and to the special trip I had made to see him in Warsaw in September 1984, right after his release from prison. I had used the occasion to make arrangements with Michnik for another surreptitious meeting, this one with Jonathan Fanton, then president of the New School for Social Research in New York. Fanton had asked me to inform Michnik that he would be the recipient of an honorary degree from the New School and to set up a meeting in Warsaw at which Fanton would present the degree. Speaking softly and passing notes to each other, Michnik and I set a time and place for the presentation. Jonathan Fanton subsequently traveled to Warsaw with several members of the New School board and presented the degree to Michnik. Under Fanton, the New School developed an extensive program for East European scholars, many of them dissident thinkers who were ostracized in their own countries.

Arranging the Michnik award was the beginning of my friendship with Jonathan Fanton, who would become a vice chair of Helsinki Watch later that year, and the chair in 1992.

.   .   .

Changes in Hungary in 1989 were as significant as those in Poland. They began with the ouster of János Kádár, Hungary's manipulative Party leader. Kádár had developed his own special leadership style: He had allowed some measure of economic freedom over the years, including private enterprises and a decontrolled yet state-managed economy. Whenever possible, he had used economic rather than political pressure to keep dissent under control. Hungarian dissidents, on the whole, were not threatened with prison; they were fined instead or they lost their jobs, status, and livelihood.

Kádár had been installed by the Soviets after they crushed the 1956 Hungarian revolution, in which ordinary Hungarians, believing the West would support them, had waged a heroic, doomed struggle against Soviet tanks in the streets of Budapest. Thousands of people had died, and nearly 200,000 had fled the country. The Hungarian revolution was a pivotal, disillusioning event for the entire region, a warning that the Soviet Union would use force to suppress uprisings and that the West could not be counted on to intervene.

Gorbachev's pledge to stay out of Eastern Europe put Hungarian leaders on the alert, especially reformers in the Party who sensed the inevitability of change. Eager to hang on to power, they removed the ailing Kádár from leadership in May 1988. After thirty-two years of rule, he was replaced as Party leader by Károly Grosz, also a conservative.

With Kádár out of the way, his former colleagues were free to bring some glasnost to a long-suppressed national tragedy. They allowed the rehabilitation and formal reburial of Imre Nagy and his close associates, reform-minded Communists who had led the 1956 revolution. Nagy had been betrayed by the nefarious Kádár, who promised him safety but instead imprisoned him and ultimately had him hanged in 1958 and buried in an obscure grave. The timing of Nagy's reburial was symbolic, for it occurred as Kádár lay dying. Kádár's death a few weeks later seemed emblematic of the death of Hungarian communism.

The daylong Nagy ceremony in Budapest on June 16, 1989, drew a crowd officially estimated at 100,000 and was televised throughout the country. It was a catalyst for the expression of long-suppressed rage. It put Party officials on notice that their efforts to control reform from above were doomed.

The public eulogies for Nagy and his executed colleagues were breathtaking in their harsh criticism of the current leaders. Viktor Orbán, speaking for the Federation of Young Democrats, praised Nagy as "a Communist [who] identified with the wishes of the Hungarian nation to put an end to the Communist taboos, blind obedience to the Russian empire and the dictatorship of a single party." He went on to say, "We cannot understand that those who were eager to slander the revolution and its prime minister have suddenly changed into great supporters and followers of Imre Nagy."

Mária Kovács, one of the four dissident intellectuals whom I had helped get passports after my first visit to Budapest back in 1981, described the occasion to me in great detail when I saw her later in New York. Marble columns were draped in black, and modern structures were built to display the coffins amid huge flaming torches. The names and ages of 260 executed victims were read aloud by two actors. The event was designed and staged by our mutual friend, the dissident architect László Rajk, whose Communist father had been betrayed by Kádár and executed as a traitor during the Stalinist purges of 1949.

Soon after the Nagy funeral, the Hungarian Communist Party came under the control of a four-person presidium in which Party leader Grosz was the only nonreformer. Talks began between the Party and the opposition and continued through the summer. The Party pressed for Polish-style controlled elections, but the opposition held out for a national referendum. The referendum, ultimately held in November, would endorse free, multiparty elections to take place in March and April of 1990. Meanwhile, Communist Party leaders, fearing failure at the polls, would dissolve the party in October and rename it the Hungarian Socialist Party. While they were at it, they changed the name of the Hungarian People's Republic to the Hungarian Republic. The Communists' misuse of words had been so Orwellian that it was only by removing the word "people" from the country's name that Hungary could once again belong to its people.

.   .   .

For a while, it looked like the developments in Poland and Hungary were being mirrored in distant China. When Mikhail Gorbachev arrived in Beijing in May, he found himself being hailed by demonstrating students as a leader of democracy. Most of them presumably did not know that Gorbachev did not tolerate demonstrations at home. Any protests against authority—in Moscow or elsewhere in the Soviet Union—were quickly put down by the police.

Gorbachev, in China for talks on restoring governmental relations, avoided any direct encouragement of the demonstrations. Yet he stated publicly on several occasions that economic change was impossible without political reform and gave an interview on May 17 that must have heartened the demonstrators. "I am convinced that we are participating in a very serious turning point in the development of world socialism," he said. "All Communist countries are headed at different paces toward greater freedom of expression, democracy and individual rights. These processes are painful, but they are necessary."

On the day of the Gorbachev interview, more than a million Chinese were marching in support of hunger-striking students in Tiananmen Square. A few days after Gorbachev's departure, the Chinese government brought troops into Beijing. Two weeks later, on June 4, the troops attacked, crushing the demonstration, killing hundreds of protesters and arresting many thousands more in the months that followed. Robin Munro, a member of our Asia Watch staff, was in Tiananmen Square when the tanks rolled in. His accounts appeared in Asia Watch reports and were later published as a book, *Black Hands of Beijing*, which he wrote with a colleague, George Black.

.   .   .

A small dinner I gave on Charlie's birthday, on July 2, 1989, turned into a double celebration. Halfway through the meal, I received a call from New Haven, where Pam and her husband, Miguel, were living while she finished graduate school at Yale. "Mom?" It was Pam. "You have a beautiful new granddaughter, Ariana Elena." It was a special moment—Pam's first child, born on Charlie's birthday. We drank toasts to Ariana and Charlie, and I decided to leave for New Haven first thing the next morning. Underlying my happiness was a deep sense of relief at the timing: I could be there with Pam as I wanted to be, not off in the field on a mission or detained by some pressing demand at work.

After dinner, we moved outside to the terrace, where I sat with Lawrie, Charlie's wise and wonderful father, whose wife, Sal, had recently died. It was a lazy summer evening, and our talk meandered, settling finally on what was happening in the Soviet Union and Eastern Europe. Although some of the most dramatic events of 1989 were yet to come, there was already plenty for us to marvel at.

Lawrie, who had been born in Boston in 1901, remembered the 1917

Russian revolution that had shaped so much of his century. Now it seemed his life might span both the birth and the *death* of Soviet communism. "You know, Jeri," Lawrie said after a few moments of quiet. "Sometimes, when Sal was alive, we would look back on life and say how content we were. We had done everything we wanted to do, we had no regrets. We didn't want to die, of course, but we were ready. We felt we had seen everything. . . . But *this*—" he held out his arms as if to encompass the entire Soviet bloc, "this is worth staying alive for."

41

By the summer of 1989, the countries of Eastern Europe could be grouped on one or the other side of the divide between reform and repression. Communism was on its way out in Poland and Hungary, but elsewhere in the bloc, repression was intensifying. Although now, with hindsight, there is an inevitability about the sequential fall of communism in Eastern Europe, at the time things were not so clear. A million people had demonstrated in Tiananmen Square, only to be crushed. The same thing could happen elsewhere.

The security police in East Germany, Czechoslovakia, Bulgaria, and Romania were abandoning their quiet, sinister presence in favor of a blatant show of force. They were beating and arresting demonstrators, using tear gas, water hoses, and police dogs to subdue them in the streets. Gradually I came to see that these ruthless tactics by the police were actually a sign of their weakness when faced with increasing unrest. We were seeing the bared fangs of cornered animals.

· · ·

Eastern Europe was a house of cards, more interrelated than I had realized. A decision by Hungary in May—to remove the barriers at its border with Austria and allow Hungarians to travel to the West—led to a series of events that snowballed out of control. The Hungarian government was trying to appease its own citizens: It assured its neighbors that it was easing travel restrictions only for Hungarians. But many East Germans traveled to Hungary for their summer holidays and then refused to go home. They became refugees in Hungary, hoping to cross the newly opened border and make their way to West Germany. These refugees were not, on the whole, political dissidents. Many of them were young and educated, with skills that could be used in the West. They were tired of police surveillance, economic shortages, and the privileges of the Party elite. They were looking for a better life in prosperous West Germany, part of their own country that was closed off to them, for some since before they were born.

On September 10, the Hungarian government went back on its word and opened the border to the East German refugees. In the first few days, some 15,000 East Germans traveled to Austria and on, and tens of thousands more followed them in the next few weeks. East German leaders were furious. They barred their citizens from traveling to Hungary, but it was too late to stem the tide.

East Germans had also been flocking to Czechoslovakia—starting in mid-August and continuing into September and October—even though the Czech borders to the West were firmly sealed. They took refuge in the overcrowded gardens of the West German Embassy in Prague, abandoning their cars and possessions as they dashed inside the embassy gates. The Czech police attacked the German asylum seekers with clubs and engaged them in hand-to-hand fighting in efforts to keep them off the embassy grounds.

On October 1, West German foreign minister Hans-Dietrich Genscher, after conducting separate talks at the United Nations with the foreign ministers of East Germany, Czechoslovakia, and the Soviet Union, announced a compromise. He arrived in Prague and told a cheering crowd of more than 5,500 East German asylum seekers that they were free to travel to West Germany by train. The train would travel through East German territory, so that the East German government could save face by taking away citizenship papers and officially expelling the asylum seekers. There were heartrending scenes of East Germans in Dresden desperately trying to board the westbound train, until the police finally sealed the doors to block them. The East German government placed a ban on travel to yet another Communist country, this time to Czechoslovakia.

East German citizens, faced with an Iron Curtain not only to the West but to the East, mounted protests. Demonstrations took place in Leipzig every Monday night, following a "prayer for peace" service at St. Nicholas Church. The police used violence against the demonstrators, and many were arrested and sentenced.

When Gorbachev visited East Berlin on October 6, he made it clear once again that the Soviet Union would not bolster an unpopular Communist regime. "I am sure the people will decide for themselves what is necessary for their own country," he stated. "We have complete faith in them."

.   .   .

With each of his visits to fraternal Communist countries, Gorbachev appeared to be encouraging popular dissent. It seemed strange to me, for I did not consider Gorbachev a great liberal. He continued to profess his belief in communism. He was wary of any real dissent at home. He publicly disapproved of the multiparty elections that were being allowed in Poland and Hungary and consistently reaffirmed his belief in a single-party system. When the Soviet Union held its first "open" elections in March, the Soviet people were given a choice of candidates but not of parties: Only Communist Party members were allowed to run.

Yet as late as October 25, with a good part of the region in a real or potential uproar, Gorbachev made one of his strongest statements yet: "We have no right, moral or political right, to interfere in events happening [in Eastern Europe]. We assume others will not interfere either." Gorbachev's press spokesman, Gennadi Gerasimov, trying to appear "cool" with the Western press corps, came out with a glib explanation I would never have expected from a Soviet bureaucrat. Moscow had replaced the "Brezhnev Doctrine" with the "Sinatra doctrine," he said jokingly. "Hungary and Poland are doing it *their* way."

I think Gorbachev initially had the same expectations for East European communism as he did for Soviet communism, that it would change from within, with controlled reforms, into what he called "humane socialism." But East Europeans had not lived under communism as long as the Soviets. Many remembered a different system and wanted to restore it and to rejoin Europe. Modern technology—videos, computers, and fax machines; radio and television programs that seeped in from the West—exposed them to a more prosperous world. They could see how poorly their countries measured up. They looked around them and saw corrupt, repressive governments, failing economies, contaminated water, polluted air, alcoholism, and apathy. They wanted change, and the West was their model.

The Party leaders of the four recalcitrant countries—Czechoslovakia's Miloš Jakeš, East Germany's Erich Honecker, Bulgaria's Todor Zhivkov, and Romania's Nikolae Ceauşescu—needed Soviet support to stay in power. After forty years of allegiance to Soviet leaders, they felt betrayed. But the Soviet Union, even if it wanted to, was no longer capable of sustaining enforced control over Eastern Europe. The Gorbachev government had inherited a stagnant economy, the grim result of decades of corrupt, incompetent state planning. It did not have the resources or the political will to support world communism. It had its own problems—among them obsolescent industries, falling production levels, substandard public institutions, and shortages of consumer goods—greater than most people realized at that juncture.

.   .   .

Disregarding Gorbachev's message, East Germany's Party leader Erich Honecker ordered that the demonstrations be stopped at any cost. The police in Leipzig prepared for a showdown. October 9, 1989, was an incredibly tense day, with heavily armed police and nonviolent demonstrators facing off in the streets in what appeared to be the prelude to a Beijing-style massacre. Local hospitals set up extra beds and ordered additional supplies of blood. There were last-ditch efforts by several private citizens, including Kurt Masur, the prestigious conductor of the Gewandhaus Orchestra, who met with local Party officials in an effort to avert a bloody police attack. Soviet military commanders stationed in East Germany also warned Party officials against the use of violence.

The police backed off. The number of demonstrators immediately increased: from 70,000 on October 9 to 120,000 on October 16 and to 300,000 a week later. On October 18, Erich Honecker was forced to resign in favor of Egon Krenz, a Politburo member who had reportedly defied Honecker by ordering the police to use restraint in Leipzig.

An opposition movement, the New Forum, formed almost overnight. Unlike the more than 150,000 East Germans who had migrated to West Germany in 1989, these new demonstrators wanted change but they did not want to leave East Germany. Nor did they necessarily want a reunified Germany. They chanted "We're staying here," and demanded freedom to express their thoughts, to criticize authority, to travel abroad, and to come back home.

42

In Prague that October, I found all eyes on East Germany, where communism was teetering on the brink of collapse. The demonstrations in Leipzig had spread to East Berlin, and the government of Egon Krenz was making frantic concessions, trying to appease the crowds. Another large group of East German refugees had recently been allowed to leave Prague for West Germany. Rita Klímová told me how jealous she was when they left. "It made the Czech people angry," she told me. "*We* have nowhere to go."

I had arranged to meet Kary Schwarzenberg in Prague. He and I and a few others from our International Helsinki Federation were planning yet another confrontation: an open meeting in a Prague restaurant with members of the Czechoslovak Helsinki Committee. We were hoping that the presence of a few foreigners would inhibit the police. But we knew our chances were slim. State Security in Czechoslovakia was doing everything it could to keep the dissidents apart: Two dissidents together in a room was considered a "meeting."

Being in Prague with Kary Schwarzenberg was an unusual experience for me, given the low profile I had always maintained there, pretending to be a tourist and housewife. Kary had a public persona he had no way of concealing, nor did he want to. When we were first in Prague together some months earlier, in March 1989, I had quickly learned the power of the Schwarzenberg name. Arriving alone, I had gone straight to the Esplanade, a once-elegant hotel at the top of Wenceslas Square, only to find that there was no reservation in my name. Groggy from a sleepless night on the plane and a one-hour police search at the airport, I was in no mood to argue with the surly woman behind the reception desk. She was a familiar type, bored and sullen, with badly dyed blond hair that accentuated her approaching middle age. A petty bureaucrat, she insisted on reservations even though the hotel was half empty; in a planned economy, all transactions were supposed to be planned.

"I'm with a group," I explained as calmly as possible. "Perhaps the reservation is under another name. Could you try 'Schwarzenberg?'"

Her demeanor changed instantly. "Oh," she purred, "Prince Schwarzenberg," primping her hair as if she were about to meet him.

"Do you know him?" I asked, egging her on.

"I saw a Schwarzenberg once," she confided coquettishly, "but he would be an old man now. This Schwarzenberg is younger, I think. . . . Tell me," she whispered confidentially, "how old *is* he?"

I had already seen the effect of Kary's name in Poland and Hungary— it always drew a response, be it respectful or quizzical—but I was not prepared for what it meant in Czechoslovakia, the family seat, where some of the Schwarzenbergs' many castles and palaces, confiscated by the Communists, were still popularly referred to by the family name. I thought of Kary's business cards with the succinct "Schwarzenberg" engraved on them: They might seem like an affectation in New York or London but would be absolutely correct in Prague.

Kary, with his straight-backed regimental bearing, did not disappoint. Whenever he entered or left the hotel, members of the hotel staff would line up at attention as if they were his personal servants. They may have been eager for his generous tips, officially frowned on in Communist countries but welcome nonetheless. But I believe they were responding for other reasons—Kary was a symbol of a way of life that had become increasingly attractive as it receded into the irretrievable past.

Although Kary and his family had left Prague when he was eleven, his roots in the city ran very deep. I learned that on our first visit there together, when he insisted on giving me an early morning tour. We began at the family's sixteenth-century palace in Castle Square, facing the president's house and the archbishop's. Still adorned with the Schwarzenberg crest, it had become a Communist military museum. Kary smiled ironically and said, "I'm sorry I can't invite you in for tea. The servants are not here today." We went on to visit several churches: In one, he showed me a statue of his great-great-uncle, the cardinal of Prague. He also told me that the altar was a gift to the church from his family. He pointed out various architectural styles—Gothic, Baroque, Renaissance, and nineteenth century—all in one church. We wandered along a cobblestone street where his grandfather had once lived: He told me that when the old man was dying, the municipal authorities arranged to have hay spread on the cobblestones to dull the noise of passing carriages.

Kary told me he had taken his young son to visit Orlík, one of his family's confiscated castles, an imposing white, neo-Gothic building almost entirely surrounded by water; the castle, several hours out of Prague, had also been made into a museum. The elderly curator gave the two Schwarzenbergs a very thorough tour. Although they never formally acknowledged their identities, he clearly knew who the two tourists from Austria really were.

Kary had traveled back and forth to Prague on business over the years, but it was only in the fall of 1988 that he had first met Václav Havel. Havel, with his tendency to see life as theater, was immediately taken by Kary— a modern prince returning to the oppressed land of his birth, intent on righting wrongs. A strong friendship developed between the two men.

.   .   .

Now, in October 1989, I was looking forward to another trip with Kary. Being with someone so important and visible, I thought, would be a kind of protection for me. But just as I was leaving New York, I heard that Kary had been refused an entry visa to Czechoslovakia and I would be on my own. I was glad I had kept a low profile all along. At least one of us would get in.

Something peculiar happened in the Prague airport upon my arrival. After the search of my belongings that had become routine for me ever since my expulsion in 1983, the young customs official, who waited around until the police were gone, turned to me apologetically. "I am sorry," he said. "I am only custom official. That is police. Police is very bad man." I was dumbfounded. Such a departure from protocol would have been unthinkable just a short time before.

When I got to my hotel, there was a message for me from Kary: He and several colleagues from Austria would be arriving the next day. He had managed to get a visa after all, thanks to the intervention of the Austrian foreign minister.

.   .   .

At an impromptu get-together at Rita Klímová's apartment the night I arrived, Jiří Hájek, chairman of the Czechoslovak Helsinki Committee, said he doubted the police would allow the meeting to take place: "They arrested me yesterday when I went to visit a friend, and they held me all day." Hájek was a courteous, mild-mannered man in his mid-seventies whose gentle demeanor concealed an iron will when it came to matters of principle. A resistance fighter who was imprisoned by the Nazis during World War II, he had served as Czechoslovakia's foreign minister during the Prague Spring and later condemned the occupation of his country at the United Nations. In 1977, Hájek was one of the original three spokespersons for Charter 77.

"It's the beginning of disintegration," Hájek continued. "Some groups in the Party want to be the first to take the initiative. One of the cards up their sleeve is a 'dialogue with society.' But no one is ready to play it yet." Hájek, I noticed, had aged noticeably over the last year. His slender frame was stooped, his thin, sensitive face seemed drawn, and the heavy lenses in his glasses—he had always been quite nearsighted—gave him an owlish appearance. He was still recovering from the sudden death of his wife some months before.

Rita joined in: "They're arresting everyone," she told me. "I carry a toothbrush with me all the time now, and a pair of panties."

.   .   .

When Kary arrived the next day, we went to Václav Havel's apartment. Havel, who had spent the first six months of the year in prison yet again, was characteristically quiet and thoughtful.

"People in Czechoslovakia always wait for support from abroad," he remarked. "Like when Gorbachev came to visit. Everyone expected him to fire [then Party leader] Husák, and they were disappointed when he didn't. It was a good lesson. We have to help ourselves."

He seemed troubled. "It's very strange," he mused, "that we who have more democratic traditions than Poland, Hungary and the GDR [German Democratic Republic] are the last island. But Middle Europe is all inter-related. One country opens its borders and we all have problems. It will be increasingly difficult for Czechoslovakia to be a museum."

Havel, whose influential essay "The Power of the Powerless" described the essential power of people who live their lives in truth, was concerned about the passivity of his countrymen. I wondered if he himself was being too passive by refusing to urge people to action. Havel told me he had actually counseled young people *not* to demonstrate in August on the anniversary of the Soviet invasion; he was afraid of bloodshed. Now, with Czechoslovakia's National Day approaching on October 28, he was again opposed to any demonstration. He knew that on October 28, *he* would either be in preventive police detention or out of town to avoid arrest. "How can we ask young people to demonstrate when we are safe in prison?"

.   .   .

We planned our strategy for the Helsinki group meeting. It was set for 11 A.M. the next day, October 18, in the restaurant U Piaristů on Pánská Street. Our Czech colleagues were worried that the police might arrest them as they left their homes that morning, so we decided that we foreigners would accompany some of them to the meeting. An Austrian colleague and I would go with Rita Klímová and Jiří Hájek; Kary Schwarzenberg would escort Havel.

It began according to plan. Rita and I walked together on that crisp, sunny October morning, chatting easily. But as we approached the restaurant we saw that it was closed. A uniformed policeman stood at attention, barring the door. A few yards away I saw a cluster of people, many of them friends I was expecting to see. As we drew closer, I saw they were arguing with a group of plainclothes police, recognizable by their short leather jackets and tough faces. Not understanding what they were saying, I stood back a little, taking in the scene.

Suddenly I heard Jiří Hájek declare loudly and firmly, first in Czech and then in English for my benefit: "You are violating my rights under Czechoslovak and international law!" Rita called to me plaintively: "Jeri, they're arresting us. Jeri, they're taking us away." I stood frozen, feeling somehow responsible. *I am the foreigner who's supposed to be protecting them. What should I do? I can't just stand here while they're being arrested. . . . The police would never behave this way in front of the foreign press. Maybe if I start taking pictures, I'll frighten them off.*

As soon as I reached for my camera—I had barely gotten it out of my bag—I was attacked by one of the security men, who tried to pull it out of my hands. I fought back, grabbing his arm and pushing him away. There was a brief, unpleasant scuffle, and a quick exchange in Czech between two policemen. The two thugs closed in on me and pushed me toward a waiting car. I felt a sharp karate chop behind my knees; they buckled, and I was quickly and expertly lifted into the car. It was a tiny Czech Škoda, with room for only two in the back seat. Ladislav Lis, who was carrying all the papers for the meeting, was already seated there, looking angry and upset behind his drooping white mustache. I knew he spoke no English. He took my hand, and we rode in silence to the police station.

At the station, the police took my passport and left me in a large room that looked like a classroom. Several of my Czech friends were already there and others kept arriving in pairs until our group grew to sixteen. Jiří Hájek had seen the police manhandle me during my arrest, and he was very distressed; "I am so sorry about our police," he kept saying, almost as if it were his fault. Rita told me she had seen Havel and Schwarzenberg walking toward the restaurant when she was already in the police car: "I yelled, 'Turn back! They're arresting us,' and they got away."

Well, now I'll find out what it's like to be in prison. I wasn't frightened, only concerned that I would be bored because I had nothing with me to read. I knew that Kary would inform the U.S. Embassy of my arrest, and I imagined I would be held no more than a day or two at the most. My deepest fear was that I'd be expelled again and that this time they would not let me back in.

.   .   .

In less than an hour I was taken to an adjoining room where two uniformed officers briefly inspected my pocketbook, showing no interest at all in my camera. They returned my passport and told me curtly that I could go. I felt strange, like a traitor, walking *away* from the police station by myself, the privileged American. I worried about what would happen to the others. As it turned out, they were all released that day, though at different times, with the last release close to midnight.

I returned to my hotel, where I found Kary and Havel waiting in the upstairs dining room. Havel had decided that our hotel was the safest place for him to be that day; he was sure he would be arrested if he returned home. After about an hour, I called Rita's apartment and found that she had just arrived home from the police station. She soon joined us at the hotel, as did some of the others as they were released from the jail. Libuše Šilhanová, one of the charter spokespersons, arrived, well-groomed and elegant despite the wear and tear of the morning's events.

She told us about a friend of hers who had been arrested and tried for calling the police "Stalinists"; at the trial, her lawyer pointed out that Stalin was a Communist hero, and the woman was acquitted. We laughed at the absurdity of it all. It was typical of that moment in history, when everything seemed topsy-turvy.

The police were bewilderingly inconsistent. A short time before, none of these people would have been allowed even to enter the Intercontinental Hotel, but now they were coming there straight from jail. Jiří Hájek described the ups and downs of his week as truly bizarre: "On Tuesday, I was arrested for meeting with Libuše; on Wednesday I was told that I could travel to the Socialist International meeting in Vienna; today I was detained again, but when they released me, they said my passport for Vienna would be ready tomorrow. They don't know what they are doing!"

I told Havel we would be trying to hold a nongovernmental meeting in Moscow the following year. Was there any chance he might attend? "I would like to be there," he said, "but it is, of course, impossible." Even if Havel were to receive a visa, which was highly unlikely, the police would probably prevent him from returning home once he was abroad.

.   .   .

I have often looked back on that long afternoon in the hotel as a pivotal moment suspended in time. No one predicted the events that would actually happen, and no one dreamed they would happen so soon—that the revolution in Czechoslovakia was only a month away. Yet slowly, imperceptibly, in the course of that afternoon, the discussion shifted from *whether* communism would end in Czechoslovakia to *when* it would happen and *who* the new leaders would be. It was the first and only time I heard Havel discuss what his future role might be.

Havel predicted that it might be as long as ten years before Czechoslovakia saw any real change.

"Why ten years?" I asked.

"Because the powerful do not want to give up power," he replied. "We certainly have the support of the society," he added. "It looks to us for more than we can supply. What we need are real political figures with charisma and a program."

"What about you?" I asked.

"I will be engaged as an amateur," he answered, his eyes downcast, "but not as a professional." He paused for thought, as is his way. "I'm prepared to serve, but I am no Mazowiecki," he said slowly, referring to the newly elected non-Communist prime minister of Poland. "I'm a writer, not a politician. I would like being a kingmaker, but not a king," he added with a little laugh.

I studied Havel during this conversation, and I believed him—that he meant it when he said he had no political aspirations and that he was right in not wanting power. In his usual attire—blue jeans and a rumpled sweater—he indeed seemed more a writer than a politician. He was small, sensitive, and appealingly shy, a comfortably familiar figure, a man of letters. But his life had taken a very different turn from what it might have been. The years he spent in prison, the unrelenting persecution that had become part of his everyday life, had given him a special kind of wisdom and strength, and a belief in his own integrity. These attributes were necessary to stand up to the Communists. They were also a preparation for leadership.

I turned to Jiří Dienstbier, a journalist-turned-janitor who had twice been a charter spokesman.

"What about you?" I asked and, remembering Jiří's former career in journalism, I suggested, half in jest: "Wouldn't you want to be minister of culture?"

Dienstbier, always bantering, grinned as he answered me: "I'd like to be minister of the interior, in charge of the secret police . . . for just one week!"

.   .   .

There was yet another paradox: Several days after my release from jail, I went to Brno and Bratislava to meet with Slovak dissidents, traveling with Kary Schwarzenberg in his fire-engine-red Porsche. I was no longer worried about calling attention to myself. The old rules seemed not to apply. We drove without police interference of any kind.

If the police *had* wished to keep an eye on us, Schwarzenberg's flamboyant car would have made it easy for them. No one missed us as we passed; there were double takes and gaping mouths all along the way. I became uncomfortable when I saw these reactions to his car, thinking of how insensitive we were to the poor, colorless lives of the villagers who were watching us go by. But when I glanced at Kary, he was smiling, enjoying every minute of it. He was the fearless prince riding through the countryside; the car was his white horse.

For some time now I had been aware of how little I really knew about Kary, his aspirations and his goals. I had met his wife and some of his children and had stayed overnight in his Vienna home. I had heard vague allusions to his jet-set social life—weekend parties at his palace in Germany, hunting trips in Spain, gallery openings in New York. Although I sensed that his human rights work had come to take precedence over many of his previous, more frivolous pursuits, I still found it hard to imagine Kary Schwarzenberg abandoning his luxurious life in Vienna for the bleakness of Prague. Yet he and Havel had spent hours closeted together in discussions to which I was not privy. *Their* business was no longer *my* business.

Until now, Kary and I had been on the same mission: to promote human rights in repressive countries. My job in Czechoslovakia would end if and when this was achieved, but Kary's might only be beginning. Turning to Kary, I asked him, tentatively, if he had ever considered a political role for himself in the new government that might someday come to be. I expected him to deflect the question with a laugh, but he did not. He answered me very soberly: "If there is a way that I can serve, I am prepared to do so."

·   ·   ·

Before that strange trip in October 1989, I had been thinking of taking a vacation in Czechoslovakia. I wanted Charlie to see Prague, to meet Anna, Rita, and some of my other friends there. I thought we might go there for the Prague Spring Music Festival. I sensed that Prague would be changing. I wanted Charlie to see the city as it was.

After my arrest, however, I lost all heart for such a trip. I would never be able to travel in Czechoslovakia as an ordinary tourist: I was suspect, and anyone who was with me would be suspect, too. I also found it distasteful to think of being a tourist in Prague while the Communists were in power.

In my brief encounter with State Security, I had experienced a little of what my friends in Czechoslovakia had lived with for decades, what I myself had written about but had never really seen unfold. And there was something else, something I had not confessed to anyone: I *wanted* to be arrested on October 18. No, that's not quite true, I did not really *want* to be arrested; as a human rights professional, my job was merely to observe and record. But I could not just stand there as if I were invisible while my friends were being taken away. That is why I took out my camera. I was asking to be part of it.

The Czech dissidents understood my feelings, better perhaps than I. They had been through such experiences many times, with very much more at stake. Their passage to dissidence, more often than not, was *not* the result of an abstract choice, but a response to seeing their friends in trouble.

"Now you understand," said Petr Uhl, a charter activist who had spent nine years in prison. When I met with him and Jan Urban the evening after my arrest, they had already heard about the day's events through a Radio Free Europe broadcast some hours before. Uhl spoke with a knowing, almost mischievous look. "Now you know," he nodded his head affirmatively. "Now you know how one becomes a dissident in our country."

43

In the month of November 1989, the Communist governments of three countries—East Germany, Bulgaria, and Czechoslovakia—succumbed suddenly to spontaneous peaceful demonstrations. Their defeat was not the result of negotiations, as in Poland and Hungary earlier in the year. It was in direct response to the demonstrators, to "the power of the powerless," in Václav Havel's words.

When I was in Bulgaria in late October, I watched that revolution begin. The backdrop was a familiar one: an official Helsinki conference—this time, an environmental forum—that was taking place in Sofia in October.

A group of Bulgarian intellectuals, many of them new to dissidence, formed a nongovernmental group called Eco-Glasnost. They wanted to use the occasion of the conference to call attention to an atmosphere that was suffocating, both literally and metaphorically. They were fed up with Communist Party chief Todor Zhivkov, the seventy-eight-year-old despot who had been running the country like a mobster for thirty-five years. He rewarded family and friends for loyalty, persecuted minorities like the Turks and the Roma, and restricted all basic freedoms, including the rights to free speech, a free press, and free assembly. For more than three decades, Zhivkov had toed the Soviet line in slavish obeisance, a model Communist dictator. Now he found himself confused and unsettled by the Gorbachev government and its reforms.

Eco-Glasnost members assumed that the Bulgarian police would not arrest members of a citizens' *environmental* group while an official environmental forum was in session in Sofia. The group gathered more than

11,000 signatures on a petition, organized demonstrations, and gave interviews to the Western press that gathered in Sofia to cover the conference.

I was a witness to a noontime Eco-Glasnost march to a park in the center of Sofia where the activists planned to get more signatures for their petition. The petition took issue, in particular, with two river-diversion schemes that threatened the ecological balance of the Rila Mountains and with a project to build a nuclear power plant on Belene Island, an earthquake zone. The march was stopped by police who directed the group to move to South Park at the outskirts of Sofia. The demonstrators refused to move, demanding to know the policemen's names and to see a written order. The police blocked them from contact with people who had lined up to sign the petition.

I latched onto a woman in her thirties who spoke good English. She was casually dressed, in pants and a loose jacket, her short-cropped hair brushed back, her pretty face distorted by anger. She was in the center of the dispute, shouting at the police, but was also willing to keep me, a total stranger, informed of what people were saying. "Of course, they won't identify themselves or show us an order," she explained to me. "That way they can say this never happened."

That evening I attended a reception given by U.S. ambassador Sol Polansky for our group to meet the leaders of the Bulgarian dissident intelligentsia. There I was formally introduced to Dmitrina Petrova, a professor of philosophy, who had been my volunteer interpreter during the face-off with the police a few hours earlier. I barely recognized her, elegant in a lace-trimmed black velvet dress, sitting demurely at her husband's side. "We're having another march tomorrow," she told me. "Please try to come. Foreigners are our protection." I asked if she was afraid of being arrested and found her answer curiously naive. "I'm a professor at the university," she responded. "I have nothing to fear."

I also met Zhelyu Zhelev at the ambassador's, a philosopher who in less than a year would be the non-Communist president of Bulgaria—a development neither of us in our wildest dreams would have predicted that evening. "I don't see things changing in the near future," Zhelev declared in words reminiscent of Havel's a week before. "We have no democratic movement from below. In fact, after the forum ends, things may change for the worse. After the conference, they will certainly be more brutal."

I already had plans for the following day, and so I missed the Eco-Glasnost march. Instead, I went on an all-day and most-of-the-night trip with two colleagues to southern Bulgaria to investigate the oppression of a Bulgarian Muslim group called the Pomaks. The trip into the Bulgarian countryside gave me an unexpected view, not of the bucolic landscape I had expected to see but of a true nightmare of unbridled pollution. In Sofia, I had already seen the results of Zhivkov's program of rapid indus-trialization. There was a foul-smelling, greenish-yellow haze outside my Sofia hotel window every morning, obscuring the fabled panoramic views of snow-capped Mt. Vitosha. This was the fallout from the unending clouds of black smoke belching from the stacks of two giant steel plants outside the city, which reportedly deposited some 20,000 tons of grime on Sofia each year. Now we were driving through one of these steel-plant complexes, our car windows tightly shut, unable to see more than a few feet in front of us through the dark haze. Encircling the factory were housing developments where the workers and their families lived, forever engulfed in black smoke, not only in the workplace but in their homes, schools, and shops.

We kept expecting the smog to dissipate, but it continued for more than twenty miles outside of Sofia as we followed trucks with black diesel-fuel emissions through a hazy mountain pass. Occasionally I caught glimpses of fall-colored trees, of snowcaps on a mountain, of tobacco drying under plastic, of algae-covered ponds. Old farming villages were interspersed with the shabby, "modern" housing projects; laundry hung limply in unmitigated gloom. It was not until we left the main road and climbed high into the Pirin Mountains that the air finally cleared and we saw sheep and shepherds and small, remote hamlets.

·   ·   ·

The next day, back in Sofia, Dmitrina told me what had happened at their demonstration the day before.

> I take back everything I told you the other night, that people like me would not be attacked. We were beaten, terribly. Alexander was dragged, struck, pushed against the step of the bus so that his back was badly wounded; Deyan was hit on the head, Krassimir kicked in the kidneys. Nikolina was dragged and lost her shoes ... They grabbed her hair and pulled her head down and gave her a horrible chop on the neck ...

They jumped over me, took my hands and dragged me while others struck me all over my body, shouting dirty things . . . I must have asked at least ten times, but the police refused to identify themselves, although they are required to by law. They know what they are doing is unlawful—and that someday they may be tried. Some of the delegates to the forum were present and saw what happened. Nine countries have raised the question of whether the conference should continue.

My interview with Dmitrina took place in South Park, to which the group had been forced to retire. She spoke nonstop as I took copious notes, yet all the while I was aware of the way she was watching me, a small smile hovering at her lips. *Is she secretly mocking me, wondering why I'm taking all these notes? Does she know why I'm doing this, what a human rights group does?*

Only a few years later, Dmitrina would be the head of a new Helsinki group in Bulgaria and would be honored in New York as one of our "human rights monitors." At a dinner for her at Jonathan Fanton's house, she was asked how she became involved in human rights work. Her response took me completely by surprise and touched me deeply.

"I wanted to be Jeri Laber," she said quietly, describing her interview with me in South Park. "I said to myself, 'I want to be this woman.' Jeri was writing very fast with her left hand, looking straight in my eyes, taking down all the details. And I was thinking: 'I want to be Jeri Laber.'"

.   .   .

Back in South Park in late October 1989, Dmitrina was angry and defiant. "The term 'state security' has been demystified," she told me. "People used to be afraid of the very words. Now we have met them face to face. We have been interrogated at their invitation. And we are no longer afraid." I understood what she meant. The secret police, I had come to realize, were no better than the governments they worked for: They were shabby, inefficient, and corrupt. They didn't believe in anything.

The Eco-Glasnost demonstrations were the start of the Bulgarian revolution. Faced with the prospect of a walkout at the official Environmental Forum, the Bulgarian authorities allowed the demonstrations to continue and the crowds grew in numbers. On November 9, less than two weeks after I had left Bulgaria, Todor Zhivkov was removed as Party leader, replaced by his foreign minister, Petar Mladenov. It was still a Communist government, but the movement toward reform and power sharing had begun.

Many factors in addition to popular protest, of course, contributed to the changes in Bulgaria. There were machinations among reformers within the Politburo. There was Gorbachev. Above all, there was the toppling of Communist leaders elsewhere in the bloc. As Havel had said: "Middle Europe is all interrelated."

.   .   .

On November 9, the same day that Zhivkov was removed from power, the world watched an unbelievable scene, perhaps the most significant and certainly the most symbolic event of 1989: the opening of the Berlin Wall.

After twenty-eight years and ninety-one days, the wall fell. No one knows who gave the order, no one even knows if an order was given, but five days before, on November 4, a crowd estimated at anywhere from half a million to a million had demonstrated in East Berlin. Then, on the evening of November 9, a senior Party official, speaking on television for a very nervous government that was unable to keep up with its citizens' demands, announced that East Germans would be allowed to make private journeys to the West. He didn't say when, he didn't say how, but people, tens of thousands of them, began streaming to the wall to find out for themselves. Bewildered border guards, under long-standing orders to shoot on sight anyone trying to cross the border, telephoned for instructions, but it was too late to stop the jubilant crowds. Some 2 million East Germans crossed into West Germany over that unforgettable weekend.

Years later, in a television interview, Gorbachev claimed that he was not consulted by the East German government on November 9: "Next morning I got a phone call. They told me what had happened. I said, 'You made the right decision,' because how could you shoot at Germans who walk across the border to meet other Germans on the other side?" How could you, indeed? Over the years, at least 475 East Germans had been killed during desperate attempts to reach the West and thousands more had been caught and imprisoned.

.   .   .

Meanwhile, in Prague, the October 28 National Day had become the occasion for a serious confrontation. Although the prominent dissidents were detained in advance, as expected—the police actually dragged Havel to jail from his sickbed—a demonstration took place. Some 10,000 people, mainly students, turned out. Havel's fears came true: The police, unprovoked, attacked the crowd with truncheons, wounding dozens of young people.

On November 17, eight days after the Berlin Wall came down, thousands of students turned out in Prague for what began as a state-sanctioned rally. The police were nervous. They attacked the demonstrators, and many were seriously injured. But this time the crowd held its ground. From November 17 on, there were massive rallies each day, growing in size from 200,000 to 800,000, and even more. The revolution had begun. It was a people's revolution, initiated by a new generation, by students too young to know of a life before communism.

Czechoslovakia's revolution, though slow in coming, was in many ways the smoothest and the most peaceful, which is why its description as the "Velvet Revolution" seems so apt. Millions of people all over the world watched it on their television screens over a period of three and half weeks—the daily throngs of ecstatic people in Prague's Wenceslas Square, jingling their keys and responding in unison to the various speakers; the thousands of lighted candles signifying bright hopes; and the dissidents blinking in disbelief as they emerged from their "ghetto" to the adulation of the crowd.

I watched it all from afar. Although I longed to be there, I didn't see any role I could play. If our organization had been better staffed and funded, as it is today, I would probably have gone to Prague to take in the scene, enjoy a time of triumph, and report back to my colleagues at home. But in 1989, I didn't have that luxury. There was too much other work to do in places where we were still badly needed.

Czechoslovakia, I assumed, would succeed. It had the best possibilities: a history of democracy on which to build and a new leader, Václav Havel, who profoundly understood the drama in which he was playing a major role.

.   .   .

Rita Klímová, with her New York accent, astounded and amused people as the English-language voice of the revolution. For a long time I thought it was she who coined the term "Velvet Revolution," but she set me straight one day, assuring me that the words were Havel's.

"But it was *you* who chose to translate it that way," I insisted, "Someone else might have used a different word."

Rita took the sleeve of my jacket between her thumb and forefinger, rubbing her fingers together. "Velvet is velvet," she declared.

One of Havel's many inspirations was the decision to send Rita to Washington as ambassador to the United States.

.   .   .

Havel was elected president in December 1989. He was inaugurated on December 29 with a twenty-gun salute, while throngs of people danced in the castle courtyard. One of his first acts was to appoint Kary Schwarzenberg chancellor of his government. For one brief moment, it seemed like a fairy tale come true. The philosopher became king and the émigré prince regained his birthright.

44

It seemed like a good idea—to take a short vacation in London over the Christmas holidays. It was the end of 1989, a tumultuous year that saw Communist governments topple in five East European countries. Things would quiet down over the holidays—they always did—and we all needed a breathing space, time to let the new governments take hold, to wait and see what they would do.

Suddenly, in mid-December, there were reports of *new* unrest, this time in tightly controlled Romania, where revolution had seemed unlikely. They were coming from a city called Timişoara that I had barely heard of just a short time before.

The uprisings in Timişoara on December 16 and 17 began as a small protest in support of a dissident Protestant minister, the Reverend László Tőkés. Tőkés, an ethnic Hungarian, was about to be removed from his church because he had criticized Ceauşescu's policy of destroying villages in the countryside. The protest struck a sympathetic chord in Timişoara, a relatively sophisticated and prosperous city. As the ranks of the demonstrators grew, the army and the secret police, the Securitate, fired on them, leaving an unknown number dead. On December 20, there were further demonstrations in the city, but this time most of the army was reportedly on the demonstrators' side.

Ceauşescu, the Romanian dictator, made several fatal mistakes. He left the country on a state visit to Iran at the start of the Timişoara events and was forced to return hurriedly when the situation got out of hand. On December 21, he organized a mass rally in Bucharest, apparently to assure people that he remained in control. Speaking from the balcony of the

Party Central Committee building, he blamed the unrest on foreign agents. But the crowd turned against him, booing and chanting *"Tim-i-şoar-a,"* so suddenly and vociferously that Ceauşescu became visibly flustered. The police began to clear the square, but his bewilderment and fear, captured on national television, brought more crowds into the streets later that day and night. They were waving the Romanian tricolor flag with a hole cut in the center where the Communist Party symbol had been. They were demanding Ceauşescu's overthrow.

The next day, December 22, there was an announcement that the minister of defense, General Milea, had committed suicide. Rumor had it that he had refused to order his troops to fire on the demonstrators. Ceauşescu attempted to appear on the same balcony again, but was forced to duck back when the crowd began throwing things and surging into the building. The dictator and his wife, Elena, fled to a waiting helicopter that took off from the roof. No one knew where they were going.

Violence increased in Bucharest and elsewhere in Romania over the next days. The airport was one of the battlegrounds, its cafeteria reportedly an improvised morgue. Tarom, Romania's national airline, was grounded, and all international flights to Romania were canceled. Foreign journalists had to take long and dangerous overland routes from neighboring countries. The initial reports we received were murky and confused. It wasn't clear who was shooting at whom.

.   .   .

It was a bad time for me to be going away. I asked Janet Fleischman, who had been following Romania for Helsinki Watch, if she would consider changing her own vacation plans to cover the situation while I was gone. Janet was an enthusiast and deeply committed to her work. She willingly agreed to change her plans, and I went home to pack for London: Charlie and I were due to leave the next day, December 23.

After all the missions I had taken, I had packing down to a science. I kept a running checklist on my computer and a small leather kit always packed, ready to go. Most of the items in my kit were common, over-the-counter drugstore products, readily available in most of the world but not in Eastern Europe: Band-Aids, eyedrops, aspirin, allergy pills, Bacitracin. I carried a prescription antibiotic in case I got sick and a disposable hypodermic needle in case I should need an injection. I don't think we fully grasped the backwardness of hospitals under the Communists—we didn't yet know of tainted blood supplies and contaminated needles—but I knew enough to bring what I might need in case of emergency. I also brought American cigarettes to use as gifts or, more often, as barter; a small flashlight to read names on doors in dark stairwells; and a pack of single dollar bills—in the late 1980s in Eastern Europe, an illicit dollar would take me anywhere I wanted to go by car or taxi.

I didn't need any of this for London, of course, but I put the prepacked kit in my suitcase nonetheless. I also added a few other things I wouldn't ordinarily have taken: warm corduroy pants, fleece-lined boots, a woolen hat, scarf, and gloves. *You never can tell,* I told myself, while barely acknowledging what I was doing. It was freezing in Romania.

. . .

Charlie and I were met at the London airport by George Soros's chauffeur-driven Jaguar. George and his wife, Susan, both members of the Helsinki Watch board, were very generous to me over the years, inviting me to their Long Island home in the summer and to parties at their city apartment. On this occasion, they had offered us the use of their London town house, which would otherwise have stood empty during the holidays.

The staff had prepared for us as if we were the Soroses themselves. They had decorated the house for Christmas, with a lovely tree, mistletoe, and platters of Christmas sweets. At our request, they had made a dinner reservation for us at the Connaught Hotel for Christmas Eve and had booked theater tickets for four of the seven nights of our stay. We slept in the master bedroom and were served a leisurely breakfast at whatever hour we wished. The London morning newspapers were waiting for us at the breakfast table. We read them, transfixed.

. . .

With the Ceauşescus in hiding since December 22, Romania was in chaos. It was impossible to get reliable information. Reports had it that the dreaded Securitate, their black-shirted elite forces numbering up to 15,000, were terrorizing the population, firing at them from building tops and from low-flying helicopters, machine-gunning demonstrators, shooting into crowds, pulling the wounded from their hospital beds, attacking ambulances. In Timişoara, where the death toll was said to be 4,500, there were reports of a mass grave containing naked, tortured bodies. In Bucharest over the Christmas weekend, 5,000 people had reportedly died. The Securitate was said to have secret hiding places all over the country and a maze of underground tunnels in Bucharest, where Securitate "terrorists" would emerge from manholes for surprise attacks. These reports were based on rumor, and most of them eventually turned out to be unfounded. Never in my experience has the press been so confused and inaccurate.

John Tagliabue, a *New York Times* correspondent I had come to know during my work in Eastern Europe, was shot by a sniper and lay wounded in a hospital in Timişoara. Other Western correspondents who managed to reach Bucharest were often forced to rely on hearsay. Although it was generally believed that the army was fighting the Securitate, it became increasingly unclear as to who was the aggressor and who was on the run. "It was the strangest situation I ever covered," a journalist told me years later. "Where were the bodies? Everyone was lying. It was a country of liars."

By the time Charlie and I arrived in London, a self-appointed group that called itself the National Salvation Front was running Romania. It claimed to have the support of the army and had taken over the television station, which was periodically reported to be under siege. The Ceauşescus had been captured. They had gone first to their villa at Lake Snagov, then headed for an army base where a jet plane was supposedly waiting to take them abroad. But the helicopter either ran out of gas or was intentionally ditched by the pilot. It landed alongside a highway, where the couple and their bodyguard then commandeered a private car. They were arrested in Tirgoviste, about fifty kilometers north of Bucharest, and taken to a military base. There they were hastily "tried" by an anonymous, kangaroo court. On Christmas Day they were summarily executed.

Video footage of their execution and a transcript of their pathetic mock trial were released as proof. Members of the Salvation Front took responsibility for the execution, claiming they had no choice, that Securitate forces were about to overpower the army base and release the Ceauşescus. Their explanation was widely questioned, and their decision generally denounced. The execution deprived the Romanian people and the world of the satisfaction of a scrupulous legal process in which Ceauşescu's crimes and those of his colleagues would have been revealed and appropriately punished. The rapid disposal of the Ceauşescus appeared to serve only the interests of the leaders of the new National Salvation Front, many of whom were former Ceauşescu henchmen who might have been implicated in a serious trial.

.   .   .

A few days into our vacation, it became clear that I would soon be going to Romania. I was in constant touch with Janet in our New York office, who was helping to organize a team to enter Romania as soon as it was possible. Jonathan Fanton, then vice chair of Helsinki Watch, told me he was ready to go. At his suggestion, I called Kary Schwarzenberg in Vienna and he immediately agreed to join us. We wanted to find out what was really happening there. We wanted to see if there were any human rights activists and to encourage the formation of a Helsinki group in Romania. We wanted to meet with the new leaders and impress upon them the importance of documenting past crimes and bringing the perpetrators to justice.

This was the plan: Schwarzenberg, Fanton, and I, accompanied by an interpreter—Sandra Pralong, a Romanian-speaking woman I had interviewed "just in case" before leaving New York—would fly into Bucharest as soon as the airport reopened. At the same time, Janet Fleischman, accompanied by David Nachman, a lawyer who did volunteer work for our organization, would enter Romania by car or train from Hungary and go to Timişoara to investigate what had happened there. Hungarian airlines informed us that flights into Bucharest would resume after the first of the year. Therefore, we would all meet in Budapest, Hungary, on January 1, 1990.

.   .   .

This was a much more frightening trip than any I had previously made. Although it was never pleasant traveling alone in Communist police states, being followed and bugged, detained and interrogated, I felt up to that kind of situation, able to handle it. But being the target of a sniper's bullet was something else. The randomness of such danger, the likelihood of being the victim of such an attack in a country where I did not understand the language and would not respond to a call in Romanian to "hit the ground"—these things truly terrified me.

I tried to take heart from the fact that others, including Fanton, a cautious and sensible man, seemed to have no hesitation about going and that Schwarzenberg had so readily agreed to join us. But I suspected they were taking their cues from me, for I had said nothing to them about my misgivings. It was the blind leading the blind. Charlie surprised me with his upbeat attitude. "Of course you have to go," he kept saying. "It's very important. It'll be fine." He calmed me down.

Together we bought a small blue canvas bag. I packed it with my warm clothes and the kit of medicines I had brought with me "just in case." The rest of my things went back to New York with Charlie on December 31, when he left London as scheduled, but by himself.

I spent my last day in London sitting at an antique desk in the Soros's living room, making phone calls to various countries in preparation for the trip, while the staff brought me coffee and sandwiches. Our mission to Romania was being funded by a Soros grant. In an unexpected confluence, the Soros's gift to me of their house for Christmas, an offer made some months before, melded neatly with the mission I was now planning. It was George's chauffeur who helped me get my visa for Hungary and drove me to the airport the next day.

While phoning New York, Washington, Vienna, and Budapest, I didn't think to check my answering machine at home. It was just as well. If I had, I would have found an urgent, unsolicited message from someone at the U.S. State Department, telling me that I should not go to Romania under any circumstances and that the U.S. government could not vouch for my safety.

.   .   .

Our plans to fly from Budapest to Bucharest were stymied when Hungarian airlines canceled the flight. Instead, we flew from Budapest to Vienna, where we were booked on an Austrian Airlines flight to Bucharest on January 3, the next morning. It was the first scheduled flight into the country since the revolt began.

In the morning, Kary, Jonathan, Sandra (our interpreter), and I met for an early breakfast at the Palais Schwarzenberg. I knew from previous trips that Kary always traveled with provisions—Scotch, salami, bread, cheese, and chocolates, enough to share with me and other colleagues and with the dissidents we met. This time, we almost missed our plane when he insisted on returning to the hotel at the last minute. He dashed into the Palais and reemerged breathless and triumphant, carrying four rolls of toilet paper, one for each of us. "It is always good to be prepared," he announced formally, with a touch of regal irony.

The Bucharest airport, ringed with tanks, looked like a war zone, with scores of soldiers milling about in the below-freezing temperature. We were met by Mrs. Berta Braun, the Austrian ambassador to Romania: The Austrian Foreign Office, at Kary's request, had alerted her to our arrival. (I had made a similar request through the U.S. State Department, but the U.S. ambassador, a political appointee brand new in his job, seemed overwhelmed by the chaos of the revolution: He had sent most of the embassy staff out of the country and remained closeted in his office, recovering from a bad fall he had taken on the icy street.)

Ambassador Braun was a stout, plucky woman who knew the country well. We were fortunate to be in her hands as she led us expeditiously through the bureaucratic entrance procedures. I don't know how we would have gotten to the city without her car, since there were no taxis at the abandoned airport. It took the better part of an hour to navigate the icy road, along which we were stopped four times by soldiers manning roadblocks. As we entered the city, passing Bucharest's small version of the Arc de Triomphe and driving along the wide, tree-lined Calea Victoriei, I remembered the city's past reputation as the little Paris of the East. It was a dark, snowy afternoon: Snow clung to the tree branches overhead, creating an unexpectedly enchanting fairyland. Then we passed an open square and got our first glimpses of the destruction—the royal palace, the university library, and the Party Central Committee building, burned and bullet marked, with tanks and soldiers everywhere. There were candles burning at various spots where people had died: Each little makeshift shrine was surrounded by a small group of people, all of them looking cold, shabby, and sad.

We were fortunate to find rooms at the Intercontinental Hotel, which was packed with foreign journalists and camera crews, about 200 to 300, we estimated. The hotel was a center of activity and information during the week we were there, and we learned a lot from people who gathered in the lobby and by moving from table to table in the dining room. Remembering my previous visit to Romania in 1983, when I could barely meet anyone and was threatened by the police for making the few contacts I did, it came as a surprise to be meeting sophisticated and knowledgeable Romanian scholars and writers in Bucharest. One of my goals was to establish a Helsinki committee there, and I found one already in the making when I arrived. One of its organizers recognized my name from articles he had read in the *New York Review of Books*.

I was relieved to learn that the sporadic fighting had just about come to an end. The only danger we faced was on the icy sidewalks and streets that had not been cleaned since the violence began and were now frozen solid. When I left the hotel the first evening, stepping briskly onto the sidewalk in my smooth-soled leather boots, my feet went right out from under me and I landed flat on my back—so quickly I didn't have time to tense up or therefore to be hurt. But my head missed a sharp ledge by an inch or two, horrifying my companions. After that, I went everywhere holding on to Kary Schwarzenberg's arm: Kary had come prepared with huge new hunting boots that had deeply ridged soles designed to cling to ice. Because walking was so difficult, we took taxis whenever possible. The rides, though short, were often hair-raising, with the car spinning around in a full circle, sometimes more than once, in the course of a trip.

·　　·　　·

It soon became clear that the estimates of casualties were highly inflated. The initial figure of 64,000 deaths was reduced during our stay to 7,000 and, ultimately, to around 700. In Timişoara, the 4,500 deaths initially reported became 115. But even these reduced figures were a matter of conjecture, because no official information was released.

·　　·　　·

I did not find what I had expected to see in Romania—the euphoria that should have accompanied the most dramatic and long-awaited overthrow in Eastern Europe. Instead I encountered skepticism about the new government, even though it had issued new decrees eliminating the repressive practices of the past and establishing the right to travel abroad, to have contact with foreigners, to publish and distribute literature independently, and so forth.

Everyone we met was suspicious and unhappy because they were not getting the full story. They were convinced that the National Salvation Front, which called itself a provisional government, intended to become a permanent one. One of the intellectuals we met described the front as "Communists with another face." We met students and young people who had fought in the streets; they were not just skeptical, they were outraged. The front has stolen the revolution from the people, they told us. It belongs to us because we fought. The same people are in place. Before they were pro-Ceauşescu; now they're against him. During one such interview, Sandra, who was interpreting, burst into tears. I chided her later for her unprofessionalism. I didn't yet acknowledge what she instinctively knew to be true, that the Romanian revolution was turning into nothing more than a palace coup.

.   .   .

We met with most of the top members of the National Salvation Front, including its leader, Ion Iliescu, a former Communist official who had fallen out with Ceauşescu. Iliescu would become the president of Romania for the next seven years, surrounded by cronies intent on dividing the spoils, but we, of course, did not know this at the time. We urged Iliescu to take immediate steps to document the events of the revolution.

- How many people were killed?
- Who did the shooting?
- Why did the violence suddenly stop after the Ceauşescus were executed?
- Where are the Securitate forces now?
- Have there been arrests?
- How many political prisoners are there, and have they been released?

We also urged him to begin an investigation of Ceauşescu's crimes— before records could be destroyed, before stories could be invented. But our questions and suggestions were not taken seriously. Iliescu listened, a patient expression on his tired face, but he responded by describing all the pressing problems he had to deal with first. Foreign Minister Sergiu Celac was more frank. When we suggested that his government release an accurate accounting of the dead, he asked sardonically: "What do you want me to do? Count the crosses in the cemetery?" We tried to explain that exposing the truth and holding people accountable for past misdeeds was necessary, not just to clear the air and give victims a sense of vindication but to establish trust. But our words fell on distracted ears. The new leaders had no intention of establishing procedures that would undermine their power and might ultimately incriminate them.

The truth had been suppressed for so long in Romania that no one in authority had much regard for it. To this day, there is no acceptable official version of what happened in the days between Ceauşescu's flight from Bucharest and his execution. Some claim it was a time of utter confusion in which soldiers were killed by the friendly fire of other soldiers who thought they were shooting terrorists. Others believe that Iliescu and a small clique had plotted against Ceauşescu months before the spontaneous eruption in Timişoara; that the booing and shouts that caused Ceauşescu to flee on December 21 were orchestrated by the clique; and that the violence that erupted between December 22 and December 26, though officially blamed on sinister Securitate forces fighting to free their master, was in fact directed *against* the Securitate, whom the clique did not trust. According to this scenario, the excuse for the Ceauşescus' execution—that they were about to be rescued by terrorists—was manufactured by those who wanted the dictator and his wife dead so that they could not implicate others or stage a comeback.

Iliescu denies there was a plot and claims the events were spontaneous. When interviewed years later, he acknowledged that there were many questions that would never be answered, that "it remains one of the contradictory problems of our revolution."

.   .   .

Establishing the truth, determining accountability, and administering justice—these basic precepts of human rights work were completely lacking in Romania at the pivotal moment in 1990 when documentation was possible. The result is an enduring puzzle—about Ceauşescu, about the revolution—with many missing pieces that may never be found. The Romanian people have been cheated once again, this time of their own history.

45

I n February 1990, President Václav Havel made his first official visit to the United States. He was hailed as a conquering hero. The dissident playwright and philosopher—whose name had been only vaguely known a short time before, except in certain literary circles—had captured the imagination of the world, his very person a symbol of 1989. Touchingly uncomfortable in his new role, he seemed to represent not just Czechoslovakia but all of the newly freed lands that were rushing to rejoin Europe and the West.

Havel's warm reception may also have reflected the special feelings many Americans have for the Czechs, for the dignity and pride with which they survived two reprehensible betrayals by the West: the Munich Pact of 1938 in which the West handed Czechoslovakia over to the Nazis without a fight, and the heartbreaking suppression of the 1968 Prague Spring, when Soviet tanks rumbled through Prague's narrow streets and the West did nothing to stop them.

. . .

Havel's visit began in Washington, where he made an eloquent speech to a standing ovation by a joint session of Congress. Rita Klímová, in her Washington ambassadorial post for less than two weeks, organized a huge reception for him at the embassy, her first major diplomatic effort. "Stay close to me, I need your support," she told me when I arrived. She had inherited a staff of Communist sycophants, who, knowing they would soon be out of their jobs, resented her presence and that of the new president, whose arrival they were supposed to be celebrating.

After the reception I attended a small dinner hosted by Katharine Graham, the *Washington Post* publisher, in the elegant dining room of her Washington home. Havel had traveled with about fifty people all eager to visit the United States ("It was hard to say no to anyone," he told me). Rita had compiled a guest list for the dinner, selecting those she thought would be of most interest to Mrs. Graham, who, in turn, invited some prominent American political and literary figures. Looking over the list, Mrs. Graham's staff did not recognize my name.

"They were so suspicious," Rita told me later. "Wanted to know all about you, why you were on the list, why you should be at the dinner."

"Did you vouch for my table manners?" I asked.

Rita gave me a playful jab in the arm. "I told them you were the unsung hero of our revolution."

.　　.　　.

Rita told me how the Czech visitors, back in their hotel rooms, would roll on the beds laughing like children, unable to believe the extravagant attention they were receiving. Havel did not put on airs: Soon after arriving in New York, he changed into blue jeans and went barhopping in Greenwich Village with his old friend, the film director Miloš Forman, staying out until the early hours of the morning.

Their one full day in New York was a whirlwind of activity—breakfast at Gracie Mansion, visits to the United Nations and the Metropolitan Museum of Art, lunch at the residence of Archbishop John Cardinal O'Connor, a talk at Columbia University, a theatrical tribute at St. John the Divine, and a dinner hosted by the *New York Review of Books*. At midday, in the midst of all these events, Havel visited Helsinki Watch.

I had seen Havel a few weeks before in Prague, my first visit with him as president. We met in the castle, in a small, gilded room with a round polished wood table and an impressive crystal chandelier. Havel, who had decided not to live in the castle, still had his feet in both worlds. He was wearing black jeans, a gray sweater, and a tan shirt, unbuttoned at the neck. "When were we last together?" he asked me. "It seems like a hundred years ago." It was during this meeting that I invited him to visit Helsinki Watch during his visit to the States. Neither he nor I anticipated the overwhelming attention he would receive. Caught up in the frenzy of events that were planned for him, it would have been completely understandable if Havel had decided not to visit Helsinki Watch after all. But the Czechs do not forget their friends.

.   .   .

On the morning of February 22, our office was in a complete tizzy. All work had ceased. The open center section was cleared out as much as possible, the cluttered desks suddenly spotless. Folding chairs were set up, as was a podium with microphones. A brand new satin banner with the Human Rights Watch name, ordered for the occasion, hung behind the speakers' platform from which I would introduce Havel. The audience included all of our staff and board plus friends and members of the press. We had ruled out television coverage but allowed the work of a small movie crew that was making a documentary film about Havel. Yuri Orlov was there, as was Henryk Wujec, a leader of the Polish Solidarity movement and of the Workers Defense Committee. There were also several student leaders from China's Tiananmen Square demonstrations, who had formed an organization in exile, working out of our office; they had translated Havel's "The Power of the Powerless" into Chinese and planned to present a copy to him that day.

Havel was late. We milled about for more than a half hour, while I worried that he would not show up at all. Then suddenly he was there, in a dark suit and tie. Surrounded by hefty American Secret Service men, he looked small and overwhelmed.

It was thrilling to have him in our office. Putting aside my prepared speech, I talked about how I was arrested in Prague on October 18, 1989, together with members of the Czechoslovak Helsinki Committee: "Václav Havel escaped arrest that day because he came late." They loved it, that audience that had waited so patiently for him to arrive.

The *New York Times* reported the next day: "In a day of high emotion, Mr. Havel seemed particularly moved by his visit to the Fifth Avenue offices of Helsinki Watch. 'I feel that I'm here as a friend among friends,' he said. 'I know very well what you did for us, and perhaps without you, our revolution would not be.'"

He's giving us the credit. I can't believe it. I looked around the room as Havel was speaking, at the rapt faces of the Chinese students and of my colleagues who were working for human rights in other parts of the world. I thought of the patience and perseverance of the small Helsinki Watch staff, how they had persisted in their work with no indication that our reports and protests were getting through. It was their triumph as much as mine.

Havel reminisced about being with me in Prague in October, several weeks before the revolution began: "Jeri was right when she said lots of things changed since October. I remember, for example, sitting in some other restaurant with Jeri and Charles [Kary] Schwarzenberg (who is now my collaborator in Prague Castle), and we discussed how to arrange it— that I would come to Moscow to some session of the International Helsinki Federation for Human Rights. We were thinking—How to do it? If I could come there or not?" He paused for effect. "Now some things changed," he continued. "I have an invitation from Mr. Gorbachev. I'll speak to him on Monday."

.   .   .

That evening 4,000 to 5,000 people, many of them holding a single burning candle to recall the Velvet Revolution, attended a gala at the Cathedral of St. John the Divine. The program, organized mainly by Miloš Forman, included readings by Arthur Miller, Paul Newman, and Elie Wiesel, among many others. A much smaller group ended the evening at a party hosted by the *New York Review of Books* at the Vivian Beaumont Theater, where we ate and drank on the darkened stage. I didn't try to break into the prestigious literary crowd that surrounded Havel but talked instead to members of his entourage, including a very serious and rather acerbic man with excellent English whom I was meeting for the first time. "That's Václav Klaus," Rita Klímová told me later. "He's an economist, very smart. We really need him." Klaus would later become prime minister and Havel's greatest political foe.

As midnight approached, the Czechs got ready to leave. They were heading for the airport and their flight back to Prague. I saw Olga Havlová conferring with her husband; then she took me aside to give me a present. It was a oversized book with photographs and text describing the Velvet Revolution. The Havels had brought copies to give to the dignitaries they met in Washington and New York. Now they were leaving and had just one copy left. They decided to give it to me.

.   .   .

Eight months later, when Havel was deeply involved as president of

Czechoslovakia and I had moved on to new problems elsewhere in the region, a fax from Prague arrived at my office, signed by Václav Havel and Karl Schwarzenberg. At first I was confused: "In remembrance of the October 18, 1989, incident in Pánská Street, we would like to thank you for everything you did for us."

Pánská Street? Of course. That was where I had been arrested with members of the Helsinki Committee and hauled off to a police station, the last foreigner to be detained in Communist Czechoslovakia. So much had happened since that incident, just one year before. They wanted me to know that they still remembered.

46

The Soviet empire was unraveling. First, it lost the countries of Eastern Europe. Then, by the end of 1989, the Baltic republics—Lithuania, Latvia, and Estonia—were demanding *their* independence. This was not really surprising. The Baltics were more prosperous, more European, more recently acquired than the other twelve Soviet republics. Like Eastern Europe, they had come under Soviet control involuntarily as part of the fallout from World War II. The United States and other Western countries had never recognized the legality of their annexation by the USSR.

Soviet leaders were experiencing what the British and French had discovered earlier: that the loss of one colony in an empire leads to the loss of others. But the Soviet Union was itself an empire: Its "colonies" were geographically contiguous, Russia being the largest and most dominant of fifteen disparate republics. If the Baltic republics were to go, would the others be far behind? Loss of empire in *this* case could mean the end of the USSR altogether.

Gorbachev drew a distinction between Eastern Europe and the republics of the Soviet Union. When events in Eastern Europe went further than he wished, he was powerless to stop them. But the Soviet Union was another story. In November 1989, while the Czech revolution was under way, he issued a two-page manifesto in *Pravda* reaffirming his belief in communism and in the Party's supremacy in the Soviet Union. He declared that the goal of his reforms was socialism—humane socialism— and not capitalism. Although Gorbachev displayed great courage in his efforts to reform the Soviet Union, he was hindered by his own worldview, by his unwavering belief in communism and his conviction that communism could change from within.

Gorbachev was deeply worried—and under attack. He was being assaulted from all sides. Conservatives in the Party criticized him for losing Eastern Europe and for what they saw as a drift toward capitalism. Liberals in the new 2,250-member Parliament, the Congress of People's Deputies elected in March, berated him for not moving faster to satisfy the people's desire for a better life. The Parliament's first session in May 1989, televised to a transfixed nation, had become a forum for airing grievances. Calls for independence coming from Lithuania, Latvia, and Estonia had been echoed by other republics and even by autonomous regions within the republics, all eager to gain some independence from the Moscow center.

Reformers in the Parliament, led by Boris Yeltsin, an immensely popular maverick politician, attacked Gorbachev for not going far enough in his economic reforms and for exercising too much power. Andrei Sakharov, a deputy to the Parliament, put his personal prestige behind his call for an end to the Party's leading role in society. Sakharov and his allies minced no words in describing the country's economic woes: They pointed to the dearth of consumer goods, the rise in infant mortality, the decrease in the life span of Soviet citizens, ecological disasters, and chemicals in the food supply.

When the Parliament met again on December 12, Gorbachev was angry and bullying. He interrupted the speeches of several delegates and rudely dismissed Sakharov by switching off the microphone while he was speaking. It turned out to be Sakharov's *last* speech. Two days later, he was dead. The dissident scientist, sixty-eight years old, collapsed in his study from a sudden heart attack on December 14, 1989, while preparing a speech on the economic crisis that he planned to deliver to the Parliament the next day.

Sakharov was widely mourned as the world's greatest human rights defender, with many thousands of Russians attending his funeral. Gorbachev praised him publicly as "a man of conviction and sincerity." His death was an incalculable loss to Russia, coming at a decisive moment in history when Sakharov had a major role to play. I often wonder if events in the Soviet Union might have developed differently had Sakharov lived.

.   .   .

In 1990, Boris Yeltsin became president of the Russian Republic. He was not as powerful as Gorbachev, who was both president of the USSR and leader of the Communist Party, but he was much more popular. Yeltsin quit the Communist Party. A pragmatic man, he was unfettered by the dogma and idealism that held Gorbachev back. The two men were natural enemies.

A few of us met with Yeltsin in Moscow on June 4, 1990, shortly after he had become the Russian Republic's president. I had seen him previously, at the Council on Foreign Relations in New York City, during his highly publicized visit to the United States in September 1989. His speech at the council had lacked substance: Rather than discuss his program for Russia, he had badgered the distinguished audience to help him get a meeting with President Bush; then, he said, they would see what his program for Russia was. Like many others at the meeting, I was unfavorably impressed.

Yeltsin had seemed obsessed during his U.S. visit with having a proper meeting with President Bush. But members of the Bush administration didn't want to offend Gorbachev while arms negotiations were in progress and were thus reluctant to receive Yeltsin at a state level. Eventually, they invited him to meet with Brent Scowcroft, the national security adviser; President Bush, according to a prearranged plan, would drop in "unexpectedly" for five minutes during the Scowcroft meeting. Yeltsin was reportedly offended by this arrangement, but the "chance meeting" with Bush did take place. According to his biographers, Yeltsin postured, criticized Gorbachev for taking half measures, warned of the imminent collapse of the Soviet economy, and gave his unsophisticated views of market economics. Washington did not take him seriously.

At our Moscow meeting, Yeltsin seemed self-assured, dignified, and statesmanlike. He told us he favored decentralization and rule from below and believed in bringing the people into decision making. He was also in favor of a free market system and the private ownership of farms.

Only once did Yeltsin seem embarrassingly petty, and that was in response to a question about his relations with Gorbachev. Yeltsin proudly showed us a recent front page of the *New York Times* on which his photograph was larger and higher on the page than one of Gorbachev. I remembered how we used to study *Pravda* back in the old days, examining photographs from the May Day parade to see who was on top in the Soviet hierarchy. Now one of the most important politicians in Russia was looking for clues in the *New York Times* to see how he was doing.

.   .   .

In the fall of 1990, Gorbachev reached a turning point. Frightened by the forces his policies had unleashed, intimidated by conservatives in the Party, trapped by his own commitment to communism and his determination that it would not be eroded in his own country as it had been elsewhere, he turned to the right. He strengthened his own powers and eliminated moderates from his government. He scrapped his economic reform plan for a more conservative one and came out firmly against private enterprise. He curtailed free press and assembly. He appointed a new minister of the interior, Boris Pugo, who was experienced in suppressing nationalist outbreaks in the republics.

Many in the West who thought highly of Gorbachev could not square his image as the father of reform with his assumption of dictatorial powers. They saw him as a congenial figure, more "Western" than Yeltsin, more reasonable. They were mindful of the very real courage Gorbachev had shown in exposing past abuses and instituting changes. They made excuses for him, saying he was hostage to the military. My friends in the East were more cynical. "Gorbachev is a Party functionary to the marrow of his bones," Sergei Kovalev confided to me in 1990. Havel, at about the same time, told me how stunned he was when he finally met Gorbachev in 1990: "I expected to speak to him as one reformer to another; instead he addressed me in Party jargon. I couldn't believe it."

In December 1990, Eduard Shevardnadze resigned as foreign minister, warning that dictatorship and bloodshed were in store. He was obliquely critical of the Soviet army, which had used violence against civilians during recent demonstrations in his native Georgia and in Azerbaijan. He said he feared a repetition of such brutality. He seemed to be warning that a crackdown on the Baltics was in the works.

47

The Baltic republics—Lithuania, Latvia, and Estonia—had long chafed under Soviet rule. They claimed their annexation in 1940 was illegal and resulted from a secret Soviet pact with the Nazis in 1939. Under Gorbachev, in the spirit of glasnost, the existence of the pact was acknowledged, giving legitimacy to their demands for independence.

In March 1990, Lithuania had unilaterally declared its independence. Latvia had done the same in May. All three republics by then had popularly elected, pro-independence Parliaments. They had rejected Russian as the official language and had begun using their national languages instead, and they were drawing up new economic and political laws. Gorbachev had reacted harshly, with threats and displays of force, including a debilitating economic blockade of Lithuania that lasted from April to the end of June.

In January 1991, the Soviet military moved against Latvia and Lithuania, seizing press buildings in both capitals in an effort to silence the outspoken media. In Riga, the Latvian capital, the attacks were by Black Berets, special Soviet riot-control forces loyal to Moscow. In Vilnius, Lithuania's capital, tanks and paratroopers stormed the television tower and the National Defense Building. Tens of thousands of Lithuanians came out into the streets to form a human shield around the besieged buildings and the Parliament; unarmed civilians defended their country by pitting their bodies against Soviet tanks. On the morning of January 14, there was a chilling photograph on the front page of the *New York Times*— a group of Lithuanians were pushing against a Soviet tank in a desperate effort to stop its advance; clearly visible under the tank's treads were the limp legs of a woman wearing black leather boots.

The Gorbachev government eventually backed off: Its troops did not go on to occupy the Parliament or other key buildings in Vilnius. Gorbachev had not expected so much violence or so much publicity in the foreign press. He hadn't anticipated protests in Moscow and must have been stunned when hundreds of thousands of Muscovites spontaneously demonstrated against the attacks in Lithuania. Nor was he prepared for the postponement by President Bush of a pending summit meeting. Most threatening of all was probably Boris Yeltsin's timely statement supporting Baltic independence. Yeltsin condemned the attacks in Vilnius and said that the Russian Republic would sign mutual defense treaties with the three Baltic republics.

Gorbachev then denied he had authorized the attacks. Interior Minister Pugo claimed that photographs of the events were doctored, that the crowd was armed and that it was *the people* who began the shooting.

·　　·　　·

Jonathan Fanton and I went to Estonia, Latvia, and Lithuania at the end of January 1991, two weeks after the violence. There had been so much disinformation in the Soviet press; we wanted to document what had happened there and determine who was responsible.

Fanton and I had traveled together in Bulgaria and Romania as part of larger groups, but on this occasion it would be just the two of us. I worried about how we would manage. I knew that Fanton was an exacting man, used to having his way paved smoothly by a large and attentive staff. But this trip was to countries in crisis; advance planning was virtually impossible. I wasn't sure whom we would see or even how we would get from place to place. I didn't know how dangerous it would be. I hoped he would understand.

Fanton proved to be a good sport, flexible and an enthusiastic investigator. Over the next few years, we would travel together on missions to Moscow, Yugoslavia, Turkey, Czechoslovakia, and Albania. Fanton, who would become the chair of Helsinki Watch in 1992, and chair of the board of Human Rights Watch in 1999, often credits me with having introduced him to human rights work, but it was by no means a one-sided relationship. I appreciated his quick grasp of the politics of each situation and his persistence in getting to the bottom of things.

·　　·　　·

We traveled to all three of the Baltic republics in 1991, hiring cars and drivers to take us through roadblocks along the snowy roads leading from one capital to the next. We met with independence-seeking officials in each country, as well as with ordinary citizens—those who had fought at the barricades, those who lay wounded in hospitals, representatives of minority groups, scholars. Our research led inexorably to one conclusion: that the Soviet military was the aggressor, that it had tried to destabilize the Baltics in order to declare their rebellious governments ineffective and then to establish direct presidential rule from Moscow. The script undoubtedly had Gorbachev's approval, and the scenario was a familiar one, used before in other, more remote parts of the Soviet Union, far from the eyes of the outside world.

.   .   .

In Tallinn, the Estonian capital, there had been no violence, but people were in a state of readiness: The inner courtyard of the lovely pink castle that housed the Parliament was filled with television trucks and stocked with food supplies and water in preparation for a siege. Large boulders and concrete blocks barred the entrances, and soldiers with Kalashnikovs were stationed there day and night, waiting for an attack that, fortunately, never came. There was a touch of dark humor in the metal traffic sign in front of Parliament that showed a black tank against a white background with a red slash running through it.

In Latvia, we determined that six people had been killed and more than a dozen injured in Riga, the capital. Five of the deaths occurred during an attack by Black Berets on the Latvian Interior Ministry Building on January 20. We walked through a park overlooking the ministry, stopping at small shrines where onlookers to the attack had been killed.

In Vilnius, Lithuania, we found the Parliament still barricaded against possible attackers. Young men were camping out in sleeping bags in the corridors, walls were plastered with posters, photographs, and press releases. The Parliament building remained brightly lit throughout the night; the president, Vytautas Landsbergis, had taken up residence there for the duration. Guards paced outside the building, where there were flowers and flags commemorating the dead and bonfires to warm the living.

President Landsbergis confirmed that at least fourteen people were killed and hundreds were injured during the January 13 attack on the television tower. He told us that when he telephoned Gorbachev to ask him to call off the tanks, Gorbachev refused to come to the phone.

Jonathan Fanton and I were shown an unedited videotape taken on January 13. It showed unarmed people, arms linked, singing the national anthem as they faced down advancing tanks. Even when they were forced to run in confusion, they continued to sing and to chant *"Leituva"* (Lithuania). Lithuania would later be known for its "singing revolution."

The scenes from the attack on the television tower during the early morning hours of January 13 were nightmarish: darkness, smoke, eerie lights, explosions, the staccato bursts of automatic weapons, the deafening roar of tanks, men and women of all ages running for safety, soldiers smashing their rifle butts into people's heads, shots, screams, bloody faces, corpses.

A young woman was shown, lying among the dead and wounded at the hospital. The camera traveled over her body, naked with unnaturally distended hips and a flattened abdomen; it lingered on her face, strangely peaceful and serene. She was speaking to someone, but her words were inaudible. This was Loreta Asanaviciute, a woman in her early twenties whose pelvis had been crushed by a tank and who died some hours later in the Vilnius Red Cross Hospital. It was her legs, protruding from under the treads, that I had seen in that *New York Times* photo. Whenever I think of Lithuania's "Bloody Sunday," I think of her. Her death destroyed any lingering vestiges of hope I may have had in Gorbachev.

48

In the spring of 1991, with 300,000 miners on strike in Siberia and nationalist unrest in many of the republics, Gorbachev banned all further public demonstrations in the USSR. He gave the Soviet interior minister, Boris Pugo, control of the Moscow police force. But even in Moscow, where the Soviet government wielded its power from the Kremlin, he did not have full control. Yeltsin defied him by organizing a big anti-Party demonstration in Moscow in March, and he got away with it.

In June, the Russian Republic decided to hold open democratic elections for its president. Yeltsin won a sweeping victory, becoming the first popularly elected Soviet leader ever. Gorbachev continued in the country's top position as USSR president, presiding over the Soviet Union's fifteen republics, including the Russian Republic. But Yeltsin had an edge on him: He had won in an open election, something Gorbachev did not dare to try.

Gorbachev seemed out of touch with the world around him. He began negotiating a new Union Treaty with nine of the republics, promising to give them increased political power. Conservative Communists in the central Soviet government knew the treaty would undermine their own power and were opposed to it, but Gorbachev failed to see how strong their opposition was. He remained unfazed, even when rumors of a possible right-wing coup began circulating in Moscow.

·   ·   ·

In May 1991, I began a four-month sabbatical. I wanted some time and distance—to absorb all the amazing events in Eastern Europe, to think about my experiences there, to write about them.

I had been working at a feverish pace since 1979 with only a few weeks off in the summers, weeks that seemed over before they began. Charlie and I were still together, but in a holding pattern that sometimes seemed to be going nowhere. We desperately needed some time together.

On the first day of my sabbatical, I forced myself to do nothing. I walked through Central Park. I sat on a bench and watched people pass by. I took deep breaths of the spring. I luxuriated in the absence of demands.

Then I got busy. I started writing—short essays about some of the people I had come to know—Anna Grušová, Rita Klímová, Gulşat Aygen, Kary Schwarzenberg. The writing was easy and enjoyable; the words just seemed to flow. I didn't have to worry about deadlines or word counts, or the need to be timely. I had been writing all my working life, but never in quite that way—from deep inside me, without a specific audience or a special political point to make.

I also embarked on a quest with Charlie—to find a weekend home that we would share, a hideaway, a place that was *ours*. Our initial goal was a modest one—a little cabin in the woods somewhere—but we fell in love with a rambling old farm in the mountains of upstate New York that soon became a second home to both of us. Charlie painted, I stenciled; he refinished floors, I made curtains. I started a flower garden that would have made my father proud. Over the years we would plant trees, repair the barns, enlarge the pond. I no longer yearned for the country home that had vanished with my divorce a dozen years before. Our new home was infinitely more rewarding because it was filled with love.

.   .   .

But the world did not stand still for my sabbatical. Serbian forces attacked Croatia that summer, starting a series of bloody wars that would rock Europe to its core and destroy Yugoslavia. Some months earlier, I had traveled through many of the picturesque villages in Croatia that were now erupting in internecine warfare. I had seen ethnic tension building among the villagers I met; ethnic Serbs were sleeping in the fields, afraid of nighttime attacks on their homes by the Croatian police. I knew their hysteria was the result of the Yugoslav government's propaganda of hate, orchestrated by President Slobodan Milošević. But I never dreamed that within the year, longtime neighbors and friends would come to see each other as mortal enemies, solely because of their different ethnic origins and religions.

.   .   .

In mid-August, there was another upheaval in the region—an attempted coup in Moscow. And with this news, my sabbatical effectively ended. It was time to get back to work.

.   .   .

The coup attempt took place while Gorbachev was on a family vacation in the Crimea. Gorbachev was placed under house arrest and completely isolated in his vacation home, while the coup plotters made their moves in Moscow. The people who betrayed him were his own close colleagues, conservatives he had put in high positions thinking he would thus satisfy and control them. Chief among them were Vladimir Kryuchkov, head of the KGB; Boris Pugo, minister of the interior; Dmitri Yazov, minister of defense; Valentin Pavlov, the prime minister; and Gennady Yanayev, the vice president, who became acting president at the time of the coup. On August 19, one day before Gorbachev's controversial Union Treaty was supposed to be signed, they formed a State Committee for the State of Emergency, proclaiming that Gorbachev had been removed for reasons of health.

It was frightening when the tanks moved into Moscow. Yeltsin and other liberals headed for the Russian Parliament building, known as the White House. Following the example of Lithuania, they made the Parliament their headquarters and barricaded it against possible attack. Tens of thousands of people turned out to defend it.

Later that day, Yeltsin climbed onto a tank and gave a speech condemning the illegal actions of the junta. A photograph of him standing there—big, courageous, bearlike—became a worldwide symbol of the Russian people's heroic resistance.

In retrospect, the coup attempt was laughably inept—ill-conceived and ill-executed by a group of disorganized Party officials, many of them incompetent, stupid, or drunk. They had no real plan and were unable to win the loyalty of the people they needed most—key leaders of the army and the KGB, who refused to storm the Parliament, and workers at the state television, who refused to doctor their reports. The coup collapsed after three days and the conspirators were arrested and eventually tried.

Boris Pugo committed suicide on August 22. Dmitri Yazov called himself a fool and said they had all been drunk when the plan was devised. Valentin Pavlov tried to use his own drunkenness as an excuse. Anatoly Lukyanov, one of the conspirators, was an old buddy of Gorbachev's from college days; he tried to prove that he was loyal by saying that he had expected Gorbachev to endorse the coup. But Gorbachev would have none of his excuses. He reportedly dismissed Lukyanov with a Russian saying I had not heard before: "Don't hang noodles on my ears, Tolya."

.   .   .

Boris Yeltsin had saved the country for its legal president, Mikhail Gorbachev, but it was Yeltsin who was the hero of the day. Gorbachev was in a weak position when he returned to Moscow; there were some who even thought he had been part of the plot. The conspirators, after all, had been *his* men; the liberators were Yeltsin's. Compounding the damage, Gorbachev gave a speech reaffirming his continuing belief in the Party as the leader of perestroika—this at the very moment when people were tearing down Party monuments and symbols. Gorbachev did not understand the mood in Moscow. By the time he realized how far behind he was, it was too late.

Yeltsin humiliated Gorbachev by forcing him to renounce the Communist Party. On August 24, Gorbachev, though he remained USSR president, resigned as the Party's general secretary. Yeltsin then banned the Party in the Russian Republic.

.   .   .

If the Party hacks who plotted the coup had accomplished anything, it was to finish off the very system they were trying to save.

49

When the much-debated human rights conference finally opened in Moscow in September 1991—less than three weeks after the aborted coup—Gorbachev was no longer worrying about his human rights record. He was fighting for his political life and for the viability of the Soviet Union. For a while we thought the conference might not open at all, due to the chaos in Moscow. Instead, it became a forum to hail the triumph of Soviet democracy.

Gorbachev gave the opening speech to delegates from thirty-five Helsinki nations who attended the official meetings. He portrayed the suppression of the coup as a human rights victory. Many of the foreign delegates, eager to support him, took up that theme. The Soviet delegation had two cochairs, one of them our friend, the veteran dissident Sergei Kovalev, who had become the leading human rights figure in the country since the death of Andrei Sakharov. His appointment was significant, for Kovalev, the outspoken former prisoner, was strong-willed and principled and determined that the government would fulfill its promises. Members of the Soviet delegation, representing Gorbachev and the central USSR government, were conciliatory: They no longer claimed that human rights problems were their own internal affair; to the contrary, they accepted all outside criticisms and promised to conform to international standards. The meeting was more open than those that had preceded it, with other countries coming in for some criticism as well. It was no longer simply an East-West debate.

But the upbeat nature of the proceedings was undercut by deep-seated worry, for the cooperation of the Soviet government had come too late— at a time when the central government was losing control of the nation's constituent parts and might not be able to prevent human rights abuses, even if it so wished. By September 1991, Gorbachev had recognized the independence of the three Baltic nations, and the leaders of other republics had begun to assume more power for themselves. Many of them had blithely shed the mantle of communism for the more popular one of nationalism. How would *they* govern? Would *they* protect their citizens from abuse? Would Moscow be able to curb any excesses? The answers to these questions were not yet clear, but the prospects did not look good.

.   .   .

The issues that had concerned us when we first began discussing a human rights conference in Moscow—political prisoners, access to information, emigration—had been largely resolved. Now, throughout the region, we faced a new set of problems revolving around the rise of nationalism, among them bloody ethnic conflicts, territorial disputes, and discrimination against minorities. Old hatreds were resurfacing, exploited by manipulative leaders seeking to shore up their own power. Hundreds of Soviet citizens had died since 1989 as a result of nationalist unrest in Georgia, Uzbekistan, Azerbaijan, Armenia, Tajikistan, Moldova, and the independence-seeking region we then called Chechen-Ingushetia. Yugoslavia was fracturing into its separate parts. Even Czechoslovakia was being torn apart.

Before 1989, when Eastern Europe was under Soviet control, it was possible to respond to events in the Warsaw Pact countries almost as if they were a single entity. Now these countries had gone their separate ways. Within a few years, the thirty-five countries that had signed the Helsinki accords would become fifty-five countries, still occupying the same geographical space. And within those countries there were still other ethnic groups, also seeking their own separate states.

.   .   .

Back in 1989, caught up in the euphoria of East European change, it seemed for a brief moment that our work might be finished. Friends and colleagues asked me: "What now?" "Now that the Communists are gone, what's left for Helsinki Watch to do?" Bob Bernstein seemed ready to consign me to heaven: When I opened his introduction to the 1989 Helsinki Watch Annual Report, I was surprised to read that "Jeri . . . could run for sainthood [in Eastern Europe] if such an office existed."

But the moment was short-lived. By 1991, we were working harder than ever before, taking full advantage of the greater freedom we had to travel to the problem countries in our region. We began sending missions to various Soviet republics that were previously off-limits. We went to Serbia and Croatia, where war had begun, and to Kosovo, a troubled region within Serbia. We began reporting on abuses in Albania, Greece, and Northern Ireland. We continued to monitor Turkey, Bulgaria, and Romania.

The Helsinki Watch staff more than tripled. We had a deputy director, Lois Whitman, who took over the responsibility for Turkey and helped expand our work to Greece and Northern Ireland, and about fourteen other staff members, not counting consultants, fellows, and interns. We had a field office in Romania, staffed by a Romanian-speaking American lawyer, Holly Cartner, and a similar one in Bulgaria, staffed by an American lawyer named Ted Zang. We had local representatives in Serbia and Croatia and a new researcher on Yugoslavia in our New York office, Ivana Nizich, an American of Yugoslav origins. Two Cathys were working on the Soviet Union—Cathy Fitzpatrick and Cathy Cosman. By the end of 1991, we would have an office in Moscow, with a Russian staff member, Alexander (Sasha) Petrov, and an American director, Rachel Denber. In 1991 alone, we sent twenty-five missions into the field and published thirty reports.

Lyuda Alexeyeva, our longtime consultant on the Soviet Union, was now permitted to travel to her former home. She was part of the rather large group we brought to Moscow for the human rights conference, where we distributed reports on minority problems and held hearings on ethnic violence in the Soviet republics. Lyuda, who had spent fifteen years in exile in the United States, serving as spokesperson for the Moscow Helsinki Group, was still completely at home in Moscow, with a large circle of friends and acquaintances from many different spheres of life. It was she who helped me find the space for a Helsinki Watch office in Moscow and introduced me to Sasha Petrov, who would become the linchpin of our Moscow operation. And it was Lyuda who brought me together with her friend Larisa Bogoraz, whom I had long admired, more or less from afar.

.   .   .

Larisa had always been a kind of legend for me, even before our first meeting in 1979 at our publishers' dinner in Moscow. I had enormous respect for the heroism she displayed when she and six other people demonstrated in Red Square in 1968 to protest the Soviet invasion of Czechoslovakia. I often tried to picture the scene—their little band entering the vast expanse outside the Kremlin, their banners and a homemade Czech flag concealed until they were ready to display them. They knew they would be arrested, as they were almost immediately, and that few would actually witness their act of defiance.

Before she was taken off to Lefortovo Prison, Larisa sent the following letter to a friend, explaining her decision:

> Don't criticize us as others criticize us. Each of us made this decision for himself because it has become impossible to live and to breathe . . . I cannot even think about the Czechs. As I hear their pleas on the radio, I cannot stay silent, I cannot keep from shouting.

And to Marchenko, her husband who was once again in prison, she wrote:

> Please forgive me and all of us for what happened today. I was simply unable to behave differently. You know what that feeling is like, when you cannot breathe.

In a taxi on our way to Larisa's home, I asked Lyuda how she and Larisa had met. Lyuda began,

> I remember my first impression. Larisa's first husband, Yuli Daniel, was a writer, as you know, and a very worldly man. He always talked about "my wife" but I had never met her; she didn't go out much. . . .
>
> When I entered the room, I noticed her. I didn't know who she was. She was sitting in a corner, reading a book, not participating in the conversation. But from time to time she said "Listen to this," and read from the book. And I was struck with how beautiful her voice was, deep and throaty. I decided she must sing Gypsy songs—she looked like a Gypsy—but it turned out she can't sing at all.
>
> I was intrigued by her at first glance. I had expected a superficial, flighty woman, a *"fifa,"* as we say in Russian slang. She was tall and thin and dressed carelessly, without any thought to how she looked. I was astonished. I thought—this is a very unusual woman and tried to imagine what she was like.

When we met again, I asked Yuli Daniel about her. I said, "You know, I looked at your wife and I think she has a heroic nature." He seemed surprised at how impressed I was. He said "But you didn't even talk to her."

I began to feel uncomfortable. "I don't mean to say that she will act heroically," I explained. "She may not have an opportunity to act on it but in certain circumstances she could be a heroine . . . in a way I know I could never be."

He listened and listened and then he said, "You know, you're right. I never thought of it, but you are right."

"I can't judge everyone that way," Lyuda explained to me, "but she made such an impression on me that I sensed it. I never dreamed that we could become friends."

In 1966, when Daniel was arrested for publishing abroad under an alias, Lyuda went to see Larisa and asked if she could be of any help. That was when their friendship began.

.   .   .

"A Moscow kitchen is a very special place," Lyuda confided with a twinkle as we sat down at Larisa's small, untidy table, covered in red oil-cloth. Through the kitchen window I saw birch trees, their leaves fluttering, still green in the early fall. Pasha Marchenko, Larisa's son with Anatoly Marchenko, had let us in. He was eighteen at the time, with dark hair, a little beard, and an appealing manner.

Pasha began clearing off the table as Larisa emerged from the bedroom, wearing a bathrobe. She served us tea, bread, and homemade blueberry jam, moving slowly about the room. At sixty-two, her gait was unsteady; her body was stooped and stiff, and racked by a hacking cough. She chain-smoked steadily and had for forty-two years. "I smoke for my health," she told me, feigning an apologetic smile. She and I had spent some significant moments together: at the publishers' dinner in 1979, with the Burlatsky commission in 1988 when we fought to get her and two others seated at the conference table, and most recently in New York in 1989, where she had been honored as one of our "human rights monitors." But we hadn't spent time together in her Moscow kitchen, where people let down their hair and really talk.

Larisa told us that Pasha was one of the people who had rushed to defend the Russian Parliament during the recent attempt at a coup. She showed us a newspaper photo of him on a tank at the barricades. This woman, whose entire life had been a demonstration of quiet bravery, told me: "I have never known what it was to be afraid until August when Pasha was at the barricades." She admonished him jokingly: "Next putsch, *I* go to the barricades. *You* stay home." Then she began coughing. We waited for a long time until she could stop.

It was hard to believe that Larisa was only two years older than I was. Her hair was gray, her skin was gray, and deep, dark circles etched her large, prominent gray eyes. She looked at me intently as she spoke, her eyes revealing everything: her intelligence, her sensitivity, her pain.

Lyuda had brought gifts—SOS pads, sneakers for Pasha, and a large quantity of roach traps. She also brought some special medicine for Larisa's heart: "Each bottle of tablets lasts 120 days and cost $150. Of course, I hide the price," Lyuda confided to me.

Larisa described a recent visit she had made to Chistopol Prison, where Marchenko had died. "I went with German television," she explained. "They were doing a documentary. We were in the very cell where Tolya died. The head of the prison greeted us when we arrived, the *very same one.* I asked for Tolya's letters; they had nothing. They even denied that his hunger strike had occurred. I couldn't sleep for a week after that."

Now she was busy preparing programs for human rights seminars that she was conducting for the newly reconstituted Moscow Helsinki Group. She and Lyuda lapsed into Russian, talking about the political situation. After a while, they began telling jokes.

.   .   .

A few days later, I was back in Larisa's kitchen, this time without Lyuda. Larisa's English was about as good as my Russian, and our conversation was frustratingly stilted. We were helped a bit by Sanya Daniel, Larisa's older son from her first marriage. Larisa was wearing a heavy sweater, a woolen skirt, and blue-and-white jogging shoes. The two of us had just come from a meeting of human rights activists with the deputy foreign minister—a lot of pleasant words, we agreed, nothing more. It had taken us a long time to get back to Larisa's apartment, for she moved very slowly and gingerly. But her voice was strong and her eyes were deep and serious.

Larisa talked about the four years she had spent in exile in Siberia, near Irkutsk, where she worked in a sawmill, carrying heavy logs. She lived in a tiny log cabin, bought with money raised by her friends in Moscow. She developed a stomach ulcer there. Her health was ruined.

She also described a visit to Prague the previous year, in the summer of 1990. Václav Havel, with his eye for theater, had invited the handful of Russian dissidents who had demonstrated for Czechoslovakia in 1968. He brought them to Prague to honor them in Wenceslas Square on the anniversary of the Soviet invasion. She said she had been wary, afraid it would be "a show," but it turned out to be very moving: "We felt very pure."

"I loved the Czech people," she told me. "I saw Havel as my friend."

Larisa's family was originally from Kharkov, in Ukraine. Her father, like mine, was an engineer. "My father was in Stalin's camps," she told me. "I was destined to become a dissident. It began with the arrest of Yuli Daniel. I knew he would be arrested but in my heart I didn't believe it. No, I believed it, but I couldn't make my peace with it. We were still married but not together any more: I was working at the university in Novosibirsk; he lived in Moscow. But in 1966, when I heard he was arrested, I came to Moscow to help him. Many friends also wanted to help. The dissident movement for human rights began."

.   .   .

Studying Larisa's face during a few moments of silence, it occurred to me that she might be Jewish. I asked her if she was. "I was born Jewish but I am a Russian," she told me firmly, with pride. It was not easy to shrug off Jewish identity in Russia, so I questioned her further, asking if she had experienced anti-Semitism. "I finished the university as a linguist, but I couldn't find work because I was Jewish," she said matter-of-factly. "Several times this happened. . . . Many of my friends left for Israel, but not me. My culture is Russian culture. It is a very important culture."

Larisa had once written: "I am accustomed to the color, smell, rustle of the Russian landscape as I am to the Russian language, the rhythm of Russian poetry. I react to everything else as alien."

I felt an affinity for this woman with a broken body, lyrical mind, and spirit of steel. We shared a lot—our Jewish origins, our passion for Russia, our commitment to human rights. Our lives might well have converged, had my grandparents chosen *not* to leave Russia, or hers chosen not to stay. An accident of geography made us who we were.

As an American, I was born with choices Larisa had never known. I identified with Larisa; I tried to help her. But I also went home again to the country of my birth, the place that had shaped me and given me the freedom to criticize any government, including my own.

Larisa believed fervently in Russia, in the culture that had produced so many great writers, composers, poets, thinkers. Her belief in Russia was the source of her strength. It emboldened her to criticize the Soviet government's brutality. It gave her the courage to walk into Red Square, plant her flag and announce: "I protest!"

"My feeling for Russia is very deep," Larisa told me in her melodic voice. Her words were like a poem, more beautiful in Russian than in translation: "I love Russia. I pity Russia. She is poor. She is unhappy. And my heart hurts for her. I don't want Russia to give me anything. I want to give her what I can."

"You've given so much," I assured her.

"It is never enough," she answered. "Anatoly gave all—his life. He also pitied Russia."

There was a long silence before she added: "Anatoly was *ashamed* for his country."

.   .   .

On December 8, 1991, Boris Yeltsin, president of the Russian Republic, met with two of his counterparts, the presidents of Ukraine and Belorussia. The three republics between them represented 80 percent of the land in the Soviet Union and 73 percent of the population. They agreed to form a new Commonwealth of Independent States, with its headquarters in Minsk, the Belorussian capital. By December 21, most of the other republics had agreed to join the commonwealth. There was no place for Gorbachev in the commonwealth structure, no role for the Soviet government or its ministries.

For the better part of a century, the Soviet Union had shaken the world with its message and its might. Suddenly, in what seemed like an instant, it was gone. On December 25, 1991, Mikhail Gorbachev, president of a nation that no longer existed, resigned. Russia was free to reclaim its soul. The Union of Soviet Socialist Republics was no more.

EPILOGUE

Prague, October 2000. More than a decade has passed since the Velvet Revolution. I am back in Prague, a city I love, the place that once broke my heart with its melancholy beauty. This time I am not alone or hiding from the police. I am with Charlie, and we have come at the invitation of the Czech government. After all this time, the former dissidents still remember a friend.

Prague is the "golden city" once again, suffused with light and life. Its freshly painted buildings gleam in the fall sun. But the new restaurants, souvenir stands, and elegant boutiques seem unnatural to me, modern intrusions superimposed on an old, familiar facade. Hordes of tourists jam the narrow streets and lounge in sidewalk cafés spilling out onto Old Town Square. A Dixieland band is drowning out the chimes of the famous astrological clock.

We walk across the Charles Bridge, its blackened statues obscured by bustling crowds. I tell Charlie about a moonlit night back in another time when I found myself all alone on the bridge, not a person in sight, feeling a mystical connection to the city's history and a deep sadness for where it had all led. I describe how, leaving a friend's apartment late one evening, I walked back to my hotel through the dark, empty streets of Old Town, imagining I was in the fifteenth century, my solitary footsteps on the cobblestones echoing in the quiet night. For a brief moment I actually feel nostalgia for the "bad old days" before Prague became filled with admiring visitors, fast-food emporiums, and pickpockets.

On Saturday night, before a crowd of 4,000 people in the Great Vladimir Hall of Prague Castle, President Havel presents the country's National Day awards. I receive a round gold medal for "meritorious service to the Czech Republic." I finger the medal's smooth edges; they seem to symbolize a full circle in my life. Many old friends are here to greet me, familiar faces, once tense and serious, now relaxed, the faces of a new Prague.

My dear friend Anna Grušová, who had despaired of doing something meaningful with her life, now works for the Czech Helsinki Committee, helping refugees seeking shelter in the Czech Republic, a place from which people once wanted only to flee. Petr Uhl, who spent nine years of his youth in prison, is the government's commissioner for human rights; looking suave and worldly in his dinner jacket, he laughs when I remind him of our first meeting when he spoke to me in English, a language he had read but never before tried to speak out loud. I see Jan Urban in the crowd—Jan, who was saved from arrest by Andrei Sakharov's attentions from Moscow; graying but still boyish-looking, Jan is now a muckraking journalist, critical of the government. Kary Schwarzenberg has left government service and spends much of his time restoring the family castle in Orlík, a few hours from Prague. He has lost the quiet reserve I remember from Vienna. His cell phone rings constantly, he seems outgoing and expansive, more at home with himself than he was in the past. Why not? He has come home.

I miss Jiří Hájek, his Old World courtesy and dignity. One of the last of the Prague Spring leaders, he lived to see the end of communism before his death in 1994 when he was in his early eighties. Above all, I miss Rita Klímová, my guide to all that happened in Prague: Rita died early, of leukemia, on December 30, 1993, when she was sixty-two. She spent her last three years in Washington as ambassador to the United States, a glorious climax to her lifelong love affair with America.

.   .   .

With the fall of communism, Europe became whole once more. But the euphoria that attended the revolutions of 1989 didn't last long. In their rush to establish political democracies and market economies, former Communist countries missed a great opportunity—to find a third way by learning from the mistakes of the West as well as from those of communism. Havel, in his address at the awards ceremony, voiced despair over the devastation of the Czech landscape, about cities and towns marred by "a banally universal architecture devoid of creativity and imagination," about broad belts of supermarkets and shopping malls that "defy both town and nature." He deplored the degeneration of language, the spread of corruption and dishonesty, and the "blood flowing from the [television] screen."

In countries like Russia, the Czech Republic, Slovakia, Bulgaria, Poland, and Hungary, communism left a painful legacy of dismay, anger, and confusion—dismay that an economic safety net no longer existed, anger that former Communists were prospering, confusion about new values and mores that were suddenly imposed. Racism and discrimination became endemic throughout the region.

In former Soviet republics like Turkmenistan, Uzbekistan, and Belarus, repressive leaders continued their tyranny with little change from Communist times. Elsewhere in the Helsinki Watch region, countries that were once darkly secretive about their behavior toward their citizens became hot spots of well-publicized but unstoppable fighting. Brutal ethnic wars broke out, in Nagorno Karabakh, Croatia, Bosnia, Kosovo, Chechnya, and Macedonia, wars that were all the more horrible because the combatants were often former neighbors or even friends, because they were armed with sophisticated weapons, because they seemed impervious to worldwide censure, and because the outside world was loath to intervene.

It was no longer sufficient for us to expose abuses and stigmatize offending governments, demanding that they change. We began urging governments and international institutions to exert pressure on offenders, including the denial of economic and military aid. Yet how are we to deal with rogue governments that seem oblivious to principles and to pressure? And with international terrorism and its shady perpetrators?

The human rights movement has become increasingly international, with many groups joining together in worldwide campaigns, such as the ones that led to the banning of antipersonnel land mines, to the establishment of two war crimes tribunals—for the former Yugoslavia and for Rwanda, and to the signing of an international treaty to create a permanent International Criminal Court. The legal punishment of torturers and tyrants may deter others from committing similar crimes and bring some degree of closure to victims and survivors.

.   .   .

Human Rights Watch went through a stormy period in the early 1990s, when we seemed unable to cope with our own momentum. The board suggested a management consultant to rethink our governing structure, but Aryeh Neier refused to consider any change in his management style. I was opposed to a proposal to bring all of the regional watch committees under the Human Rights Watch name—I didn't want to lose the name recognition I had established for Helsinki Watch, and I also worried about losing my own independence.

Neier left abruptly in 1993. He had lost the goodwill, though not the respect, of many on the board and staff; rather than try to retrieve it, he moved on to a new challenge—running George Soros's Open Society Institute. He left without fanfare and, as far as I could tell, hardly a backward glance—one day I arrived at work to find his books and his big black chair gone. He had given much to the organization—its direction, its high standards—and these continue as his legacy.

Ken Roth, the new director, adopted the recommendations of a management consultant and created a core management group to ensure uniformity in our standards and policies. A gifted young lawyer and former prosecutor, Roth used persuasion rather than fiat to convince me of the importance of consolidating under one name, that it was necessary to increase our leverage and our constituency. The names of the original watch committees were gradually phased out: Helsinki Watch ultimately became the Europe and Central Asia Division of Human Rights Watch.

By the end of 2001, Human Rights Watch employed more than 180 people in its eight regional and thematic divisions, covered seventy-six countries, and had seven permanent offices worldwide. The annual budget—$200,000 when we began in 1979—was estimated at $20 million for 2002.

The New York office of Human Rights Watch occupies a floor and a half of the Empire State Building. It's a very different place now, with only a handful of people left from the early 1980s. Many on the staff are talented, dynamic women. Despite an inevitable trend toward bureaucratization, the atmosphere remains hardworking and friendly. Our scope has become broader, focusing on the rights of many groups: war victims, prisoners, women, children, refugees, workers, migrants, gays and lesbians. Our meetings deal mainly with policy issues and strategies. There is seldom talk of individual victims.

The ongoing relationships I was able to maintain with dissidents back in the 1980s—documenting their tragedies, admiring their heroism, mourning their deaths—now seem like part of a distant past. It's a different world now, with more complex problems and more complicated moral issues, a world in which the victim one day may be the abuser the next, in which the testimonies we take come mainly from refugees, numbered in the tens of thousands.

I take great pride in this large professional organization, especially when I recall how we grew from a handful of people with little more than ideals and hubris to spur us on. I also feel nostalgia for that less complex time when so many of the victims were people we knew.

.   .   .

One spring day back in 1994, Bob Bernstein appeared in my office unannounced. He had just been meeting with Ken Roth, the new young director of Human Rights Watch. "If you never do another thing," Bob began, without any preamble, "you've proved yourself to me, to everyone. You've done a fantastic job." I wondered what had inspired this sudden outburst of praise. Then he asked me: "Do you think you're slowing down?"

"*Slowing down?*" My words exploded. Why just the past weekend Charlie and I had painted two whole rooms and a staircase in our country house—walls, floors, trim, stencils—working from dawn to midnight, impressed by how much we had accomplished. We were creating a home for ourselves, making up for lost time. "I've never felt more energetic in my life," I declared.

"Okay, okay." Bob changed the subject quickly, taken aback by my vociferous response.

But later, after he was gone, I began to think about his question. Bob wasn't talking about my energy in general, he was talking about my *work*. What *was* I doing, painting an old farmhouse over the weekend when I could have been in the office, editing a report, or traveling to one of the hot spots where we now had local staff in need of direction? For a while now, I had been finding reasons *not* to travel—not because I was afraid of losing Charlie, as I had once been, but because I wanted to be with him.

Through the many years when work dominated my life, I had tried to hold on to the interests and friends that had sustained me at an earlier time. Lately, I seemed to need them more and more. I had been at my job for sixteen years, traveling to far-flung places, managing a large and scattered staff, reading and editing hundreds of reports, and dealing with human suffering on a day-to-day basis. By 1994, the work was taking a toll. The ethnic warfare in Yugoslavia—a country directly under my watch—was unbearable to contemplate: "ethnic cleansing" and concentration camps recalling the dark days of the gas chambers; fathers and sons spending their weekends at target practice with defenseless residents of Sarajevo as their targets; 7,000 men and boys massacred in cold blood in the "protected safe zone" of Srebrenica. I felt helpless in the face of that war raging in the heart of Europe, a war to which Europe had turned a cold heart. As I write this, the reporting we did on Croatia and Bosnia in the early 1990s is being used as evidence by the international war crimes tribunal prosecuting Yugoslavia's former leader, Slobodan Milošević; he is finally being brought to justice and our work has played a role. But the fact remains that we were unable to stop the killings when they were occurring or to get any nation to intervene. Bosnia, and the concurrent nightmare in Rwanda, were crucibles for many of us at that time: a recognition of how little the world had progressed—and of our own limitations.

On the positive side, the human rights movement had taken hold worldwide by 1994. Our cause had become a profession. Courses in human rights were being offered in universities, law schools, and graduate schools. Although I no longer could keep track of the names of all the new young people on our staff, I was proud of them: they were hard-working, well trained, and professional. More realistic than I was when I first began, they didn't expect to change the world. Yet they woke each morning with renewed dedication, determined to do what they could. A new generation, inspired by our example, had entered the fight for human rights.

Human Rights Watch was no longer dependent on any single person or group of persons for its continuing existence. People who had joined the staff *after* me were leaving the organization for other jobs. Even Bob Bernstein, without whom there would be no Human Rights Watch, was talking about stepping down as chairman. Was Bob looking out for my interests, telling me something I should have seen for myself?

.   .   .

Charlie and I were married in June 1994 at the start of my second three-month sabbatical. We spent the summer at our upstate farmhouse. I didn't do much writing this time. Instead, I worked long days in the flower garden. The earth that I shoveled, the plants I tamped in, seemed part of a healing process after many intense years of dealing with death and destruction. The garden became larger and larger. I began to wonder how I could possibly care for it once I went back to being a weekend visitor.

In the course of that summer, I reached a decision—to give up my job and its administrative responsibilities, to begin a new phase in my life. In January 1995, I stepped down as Helsinki Watch director, though I would continue as senior adviser to Human Rights Watch on a half-time basis for the next six years. At last I had some unbroken time, time for myself, to reflect, to write.

.   .   .

My life, like all lives, has been a journey, following a path that seems clear and purposeful only now, when I stop and look back. I crossed closed borders, some of them delineated by watchtowers and barbed wire, others existing only in my mind. I traveled behind the Iron Curtain. I spoke out and people heard my voice. I removed the cloak of mystery that my father had wrapped around Russia. I explored my own origins—both Jewish and Russian—and came to value being an American all the more.

I am no longer the idealist I was at the start. It all seemed black and white back then, a world of absolutes in which Good and Bad stood diametrically opposed, as they were in the "just war" of my childhood. I now believe that the capacity for cruelty exists everywhere—in every country, perhaps in every person—and that we need laws and punishments to keep it in check. The human rights movement has been instrumental in saving lives and bringing down dictatorships. It will never bring an end to acts of inhumanity.

Evil constantly reinvents itself—"ethnic cleansing" in Bosnia, butchery in Rwanda, brutal imprisonment in China, saturation bombing in Chechnya, stonings in Afghanistan, massacres in Kosovo, amputations in Sierra Leone, suicide attacks by terrorists—the list seems endless. But there is a movement now to fight such depravity and uphold our basic principles, a worldwide movement of which Human Rights Watch is a small part. The movement is huge, respected, and capable.

It has come of age. It is here to stay.

SOME PEOPLE
IN THIS BOOK:

Who They Are;
Where They Are Now

Elliott Abrams, assistant secretary of state for human rights and humanitarian affairs under President Reagan (1981–1985), was later implicated in schemes for illegally supplying aid to the Contras in Nicaragua. In 1991, he pleaded guilty to two counts of withholding information from Congress. He was pardoned in December 1992 by President Bush. In 2001, President George W. Bush named him senior director for democracy, human rights, and international operations at the National Security Council.

Ludmilla Alexeyeva, a founding member of the Moscow Helsinki Group in 1976 and for many years its official spokesperson abroad, is the author of *Soviet Dissent: Contemporary Movements for National, Religious, and Human Rights* (Wesleyan University Press, 1985). She returned to Russia in the early 1990s, where she chairs a newly reorganized Moscow Helsinki Group, modeled after the U.S. Helsinki Watch, which she had observed closely while working for many years as our consultant. Lyuda also became chair of the International Helsinki Federation for Human Rights, a position first occupied by Kary Schwarzenberg.

Gulşat Aygen, arrested and tortured in Turkey when she was twenty-one and released as a case of mistaken identity when she was twenty-seven, is now writing her thesis in linguistics and teaching at Harvard University in Boston, Massachusetts.

György Bence, the Hungarian philosopher who had been denied work at the university for ten years when I first met him in 1981, is now a professor of philosophy at ELTE University of Budapest.

Robert Bernstein, chairman and chief executive officer of Random House until 1990, was the chief founder of Helsinki Watch in 1978 and the founding chair of Human Rights Watch until 1999. He remains an active member of the Human Rights Watch board. He is also a co-chair of Human Rights in China and devotes much of his energy to helping that cause.

Larisa Bogoraz, Russian human rights veteran who spent four years in internal exile and is the widow of Anatoly Marchenko, lives in Moscow, where she is revered by many human rights activists. She joined the new Moscow Helsinki Group in 1989 and headed the Seminar on Human Rights until 1996.

Elena Bonner is the author of *Alone Together* (Alfred A. Knopf, 1986), describing her life in exile with her husband, Andrei Sakharov. She has established several institutions to honor her late husband's memory, both in Russia and at Brandeis University in Massachusetts. She is an outspoken critic of the Russian government's policies in Chechnya and on other human rights issues.

Mihai Botez, the Romanian mathematician who helped me during my first visit to Romania in 1982, received political asylum in the United States in 1987. In the fall of 1988, he was a fellow at the Woodrow Wilson Center in Washington, D.C. He became Romania's ambassador to the United Nations in 1993 and to the United States in 1994. He died in 1995.

Vladimir Bukovsky, whose case I worked on in my Amnesty International group back in the 1970s, was first arrested in 1963 when he was twenty-one and spent most of the following years in prisons and psychiatric hospitals until his release to the West in a prisoner exchange in 1976. Bukovsky subsequently graduated from Cambridge University (1981) and received a Ph.D. in biology from Stanford University (1986). He has written a number of books and articles, including *To Build a Castle* (Viking, 1979) and *Reckoning with Moscow* (Alfred Regnery, 1999). He lives in Cambridge, England.

Fyodor Burlatsky, chair of the officially sanctioned Soviet human rights organization with which we met in January 1988, later lost his job as editor of *Literaturnaya Gazeta*. He continues to write and to speak at conferences, often about the Gorbachev years and the Cuban missile crisis of October

1962. He is currently president of the International League for the Protection of Culture and has spoken out in favor of reviving cultural institutions in the Chechen Republic.

Yuli Daniel, Larisa Bogoraz's first husband, is the poet and short story writer who was tried and convicted with Andrei Sinyavsky in 1966 for several works he published abroad under the pseudonym "Nikolai Arzhak." He died in Moscow on December 30, 1988.

Josef Danisz, Anna Grušová's ex-husband, was revealed in 1990 to have had illicit dealings with the Communist secret police in Czechoslovakia. When I visited him in Prague in 1992, he acknowledged the validity of the charges but assured me that he had never implicated any of his colleagues in the Charter 77 dissident movement.

Jiří Dienstbier, who worked as a janitor when I first met him in the 1980s in Prague, had been a foreign policy commentator for Czech radio at the time of the 1968 Soviet invasion and had spent three years in prison for his dissident activities. After the 1989 revolution, he became Czechoslovakia's minister of foreign affairs, from December 1989 to 1992. From 1998 to 2001, he was the United Nations special rapporteur on human rights in the former Yugoslavia.

Ágnes Erdélyi, one of the Hungarian philosophers I met in 1981, is now professor of philosophy at ELTE University of Budapest.

Jonathan Fanton, president of the New School for Social Research (now New School University) until 1999 and chair of Helsinki Watch from 1992 to 1999, became chairman of the board of Human Rights Watch in 1999, replacing Robert Bernstein. He is now president of the John D. and Catherine T. MacArthur Foundation.

Catherine Fitzpatrick worked for Helsinki Watch for almost a decade as research director for the Soviet Union and Yugoslavia. She left in 1990. She is currently executive director of the International League for Human Rights.

Janet Fleischman was Helsinki Watch's researcher on Eastern Europe until

1990. She has worked for Human Rights Watch for almost two decades, currently as Washington director of its Africa division.

Arthur Goldberg, former Supreme Court justice, U.S. ambassador to the United Nations, and U.S. ambassador to the 1977 Helsinki Review Conference in Belgrade, played an important role in getting the initial funding to launch Helsinki Watch in 1978. He died in January 1990.

Anna Grušová, my Czech dissident friend who despaired of finding meaningful work in Prague, now works for the Czech Helsinki Committee, where she is deeply involved in helping refugees in the Czech Republic.

Jiří Hájek, Czech foreign minister during the Prague Spring and one of the original three spokespersons for Charter 77, became chair of the underground Czechoslovak Helsinki Committee in the late 1980s and continued in that role after the revolution. He died in 1994.

Václav Havel, Czech playwright and one of the original Charter 77 spokespersons, became president of Czechoslovakia in December 1989 and president of the newly created Czech Republic in 1993.

Human Rights Watch in 2001 covered seventy-six countries, maintained seven permanent offices worldwide, and employed more than 180 people. Its operating expenses for the fiscal year ending March 31, 2001, were $17,095,768.

The **International Freedom to Publish Committee** of the Association of American Publishers continues its activities worldwide. I have been its director since 1977. It is currently chaired by Nan Graham, editor in chief of Scribner.

The **International Helsinki Federation for Human Rights,** founded in Bellagio in 1982, now includes thirty-nine national Helsinki committees, many in the former Soviet republics and throughout Eastern Europe. Its offices remain in Vienna. Yuri Orlov is its honorary chair, Ludmilla Alexeyeva its chair.

Reha İsvan, wife of the former mayor of Istanbul who was arrested as a member of the Turkish Peace Association in 1982, served a prison sentence from 1983 to 1986. After her release, she wrote several books about her prison experiences and traveled throughout Turkey, speaking on human rights issues.

Hasan Kakar, the imprisoned Afghan professor whose wife I interviewed in 1986, was subsequently released from prison. In 1988, he was honored by Human Rights Watch as a "human rights monitor."

Max Kampelman's career as a lawyer, diplomat and educator includes his role as U.S. ambassador to the Helsinki Review Conference in Madrid from 1980–1983 and as U.S. ambassador to the Moscow Conference on the Human Dimension in 1991.

Rita Klímová, who became active in the underground Czechoslovak Helsinki Committee in the late 1980s and was my key contact person in Prague, was appointed Czechoslovakia's ambassador to the United States after the 1989 revolution. She died of leukemia in December 1993.

Edward Kline, publisher of Soviet samizdat in English and editor of the *Chronicle of Human Rights in the USSR*, is now president of the Andrei Sakharov Foundation.

György Konrád, the well-known Hungarian writer and former dissident, continues to write novels and essays and is the head of the Berlin Academy of Arts.

Lev Kopelev, Soviet writer and former political prisoner, and his wife **Raisa (Raya) Orlova** hosted a literary salon in Moscow in the 1970s until they left for Cologne, Germany, in 1980, where they were both stripped of their Soviet citizenship. Raya, who had written several books in Russian about American literature, later published *Memoirs* (Random House, 1983). She died of cancer in 1989. Lev is the author of a number of books, including *To Be Preserved Forever* (J. B. Lippincott Company, 1977), *The Education of a True Believer* (Harper & Row, 1978), and *Ease My Sorrows: A Memoir* (Random House, 1983). He died in 1997 at the age of eighty-five.

Mária Kovács, one of the four Hungarian intellectuals I befriended in 1981 and subsequently helped bring to the United States, is now director of the Nationalism Studies Program at the Central European University in Budapest.

Sergei Kovalev, biologist, former political prisoner (1974–1984), and close friend of Andrei Sakharov, has been a member of the Russian Parliament since 1990. In 1993, he became Russia's first human rights ombudsman. He lost that position in 1995 because of his protests against the behavior of Russian troops in Chechnya.

Jacek Kuroń, a leading Polish human rights activist, one of the founders of KOR (Workers Defense Committee) in 1977 and a Solidarity activist in the 1980s, became minister of labor in the first Solidarity government, founded the Democratic Union in 1990, and until recently served as a deputy in the Polish Parliament.

June Lidsky, my troubled sister, remained forever estranged from her family. She died of cancer in 1999. I learned of her death indirectly, two years after she had died.

Helena Łuczywo, an underground newspaper editor in the 1980s and my guide during my first missions to Poland, is now the managing editor of *Gazeta Wyborcza*, the most successful newspaper in Central Europe, with a daily circulation of over 500,000 copies.

Anatoly Marchenko, the dissident Soviet writer of several books including *My Testimony* (Dutton, 1969) and *To Live Like Everyone* (Henry Holt and Company, 1989), died on December 8, 1986, of a cerebral hemorrhage while on a hunger strike in Chistopol Prison.

Adam Michnik, Polish intellectual and essayist, a founder in 1977 of KOR (Workers Defense Committee), and a Solidarity activist in the 1980s who spent six years in Polish prisons, served in the Polish Parliament from 1989 to 1991. He is the editor in chief of *Gazeta Wyborcza*, Central Europe's most successful newspaper.

Vladimír (Vlaďya) Mlynář, Rita Klímová's son, wrote for the Czechoslovak underground newspaper *Lidove Noviny* before the revolution, became editor in chief of the political weekly *Respekt,* where he worked for seven years before joining the government as minister without portfolio with a special interest in national minorities.

Valentin Moroz is the Ukrainian nationalist and political prisoner, author of a prison memoir *Report from the Beria Reserve,* whose case I worked on in my Amnesty International group in the 1970s. He spent almost thirteen years in Soviet prisons until 1979, when he was exchanged with four other Soviet prisoners for two spies held by the United States. Moroz became a freelance writer for Radio Free Europe/Radio Liberty. In 1984, he was accused of expressing anti-Semitic views in his writings.

Gerald Nagler, executive director of the International Helsinki Federation for Human Rights (1984–1992), remains the chairman of the Swedish Helsinki Committee in Stockholm and became actively involved in helping human rights activists in Yugoslavia.

Aryeh Neier, executive director of the American Civil Liberties Union for fifteen years and one of the founders of Helsinki Watch in 1978, was executive director of Human Rights Watch until 1993. He is now president of the Open Society Institute.

Yuri Orlov, the founder of the Moscow Helsinki Group who spent nine years in Soviet prisons and internal exile, was released to the West in September 1986, where he wrote *Dangerous Thoughts: Memoirs of a Russian Life* (William Morrow and Company, 1991). He became the honorary chair of the International Helsinki Federation for Human Rights and works in physics at Cornell University in Ithaca, New York.

Dmitrina Petrova, the Bulgarian professor who aspired to become a human rights activist after our first meeting in 1989, became active in the Human Rights Project in Bulgaria. She is now the director of the European Roma Rights Centre in Budapest.

László Rajk, the Hungarian architect who ran a samizdat boutique in his apartment, works as an architect in Budapest.

Zbigniew Romaszewski, head of the first underground Polish Helsinki Committee and a Solidarity activist, became a Polish senator and chairman of the Human Rights and Rule of Law Committee.

Zofia Romaszewska, who worked with her husband in Solidarity's Intervention Committee, became the executive director of the Foundation for the Defense of Human Rights in Warsaw.

Andrei Sakharov, nuclear physicist and the Soviet Union's most famous dissident, died of a heart attack on December 14, 1989, while preparing a speech to deliver in the Soviet Parliament the next day.

Orville Schell, a prominent lawyer, one of the founders of Helsinki Watch and the first chair of Americas Watch, died in June 1987.

Karl (Kary) Schwarzenberg, the prince who was the first chair of the International Helsinki Federation for Human Rights, became chancellor to President Havel after Czechoslovakia's Velvet Revolution. He now divides his time between Vienna and Prague, managing his extensive holdings.

Natan Sharansky, formerly Anatoly Shcharansky, was a Soviet refusenik and human rights activist who spent nine years in the gulag. Since his expulsion from the USSR in 1986, he has lived with his wife, Avital, in Israel, where he has held many influential government posts, most recently deputy prime minister and minister of housing and construction.

Andrei Sinyavsky, author of *Fantastic Stories* and *On Socialist Realism,* among other works written under the pseudonym "Abram Tertz," was tried and sentenced in the infamous Sinyavsky-Daniel case of 1966. He immigrated to Paris in 1973, where he continued his writing, including *A Voice from the Chorus* (Farrar, Straus, and Giroux, 1976). He died in Paris in 1997.

Alexandr Solzhenitsyn, the writer and former political prisoner expelled from the Soviet Union in 1974, is most famous for his masterpiece *The Gulag Archipelago* (Harper & Row). He won the Nobel Prize for literature in 1970 and claimed it when he reached the West, where he lived in exile in the United States until after the collapse of the Soviet Union. In 1994, he returned to Russia.

Vilmos (Vili) Sós, one of the four Hungarian intellectuals I befriended in Budapest in 1981, a philosopher who was denied work for many years, is now a research fellow in the Institute of Philosophy at the Hungarian Academy of Sciences.

Mümtaz Soysal was a member of Amnesty International's international executive committee in the 1970s and represented Turkey at our Bellagio meeting in 1982. A professor of political science at Ankara University and a columnist for *Hurriyet* and other publications, he was Turkey's minister of foreign affairs in 1994.

Jacobo Timerman, the Argentine newspaper publisher who was imprisoned and tortured for publishing the names of the "disappeared," was expelled from Argentina in 1979. He described his prison experiences in *Prisoner Without a Name, Cell Without a Number* (Alfred A. Knopf, 1981) and went on to write a number of other books, including *The Longest War: Israel in Lebanon* (Alfred A. Knopf, 1982) and *Cuba: A Journal* (Alfred A. Knopf, 1990). Timerman lived in Israel from 1980 to 1983 before returning to Argentina and his work as a publisher and editor. He died in 1999.

Lev Timofeyev, the former political prisoner who founded the Glasnost Press Club in 1987, lives in Moscow, where he has written a number of books, including *Russia's Secret Rulers: How the Government and the Criminal Mafia Exercise Their Power* (Alfred A. Knopf, 1992).

Jáchym Topol, the young poet chosen by Václav Havel to represent him at Human Rights Watch's 1988 annual dinner, has become a well-known writer in the Czech Republic.

Dorin Tudoran, the Romanian poet I met in Bucharest in 1982 and who came to the United States several years later, is back in Bucharest, writing poetry and essays.

Petr Uhl, Charter 77 activist and former political prisoner in Czechoslovakia, became a member of Parliament after the revolution and the director of the Czech News Agency. He is now the Czech Republic's commissioner for human rights.

Jan Urban, the Czech dissident who was one of the founders of the underground magazine *Lidove Noviny*, was active in the Civic Forum, the coalition that defeated the Communists. He subsequently left politics and now works as an independent writer and journalist with a continuing interest in human rights issues.

Lech Wałęsa, the leader of Solidarity in Poland who won the Nobel Peace Prize in 1983, was president of Poland from 1990 to 1995. He now heads a foundation he established in Poland.

Joanna Weschler, a former Solidarity journalist, began work at Helsinki Watch in 1983 after martial law in Poland left her stranded in the West. In the 1980s, she covered Poland for Helsinki Watch as well as several Latin American countries for Americas Watch; she also ran the Human Rights Watch prison project. She is now the United Nations representative for Human Rights Watch.

Zhelyu Zhelev, the Bulgarian philosopher I met in Sofia in 1989, was chosen president of Bulgaria in August 1990 by the Grand National Assembly and was popularly elected president in 1992. He served as president until 1996, after which he formed the Dr. Zhelyu Zhelev Foundation to further political activity in Bulgaria.

Warren Zimmermann, the U.S. ambassador to the Helsinki Review Conference in Vienna (1986–1989), went on to become the last U.S. ambassador to Yugoslavia, from 1989 to 1992. He then left government service, wrote *Origins of a Catastrophe: Yugoslavia and Its Destroyers* (Times Books, 1996) and is now a full-time writer.

ACKNOWLEDGMENTS

I am grateful for the love and support of my family—Charlie and my daughters Abby, Pam, and Emily. I also thank my brother Bob for his unflagging enthusiasm and his insights into our early life together.

There is also my other family—the Human Rights Watch family, past and present—members of the staff and board and all our friends and supporters. Their commitment to our cause remains a constant source of inspiration to me, and their curiosity and interest in seeing this book has spurred me on. I appreciate the alacrity with which so many responded to my queries and let me test my memory against theirs, among them: Ludmilla Alexeyeva, Roland Algrant, György Bence, Bob Bernstein, Rachel Bien, Cynthia Brown, Holly Cartner, Istvan Deak, Rachel Denber, Helen Epstein, Catherine Fitzpatrick, Janet Fleischman, the International Helsinki Federation staff, Alice Henkin, Sidney Jones, Krassimir Kanev, Mária Kovács, Sidney Orlov, Yuri Orlov, Susan Osnos, Petr Petr, Jemera Rone, Ken Roth, Barnett Rubin, Barbara Sproul, Jonathan Sugden, Kumru Toktamış, and Joanna Weschler.

A grant for Research and Writing from the John D. and Catherine T. MacArthur Foundation made it possible for me to devote myself full-time to my writing. I am also grateful to Furthermore, the publication program of The J. M. Kaplan Fund, for its help in the writing and production of this book.

The Promises We Keep: Human Rights, the Helsinki Process, and American Foreign Policy, by William Korey (St. Martin's Press, 1993) proved invaluable in reconstructing Helsinki events and finding my own place within them. *Soviet Dissidents: Their Struggle for Human Rights*, by Joshua Rubenstein (Beacon Press, 1980) and *The Thaw Generation: Coming of Age in the Post-Stalin Era*, by Ludmilla Alexeyeva and Paul Goldberg (Little, Brown and Company, 1990) provided helpful background on the early days of Soviet dissent. Jonathan Fanton's *The University and Civil Society* (New School for Social Research, 1995) helped me remember details of the missions he and I took together.

I am indebted to Robert Silvers and Barbara Epstein, editors of the *New York Review of Books,* for all their help over the years: Bob for providing me with a venue to describe my various missions and for helping me crystallize my thoughts, Barbara for generously volunteering to read and comment on a much earlier version of this memoir. Parts of my articles that appeared in the *New York Review* have been adapted for use in this work.

It was my agent, Joe Spieler, who got me to write this memoir in the first place. Without his advice on how to tackle it, his gentle prodding during a long period of incubation, and his careful editing of my initial proposal, this book might never have seen the light. My thanks also to Peter Osnos for wanting to publish my book, to Lisa Kaufman, an enthusiastic and understanding editor, to Michele Wynn for her thoughtful, intelligent copyediting, and to the entire staff of PublicAffairs for making the publication of this book such a pleasant experience.

Emily Laber, a professional editor and my first reader, approached my work with her usual high standards and sense of responsibility; her marginal comments ("Go, Mom!"; "kinda boring") lightened the task as she skillfully helped me find my voice and set the right tone. Abby Laber, a gifted teacher with a passion for literature, helped me discover underlying themes and encouraged me to develop them. Judy Crichton, a good friend and an equally good writer, was always there to read and comment along the way. Other close friends—Aaron Asher, Linda Asher, and Barbara Davis—generously applied their years of experience to the finished manuscript and gave me helpful suggestions. Jim Finn, Jess Korman, and Toby Talbot gladly pitched in when I needed them. And Charles Kuskin read the work in part and as a whole more times than I can recall, bringing to it his musician's ear for cadence and a knack for picking up on subtle nuances; he involved himself so deeply in my words it was as if they were his own.

To all of these dear people I am truly indebted, as well as to many other good friends, equally talented and generous, who also offered to read my book and whose help, time permitting, would undoubtedly have enhanced it.

Finally, I want to thank Bob Bernstein for starting me on a journey that became my life. This book, in many ways, is his story as well as mine. It is my thank-you note to him.

INDEX

luncheon for Gorbachev, 285–286; and
Romania, 188, 192–193, 195–196, 342,
343; and Turkey, 213–214, 216; and visa
denials, 277; and Zimmermann, 261–262
Uzbekistan, 39, 234, 365, 375

Veliotes, Nicholas, 277
Velvet Revolution, 335–336, 350, 373
Vienna Review Conference, 258–263,
283–284, 305
Vietnam, 9, 70, 168
Village Voice, 161
Visas, 36, 109–110, 112, 185, 207, 260, 267,
277
Vladimov, Georgi, 119
Vladislav, Jan, 136
Voice of America, 144, 182
Voinovich, Irina, 119
Voinovich, Vladimir, 115, 119, 278
Vonnegut, Kurt, 83, 101, 102
Voznesensky, Andrei, 55, 115

Wałęsa, Lech, 4, 147, 149, 311
Wallach, Ira, 185
Wallenberg, Raoul, 120
Wall Street Journal, 94, 122
Warsaw, 146–153, 266–267
Warsaw Pact countries, 137–138, 146, 184,
241, 264, 284, 365. *See also specific countries*
Washington Post, 86, 114, 221, 280, 348
Weapons of mass destruction, 48, 79, 93–94
Weschler, Joanna, 212
Weschler, Lawrence, 171
West Germany, 94, 316–317. *See also* GDR
(German Democratic Republic)

"White Book," on the Sinyavsky-Daniel
trial, 59
Whitman, Lois, 366
Willam Morrow Publishers, 115
Willen, Paul, 51
Williams, Marta, 123
"'Wire Skeleton' of Vladimir Prison"
(Laber), 73
Wood, Elizabeth, 178
Woods, Donald, 86
Woodstock, 61
World War II, 23, 120, 155, 265, 352; resist-
ance fighters during, 53, 323; and
Czechoslovakia and Poland, 150, 151;
Soviet Union after, 47. *See also* Holocaust;
Nazis
Wujec, Henryk, 349

Yanayev, Gennady, 362
Yazov, Dmitri, 362–363
Yegides, Pyotr, 119
Yeltsin, Boris, 353–354, 357, 360, 362–363,
371
Yevtushenko, Yevgeny, 115
Yıldırım, Hüseyin, 223–224
Yugoslavia, 133, 181, 361–362, 365–366,
375, 378

Zang, Ted, 366
Zeb, Ahmed, 254
Zhdanovism, 54
Zhelev, Zhelyu, 331
Zhivkov, Todor, 318–319, 330, 332–334
Zimmermann, Warren, 261, 262
Zorin, Leonid, 54

PUBLICAFFAIRS is a publishing house founded in 1997. It is a tribute to the standards, values, and flair of three persons who have served as mentors to countless reporters, writers, editors, and book people of all kinds, including me.

I. F. STONE, proprietor of *I. F. Stone's Weekly,* combined a commitment to the First Amendment with entrepreneurial zeal and reporting skill and became one of the great independent journalists in American history. At the age of eighty, Izzy published *The Trial of Socrates,* which was a national bestseller. He wrote the book after he taught himself ancient Greek.

BENJAMIN C. BRADLEE was for nearly thirty years the charismatic editorial leader of *The Washington Post.* It was Ben who gave the *Post* the range and courage to pursue such historic issues as Watergate. He supported his reporters with a tenacity that made them fearless, and it is no accident that so many became authors of influential, best-selling books.

ROBERT L. BERNSTEIN, the chief executive of Random House for more than a quarter century, guided one of the nation's premier publishing houses. Bob was personally responsible for many books of political dissent and argument that challenged tyranny around the globe. He is also the founder and was the longtime chair of Human Rights Watch, one of the most respected human rights organizations in the world.

·   ·   ·

For fifty years, the banner of Public Affairs Press was carried by its owner Morris B. Schnapper, who published Gandhi, Nasser, Toynbee, Truman, and about 1,500 other authors. In 1983 Schnapper was described by *The Washington Post* as "a redoubtable gadfly." His legacy will endure in the books to come.

Peter Osnos, *Publisher*